# INDIRA GANDHI

# INDIRA GANDHI

## A PERSONAL AND POLITICAL BIOGRAPHY

### INDER MALHOTRA

Hodder & Stoughton

LONDON SYDNEY AUCKLAND TORONTO

British Library Cataloguing in Publication Data

Malhotra, Inder
  Indira Gandhi: a personal and political biography
  1. India (Republic) Gandhi, Indira, 1917–1984
  I. Title
  954.04'5'0924

  ISBN 0-340-40540-6

First published in Great Britain 1989

Published by Hodder and Stoughton,
a division of Hodder and Stoughton Ltd,
Mill Road, Dunton Green, Sevenoaks, Kent TN13 2YE
Editorial Office: 47 Bedford Square, London WC1B 3DP

Photoset by Rowland Phototypesetting Ltd,
Bury St Edmunds, Suffolk

Printed in Great Britain by St Edmundsbury Press Ltd,
Bury St Edmunds, Suffolk

To REKHA

# Contents

# Illustrations

ACKNOWLEDGMENTS
1  Press Information Bureau, Government of India
2  Raghu Rai
3  R. K. Laxman
4  *The Times of India*
5  Virendra Prabhakar
6  R. K. Dhawan

# Foreword

More books have been written on Indira Gandhi than on even her illustrious father, Jawaharlal Nehru, independent India's first Prime Minister for seventeen years and, in modern Indian history, unquestionably a more towering figure. An obvious reason for this is the high drama in her life. Her phenomenal rise to power and popularity was followed by a fantastic fall and then by an even more rapid and remarkable political resurrection less than four years before her assassination in the autumn of 1984.

However, the problem about the plethora of books and publications on and about Indira is that the bulk of these appeared in two big spurts at the highest and the lowest points in her chequered career, separated from each other by only a few years. In the early Seventies, after Indira's tremendous success in the 1971 General Election and India's victory in the war with Pakistan that led to the liberation of Bangladesh, there was a virtual avalanche of adulatory biographies of Indira. In these, she was praised to the skies, judged to be totally free from fault or blemish and extolled as Durga, the invincible goddess in the Hindu pantheon. In the latter half of the decade, when the people of India voted her out of power, largely in protest against her declaration, in 1975, of a State of Emergency that suspended Indian democracy for nineteen months, there was a torrent of instant books that tarred Indira with the darkest of dark brushes and indeed depicted her as irredeemably evil. In some cases at least the authors of the adulatory and abusive books were the same.

Surprisingly, despite the passage of years, both the extreme views of Indira are strongly held in India even today. She is either revered or reviled. There is hardly a neutral opinion about her though it should be added that the reviling is usually done by the educated upper middle class, while reverence to her is shown by the people at large.

After Indira's return to power, in January 1980, several hurried books once again put her on the pedestal, while a number of recent volumes on the traumatic problem of Punjab and the Sikh minority have made her out to be an ogress. My primary purpose in writing this book is to break the cycle of hagiography and demonology and present her life story in its entirety, not in bits and pieces, as objectively as humanly possible. It is not an easy standard to live up to, if only because the very mention of her name invites an outpouring of vitriol

11

and venom in many Indian gatherings even today, but I have tried my best. In making this attempt I have been acutely aware that a personal and political biography of Indira is also a history of India at least for the two decades during which she dominated the Indian scene, whether she was in power or out of it.

From shortly after the day her father took over the leadership of independent India's government and Indira became his châtelaine and confidante, I have been lucky to have been a witness to most of the events described in this book, often from a ringside seat. I also had the good fortune to know Indira Gandhi though it would be presumptuous to claim either that she was a friend or that I knew her well. She was a very private and reserved person and had very few friends, and even they could not claim to have known her well because she revealed so little of herself.

However, I did know Indira. I began seeing her in the mid-Fifties, initially at the instance of her husband, Feroze Gandhi, who was a friend of mine. I was at that time a special correspondent of *The Statesman*. By the time of her father's death in May 1964, I had become the paper's Political Correspondent and chief of the New Delhi News Bureau. In this capacity, I saw a lot more of Indira during the eighteen months when, as Minister for Information and Broadcasting in the cabinet of Lal Bahadur Shastri, her father's successor, she was most unhappy with what she perceived to be his scant regard for her. Not many people visited Indira those days. My regular visits perhaps accounted for the rather easy access I had to her even after she became Prime Minister in January 1966.

At the end of 1967 I was transferred to Calcutta, the headquarters of *The Statesman*, from where I migrated in 1971 to Bombay, where I joined *The Times of India*. Even so, I continued to see her often enough, either when I went to Delhi or when she visited the city I was living in.

This pattern was broken by the Emergency, during which I made no attempt to see her, nor she to send for me, as she used to do sometimes in the past. In April 1978 I returned to Delhi as the Resident Editor of *The Times of India*. She was then out of power. The Janata government was determined to call her to account for her excesses during the Emergency but its drive to do so had degenerated into a vendetta. I took the earliest opportunity to call on her and the old pattern of communication was restored.

In writing this book I have drawn upon nearly thirty off-the-record conversations I had with her over the years at which no one else was present and also on an almost equal number of discussions with her by small groups that included me. Contents of group discussions can be confirmed or contradicted by other participants. For the accuracy of my account of one-to-one meetings the only surety I can offer is my record as a reporter and commentator for *The Statesman* and *The Times of India* in my country and for *The Guardian* in Britain.

The reader is entitled to know why I refer to Indira, and not to Gandhi or Mrs Gandhi, as would have been the case normally. The reason is not to claim familiarity with her but a purely practical one. Gandhi or Mrs Gandhi would have created endless confusion. Gandhi could be mistaken even for Mahatma Gandhi, the Father of the Nation, who was no kinsman of Indira's, to say nothing of the confusion between her and her two sons, Rajiv, who succeeded her, and Sanjay, who died in 1980. Even the use of the suffix Mrs would not have helped. For Indira's two daughters-in-law, Rajiv's wife Sonia, a great favourite of the late Prime Minister, and Sanjay's widow, Maneka, who was at war with her mother-in-law, also figure in the narrative frequently.

A brief word may also be said about the foot and notes disease from which no author can be free. At the suggestion of my publishers I have adopted a somewhat unusual technique and have dispensed with the practice of cluttering the text with numerals for the sake of notes on sources and other explanations. These notes have now been given according to the page and the lines on it and in a manner the reader should have no difficulty in following.

For any conclusions drawn or opinions offered in this book, unless specifically attributed to anyone else, the responsibility is entirely mine. But a great many people who knew Indira better than I did, or, by virtue of their political or official association with her, were privy to information still classified or outside the public domain have given me invaluable assistance and advice. They helped me sift fact from fiction and put arcane developments, elliptical hints and Byzantine intrigue into proper perspective. It would have been difficult to thank them individually in any case because of their large number. But, as it happened, a surprising proportion of them, including Indira's confidants and supporters, turned adversaries; and some inveterate critics who appeared to have developed some respect for her after her death, spoke to me, often at great length, only on condition that they would not be quoted or identified by name. I am most grateful to them, as I am to those who graciously allowed me to quote them and have been cited in the source notes. To Pupul Jayakar, P. N. Haksar, H. Y. Sharda Prasad and L. K. Jha I owe a special debt of gratitude because they spared a great deal of their valuable time answering my repeated and sometimes nagging queries with which I continually returned to them. The last of them, to my sorrow, died when this book was in the last stages of preparation for publication.

It has not been an easy book to write. I fell behind schedule more than once. An even bigger problem was that at almost every stage of writing and rewriting, the length of the text got out of hand. There were days when I despaired of ever being able to complete the book. I was rescued from these dire straits by Jane Osborn, my editor at Hodder & Stoughton, who showed exemplary patience and gave me both wise suggestions and much-needed encouragement. I cannot thank her adequately.

I am extremely grateful to Raghu Rai and Virendra Prabhakar for graciously allowing me to choose and use some of the excellent photographs of Indira Gandhi taken by them; to the government of India, especially its Principal Information Officer, Rammohan Rao, for permission to use pictures the copyright for which is held by the Indian government's Press Information Bureau (PIB); to *The Times of India* for letting me publish the photograph of Jayaprakash Narayan (J.P.); and to R. K. Dhawan, Indira's special assistant for many years, for readily opening up his private album to me and telling me to use whichever photographs I liked. R. K. Laxman, India's premier cartoonist and a dear friend, equally generously allowed me to reproduce his caricature of Indira as the Empress of India. To him also I offer profuse thanks.

My family put up cheerfully with my total neglect of them because of my preoccupation with writing this book and with my tantrums born of frustration over lack of adequate or timely progress. My son, Anil, would call frequently from New York where he lives to enquire how I was doing or to fret that I wasn't writing fast enough. It was my wife, Rekha, who bore the brunt of what at times seemed nothing less than an ordeal. But for her love, support and occasional prodding and cajoling this book might never have been written or, if written, reduced to requisite length. The dedication of the book to her is but a small recompense for what she went through.

INDER MALHOTRA

# 1   Murder in the Morning

On the cool, crisp morning of October 31st, 1984, Indira Gandhi, India's Prime Minister for all but three of the preceding eighteen years and often described as the world's most powerful woman, breakfasted on fruit and toast and stepped out of a side door of her official residence, 1, Safdarjung Road, in a most exclusive, tree-lined part of New Delhi, which the British had built as their imperial capital just over half a century earlier.

The short, slim and strikingly handsome woman looked as fresh as the flowers blooming in her beautifully maintained garden. Briskly, as was her wont, she started walking along a pathway connecting her house with the adjoining bungalow, 1, Akbar Road, that served as the Prime Minister's office. Once entirely separate, the two bungalows had for years formed part of a single complex, divided from each other only by a fence broken by a single wicket gate.

As always, except on rare occasions when a carefully cultivated dishevelled look served a political purpose, Indira was superbly turned out. In fact, she had taken particular care with her dress, appearance and coiffure because she was on her way to a television interview she had agreed to give Peter Ustinov, the British playwright, actor and humorist, on the lawns of her Akbar Road office. She had chosen a saffron sari because she had been advised that this colour showed rather well on the screen. Whether she realised that saffron is also the colour of martyrdom, according to Indian, especially Sikh, belief, will never be known.

If Indira had put on a saffron sari for the sake of the TV camera, she had, for the same reason, left off the bullet-proof vest that she had been virtually forced to wear under her blouse because of repeated threats to her life. These threats had suddenly multiplied during the four months since June when she had ordered the Army to storm the Golden Temple at Amritsar in Punjab. This holiest of the holy Sikh shrines had been converted into a fortress and the headquarters of the Sikh terrorists trying to carve out of India an independent Sikh homeland to be called 'Khalistan'.

Besides discarding the bullet-proof vest, Indira had dispensed with an important routine dating back to the days of her illustrious father. For about an hour every morning the Prime Minister's home used to be an open house. Hundreds of people, including the poorest of the poor, were allowed access to the head of the government to submit a petition, ventilate a grievance or simply to have the Prime Minister's *darshan*, a singularly Indian phenomenon through which a person is supposed to earn much merit just by having a glimpse of a noble soul. On October 31st, 1984, however, there was no time for the daily *darshan*.

As independent and impartial observers have testified, Indira's decision to order the troops to flush the terrorists out of the Golden Temple did not stem from 'enmity' for the Sikhs, 'a community Mrs Gandhi regarded with great affection'. But this is not how the Sikhs in general and extremists and terrorists in particular saw things.

To most Sikhs, including those who had hailed Indira's return to power only four years earlier, the military action in the Golden Temple, during which casualties were heavy and damage to the holy precincts extensive, was 'intolerable desecration' of what was, in their eyes, the most hallowed spot on earth. The Sikh terrorists, feeding on the community's collective rage, had vowed vengeance. Not a day passed when they did not threaten the Prime Minister, her son and her grandchildren with death.

Barely forty-eight hours earlier Indira herself had spoken of the possibility of her being killed. But she had told a huge public meeting in the eastern state of Orissa that 'such things' did not worry her because 'when I die every single drop of my blood will invigorate the nation and strengthen united India'. The audience had cheered her to the echo not because it believed her death to be imminent but because of its admiration for the courage of this seemingly frail woman.

In Indira's mind, however, the thought of death appears to have lingered. At dinner that night, she had told her host, the Orissa Governor, Bishamber Nath Pandey, that having seen her mother, grandfather and father die painfully in bed, she was keen to die 'on my two feet'. Then, cutting short her stay in Orissa by a day, she had rushed home to Delhi. She had received word that her grandchildren had been involved in a car accident which, she suspected, could have been an attempt on their lives by terrorists.

It took Indira only a minute to reach the wicket gate where she smiled at Sub-Inspector Beant Singh, a Sikh who had been a member of her bodyguard for nine years, had travelled abroad with her several times and was now on duty at the gate. His reponse to her smile was to shoot her in the abdomen with his revolver. As she collapsed on the concrete, Constable Satwant Singh, also a Sikh, emptied his Sten gun into her.

In two terrible minutes it was all over. The time was just after ten past nine. For a few seconds after the ghastly gunshots, almost everyone within the heavily guarded compound was stunned. Then all hell broke loose. Officials and guards, including those whose first impulse had been to scurry to safety, started running around, shouting and cursing.

During the brief moments of shocked silence, Beant Singh had had time to hang his walkie-talkie on the fence, raise his arms and declare: 'I have done what I had to do. Now you do what you like.' This was his way of saying that, on behalf of the Sikhs, he had avenged the gross sacrilege at the Golden Temple.

Commandos of the Indo-Tibetan Border Police, in charge of guarding the outer periphery of the Prime Minister's house and office, surrounded Beant and Satwant and marched them off to a nearby security hut. There, in a scuffle, the result allegedly of their attempt to escape, they were fired upon. Beant was killed on the spot. Satwant, though badly wounded, lived to face trial for murder and was executed in January 1989.

From a distance of only eighty yards, Peter Ustinov heard the horrible shots that shattered the peace of the lovely garden and ended Indira Gandhi's life. He later recalled:

> We were ready with the mike and the camera. A secretary had gone to fetch her, and then it happened. I heard three single shots. We looked alarmed but the people in the office said it must be firecrackers. Then there was a burst of automatic fire as if the attackers were making sure of it. I didn't think she had a chance in hell. We saw soldiers running. They kept us there for five hours. It became like a prison.

The security authorities were understandably anxious to ascertain whether Ustinov's crew had filmed the assassination and, if so, to confiscate the film. They were told that no such film existed because none had been taken, the TV crew being unsure of what exactly was going on. But the officials, thoroughly shaken by the morning's macabre events, pursued their inquiries at too great a length and with excessive zeal.

From early childhood Indira had identified herself with Joan of Arc. The Maid of Orleans had been betrayed and brought to death by people she had trusted. Indira was gunned down by men whose job it was to protect her. But there was a difference between her death and that of the heroine of her girlhood fantasies. The utter degeneration of the governmental system Indira herself had presided over for so long had contributed to both the insane hatred motivating her murderers and the incompetence of the elaborate security apparatus guarding her.

For instance, had elementary security norms been observed Satwant

Singh could not have been at the wicket gate inside the Prime Minister's compound on that fateful morning. For him to be there along with Beant Singh would have been unthinkable.

An impressionable young man, not yet twenty, Satwant had just returned from long leave in his village in Punjab's Gurdaspur district, a hot-bed of Sikh extremism. It should have been imperative that his superiors post him only at the periphery of the Prime Minister's house and not allow him anywhere near her until they had watched him carefully and made sure that he had not been infected by the virulent anti-Indira campaign raging in the area where he had spent his vacation.

Beant, too, had attracted adverse attention in the capital because of his meetings with hot-heads in Sikh shrines, or *gurdwaras*. Senior officers had, therefore, transferred him back to the Delhi Armed Police to which he belonged. But, having served the Prime Minister for years, he appealed to her directly and got the transfer order rescinded.

This had happened in spite of the agony which top security officials were going through for fear that Sikhs serving in the security guard might themselves become a security risk. In fact as soon as the Sikh community's rage against the military action in the Golden Temple had erupted, the Director of the Intelligence Bureau, technically also the head of the Prime Minister's security, had felt that it would be prudent to remove all Sikhs from her security guard, at least for some time. But rather than act on his judgment, he forwarded his proposal to the Prime Minister for approval.

On the 'Top Secret' file that saw the light of day only after her assassination, Indira had scribbled just three words: 'Aren't we secular?' This had put paid to the Intelligence Bureau Chief's idea. But to this day no one has explained why the file was sent to Indira in the first place. After all, a head of government in need of protection is not usually asked to be the judge of the arrangements necessary for the purpose.

In fairness to the harassed Intelligence Chief, it must be added, however, that the exclusion of all Sikhs from the Prime Minister's security guard was an extremely sensitive issue. And since Indira's highly centralised and personalised style of government had robbed most functionaries of the Indian state of initiative, the poor man was evidently scared of acting on his own.

While rejecting the proposal to banish all Sikhs from her security guard, Indira had endorsed, however, a decision taken at the instance of Ramji Nath Kao, a father figure in the Indian Intelligence establishment whom Indira had recalled from retirement to serve as her security adviser. The decision was that no two armed Sikh guards should ever be posted together anywhere inside the compound housing the Prime Minister's residence and office, and this was supposed to be an inflexible edict. And yet Satwant got round it simply by pretending that he had an upset stomach and, therefore, needed to stay close to a lavatory. Since there was one near the wicket gate, Satwant and his accomplice, both evidently burning with the desire to take revenge, managed to be together at a critical spot.

To cap it all, the regulation requiring that the Prime Minister should always be surrounded by bodyguards to screen her from the bullets of would-be assassins was also flouted. Indira was walking ahead of everyone else, with her devoted special assistant, R. K. Dhawan, at her elbow and the security guards ambling several steps behind. To their shame, they fled in different directions on hearing Beant's first shot.

Somewhat uncannily, Indira had foreseen this disgraceful denouement. As threats to her life had escalated, Kao had got rather alarmed by the very short distance between the boundary wall and her residential quarters. He had sought her permission to landscape the lawn so as to raise mounds of earth that might offer some protection from explosives thrown over the outer wall.

Indira had laughed and told him not to worry. 'When they come to kill me,' she remarked, 'nothing would help. Those supposed to save me will be the first to run away.'

Was this mere premonition or also a belated realisation that she had allowed instruments of the Indian state to run down dangerously? It is hard to say. But the fact remains that when the crunch came, things turned out to be even worse than she had anticipated.

There had clearly been a criminal neglect of her security. But this was not the only lamentable lapse on that melancholy morning. There was also a scandalous lack of timely medical aid to the Prime Minister.

An ambulance was routinely stationed at 1, Safdarjung Road. But at the critical moment it was unavailable. Its driver had gone for his tea break. There was no standby blood supply either. The fatally wounded Indira was, therefore, bundled into an Ambassador, an Indian version of the Morris Oxford, of 1954 vintage, by Dhawan and her Italian daughter-in-law, Sonia, still in her housecoat, who came rushing out, shouting: 'Mummy, Mummy'. Indira was taken to the prestigious All India Institute of Medical Sciences, nearly three miles away.

Since no one had thought of sending a wireless message to the medical institute, its junior doctors, on seeing the Prime Minister being carried in, panicked. Their seniors arrived on the spot fast enough and rushed Indira to the operating theatre where she was put on the heart-lung machine. She was given almost continuous blood

19

transfusion. At one stage a public appeal for blood was made. There were fist fights among volunteers wanting to be the first to donate blood. This aggravated the confusion and restiveness of the vast, constantly increasing crowd swirling around the institute which had started collecting from the moment Indira was brought in. It was swelling fast and its mood getting angrier by the minute.

All the pumping of blood into the Prime Minister was, however, little more than an elaborate essay in make-believe. In retrospect at least, it is clear that Indira, with no fewer than twenty bullet wounds, was clinically dead on arrival at the medical institute. But the doctors did not declare her dead until two twenty in the afternoon, though the news of her death had been broadcast by the BBC, and even circulated by Indian news agencies, several hours earlier.

Millions of Indians who wept for Indira first heard of her death from the external services of the BBC. One of them, who switched on his transistor in the marshy outskirts of Calcutta, was her sole surviving son, Rajiv Gandhi. Rajiv was absent from Delhi because he was campaigning for the ruling party in West Bengal as part of his apprenticeship for eventually succeeding his mother. How was he to know that the day of succession was to arrive so soon, so suddenly and so sadly?

Nor was Rajiv the only important person desperately needed in Delhi to be absent. The republic's President, Giani Zail Singh, himself a Sikh, was even further away, on a state visit to San'a, the capital of Northern Yemen. He decided to fly back home at once but could reach Delhi only late in the afternoon, a few hours after Rajiv's return. All this had a lot to do with the long delay in the official announcement of Indira's death.

Under the Indian constitution when a Prime Minister dies another one has to be sworn in immediately to avoid a vacuum. There can be no government without a council of ministers and no council of ministers without a Prime Minister at its head. At the same time, the President, even if he be travelling abroad, remains the only authority competent to pick a new Prime Minister (there is no provision for an acting Prime Minister) and to swear him or her in. Over the years Indian officials have had to be flown to such far-away places as Kiev in the Soviet Union and Ottawa in Canada to obtain a travelling President's signature on state papers that could not wait until his return home.

In an emergency the Vice-President can perform the President's functions only if these are formally and specifically transferred to him by the council of ministers which itself would cease to exist if the Prime Minister's death were officially admitted.

This Catch-22 situation was further complicated by the problem of whom to swear in. Past practice ran completely counter to the widely perceived current need: to transfer Indira's mantle to Rajiv immediately. When Indira's father and later his successor, Lal Bahadur Shastri, had died in harness, the then President, Dr Radhakrishnan, had sworn in the most senior cabinet minister, Gulzarilal Nanda in both cases, and asked the ruling party to elect a new leader after the customary thirteen-day mourning period. That was how Shastri had emerged as Nehru's duly chosen successor and Indira his.

However, in the changed and traumatic circumstances, a leisurely succession, spread over two weeks, seemed a luxury India could hardly afford.

Moreover, the selection of a stop-gap Prime Minister, pending the election of a permanent one by the ruling Congress party, even if still considered desirable, was hardly feasible. Indira had spent her last years making sure that no one except her son could succeed her. In the process she had so thoroughly downgraded and even denigrated her cabinet colleagues, state chief ministers and the party leaders that no one of any stature was left around to be a contender for her office. Even the pecking order among cabinet ministers holding important portfolios had been deliberately blurred. There was no identifiable Number Two to be treated as Nanda had been at the time of Nehru's and Shastri's deaths. A search for an interim successor could, therefore, prove even more contentious and perhaps divisive than the immediate coronation of the Crown Prince.

No wonder then that the inner councils of the Congress party, such as they were, quickly veered round to the view that Rajiv Gandhi should be sworn in as Prime Minister right away and that the party should meet after Indira's funeral to endorse the decision and formally to elect him as its leader.

Party elders, though not particularly happy to have to defer to a 'youngster', consoled themselves with the thought that the Nehru–Gandhi charisma, inherited by Rajiv, would be an asset in the General Election due only a few months hence.

During the long and rather tense flight from San'a to Delhi the President, too, had concluded that there was no viable alternative to making Rajiv Prime Minister right away. To Giani Zail Singh the presidency had been Indira's gift. Her decision to make him head of state had, in fact, surprised the country, dismayed many and overwhelmed the Giani himself. In a less than edifying display of gratitude he had declared: 'If Madam asks me to pick up a broom and sweep the floor, I would happily do so.' Later, however, his relations with the Prime Minister had begun to sour. They reached a very low point after the military action in the Golden Temple of which he was extremely and openly critical. This, however, had not mollified the Sikh community which blamed him for what had happened, next only to Indira. In fact, it held him 'guilty' of 'sacrilege' by virtue of being the supreme commander of the armed forces that had 'invaded' the holiest of Sikh shrines.

Nevertheless, as he confided to some of his travelling companions, his estrangement from Indira had little to do with the question of appointing Rajiv Prime Minister, which had to be decided on merit. Consequently, his first act on returning to Delhi and after paying homage to Indira at the medical institute was to swear Rajiv Gandhi in as the new Prime Minister. Only a minute or two before the brief and subdued ceremony at Rashtrapati Bhavan, the British-built presidential palace, formerly the abode of Viceroys, were the state-owned Indian TV and All India Radio allowed to announce that Indira Gandhi was dead.

Indira Gandhi was the third Indian Prime Minister to die in office but the first to be killed. She was not, however, the first great Indian to be gunned down. Thirty-six years earlier, Mohandas Karamchand Gandhi, better known as the Mahatma – Great Soul – and hailed as the Father of the Nation, was shot dead by a Hindu fanatic, Nathu Ram Godse, on January 30th, 1948.

The Mahatma – who, let it be repeated, was no kinsman of Indira – was a lone but heroic crusader against the Hindu–Muslim butchery and the mass migrations that accompanied the subcontinent's independence and partition into India and Pakistan in August 1947. Godse and other Hindu zealots accused him of being 'soft' on the Muslims, whom they held responsible for 'vivisecting Mother India', and hostile to his own Hindu community. They also believed that the only way to stop Gandhi from doing further 'damage' was to eliminate him.

They discovered, however, that their brutal act had had precisely the reverse effect to the desired result. The Mahatma's murder shocked Indians out of madness into sanity; indeed, it even had a salutary effect across the subcontinental divide, in Pakistan. Mindless killings stopped on both sides.

Whether Indira's assassination by two of her Sikh security guards would have similarly shocked the Sikh community out of its enraged and vengeful mood would never be known. For this hope was dealt a deadly blow almost instantly by the anti-Sikh riots that began in Delhi as soon as the news of Indira's assassination was officially announced and quickly degenerated into one of the worst orgies of murder, arson and looting that the Indian capital has witnessed in its long and often bloody history. Nearly 2,500 people, mostly Sikhs, were killed, according to official statistics; many of them were burnt alive. Fifty thousand Sikhs 'fled the capital of their own country' to seek shelter in Punjab; an equal number sought safety in hurriedly set up refugee camps in Delhi itself.

Many Sikhs were saved from frenzied mobs by their Hindu neighbours for which they were duly grateful. But the dominant sentiment among the Sikhs was one of bitterness and outrage. The killing and burning went on virtually unchecked for two days. The police, when not actually colluding with rioters, looked the other way. There was inexplicable delay in calling out the Army which eventually restored order.

The grim situation was worsened by highly exaggerated reports of rejoicing among Sikhs over Indira's murder, wholly baseless rumours of the slaughter of Hindus by Sikhs in Punjab – though Punjab, significantly, was free from Hindu–Sikh riots during those tense and terrible days – and by the slogan 'Khoon ka badla khoon' (blood for blood), shouted by interminable queues of mourners waiting for a last glimpse of Indira at Teen Murti House, her residence during seventeen years of her father's prime ministership, where her body lay in state.

What infuriated the Sikhs the most was their suspicion, strengthened by the government's refusal for many months to hold an inquiry, that the riots were organised. Independent opinion held that the riots had begun spontaneously but were soon taken over by ruling party activists, including perhaps some ministers and Delhi MPs, who then proceeded to provide direction and stewardship to the death dance.

I flew into curfew-bound Delhi from London some forty hours after Indira's assassination. From the airport itself it was clear that it was not the same city I had left six weeks earlier. Every inch of space at the airport was crowded by harried and stranded passengers. They had been stopped in their tracks not by the curfew alone but also by an almost complete breakdown of public transport.

During the dreary drive home, in a newspaper jeep exempt from the curfew, it was heartrending to see burning vehicles along the broad, beautiful but eerily deserted boulevards leading to the city. The real devastation and savagery were not, however, visible because they had taken place and were continuing several miles away, in the poorer parts of the capital, across the River Yamuna.

For days the riots against the Sikhs, unthinkable until the eruption of Sikh terrorism in Punjab and considered unlikely even afterwards, turned Delhi into a desolate and haunted city. Few moved about in the normally bustling bazaars and teeming townships. One poignant result of this was that Indira was denied the funeral she deserved.

Her predecessor, Lal Bahadur Shastri, had lacked her charisma and had ruled for only a short eighteen months. But he had died a national hero, having first successfully presided over a war with Pakistan and having then made peace with her at Tashkent in Soviet Central Asia. His funeral was a massive affair, yet it was nothing compared with the funeral of Indira's father, Jawaharlal Nehru, during which the ten-mile route to the cremation ground had become the 'most overpopulated area on earth', with crowds standing thirty deep and precariously perched on every lamp post and every tree.

Like her father, Indira had been a darling of the crowds, often attracting even larger numbers than had gathered around Nehru. In power or out of it, she could hardly take a step without being virtually mobbed. But on her last journey to a specially selected cremation spot – close to the place where the remains of her father and younger son, Sanjay, were consigned to the flames – her cortège passed through grim, grimy streets, only sparsely lined by mourners.

At the cremation ground the crowds were large enough. But no one failed to notice that there were only a handful of Sikhs, of whom most held some position in the government or the ruling party.

From the gun-carriage Indira's bier was lifted by Field-Marshal Manekshaw, the most senior Indian soldier, and the Chiefs of the Indian Army, Navy and Air Force and handed to the bereaved family. It was then placed on a sandalwood pyre on a raised platform.

While many wept and others shouted *'Indira Gandhi Amar Rahe'* (Indira Gandhi will live for ever), the pyre was lit by her son and successor, Rajiv, a picture of stoicism and dignity, who stood on the platform, flanked by his wife and two children, while the priests recited the *mantros* (litany) appropriate for the occasion.

The lighting of the pyre was not the only painful filial duty Rajiv had to perform. After the flames had risen high, he also had to bow to another dictate of the brutal finality of Hindu death rites: to tap Indira's cranium with a bamboo pole so that all her remains could be consumed fully by the fire.

Nehru, a lover of both the mountains and the rivers of India, especially the Ganga, sometimes called the Ganges, had willed that his ashes should partly be immersed in the rivers and partly scattered over the Indian earth in all parts of the country.

Indira, declaring that she was a 'daughter of the mountains', had left instructions that her ashes be scattered over the majestic Himalayas. This task, too, was completed by Rajiv Gandhi, flying in an Indian Air Force transport plane, on the thirteenth day after Indira had passed into history.

# 2 Invaluable Inheritance

The life that was so cruelly cut short on the last day of October in 1984 had begun almost exactly sixty-seven years earlier. Indira Nehru Gandhi had been exceptionally lucky in the choice of both her birthplace and the family into which she was born.

A sadly run down provincial town today, Allahabad was for centuries a major cultural and administrative centre of Northern India. It also was, and still is, an important place of pilgrimage for the Hindus, situated as it is at the confluence of the three most sacred of India's rivers, the Ganga, the Yamuna and the mythical Saraswati which flows only 'below the level of awareness'.

In the sixteenth century, Emperor Akbar renamed the city Allahabad, or Allah's Abode, and made it a seat of the Mughal Empire. With the advent of the British, its fortunes flourished further. It became the second city in the United Provinces (UP), now called Uttar Pradesh. A High Court, transferred there soon after the Mutiny of 1857 – feudal India's last and unsuccessful attempt to overthrow British rule – and the no less famous university, combined with the easy transport of goods on the River Ganga, made Allahabad a notable centre of administration, justice, politics, education and commerce.

At the time of Indira's birth on November 19th, 1917, Allahabad was truly a premier city and her grandfather, Motilal Nehru, a tall, leonine, highly successful and extremely wealthy lawyer, very much its premier citizen. She was his first grandchild and the first child of his only and much-adored son, Jawaharlal. Motilal's family lived in a palatial house called Anand Bhavan (House of Happiness) and it was here that Indira was delivered by a Scottish doctor whose name no one seems to remember.

Normally, Indira should not have been born at Allahabad at all. Custom demanded that her mother, Kamala, should go to her parents in Delhi for her first delivery. This time-honoured practice had a sound psychological basis: one's own mother's presence lessens the pains of childbirth. Kamala had, in fact, more reason than most women in her position to be near her mother during her first confinement. For she was not on the best of terms with the Nehru women. But Motilal, a proud patriarch genuinely fond of his comely daughter-in-law, would hear nothing of Kamala's travel plans. He wanted his first grandchild to be born under his own roof. He was also worried about her frail health. His affectionate pressure proved irresistible.

Understandably, the whole of the Nehru clan had assembled for the birth of Motilal's first grandchild. Inevitably, there was suspense and tension, relieved somewhat by the soft drinks served to women and Scotch and soda to men by the household servants scurrying round with trays. 'Had Father not been so excited,' recalled Indira's aunt, Krishna, only ten years older than her niece, who later married Raja Hutheesing, 'he would have remembered to celebrate the occasion with champagne, as he did some days later.'

'It's a bonnie lassie,' announced the Scottish doctor. Jawaharlal was delighted. Others clearly were not but were polite enough to remain silent. Jawaharlal's mother, Swarup Rani, gave voice to their and her own thoughts as well as to the deep-seated sentiment of the male-dominated Indian society when she burst out: 'It should have been a son.'

She succeeded only in inviting a sharp retort from her infuriated husband, Motilal. 'Have we made any distinction between our son and two daughters in their upbringing?' he demanded of his wife. 'Don't you love them equally? This daughter of Jawahar, for all we know, may prove better than a thousand sons.'

No less memorable than Motilal's outburst was little Indira's first outing only a few days later. Swaddled in heavy woollens – in November, North India can be very cold – she was taken across the compound to visit an old family retainer, Munshi Mubarak Ali, whose cottage was on the estate's edge. Treated by Motilal as more a brother than an employee, Mubarak Ali, suffering from terminal cancer, had tenaciously hung on to life with the sole objective of holding Jawaharlal's son in his hands. Joyfully he started to bless the child, exclaiming to Motilal: 'May he be a worthy successor to Jawaharlal, just as Jawahar has proved to be a worthy and wonderful son to you. May he illumine the name of the Nehrus.' The old man died without knowing that he had held a girl, not a boy, in his enfeebled arms.

For his granddaughter, Motilal chose the name Indira, after his own mother, Indrani, who was as formidable a woman in her life as Indira was to grow into later. To this, her parents added a middle name, Priyadarshini, which means 'Beautiful to the Sight'.

Congratulatory telegrams and letters from all parts of the country flooded Anand Bhavan. One of these, from Sarojini Naidu, a rare blend of politician and poet, often hailed as the 'nation's nightingale', described the baby as a 'new soul of India'. Mrs Naidu was being more prophetic than she could possibly have realised.

The Nehrus are Kashmiri Pandits, a small, exclusive community consisting of the highest of the high-caste Hindus. They belong to the lovely valley of Kashmir in the mountains of India's north-west which has, in present times, been a bone of contention and three times a battlefield between India and Pakistan. Indira's family traces its ancestry to Raj Kaul, a distinguished Persian and Sanskrit scholar, who left his home in the hills and migrated to the Mughal imperial capital of Delhi early in the eighteenth century.

In doing so, Raj Kaul was following the path traditionally trodden by other Kashmiri Brahmins, men of both learning and ambition but no great wealth and, therefore, in need of jobs in the plains. The Mughal empire was already in its decay but Emperor Farrukhsiyyar, still in a position to dispense patronage, gave Raj Kaul a *jagir* – land grant – and a house on the banks of a canal on Delhi's outskirts. Presumably to distinguish himself from other Kauls, the newcomer added Nehru, derived from the Urdu word for canal, *nehar*, to his name. The family came to be known as Kaul-Nehrus but some years later Kaul was dropped from the family surname.

Raj Kaul's brilliance, which had so impressed Farrukhsiyyar, must have been inherited by his descendants because through all the travails and vicissitudes of the empire, a Kaul-Nehru always occupied an important official position in it.

The first descendant to seek employment elsewhere was Lakshmi Narayan Nehru. Perhaps sensing the change in the wind, he became the East India Company's first Indian *vakil*, a lawyer and representative rolled into one, at the court of the now practically powerless Mughal emperor in the late eighteenth century.

His son, Gangadhar, was a *kotwal* or police chief in Delhi around the time of the 1857 Mutiny. He and his family were among the tens of thousands who fled the Mughal capital to escape the wrath of the infuriated British soldiery. They did not flee very far but tried to make a fresh start in Agra, once the empire's second city but now so tattered that even the Taj Mahal, the magnificent monument to Emperor Shahjahan's love for his wife, was being used as an armoury.

Four years later, in 1861, Gangadhar died in Agra at about the time when Bahadurshah Zafar, the last of the Mughals, lay dying in captivity in far-away Rangoon, reciting some of his own verses on the woes of exile. Gangadhar's wife was six months pregnant. The son born to her three months later was Motilal.

The burden of bringing up the infant, and indeed the whole family, fell on Nandlal, the younger of Motilal's two older brothers, who was practising at the Bar in Agra, having qualified in law while working in a princely state. When the High Court moved from Agra to Allahabad, so did Nandlal. Motilal went with him.

For the first twelve years of his life, Motilal was educated at home and taught Arabic and Persian, the languages of the once ruling Muslims. But he had also imbibed, especially from the women of his family, a great deal of Hindu thought, belief and folklore. He thus became, like other members of the élite groups of his times, a man of two cultures, best described as Indo-Persian. The broad secular outlook of Motilal and his family, which must be reckoned as one of the finest legacies of the Nehrus to modern India, grew from these roots.

While Motilal was struggling with Arabic and Persian lessons, the men of two cultures had started acquiring a third, the Western one, from their new rulers. They had welcomed the job opportunities offered by the British Raj and were enthusiastic about English education, introduced, as Thomas Babington Macaulay recorded in a celebrated minute in 1835, to raise up a new class – 'Indian in blood and colour, but English in taste, in opinions, in morals, and in intellect' – who could act as interpreters between the British and their subjects. However, once started, the English education could not be confined to the straitjacket prescribed for it by its advocates. It brought along with it the best of the British liberal thought and values which called into question the very basis of the imperial enterprise in India that had introduced schooling in English in the first place! The Raj had, in fact, sown the seeds of its own destruction – though this was not to become obvious until much later.

Motilal was among those who took to English education keenly. But he failed to get a BA degree. In the law examination, however, he did extremely well and topped the class. His subsequent success at the Bar was instant and phenomenal. He needed it, too, because Nandlal had died suddenly, leaving to Motilal, then only twenty-six, the responsibility of bringing up a large joint family.

With English language and education came the English lifestyle and Western ways which Indian élite groups started adopting with varying degrees of alacrity and enthusiasm. No one took to them more speedily or with greater gusto than Motilal.

Until Jawaharlal was three, Motilal's family lived in the old city amidst congestion, crowds, dust, din and sundry smells. But then they moved to the exclusive and antiseptic Civil Lines where, apart from the British rulers, only one other Indian family lived at that time. Anand Bhavan, the mansion where Indira would be born, was built seven years later, at the turn of the century.

As Motilal's wealth increased, so did his penchant for Western ways. He became an ardent Anglophile and spared no effort or expense to live like an English aristocrat. He employed English governesses for his two daughters and sent his son to be educated at Harrow, Cambridge and the Inner Temple, from where he returned in 1912 'more an Englishman than an Indian'. A commanding figure, Motilal dominated his household, as indeed he dominated the Allahabad Bar or any other group he happened to be in, spent lavishly and entertained royally, maintaining three kitchens – European, Indian non-vegetarian and a strictly vegetarian one.

In later life Indira was shy of talking about the feudal splendour and dazzling affluence amidst which she was born but she remembered the sprawling and luxurious Anand Bhavan as a 'delight for children, for it had a lot of space for play and hiding'.

To his children, grandchild and nephews and nieces, many of whom lived under his roof – at one time there were forty members of the clan and more than a hundred servants and retainers – Motilal was a tower of strength. His grandeur commanded respect from them, of course. But it also conferred on them a deep feeling of security. They knew, as Indira recalled repeatedly several decades later, that he was there to protect them.

His one fault, as many have testified and his younger daughter, Krishna Hutheesing, has recorded, was his imperious temper which he seems to have passed on to his descendants. Jawaharlal, having had a taste of it once, developed a dread of his doting father that never really left him. In Indira's view, however, Motilal's fiery temper was 'softened by quick forgiveness and infectious laughter'. She also admitted that in her childhood years her grandfather had a far greater impact on her than her father, whose influence came much later.

She could afford to take a relaxed view because she alone in the entire household was in the happy position of never being at the receiving end of Motilal's temper and tantrums. On the contrary, he indulged her endlessly and indeed spoiled her by meeting her every wish and whim. Others, including the womenfolk of the house and the hordes of visitors to Anand Bhavan, vied with Motilal in petting and pampering her. The rigid discipline Motilal's own children had had to observe was conspicuous by its sheer absence in Indira's case.

And yet, despite all the love and affection showered on her, Indira was a troubled child almost from the day she became conscious of the world around her. The source of her unhappiness was the harsh treatment her mother, Kamala, was receiving at the hands of the Nehru women, especially the vivacious Vijayalakshmi, nicknamed Nan but to be better known to the world in later years as Mrs Pandit, the elder of Jawaharlal's two sisters, and until Indira's birth, the darling of Anand Bhavan.

Mrs Pandit, now ninety and the oldest Nehru alive, emphatically denies having ill-treated Kamala and blames Indira for spreading this canard and harbouring ill-will against her on this score. If Mrs Pandit's vehement denials are usually disbelieved it is because too many friends and acquaintances of the family witnessed the taunts Kamala had to endure.

Kamala's family, also Kashmiri Pandits, matched the Nehrus in both lineage and wealth. But they were very orthodox and untouched by Western ways. This became a grave handicap for Kamala in the highly anglicised Nehru household. Motilal asked Miss Hooper, his daughters' governess, to teach Kamala English. But this did not help because it was her general lack of sophistication, not lack of fluency in English alone, that had made her the target of taunts by Mrs Pandit and others. Jawaharlal's mother, Swarup Rani, made no secret of her conviction that Kamala was not good enough for her beloved son.

Kamala might have borne her humiliation more stoically and little Indira might have been less troubled had Jawaharlal sometimes sprung to his wife's defence against unfair criticism or done something to assuage her wounded feelings. But he did nothing of the kind, and not merely because of his preoccupation with bigger things. As he candidly, even remorsefully, admitted many years later, when it was too late, he was simply indifferent to a wife with whom his arranged marriage had not been a resounding success.

For nearly half a century Indira kept her pent-up resentment to herself. But then it gushed forth, and the niece started repaying in kind the aunt, Mrs Pandit, for the barbs directed at Kamala. The hostility between the two grew steadily and got intertwined with the political conflicts that marked Indira's long, chequered and at times stormy career as Prime Minister. In the crucial General Election in 1977, in which Indira lost not only power but also her seat, Mrs Pandit campaigned vigorously against her though she studiedly avoided going to Indira's own constituency.

As a child at Anand Bhavan, however, little Indira could only suffer helplessly along with her mother. Kamala withdrew into her shell and sought refuge in religion. For hours she would lock herself in her room while Indira would sit by her side in silent sympathy. Of the close bond that developed between the two, Indira spoke five decades later: 'I loved her deeply and when I thought she was being wronged I fought for her and quarrelled with people.'

What she did not add but became obvious in later years was that the humiliation heaped on her mother's head also instilled in Indira a steely determination not to let anyone treat her in the same manner.

Kamala's deep and lasting impression on her daughter's personality was to prove to be the strongest influence on her. But, from early childhood, Indira's life was being moulded also by forces more powerful than personality clashes and personal bickering in the Nehru household or even her own intense love for her suffering mother.

As it happened, Indira was born exactly twelve days after the Russian revolution. But this remarkable, if only symbolic, coincidence went practically unnoticed in an India that was then noticeably placid. In the first decade of the century there had been an upsurge of revolutionary nationalism and even determined terrorist attacks on leading members of the government. But both had subsided. Western-educated men of moderation, dominant in the political institutions of the day, simply drowned the demands of more strident nationalism in their apathy. They were committed to the slow, evolutionary method of forging a new constitutional relationship between Britain and India and had no use for the extremists' demand for *swaraj*, complete independence. The terrorists were crushed by the Raj with an iron hand.

In 1912, when Indira's father, Jawaharlal, returned from England, the Indian National Congress – the principal political institution of the country, founded in 1885 – was once again firmly under the control of the moderates. And prominent within the moderates' leadership was Motilal. He had been attending Congress sessions since 1888. As a legal luminary, he had found a slow, constitutional approach to politics entirely to his taste, temperament and training.

The Indian National Congress, not to be mistaken for anything like the US Congress or British Parliament, was at that time nothing like the mighty national movement for independence that it was to become later. Nor was it even remotely comparable to the ruling party into which it was to be transformed after the advent of independence in 1947. It was then little more than a debating society humbly petitioning the government for more jobs and other opportunities for the élite classes that alone had profited from the British rule.

Young Jawaharlal, having attended the Bankipore session of the Congress in December 1912, denounced the organisation, accurately enough, as an upper-middle-class social gathering of English-speaking gentlemen in 'morning coats, top hats and well-pressed trousers'.

At the start of the First World War, the Congress attitude towards the Raj became even more accommodating, indeed submissive. It loyally declared its support for the war in Europe though in the explicit expectation that, at the end of the war, India would be given Dominion status within the British Empire and Commonwealth.

Unsurprisingly, this stirred into action those favouring the more populist and exciting slogan of 'complete independence here and now', though it took them some time to disturb the surface calm. Signs of discontent grew, however, as the war drew towards its end. The main reason for this was the British government's niggardly response to the demand for Dominion status which had been joined, interestingly, by a tall, gaunt and highly Westernised Muslim lawyer from Bombay, Mohammed Ali Jinnah, later to be the founder of Pakistan.

The Montague–Chelmsford reforms, announced in 1918, conceded partial self-government only in the provinces. The Viceroy's government in New Delhi, with absolute authority over the entire country, was to be left untouched. Even in the provinces concessions were to be doled out in driblets.

The British compounded their parsimony in political reform with provocation. They passed the Rowlatt Act which gave the government sweeping powers of preventive detention of all suspected nationalists and summary trials. Against their sentences, often for specially created offences, there could be no appeal. Indian discontent was instant, deep and nationwide. And, in the continuing conflict between moderates and extremists in the nationalist movement, the scales were tipped in favour of the latter.

The flawed reforms and the Draconian law also had a powerful, if curious, impact on a persistent conflict in the Nehru household. Motilal had always made a virtue of his moderation. To Jawaharlal, who had been exposed to Fabian socialist ideas during his stay in Britain, his father was 'immoderately moderate'. Arguments between father and son became increasingly heated.

Motilal had watched Jawaharlal fret at the slow pace of political progress in India and search vainly for some mode of action to accelerate this pace. But he had continued to hope that this youthful restlessness would pass and his son would join him in the lucrative law practice he had built up. But, as the political temperature rose, he saw his hopes fade away, and this made him angry. His son was even angrier because of his failure both to convert his father to his point of view and to find a way effectively to canalise the country's feelings against its alien rulers.

The way was eventually shown by a frail little man who burst on the Indian scene with cosmic force. In next to no time he was to revolutionise Indian politics and shake not only the Nehru household but practically every home and hamlet in the vast and until then dormant subcontinent. The shock was duly felt by the mighty British empire on which the sun was supposed never to set.

His name was Mohandas Karamchand Gandhi, soon to be called the Mahatma. Gandhi, eight years younger than Motilal, was, like him, a lawyer. But, unlike Motilal though like his son, Jawaharlal, the newcomer had taken his law degree in England – without in any way becoming anglicised.

After a few years at the Bar, Gandhi had gone to South Africa to plead a case on behalf of the Indian community settled there. He had planned to stay a year but stayed twenty. During this period he conducted his famous experiments with *satyagraha*, literally the 'path of truth' but in actual fact non-violent non-cooperation. Sometimes he also called it civil disobedience. He had found it a powerful instrument against the tyranny and racism of the Smuts government in South Africa. He now recommended the same weapon to his countrymen for use against the British, provided everyone wielding it observed the exacting code of conduct he absolutely insisted on.

Gandhi's call for *satyagraha* against the Rowlatt Act electrified the country and fired the imagination of tens of thousands of young men. Jawaharlal was among the most ardent converts to the new methodology and anxious to jump into the fray without a moment's delay. This brought him into a head-on collision with his father.

Motilal viewed *satyagraha* as nothing short of 'midsummer madness'. Law-breaking was anathema to him. This was natural in a man deeply steeped in law. But, in his vehement opposition to *satyagraha*, there was also an equally strong subjective element. The thought of his much-loved son going to jail was abhorrent to him, though often, during the night, he would descend from his comfortable bed to sleep on the floor to sample the hardship he knew awaited his son in His Britannic Majesty's jails.

However, Motilal would not relent to the extent of permitting Jawaharlal to embark on non-cooperation and jail-going. Tension between father and son mounted hourly. 'The atmosphere,' testified Krishna Hutheesing, 'was tense all the time and one hardly dared to utter a word for fear of rousing Father's anger or irritating Jawaharlal.' The harassed family did not know how and when, if at all, the conflict would be resolved. In the event it was settled simply and speedily by a grim tragedy in Punjab, the land of five rivers, the centre of Sikh religion and the main recruiting base of the British Indian Army.

The decisive event is known to history as the Jallianwalla Bagh Massacre and rightly regarded as the most infamous atrocity of the British Raj in India.

On April 13th, 1919, which was the Hindu New Year's Day, an unarmed crowd of about 20,000, including women and children, assembled in a public park called Jallianwalla Bagh in the holy city of Amritsar, later to play, as we have noted, a crucial, indeed critical, part in Indira's life. The park was then, as it is today, an enclosed one, hemmed in on three sides by the high walls of the surrounding houses and with only one very narrow exit.

General Dyer, enraged by the violence in the city in the week preceding the Hindu New Year's Day, during which an English woman missionary was beaten up and left for dead, arrived on the scene at the head of 150 soldiers and ordered the crowd to disperse. But there was just no way out. The only exit, through which no more than five people could pass at a time, was sealed by the troops. Within three minutes the soldiers were asked to fire on the crowd at point-blank range. Some tried to scale the walls but could not. Others died in an attempt to save themselves by jumping into a well. Most were cut down by bullets.

According to the Hunter Committee of Enquiry, 379 men, women and children had been shot in cold blood and another 1,200 badly wounded and left without any medical aid whatever. If more were not killed at Jallianwalla Bagh, Dyer cockily testified to the Hunter Committee, it was because he had 'exhausted his ammunition'.

The whole of India was outraged, Motilal no less than his fellow countrymen. Like them, he realised that Gandhi was right. Freedom would have to be fought for; it would not be given by the British as a gift. Almost overnight he moved closer to Gandhi than even the firebrand Jawaharlal. From now on father and son were at one in the cause of independence despite their many disagreements.

It was entirely typical of Gandhi to decide that the next Congress session should be held at Amritsar at the end of 1919. Motilal was in the chair but Gandhi was the gathering's moving spirit. Jawaharlal was present, though in a subsidiary and largely silent role. Even so, this was the start of what a British journalist was to call some years later, in a memorable phrase, the 'Nationalist Trinity of Father, Son and the Holy Ghost'.

By now Gandhi, whom Churchill was to describe as a 'half-naked fakir', had become a powerful influence on the Nehrus. He became their guide, philosopher and friend on matters political as well as personal. 'Everything changed miraculously from the time Gandhiji [ji is a term of respect usually added to a person's name as a suffix] entered our house. He came, we saw and he conquered,' recalled Mrs Pandit over sixty years later. 'My brother has called Gandhiji's entry into politics a gentle breeze. That makes me laugh because he came into our family like a hurricane.'

Indira was no more than five when she first met the Mahatma. As she stated afterwards, she then looked upon him 'not as a great leader but more as an elder in the family to whom I went with difficulties and problems which he treated with the grave seriousness which was due to the large-eyed and solemn child I was'.

Gandhi's call for a boycott of British legislatures, law courts, colleges, schools and even British goods was obeyed at Anand Bhavan instantly. Motilal's decision to give up his fabulous legal practice meant a sudden change in the family's luxurious lifestyle but he and his children made the sacrifice willingly. Discarding Savile Row suits, the old man took to loose Indian garments made of simple homespun *khadi* cloth, proudly described by his son as the 'livery of freedom'.

However, the loss of luxury at Anand Bhavan should not be exaggerated. Motilal's current income may have gone, but his wealth was more than ample. Life for the family continued to be comfortable. Indira, in any case, was deprived of nothing. All her wants and demands were still promptly met.

Motilal's and his family's metamorphosis made Indira's first memory highly political. It was that of a ceremonial bonfire of the family's foreign clothes – she remembered the 'rich materials and the lovely colours' all her life – on the terrace of the family's mansion. That evening, in her own words, she also discovered her power over her parents.

Both Jawaharlal and Kamala thought that Indira was too young to be allowed at the bonfire. She appealed to her grandfather who 'then, as always later' took her side. However, when the flames eventually went up, little Indira, exhausted by the day's excitement, was fast asleep.

The symbolic burning of foreign clothes had a searing sequel. A woman relative, returning from a visit to France, had brought Indira a lovely frock. When told by Kamala that the family now wore 'only handspun and hand-woven cloth', the Paris-returned lady lost her temper. She argued that while the adults of the family could do what they liked, the child must not be forced to forgo little pleasures.

Kamala then called Indira and gave her the choice to accept or reject the garment. After only a brief hesitation she rose to the occasion, or at least to her mother's expectations, and returned the frock to the visitor. The rebuffed relative chose to needle the child. 'All right, Miss Saint,' she exclaimed, 'I will take back the frock but how is that you have a foreign doll?'

All day Indira was torn between her passionate attachment to her doll and the call of duty and conscience. At dusk she took the doll to the terrace and set fire to it. The trauma never left her. 'To this day I hate to strike a match,' she wrote more than four decades later.

As the family plunged into Gandhian *satyagraha* there appeared in Indira's troubled world a welcome bright spot. Having watched her mother, Kamala, suffer at the hands of the Nehru women, Indira had developed a protective feeling towards her and deep resentment against her tormentors. She was not resentful against her father but his indifference to his wife's suffering did trouble her.

Now, however, Indira noticed that, to her father's delight and perhaps surprise, her mother had suddenly become his political ally and supporter. Jawaharlal remained absorbed in the great tasks he had set himself. He was so mesmerised by Gandhi's magic and so inebriated by his own 'discovery of India', especially of the hungry, half-naked peasantry he met at close quarters for the first time, that

35

he virtually forgot his family, his wife and his daughter. Only years later did he realise 'what a burden and trial' he must have been to them in those days and 'what amazing patience and tolerance' his wife had shown towards him. But Kamala, for her part, was full of joy, even euphoric. To be able to lend support and strength to her husband worked on her like a tonic. Even her health improved.

She was better suited, by temperament and upbringing, to the austerity that Gandhi preached than the Nehrus who, with the conspicuous exception of Jawaharlal, were luxury loving. She, therefore, took upon herself the task of transforming Anand Bhavan into the nerve-centre of the nationalist struggle unleashed by Gandhi.

Indira, who observed and absorbed all this, was to tell a women's seminar many years later:

> Many people knew the part which was played by my grandfather and my father. But, in my opinion, a more important part was played by my mother. When my father wanted to join Gandhiji and to change the whole way of life . . . the whole family was against it. It was only my mother's courageous and persistent support and encouragement that enabled him to take this step which made such a difference not only to our family but the history of modern India.

Little Indira's joy over the change in her mother's role was not unmixed with sorrow. She was frequently parted from the protective family elders because *satyagraha* and nationalist politics became synonymous with going to prison.

Indira was only four years old when, in 1921, balanced on her grandfather's knee in the dock of an Allahabad court, she watched the proceedings, inquisitively but uncomprehendingly, as he and her father were sentenced to six months' rigorous imprisonment each.

Thereafter jail-going by the family elders became a regular pilgrimage. Every spell of forced separation from the loving elders was naturally a big wrench for the child. Ironically her father's and grandfather's return from prison produced even greater agony because of uncertainty over when they might be hauled to jail again and the family reunion come to an abrupt end. Nor did all returns from behind bars take place in happy circumstances. Some were the result of the *satyagraha* petering out; at other times Gandhi called it off because of his followers' inability to live up to the exacting standards of non-violence prescribed by him.

No wonder Indira's childhood was extremely unsettled. She worried about her mother and shared the occasional political frustrations of her elders and she lived in a state of high excitement, with which Anand Bhavan was charged. From a very early age she also became used to huge crowds converging on her home and depriving her and her family of their privacy. And yet even amidst crowds, there were terrors in the child's life of which the grown-ups, absorbed in their own concerns, knew nothing. For instance, every night after supper she had to walk along a dark corridor to reach her room, where she had to climb a stool to switch on the light. She was scared but never told her parents or anyone else. Her lifelong refusal to share her fears with others was thus deep rooted.

Indira's games during her childhood were primarily political. She would divide her dolls into rival teams of freedom-fighters and baton-wielding police and arrange a confrontation between the two. Needless to say, the freedom-fighters would always win. She would also climb a table and deliver thundering speeches to the bemused servants of the household, repeating slogans she had picked up from her elders.

Somewhere along the line, she started having visions of heroism and martyrdom, a consequence perhaps of reading, under her father's influence, a great many serious books before her time. One day her younger aunt, Krishna, noticed that Indira was striking a rather curious pose. Her eyes flashing, her arms outstretched, she stood in the verandah muttering something to herself. Asked what was going on, she solemnly replied that she was practising being Joan of Arc. 'I have just been reading about her,' she added, 'and some day I am going to lead my people to freedom as Joan of Arc did.' Whether or not she outgrew these childhood fantasies, the Joan of Arc syndrome was to be with her until her life did end in martyrdom.

At first only Indira's father and grandfather went to jail. But the family women joined them nearly a decade later, starting a trend of women's awakening in a traditionally conservative society which far outpaced the movements for women's equality in the advanced societies of the West. Indira's mother, Kamala, was arrested first and then her grandmother. Her aunt, Vijayalakshmi, followed. Her own turn was to come much later. Meanwhile, on a celebrated occasion, she greeted some visitors to Anand Bhavan with the words: 'Everybody has gone to jail.'

Between Gandhi's first *satyagraha* and the advent of freedom a quarter of a century later, Jawaharlal underwent six terms of imprisonment totalling over nine years. These were critical years for Indira's childhood and adolescence when she needed her father's company the most. Her desolation and loneliness might have been mitigated somewhat if she had had a brother or a sister. But she was an only child. No wonder then that at a very young age she resolved never to have an only child when the time came for her to be a mother.

Her loneliness, lack of an even tenor of life and her vision of the great tasks expected of her appear to have developed in her a feeling of great vulnerability and inadequacy, goading her to develop a dual defensive mechanism. On the one hand, despite her painful shyness, she strove to excel in whatever she had to do. On the other, she enveloped herself in impenetrable reserve. She was unable to confide her thoughts and emotions to anyone except a very few and she guarded her privacy most zealously. All these traits were to remain with her even when she filled for close to two decades a position of very high visibility in a nation that is the second largest in the world and perhaps the most inquisitive.

It was the Congress policy not to pay the fines imposed by law courts on those offering *satyagraha*. The police therefore visited Anand Bhavan frequently, to realise Motilal and Jawaharlal's unpaid fines by attaching furniture and other household goods. Indira, only four years old when this process of despoliation first began, was 'greatly annoyed and protested to the police', as her father recorded in his *Autobiography*. He also wondered if this might have coloured Indira's view of the police for life.

Incidentally, this is Nehru's first reference to his daughter in his autobiography and it occurs on page 91. Mention of her birth is left until pages 332–4, in the course of his belated remorse, after Kamala's death, over his neglect of his wife. In a revealing remark, Nehru says at one place that Kamala and Indira looked like 'sisters, not mother and daughter'.

In the circumstances in which she grew up, Indira's education inevitably suffered. It became episodic, uneven and indeed nomadic. Her father, unable to take charge of the situation because of his frequent imprisonment, was worried. On hearing from his wife that Indira was becoming 'more and more intractable and pays no heed to any kind of study', his concern turned into alarm. In a letter to his father in 1922 he demanded that something be done about his daughter's schooling.

This was easier said than done. Allahabad's Modern School, where Motilal sent Indira, was a nationalist institution but apparently deficient in resources. The grand seigneur did not consider it good enough for his granddaughter. So he withdrew her from there and sent her to St Cecilia's, run by three Englishwomen, the Cameron sisters. This led to a fearful row between father and son. The younger Nehru insisted that St Cecilia's was covered by the Gandhian ban on British government schools. Motilal disagreed violently. Gandhi, whose intervention was sought, upheld Jawaharlal who had vowed that he would not allow her daughter to be brought up by the Camerons as a 'little Miss Muffet'. Indira was withdrawn from this school, too, and arrangements were made for private tutors to coach her at home.

This made her isolation from children of her own age complete.

Soon, however, a nagging worry about her mother's health super-seded her loneliness and other insecurities. Frail and delicate at the best of times, Kamala had known illness before but had recovered remarkably well, especially after plunging into political activity. But the exhilaration of participation in the freedom struggle had not lasted long. She was struck by pulmonary tuberculosis, at that time a dreaded disease and a killer. Doctors advised treatment in a Swiss sanitorium, then the destination of all those afflicted by consumption and able to afford a journey to Europe. The year was 1926. Indira accompanied her parents to Geneva.

It took over a year's treatment for Kamala to be pronounced cured. During this period Indira went to L'Ecole Nouvelle at Bex. Though still aloof from other students, she was happier than at any time before. Her mother was slowly getting better. And, for the first time in her nine years, she and her parents were together by themselves. She picked up enough French to be able to move around on her own and learnt music and skiing.

Back in Allahabad in December 1927, Indira went to St Mary's Convent School. Her father, in prison yet again, had apparently withdrawn his objection to missionary teaching. But, as a compromise, he had insisted on hiring a tutor to teach her Hindi at home. This was perhaps superfluous because Kamala was already teaching her both Hindi and Hinduism assiduously.

Indira was thirteen, according to the Hindu calendar (which varies from the Gregorian one by a few weeks), when her father felt compelled to make a contribution of his own to her education. On October 26th, 1930, from the Naini prison, across the river from his hometown, he started writing to her a series of letters which was soon to turn into a unique correspondence course in world history 'from early man to present-day civilisations'. Though written from jail without the benefit of a reference library and therefore suffering from many flaws, these letters, when published under the title *Glimpses of World History*, were justly hailed as among the best of Nehru's writings, their strong merit being a sensitive selection of significant events in the flow of human history, a lucidity of style that made the narrative intelligible to a teen-aged girl and an Asia-centred approach until then unknown to historians.

To the young and lonely Indira they were 'just letters' at that time, though she dutifully read them. Even when she re-read them in book form, she found that 'much of it was above my head. Some things I retained. Others I forgot. The same happened with other books.' However, after becoming Prime Minister she did remark: 'Now I realise that they [her father's letters] helped to form my mind in a way

39

that no other education did because they helped me to see things in perspective.'

Even before receiving the first of the letters that were to grow into the *Glimpses of World History*, Indira started experiencing the heady excitement of watching history in the making in her country, indeed in her own family.

At the stormy session of the Congress in Calcutta in December 1928, presided over by Motilal, there was a classic clash between father and son over the issue of Dominion status, favoured by the elder Nehru and the Congress old guard, as against full independence, insisted upon by Jawaharlal and his young and radical supporters. Gandhi, using his enormous prestige, brought about a one-year truce between the two sides. But the scales of Congress opinion had turned decisively in favour of the radicals well before the truce neared its end. The Congress was due to meet in Lahore, the capital of Punjab, now a premier city of Pakistan, at the end of 1929. At Motilal's suggestion and with Gandhi's active support, Jawaharlal was elected president of the Lahore Congress, the first and so far only instance of a son succeeding his father in this position.

Twelve-year-old Indira was among the hundreds of thousands of delirious Indians who saw Motilal, in the manner of a monarch, pass on the Congress crown to the son whom he loved so dearly despite their many disagreements.

On January 26th, 1930, on the banks of Ravi, the river that flows past Lahore, Indira was again present when thousands took a pledge, under her father's leadership, not to rest until they had attained full independence. The ceremony was repeated all over the country at the same time. At Lahore her grandfather now stood behind, not ahead of, her father. The greatly excited gawky girl could not have known that she was witnessing the making of what was to be one day her own inheritance.

The British chose to treat the demand for full freedom with supreme indifference. Gandhi responded by a plan of action which stunned friends and foes alike. He announced that he would personally defy the salt tax, imposed by the British, which he held to be the most iniquitous of all laws as it taxed the daily necessity of even the poorest of the poor. To ensure that no violence occurred during the salt *satyagraha*, Gandhi said he and a few hand-picked followers would march from his *ashram* or retreat in Ahmedabad to Dandi on the seashore, nearly 240 miles away, where he would pick up salt from the sea without paying anyone any tax.

Jawaharlal was not alone in exclaiming that this was a 'rather curious approach to political warfare'. But subsequent events showed that

Gandhi had once again captured the imagination of the masses by tailoring his tactics to suit their temper. Starting on March 12th, 1930, it took Gandhi twenty-three days to reach Dandi. Each day more and more people joined the march, turning a trickle into a torrent and electrifying not only the surrounding countryside but the entire country. Overnight, salt became a magic word. The Raj met the tremendous upsurge with predictable repression and mass arrests. Indira's father was among the first to be imprisoned.

As men were marched off to prison in tens of thousands, women decided to leave their homes and even *purdah* – the veil – to court arrest, braving police batons and bullets. Indira's mother, Kamala, took the plunge on New Year's Day, 1931. She was proud of 'following in my husband's footsteps' but worried about Indira, then at an 'awkward age'. Her daughter assured her that she would 'remain cheerful and look after herself'.

Still too young to be able to follow her mother to jail, Indira joined other women members of the family in nursing the victims of police volleys and *lathi*-charges (beating up with long staffs), who were brought to her previous home, now renamed Swaraj Bhavan and turned into the headquarters of the Indian National Congress. The Nehru family, in the meantime, had moved into another house, also called Anand Bhavan, which Motilal had planned as a small and modest home but which turned out to be no less palatial and opulent than the original one.

Told by her elders that at twelve she could not be a member of the Congress party, Indira reacted angrily and formed an organisation of her own. It was *Vanar Sena* or Monkey Brigade. Modelled on the legendary monkey army that helped Lord Rama, the hero of the epic Ramayana, to conquer Sri Lanka, Indira's *Vanar Sena* acted as an auxiliary of the Congress, putting up posters, writing notices, addressing envelopes, getting messages past unsuspecting policemen and, in short, acting, in Indira's words, 'not unlike monkeys'.

Busy leading the Monkey Brigade, Indira seemed less disturbed, more settled and indeed 'quite happy', as Motilal, released from prison ahead of his son, was quick to notice. But her happiness was not destined to last long. Motilal's death, on February 6th, 1931, came to her as a shattering blow and a deep emotional shock. With the disappearance of his protective presence and given the constant uncertainty of her family life, it also became difficult for her to stay at Allahabad and study at St Mary's. She was sent to Pupils' Own School, a residential and experimental school at Poona (now called Pune), in the Western Indian hills, run by a dedicated couple, Jehangir and Coonverbai Vakil, who were known to the Nehrus. With 'Aunty Vakil', Indira was to develop a lifelong relationship of devotion and

41

respect. Four decades later, in the mid-Seventies, when India was temporarily under Indira's authoritarian rule, thanks to the Emergency imposed by her, Mrs Vakil was perhaps the only Indian in a position to admonish the Prime Minister.

For all the mutual affection between her and the Vakils, Indira's stay at Poona was unhappy. During the classes and school outings and functions she behaved with commendable discipline. But she felt utterly lonely and miserable and often cried at night. In 1933, on being released from jail, her father made a beeline for Poona to see her. Indira was overjoyed to be reunited with her 'Papu', as she always called her father, and returned home with him. Both her parents began to wonder where to send her next.

Their choice fell on Santiniketan, an institution started and benignly presided over by Rabindranath Tagore, a poet-philosopher, Nobel Laureate and admirer of Jawaharlal. Before enrolling Indira there, Nehru decided to visit Santiniketan and then go to Calcutta. Kamala and Indira went with him. In Calcutta, while Nehru busied himself with political speeches, mother and daughter spent long hours together visiting the headquarters of the Ramakrishna Mission, a reformist Hindu religious order, into which Kamala had been initiated, at Belur on the bank of the Hoogly river. She used the occasion to introduce her daughter to *Vedanta*, the philosophy of the Vedas, the ancient Hindu scriptures, as well as to Anandmayee Ma (Mother Anandmayee), a holy woman who is still alive and was an important influence on, and source of solace to, Indira all through her life.

Tagore's academy, situated in idyllic surroundings, exuded tranquillity, as indeed its name implied. Indira loved the place, above all, listening to Tagore talk of a wide variety of things or watching him paint. These moments became for her 'moments of supreme joy, memories to cherish'.

However, her happiness was once again cruelly cut short when, in May 1935, her mother's health took a sharp turn for the worse. Doctors decreed that she be taken to Switzerland at once. Jawaharlal could not accompany her because he was in prison. Of course, the British were ready to release him but only if he undertook to stay away from politics. It would have gone against the grain to give this assurance and Kamala was even more adamant that no such assurance be given. Indira, now over seventeen, immediately took over the responsibility of conveying her mother to the Swiss sanitorium.

In a letter to Nehru Tagore expressed the hope that Indira would soon 'return here and get back to her studies'. However that was not to be.

In February 1936, Kamala Nehru died at Lausanne. Jawaharlal was by her side, having been set free unconditionally three months earlier.

He was desolate. Indira's grief was even more numbing. Coming five years after her grandfather's passing, her mother's death at the age of only thirty-six was a hammer-blow to her. Indira loved and adored her father, of course. But her bond with her mother was much stronger. The memory of her frail and much-harassed mother was to stay with her for the rest of her life. There are not many people who claim to have known Indira well. But of the few who were close to her most say that by the time of her mother's death the essential mould of Indira's personality had been formed firmly and that, in subsequent years, there was no influence on her even remotely comparable to Kamala's.

At Lausanne, at the moment of the biggest tragedy in their lives, Indira and her father did not have time even to console each other. Nehru had to rush back home where duty beckoned. But before doing so he had to settle the question of where to send his daughter for her education, constantly disrupted and much neglected until then.

Indira rejected the idea of going to the United States and preferred going to Britain instead. After all had not her 'Papu' been educated there? The real reason for her choice, however, was that at the London School of Economics there was a young student from Allahabad, Feroze Gandhi, whom she had known from the early days of the freedom struggle, who had helped her look after Kamala during that terrible and terminal illness at Lausanne and whom she was to marry six years later. Thus it was that she went first to Badminton School near Bristol and then to Somerville College, Oxford.

Iris Murdoch, the British novelist who was with Indira at both Badminton and Somerville, has recorded that the shy, aloof and delicate Indira seemed 'intensely worried about her father and her country and thoroughly uncertain about the future'. She has added that even then Indira 'was regarded by us as a "princess" with some sort of "destiny"; though we did not then foresee how extraordinary that destiny was to be.'

Indira's stay at Somerville to read Modern History – interspersed with a visit to Europe with her father who, appalled by Chamberlain's appeasement of Hitler, was keen to go to Czechoslovakia and the Sudetenland, and another to her home in Allahabad – was happier than at Badminton or any other school except Santiniketan. She liked, indeed loved, the city of Oxford and relished taking long walks in it. But, for all the joy she got from Oxford, her heart was not in it and certainly not in her studies.

She longed to be by the side of her father, now a widower and in need of being looked after. Her health was also not of the best. One winter she was taken ill with pleurisy and had to be sent to Switzerland for recuperation in the invigorating alpine air. Her return journey to Oxford turned out to be both circuitous and arduous because by that time the Second World War had begun. For a while she was stranded in Lisbon.

Shortly after returning to Oxford, Indira announced her intention to leave and return home as soon as a passage could be secured. Feroze Gandhi, who had been courting her assiduously, unsurprisingly decided to go back with her.

From then onwards, until very recently, Indira's own version of her reasons for saying farewell to Oxford – that she believed formal education to be a waste of time, was in poor health and, in any case, wished to be with her father – were generally believed. It was also fostered by the official profile, issued after she became Prime Minister, and her numerous biographies published in later years. Then, all of a sudden, it was discovered that Indira had no choice but to leave Oxford because of 'her failure to pass her Latin examination even in her second attempt'.

There is, however, a pleasanter sidelight to Indira's sojourn in Somerville. On the day in January 1966, when she became Prime Minister, novelist Naomi Mitchison happened to be dining at High Table in her, and Indira's, old college. 'We all,' she recorded later, 'toasted her – the first Somerville Prime Minister.' Margaret Thatcher was to become the second, over a decade afterwards.

Were the years that Indira spent in England wasted ones? Not by any means. She may have failed to get a degree but she had learnt a lot. Through Agatha Harrison, a devotee of Gandhi, and Krishna Menon, the brilliant but waspish associate of Nehru and leader of the London-based India League, she had met a great many eminent people, including Harold Laski, Edward Thompson, Ernest Bevin, Stafford Cripps, Ernst Toller, Fenner Brockway, and so on. Most of them were kind to her largely because she was Nehru's daughter. Some were clearly unimpressed by her. But in her quiet, unobtrusive style that was to become apparent later, she listened to them carefully and tried to imbibe from them whatever wisdom she could without necessarily being overawed by them. On a famous occasion, she coolly disregarded Laski's advice not to 'tag along' with her father or else she would 'just become an appendage'.

Feroze, who had a clearer grasp of contemporary affairs and was closer to Menon than she was, encouraged her to take an interest in Labour party politics, and particularly in the anti-fascist movement then growing in Britain and the Left Book Club. She and Shanta Gandhi, a school friend from her Poona days with whom Indira sometimes shared rooms in London, would stand in the rain for hours to catch a glimpse of La Pasionara, the Spanish revolutionary.

All in all, Indira's stay abroad, though bereft of academic laurels, strengthened her innate self-reliance, widened her mental horizon and invested her with a cosmopolitan outlook. All these were gains which were to stand her in good stead in later life.

# 3   Against the Whole World's Wishes

To get home Indira and Feroze had to take a slow boat around the Cape of Good Hope. The ship had to steer an erratic course to avoid German U-boats. The long journey had to be broken, moreover, by a week's halt at the South African port of Durban where Nehru's name was already well known. It was understandable therefore that Durban's Indian business community decided to give a reception in honour of Nehru's daughter.

Indira accepted but strictly on condition that she would not be asked to speak, not even to thank the hosts. She was evidently haunted by the memory of the evening in London's Caxton Hall when, suddenly asked by Krishna Menon to speak, she found herself paralysed. Words stuck in her throat. A drunk in the audience shouted: 'She doesn't speak; she squeaks.'

At the reception, however, Indira startled her hosts by insisting on speaking. She and Feroze had been driving round the city and had seen for themselves the horrors of apartheid. Indira could not contain her anger. She lambasted not only South Africa's racist rulers – who, she said, were no different from the Nazis – but also the Indian businessmen for their greed, servility to white racists and callousness to the suffering of the blacks exploited by the British and the Boers alike.

Taking a train from Bombay, where she had landed, Indira reached home in Allahabad in March 1941. No great welcome awaited her. Her father was still in jail. Gandhi had launched individual *satyagraha* and thousands had consequently courted arrest. The Second World War was raging in Europe, in the Middle East and even in the jungles of Burma. But to most Indians, absorbed in dreams of independence, it looked remote and unreal, even though massive mobilisation was going on, hundreds of thousands of Indians were volunteering to fight Britain's battles and there were sporadic talks between Indian leaders and the British Viceroy on ways to enlist the willing support of nationalist India in the war effort in return for mutually acceptable advance towards self-rule. The exercise, however, was to prove sterile. An offer brought by Sir Stafford Cripps in 1942 on behalf of the British war cabinet was to be denounced by Gandhi as a 'post-dated cheque on a crashing bank'.

A further complication, which was profoundly to influence the future of the sub-continent, had also taken place. The breach between the Congress and the Muslim League, led by the stern and dapper Mohammed Ali Jinnah, was complete. An astute and aloof lawyer who had once championed Indian unity, he now insisted on partition to create a Muslim state, Pakistan. Another prominent nationalist leader, Subhas Chandra Bose, who had once challenged Gandhi and had a radical image even stronger than Nehru's, had also embarked on a separate course.

Hoodwinking his jailer, Bose escaped from India. He had first gone to Germany and then, by submarine, to Japan. Eventually, he had made Singapore his base. There he had organised, obviously with Japanese support, the Indian National Army. Indian troops and officers taken prisoners-of-war by the Japanese either willingly joined him or were 'persuaded' to do so. Those who refused were treated brutally. Bose hoped to march at the head of his army to Delhi and liberate India from the British. Not many Indians seemed to realise, Nehru being a notable and very vocal exception, that to trade Japanese tutelage for British would be to opt for the fire rather than the frying pan.

It was in this confused, confusing and dispiriting atmosphere that Nehru was released from prison to be told by his daughter that she wanted to marry Feroze. Trouble ensued almost instantly. Nehru, among the most civilised of men, usually tried not to interfere with his daughter's decisions. But her marriage was no ordinary matter and, for once, the doting father did decide to interfere.

Nehru had known Feroze for many years. The young man, as a Congress activist, was indeed a fixture at Anand Bhavan and was regarded as a protégé of the Nehrus, especially of Jawaharlal's wife, Kamala, to whom he was greatly devoted. Feroze had, in fact, helped to nurse the ailing Kamala, first at the Bhowali sanitorium in India and then, right up to her death, in Switzerland. Many people believe that Indira decided to marry Feroze at least partly because of her gratitude for the deep and loving care he had bestowed on her mother. That he had been her only friend and companion during the lonely years in Europe could well have been another powerful reason influencing her decision.

It has also been said that opposites often attract each other. This may not be always true, but it is indisputable that Indira and Feroze were opposites in most respects. She was slender, frail and beautiful; he was short and squat. She was given to impenetrable reserve and prone to long silences; he was gregarious and exuberant, sometimes boisterous. Feroze's lower-middle-class origin contrasted with Indira's aristocratic background.

All this was repeatedly brought home to Indira. But her mind was made up. She was adamant on marrying the man of her choice, arguing that she 'did not like Feroze but she loved him'. Feroze had been proposing to her since she was sixteen but it was only in 1937 that she finally said yes on the steps of the Basilica of Sacré-Coeur in Paris. The venue seemed delightfully appropriate. 'It was the end of summer,' Indira recorded many years later, 'and Paris was bathed in sunshine and her heart truly seemed to be young and gay . . . the whole city was full of people who were young and in a holiday mood.'

Nehru's opposition to Indira's decision to marry Feroze was an amalgam of several complex factors, including every fond father's resentment of his daughter's first suitor. In fact, he did tell her that she was needlessly hastening to take the plunge, that she had been thrown into Feroze's company only by her loneliness in Europe and that she ought to give herself time 'to meet other young men and then decide'. But Indira was unmoved.

Feroze, though no stranger to Nehru, was not sure exactly what the older man thought of him. Their infrequent conversations at Anand Bhavan in the past were no more than an Olympian leader's graciousness to a young devotee and their correspondence was formal and stilted. Nehru was aware of the care lavished by Feroze on Kamala during her prolonged illness but he did not particularly care for the young man's constant shadowing of Indira. This irritation showed through his correspondence with Feroze. On one occasion, for instance, Feroze wrote to him from Switzerland enthusiastically describing some photographs of Indira that he had taken. He also sent the photographs to Anand Bhavan. '*If* you have taken these photographs,' Nehru replied, 'I must congratulate you.' Feroze felt rejected but refrained from complaining.

Interestingly, it was not to Feroze the person that Nehru objected. Nor did he make any mention of temperamental and other incompatibilities between his daughter and the man she wanted to wed. The fact that Feroze was a Parsi, a follower of the ancient and fire-worshipping religion of Zoroastrianism, not a Hindu, did matter a great deal to most members of the Nehru family, proud of their Kashmiri Brahmin lineage and anxious to preserve their exclusivity. But Nehru was far above such considerations.

He was deeply devoted to liberal values and did not have much use for religion. Some believed that he was an atheist though he preferred to call himself an agnostic. Moreover, both his sisters had married outside the Kashmiri Pandit clan and the younger one, Krishna, even outside the Brahmin caste. But both had married into wealthy families. At the time of the younger sister's wedding, Nehru had written to Gandhi:

I would welcome as wide a breach of custom as possible. The Kashmiri community – there are exceptions in it, of course – disgusts me. It is the very epitome of the petty bourgeois vices which I detest. I am not particularly interested in a person being a Brahmin, a non-Brahmin or anything else. As a matter of fact, I fail to see the relevance of all this; one marries an individual not a community.

In view of this, his opposition to or even reservations about Indira's choice of marriage partner could only mean that he was objecting to Feroze's relative poverty though he expressed himself, as was his wont, hesitantly, weighing pros and cons and raising questions rather than laying down the law. He appealed to Indira to ponder the difference in the 'backgrounds' of Feroze and herself (a euphemism for class) which could cause difficulties. He also suggested gently that Feroze might not be able to keep her happy or in the comforts she was used to.

Indira obviously had had enough. She told him that her mind was made up and that was that. She even threatened to stop talking to him, a threat which, according to her cousin, Nayantara Sahgal – a charming novelist and daughter of Vijayalakshmi Pandit, who later became very embittered against Indira – she had 'earlier carried out once to her father's great distress'. A man of reason and an overwhelmingly affectionate father, Nehru gave in. In the first contest of wills between father and daughter, the daughter had won hands down.

Nehru's acquiescence in Indira's decision was not, however, the end of the controversy. The family might have yielded. But the Nehru family, having by now become a national institution, had to contend with public opinion which was surprisingly inflamed. Indira was entirely right in claiming that the 'whole world seemed to be opposed to my marriage to Feroze'. As soon as the first news about Indira's engagement to Feroze leaked out, in February 1942, there was an outcry against the proposed 'mixed' marriage. From Calcutta, where he was entertaining the Chiang Kai-sheks, Jawaharlal rushed to Allahabad and sprang to his daughter's defence. Forgetting his own earlier reservations, he issued a statement declaring that a marriage was a 'personal and domestic matter, affecting chiefly the two parties concerned, and partly their families!' But protest did not subside until Gandhi, who had been receiving abusive letters about the impending nuptials, took up the cudgels on behalf of the young couple.

Opposition to the marriage was by no means confined to the Hindus. The Parsi community, too, was displeased though it was much less vociferous. Indeed, Feroze's association with the Nehrus had caused distress to his family long before anyone had imagined that he and Indira would want to marry. The situation is best explained by a letter Nehru wrote to his sister, Vijayalakshmi Pandit, from Bhowali in the Uttar Pradesh hills, where Kamala Nehru was under treatment for tuberculosis and Feroze was around worrying about her health.

Written on November 2nd, 1935, long before Indira agreed to marry Feroze and a good six years before she told her father, the letter did not become public until almost exactly four decades later. It merits detailed attention because it speaks eloquently of the background to the row over the Indira–Feroze marriage:

> And now a rather delicate matter and perhaps a troublesome job for you. It appears that Feroze Gandhi has got into hot water with his people, because of his association with us, and especially his long stay at Bhowali. Even before this his political activities were greatly resented by his mother and the blame for them was cast on Kamala and me. It had been settled that he was to sail for Europe with his aunt, Miss Commissariat . . . but suddenly everything has fallen through and the poor boy is landed high and dry . . . My sympathy is with the poor mother. I think also that we have been remiss in almost ignoring her. It is difficult to understand other people's family quarrels and even more difficult to interfere in them. Still something has to be done to save the boy from endless trouble . . . and put ourselves right with the family.

Nehru suggested to Mrs Pandit that she should visit Feroze's family and reassure them that he and his wife 'had no intention to come between them and their boy'. She went but it is not known how far she succeeded in soothing the family's ruffled feelings.

In any case, at the time of Feroze's engagement to Indira his family objected and raised the pertinent question of whether he could be happy with her. But Nehru, now fully reconciled to the marriage, talked them out of their misgivings. The danger of a demonstration by the local Parsi community on the wedding day was averted by an appeal to the elders of the community by Feroze's mother, at Nehru's suggestion.

One major difficulty remained, however. It related to marriage rites. Laws on civil marriage, which remained unchanged until several years after independence, required that both parties should renounce their respective religions. This practice had indeed been followed when Indira's aunt, Krishna, had married Raja Hutheesing. Neither Indira nor Feroze was particularly religious at that time. But both were stoutly opposed to the renunciation of religion. A way out was found by a Delhi professor who said that some Vedic hymns were eminently suitable for mixed marriages. He also cited a precedent. One of Indira's cousins, B. K. Nehru, a member of the 'heaven-born' Indian civil service who has since been Ambassador to the United States, High Commissioner to Britain, and Governor of several states, had married a Hungarian in this manner.

Indira's marriage took place on March 26th, 1942, a doubly auspicious day, being *Ram Navmi* or the birthday of Lord Rama, the hero of Ramayana, the epic that had earlier inspired her to set up the Monkey Brigade. Sir Stafford Cripps was one of the house guests and was greatly amused when, at the dinner table, a nervous Indira pressed him: 'Do have some potato cripps, Sir Stafford.'

From early childhood Indira had responded strongly to colours. She was particularly fond of all shades of orange, pinks and later reds. During the Bangladesh war in 1971 her mind is said to have been 'suffused with reds'. At times of crisis, personal or political, in later years she tended to wear yellow or orange. Just before her wedding, she indulged her passion for colours by buying glass bangles of various hues. This fascinated another foreigner staying at Anand Bhavan, Eve Curie, a French journalist and the daughter of the famous scientist.

Both Indira and Feroze wanted a quiet wedding. In this resolve they were strengthened by unsolicited advice from the Mahatma. But a large number of family friends insisted on attending the wedding though ostentation, usual at Indian weddings, was strictly avoided.

Indira wore a simple pink cotton sari hand-woven, to her great pleasure and pride, from the fine yarn spun by her father during his latest spell of imprisonment. Only one other gift she treasured as much as her wedding sari. It was a piece of *khadi* made from yarn spun by Gandhi. Some of Kamala Nehru's jewellery had been sold by the family after Motilal's death and especially during her terminal illness, despite her protests that her jewellery was the only security she could bequeath to her daughter. But much of it remained in the family coffers which Indira later inherited. On her wedding day, however, she shunned ornaments. She wore instead fresh flowers.

For their honeymoon the newly-weds inevitably chose Kashmir. The Nehrus might have migrated from Kashmir to the plains generations ago, but their heart was still there. Indira had heard of the Kashmir valley's magic and beauty from her grandmothers, both paternal and maternal, and from her father who, after a visit to it, wrote lyrically: 'The loveliness of the land enthralled me and cast an enchantment all about me. I wandered about like one possessed and drunk with beauty . . . Like some supremely beautiful woman whose beauty is almost impersonal and above human desire, such was Kashmir . . .'

Indira Gandhi was also fascinated from her infancy by the mountains. Every summer Motilal and later other members of her family

51

took her to the hills which she loved. She climbed the mountains so nimbly that her grandfather said she must have been a 'mountain goat in her previous incarnation'. He added that given the choice, she would take the most difficult path up a mountain, never an easy one – as she was to recall decades later during a period when she was facing acute turmoil.

From the mountain resort of Gulmarg, Feroze and Indira telegraphed Nehru: 'Wish we could send you some cool breeze from here.' He shot back: 'Thanks, but you have no mangoes.' In July he cabled them again: 'Don't hurry back. Live in beauty while you may.' But no honeymoon can last for ever. The political temperature in the country was rising. Another major struggle against the Raj looked like being in the offing. Indira felt that her place was by her father's side.

Back in Allahabad, Feroze rented a small house of his own in Tagore Town, not far from Anand Bhavan. But if he and Indira were hoping to settle down in marital bliss or quiet domesticity, they were mistaken. Their hopes, like much else in the country, were to be overtaken by the long-expected show-down between the Raj, presided over by Churchill in London and a particularly obtuse Viceroy, Lord Linlithgow, in Delhi, and the rising tide of the freedom struggle, with Gandhi riding the crest of the wave.

The issue between the two sides was clear and their differences unbridgeable. With the Japanese knocking at India's doors, it was imperative that the Raj and nationalist India should fight them jointly. Nehru, with his sympathy for the allied cause and his abhorrence of fascism, was anxious to help. But Britain remained blind to the Indian sentiment that the fight against Japan could be effectively carried out only by a genuinely national government. This destroyed such prospects of compromise as might have existed. Promises of freedom after victory were insultingly reminiscent of what had happened after the First World War. Free India, Gandhi declared, would 'join Britain in fighting Japan and Germany; unfree India would fight Britain'. Neither the Viceroy in his palatial residence in Delhi nor his bosses in Whitehall took any notice. Nehru, overcoming his own earlier reservations, once again bowed to the Mahatma's will and wisdom. It was he who moved at a meeting of the All India Congress Committee in Bombay on August 7th, 1942, the famous 'Quit India' resolution, asking the British to pack up and go. 'Do or Die' was the slogan Gandhi gave this gathering. He indicated that individual *satyagraha* would soon be replaced by mass civil disobedience. This the beleaguered British government simply could not countenance.

In a pre-emptive swoop in the early hours of August 9th, the authorities arrested Gandhi, Nehru and other Congress leaders and whisked them away to an 'unknown destination'. Soon it became known that Gandhi had been taken once again to the Aga Khan's palace in Poona, while Nehru and other Congress stalwarts had been locked up in Chand Bibi's fortress in Ahmednagar, a hundred miles southwards.

Instead of forestalling trouble, the government, by its abrupt and arbitrary action, fanned the flames of unrest. Released from the restraints imposed on it by the Gandhian leadership and emboldened by countrywide resentment and anger against the British, the Congress Left seized the initiative to launch a general insurrection against the unwanted Raj. It spread surprisingly fast and far. The 'August Revolt', as it came to be known, was eventually contained but not before it had turned into the most serious challenge to the British in India after the Mutiny in 1857.

Feroze and Indira were present at the historic session of the All India Congress Committee (AICC). After the countrywide crack-down they thought it prudent to find separate ways home. Feroze, along with some associates, went underground. During a bizarre exploit, he saved himself from arrest by impersonating a British soldier, a caper made possible by his fair complexion. Indira took a train to Allahabad. The day she reached there, her aunt, Mrs Pandit, was arrested. Indira had to forget her own little home in order to take charge of Anand Bhavan, now under strict and continuous surveil-lance. She managed, however, to shelter a number of Congressmen wanted by the police, among them a diminutive but tenacious man, Lal Bahadur Shastri, who would one day be her father's successor and her own predecessor as Prime Minister of independent India. Through Feroze, she was also maintaining contact with the under-ground; this was useful for passing money and messages to the Congress activists. One day she was caught in the midst of a crowd that was being lathi-charged by the police. She received some blows but held aloft a Congress flag someone had handed her.

Not long afterwards word reached her that she herself was to be arrested. She decided not to wait for the police to come to her but to go out and meet them halfway by addressing a public meeting which was surprisingly well-attended, considering that it could be organised only by word of mouth. She had barely begun speaking when the police pounced on her. Feroze was watching the proceedings from a nearby window because he had decided not to get involved. But when he saw that the barrel of a policeman's gun was only a yard away from his wife's head, he jumped into the fray and angrily asked the constable to lower the gun. He was promptly arrested, though he and his wife were driven away in different Black Marias.

For Indira it was a proud moment. She felt fulfilled. For two

53

decades she had seen her father, grandfather, mother, grandmother, aunts and others go to jail. Now this honour was hers. Two and a half decades later, as Prime Minister, she spoke of her arrest and imprisonment in 1942 as the 'most dramatic incident' in her life. 'I had made up my mind that I had to go to prison. Without that . . . something would have been incomplete.'

Indira Gandhi was taken to the Naini prison where her aunt, Mrs Pandit, was already lodged and was meticulously maintaining a diary. In an entry dated September 11th, 1942, she records: 'Half an hour after lock-up yesterday there was a tremendous knocking at the outer gate and the matron came in excitedly announcing "Mrs Indira is here".' Conditions in Indian jails were appalling then and they certainly have not improved since. Jail life was, therefore, something of a trial for the young, newly-married Indira. But there is no evidence to corroborate her subsequent claim that she was considered 'so dangerous' as to be denied 'regular prison facilities'.

On the contrary it seems that Indira was better off than most other political prisoners and detainees. She shared the dormitory with her aunt, Mrs Pandit, her cousin, Chandralekha Pandit, seven years younger than herself, and a number of associates and acquaintances. All were subject to the same regulations and regimen. The nine months that Indira spent in prison constituted the only period when she and Mrs Pandit lived in harmony. This lends an edge to the aunt's statement, in the introduction to her prison diary, published in 1945: 'The treatment given to me and to those who shared the barrack with me was, according to prison standards, very lenient – the reader must not imagine that others were equally well treated.'

It was in Naini prison that Indira celebrated her twenty-fifth birthday on November 19th, 1942. Feroze, who was in a nearby jail, was allowed his fortnightly interview with her on that day. From the interview she 'came back looking happy', according to Mrs Pandit, who also wrote: 'In the evening, Purnima [a family friend and vivacious nationalist only a little older than Indira] invited us all to tea on her side of the barrack and we had quite a good time.'

The idea of 'allotting', by mutual consent, a particular part of the barrack to each of the inmates had its merit. It encouraged competition in keeping the place clean and in decorating it imaginatively. Everyone gave her 'abode' a name of her choice. Indira called hers 'Chimborazo', a testimony to her love for even distant mountains from an early age, while Chandralekha Pandit called her bit 'Bien Venue'. The central space, covered by a blue rug Mrs Pandit had brought in her bedding, where all the inmates ate their meals or read at night, was given the high-sounding name 'Blue Drawing Room'.

Indira was released from prison on May 13th, 1943, and Mrs Pandit nearly a month later. With the August Revolt fizzling out, more and more prisoners were being set free. Feroze was released in August and was happy to be reunited with his wife. He started earning a living of sorts as an insurance agent and freelance journalist.

A year later the first of their two sons, Rajiv, was born. For her confinement Indira went to Bombay to her younger aunt, Krishna Hutheesing. Rajiv was an easy delivery. Indira recalled that she had just ordered a piece of toast and was busy eating it when 'Rajiv came out'. She was sorry she was unable to finish the toast. But her joy in motherhood was unbounded. 'To a woman, motherhood is the highest fulfilment,' she remarked later. 'To bring a new being into this world, to see its tiny perfection and to dream of its future greatness is the most moving of all experiences and fills one with wonder and exaltation.'

Nehru, along with other top leaders of the Congress, was still in prison when his grandson was born. He first saw Rajiv when the little one was nearly a year old. He was thrilled by the boy and delighted to see his daughter again. He also found time to devote some thought to the problem of finding his son-in-law a steady job.

Newspapers and journals have played an important part in the lives of Indian nationalists, including the Nehrus. Motilal had founded a daily called *The Independent* in Allahabad. Gandhi edited *Young India* and *Harijan*, both weeklies, the latter devoted to the cause of the untouchables, officially called the 'scheduled castes' by the British Raj. Gandhi preferred, however, to rename them Harijans or 'God's children'. Jawaharlal had founded *The National Herald*, a daily based in Lucknow, which had suspended publication in 1942 rather than submit to censorship. Three years later it was being revived and Nehru thought Feroze could be usefully and gainfully employed as its managing director.

In this job, more managerial than journalistic, Feroze was to prove himself proficient and resourceful. But if he was hoping for a settled existence with his wife, he was to be disappointed a second time. Politics once again disturbed domestic bliss, but this time the problem was compounded by personal foibles and irritations.

In 1972, when a number of laudatory biographies of Indira Gandhi appeared simultaneously, she was far from pleased. It was not the fulsome praise showered on her by the authors that displeased her. She was human enough to like it though she never admitted to having read any of these or subsequent books or even articles about herself. What made her angry was the treatment of her married life by even the most adulatory authors. Almost all of them had said, or at least hinted, usually with great tact and discretion, that a rift between her and Feroze had started early during their married life and that later they were virtually separated.

To Indira any suggestion that her marriage to Feroze was anything less than perfectly happy was anathema. She practically said so in an interview that was granted rather than sought.

Not much credence was given to her testy disclaimers though no one flatly contradicted her at that time. Some evidence of marital discord was available even then. Much more has surfaced since – a lot of it, ironically, from her own pen. Even so, the story is best told chronologically.

Some minor signs of trouble were discernible almost from the start. Even when he was begging Indira to marry him, Feroze used to wonder whether 'Indira would become a Gandhi or whether he would be expected to become a Nehru'. He did not like the first indication of the likely answer to this question. He had, as we have noted, rented a house in Allahabad's Tagore Town. Blessed with green fingers and a penchant for gardening, he grew roses in his small compound. Indira, with a passion for flowers, especially for arranging them, that was to last throughout her life, delighted in decorating their modest home. But the pull of Anand Bhavan was much too strong. Someone was needed to look after the sprawling mansion. Nehru, when not in prison, was otherwise busy; his sisters had got married and had gone away. Moreover, moving back to Anand Bahvan would be an economy, and the young Gandhis were not flush with money. Feroze agreed to return to Anand Bhavan but he was to regret this decision later. The move to Lucknow, when he became managing director of *The National Herald*, was expected to improve the situation. In the event it had precisely the opposite result.

At the end of the war in Europe the doors of the Ahmednagar fort had been opened and the Congress leaders, headed by Nehru, had stepped out. Gandhi had been released earlier, after yet another self-inflicted ordeal of a prolonged fast and the death of his wife, Kasturba, in captivity. By this time it was clear that 1945 was going to be a major turning point in history. Yalta had laid down the framework for the post-war international order. The British public had disowned Churchill on the morrow of victory. Bled and enfeebled by war, Britain was simply in no position to sustain its far-flung empire of which India was the linchpin. No one perceived this reality more clearly than the unfairly underrated head of the Labour government, Clement Attlee. Serious negotiations for transfer of power in India ensued and Nehru was amongst the most important participants. The impact of all this on a small household in Lucknow was immense. But no great notice was taken of it amidst the stupendous developments affecting the future of the fifth of mankind inhabiting the Indian sub-continent.

# 4   Father's Châtelaine and Confidante

Nehru, a widower since 1936 and immersed in the nation's chores, sometimes needed Indira to look after him. She, on her part, was greatly worried about him and considered it her duty to help him as best she could. This meant that she must constantly commute between Lucknow, where her husband lived, and Delhi where her father was engaged in gruelling and usually frustrating negotiations that eventually led to the ecstasy of independence and the agony of partition. On all her journeys to Delhi Indira took little Rajiv with her. She was unwell at that time and she found the arrangement tiring. To Feroze it was tiresome. Deprived of the company of his wife and child he became moody and increasingly resentful of both her and his father-in-law. Temperamental differences between husband and wife, ignored during courtship and honeymoon, also began to surface and accentuate the strain. Nor was the situation improved by the wider and more ominous tensions within the country, born of the Congress party's desperate efforts to maintain the sub-continent's unity and the Muslim League's determined struggle to secure a sovereign state of Pakistan in Muslim-majority areas.

On August 16th, 1946, the Muslim League gave a call for 'direct action' in support of its demand for Pakistan. This led to the 'Great Calcutta Killings' which became the precursor of the worst butchery India had seen in its long and bloody history. Wavell, the British Viceroy, privately advised Whitehall that the answer to the deadlock between the Congress and the League was a deadline for the British withdrawal and publicly invited Nehru to become Vice-President of the Viceroy's Executive Council and head the interim government that would pave the way to whatever dispensation might be agreed upon by all concerned. Nehru accepted the 'crown of thorns', in a sombre mood on September 2nd, 1946. The Muslim League, having boycotted the interim government at first, joined it some weeks later purely as a tactic to 'wreck it from within'.

Burdened with awesome responsibilities amidst a developing holocaust, Nehru needed Indira more than ever before to keep house for him and act as his official hostess. She, therefore, practically left Lucknow and migrated to Delhi where her father then lived in a relatively small, two-storey bungalow at 17, York Road, later renamed Motilal Nehru Marg. Just over three months after Indira moved to Delhi, her second son, Sanjay, was born on December 14th, 1946.

Unlike Rajiv's, his delivery was 'difficult and painful'. This was perhaps an appropriate omen. For, in later years, Sanjay was to be not only the light of his mother's eyes but also the main architect of her misfortunes and sorrows, especially during the last decade of her life.

A minor sideshow at the time of Sanjay's birth was pregnant with symbolism. Because of overcrowding at Nehru's house, Feroze, who had come to Delhi to be by his wife's side, was 'asked by her to move into one of the tents in the bungalow's compound where some other guests were also camping'.

Nothing, not even savage butchery and the country's partition, could dampen popular enthusiasm for independence. At the magic midnight hour on August 15th, 1947 – a date fixed by the last Viceroy, Lord Mountbatten, who had succeeded Wavell only five months earlier – Indira was at her father's elbow, as she was to be during the succeeding seventeen years. She was 'overwhelmed with pride and excitement', as she was to record later.

Independence also meant greater burdens on her slender shoulders. Shortly after becoming Prime Minister, Nehru moved to a bigger mansion, previously tenanted by the British Commander-in-Chief in India, and now the Nehru Memorial Museum and Library. Redecorating this huge and rambling house was itself a daunting task. Lifesize portraits of British generals, former guardians of the empire, seemed to be the only decorations on the walls, practically glaring at whoever happened to be in view. Indira got them despatched to the defence headquarters and soon succeeded in her mission of making the mansion habitable. Her two growing children and the family's deep love for animals and birds, which led to the creation of a virtual zoo in the compound, greatly helped.

Apart from the fast increasing flow of guests and visitors to the Prime Minister's house, Indira had to cope with small floods of refugees, 'wounded in body and spirit, knocking at Nehru's door' in search of relief. Even in the smaller house in York Road, two rooms had been set aside for use by refugees. In the new mansion bigger space was found for them. Some of the refugees were taken on the Prime Minister's personal staff; several stayed on to serve Indira when she stepped into the office that was once her father's.

The refugees from Pakistan were not mollified, however, by either Nehru's personal graciousness or his government's gigantic efforts to rehabilitate them. To 'avenge' what had happened to them they started a riot against the Muslims. Frightened Muslim families fled the walled city to take shelter in a camp where Indira, along with some friends, joined the dedicated band of social workers to look to the inmates' well being. Displaying exemplary courage and endangering her own life, she once rescued a poor man being chased by a 'howling mob evidently intent on hacking him to pieces.'

Gandhi was by now a broken man, though also unbowed. His message of non-violence lay shattered around him. He was ignored by many of his former followers, but he was intent on carrying on his lone crusade against the prevailing madness. He asked Indira to help him, especially in reassuring terror-stricken Muslims cowering in their ghettos or in refugee camps, totally suspicious of any stranger approaching them. She, helped by a handful of intrepid Congress workers, won their confidence and persuaded them to stay on in their homes and stop thinking of migrating to Pakistan. Gandhi was both impressed and delighted. It was during this period that Indira felt really close to the Mahatma though she had known him as a family elder ever since she was a toddler.

Purely by coincidence, Indira called on Gandhi at Birla House, the sprawling mansion of a rich Indian industrialist where he was staying, on January 29th, 1948. Communal riots in the capital had mercifully abated, but refugees from Pakistan were still seething with bitterness. Their anger was directed against Gandhi. In common with local Hindu fanatics, the refugees blamed him for 'pampering' the Muslims. But Gandhi was unconcerned. Indira found him wholly relaxed, basking in the winter sun, sporting a Bengali straw hat. She was accompanied by her aunt, Krishna, one of Vijayalakshmi's daughters, Chandralekha, and little Rajiv.

Twenty-four hours later Gandhi, father of the nation, apostle of non-violence and messenger of peace, was shot dead on the way to his evening prayer meeting by a Hindu zealot. India was overwhelmed by mourning and gloom. 'This comes of being too good,' remarked George Bernard Shaw. Nehru, inconsolable with grief, climbed the high gate of Birla House to tell the benumbed nation in an impromptu speech: 'The light has gone out of our lives and there is darkness everywhere. I do not know what to tell you and how to say it . . .'

For Indira, as for almost every other Indian, the disappearance of 'that famous toothless smile' and of the protective warmth of Gandhi's personality was a shattering blow. But she was more worried about the trauma caused to her father by the Mahatma's sudden assassination. She knew that, since 1931, the Mahatma had played in Jawaharlal's life the role that was previously Motilal's. She also 'sensed instinctively that with Gandhi gone, her father's dependence on her had increased'. This reinforced her resolve to stay by his side in Delhi.

Meanwhile, Feroze moped in Lucknow. Being an extrovert, unlike his taciturn wife, he did not hesitate to give vent to his hurt and resentment over being a grass widower while his wife and two sons lived in style in the Prime Minister's house. The children visited him, of course. His own work took him to Delhi occasionally. But such short and sporadic reunions could hardly be a substitute for normal family life.

Since the Nehru family's affairs were traditionally treated as the nation's business, tongues wagged about what was seen to be a separation between Jawaharlal's daughter and her husband. Some said that she had forsaken Feroze in order to be near the seat of power. Others alluded to 'difficulties' caused by Feroze's 'reputation for a roving eye'. Rumours about his peccadillos were never really substantiated, nor were they fully scotched. In fact, they multiplied and apparently contributed to the eventual estrangement between husband and wife.

Indira was not dissimulating when she asserted years later that she decided to help her father because she felt that 'he had a real need' for this help. From early childhood she had felt protective towards him. Now the thought that he would lead a 'lonesome life, helped only by civil servants and domestic retainers', appalled her. She felt that her 'duty was to her father'. But the fact also remains, as we shall see more clearly later, that incipient marital discord made it easier for her to resolve that her father's 'needs took precedence over everything else'. Devotion to Daddy was at least partly a compensation for a disintegrating marriage.

Of her duties as the hostess at her father's house, Indira has spoken and written elaborately and wittily. She practically compiled a manual of the combinations and permutations of her countrymen's bewildering food fads. And her accounts of some 'near-disasters narrowly averted' – such as when a strictly vegetarian meal specially prepared for the Dalai Lama had to be scrapped when the Buddhist leader, just before arrival, sent word that he was looking forward to a non-vegetarian repast – are hilarious. Being a perfectionist, she saw to it that nothing went wrong.

However, Indira was not just housekeeper and hostess to her father. Slowly but surely and initially imperceptibly her role was expanding. She soon became her father's confidante and counsellor as well. She joined him in all his foreign travels and was virtually treated as the First Lady. This enabled her to establish an easy rapport with world leaders and facilitated her task when the time came for her directly to deal with them. As later events showed, she effortlessly imbibed statecraft simply by watching her father at work.

During Nehru's talks with world leaders, apart from seeing that tea was properly served and everything else was in order, she usually sat silently. But not always. At times her cryptic interjections could be useful, indeed crucial, as happened during Nehru's first official visit to the Soviet Union, in June 1955. One of the items in his brief was to ask for Soviet financial and technical assistance for developing heavy and basic industries in India, for which aid from Western countries was not available. But being an inordinately proud individual, he seemed unable to 'bring up the subject and let slip a number of opportunities of doing so'. Indira, as she was to demonstrate in later life, was no less proud than her father. But she was more practical. It was she who introduced the embarrassing subject during her father's talks with Khrushchev and Bulganin. An agreement was quickly reached.

Since one of Indira's functions was to protect such privacy and leisure as Nehru could snatch from his gruelling sixteen-hour-a-day routine, hordes of party functionaries seeking Nehru's ear often had to be content with saying their piece to her. Nehru, for his part, started telling party colleagues to talk to 'Indu', as Indira was affectionately called by family and friends. She became an important and influential conduit between her father and the party he presided over. The process was accelerated by her own inclusion in the party's higher councils. In 1955, U. N. Dhebar, who had succeeded Nehru as Congress President, invited Indira to become a member of the Congress Working Committee, the highest policy-making body of the organisation. She agreed but chose to take an elective seat on the committee, rather than be nominated by the President. In the next two years she rose further, eventually to become a member of the Parliamentary Board which is to the Congress what the Politburo is to Communist parties.

This was a remarkably rapid rise in the party hierarchy. But there was more to come. In 1959, Dhebar, having sat in the party president's chair for four years, vacated it. At his suggestion, backed by other party elders, most notably Govind Ballabh Pant, former chief minister of UP and now Central Home Minister, Indira was elected Congress President unopposed.

This was a landmark in her political career and Indian history. It was also destined to become a focus of controversy. For even those who suspected nothing of the kind at that time began to say later that her elevation to the Congress President's post was Nehru's first 'Machiavellian move' to groom his daughter as his successor.

It is arguable, to say the least, that Indira might never have become Prime Minister had she not been Nehru's daughter. But equally, there is nothing to show that he did anything to pitchfork her into this or any other position. Dhebar was probably trying to ingratiate himself with Nehru by projecting Indira as the right occupant of the Congress President's *gaddi* (mini-throne). Nehru never asked him to do so. On the contrary, he told a press conference: 'Normally speaking, it is not a good idea for my daughter to come in as Congress President when I am Prime Minister.' But he did nothing to oppose Dhebar's move either. Had he wanted to scotch the idea, he could have easily done so.

Indira's version of the event was that she did not want to be Congress President but was 'bullied into accepting the post' by Pant. She also claimed that she might have retracted her acceptance but for Dhebar's plea that this would only vindicate those newspapers which had already started saying that 'she couldn't do the job'. 'That,' remarked Indira, 'was the clinching argument.'

At forty-one Indira was a year older than her father had been when he first became Congress President three decades earlier, in 1929. Since then the importance of the Congress presidentship had declined because power had inevitably passed to the office of Prime Minister but it still retained a great deal of prestige which Indira was expected to enhance because of her youth, special access to Nehru and a mildly radical image. It cannot be said that she lived up to these expectations, though she did buckle down to her task with conspicuous energy and panache.

For one thing, though she was elected for a two-year term, she gave up the party post after only a year partly because of ill health. For another, it was beyond her, or anyone else, to change the deeply entrenched nature of the Congress which had transformed itself from a freedom movement into an efficient election machine and little else. It was adept in reconciling rival factions, conflicting groups and clashing interests by making whatever compromise on principle or policy might be expedient. Party leaders, especially in the states, maintained their hold on the machine and their influence with the electorate largely through a judicious disbursement of the virtually unlimited patronage over which the Congress party had a monopoly, by virtue of being in power at the centre and in almost all states since independence.

Indira suffered also from another handicap. At the Nagpur session of the Congress, at which she was elected party President, a resolution was passed for joint cooperative farming in the country's half a million villages. In a society in which even marginal farmers are passionately attached to their miserable patches of land and feudal interests have frustrated even modest land reforms to this day, cooperative farming was a wildly impracticable proposition. But delegates had duly voted for it only to humour its author, Nehru, and in the full knowledge that it would never be implemented.

The new Congress President, however, wasted some of her limited time in drumming up support for cooperative farming. She even set up a training centre at Madras to impart to Congress workers skills for spreading the cult of cooperation. But it flopped because few enrolled themselves.

In any case, Indira's truncated tenure as Congress President was so completely dominated by two major events that anything else she did or failed to do was overshadowed.

One, which won her kudos all round, was the reversal, at her initiative, of a decision concerning Bombay taken by her father over two years earlier. In 1957 when the country's political map was redrawn along linguistic lines, two exceptions were made. In Punjab, the Sikh community's demand for a purely Punjabi-speaking state was rejected on the grounds that people there used both Punjabi and Hindi. The old Bombay presidency that sprawled across both Gujarati-speaking and Marathi-speaking areas was also retained as a bilingual unit. This was done even though both language groups were insistent on separate states of their own. Their difficulty was that they could not agree on the future of the flourishing city of Bombay which geographically belonged to Marathi-speaking Maharashtra but had become the country's commercial capital because of massive investments by Gujaratis and other non-Maharashtrians. A suggestion that Bombay be made a separate city-state caused widespread riots in Marathi areas. Gujaratis were equally adamant that the city must not be merged with Maharashtra.

The enforced union of the two in bilingual Bombay was thus continued. But the arrangement did not work. The sentiment in favour of linguistic states was too strong on both sides. Gujarati resistance to Bombay's inclusion in Maharashtra wore down fast. The only problem now was how to persuade Nehru and other sceptics in the Congress leadership that the old decision had to be undone. Indira did this with aplomb. On May 1st, 1960, when the separate states of Maharashtra and Gujarat were inaugurated amidst tremendous popular enthusiasm, Indira was much praised though she was no longer Congress President.

On the second major event during her stewardship of the Congress Indira's impress was even deeper. But it turned out to be highly controversial, even emotive, and brought her bouquets and brickbats in equal measure. Moreover, her political role got inextricably entangled with her personal life, aggravated the discord between her and Feroze and strained their marriage to almost breaking point.

The underlying issue in this case had to do with Kerala, a small state at the south-western tip of the Indian peninsula, and with Communism.

Kerala had then, as it has now, the highest rate of literacy in India. Other distinctive features of the state included notorious political instability, a remarkably balanced mix of Hindus, Muslims and Christians in its population, which accounted for the powerful influence of the Christian Church, the Muslim League and socio-religious organisations of Hindus, particularly those belonging to the Nair and the Ezhava castes, and a sizeable following of the Communist party, indeed the second largest after that in West Bengal.

In India's second General Election held in 1957, the Communist party of India made history by coming to power in Kerala through a free and fair poll. Alarm in India was considerable but insignificant, especially when compared with that in the outside world, particularly the United States where the ghost of Senator McCarthy had not yet been laid. There was panicky talk of Kerala having become 'India's Yenan', Yenan being the region from where the Chinese Communists had spread all across China.

The parallel was totally untenable. Mao Zedong had carved out a base in Yenan by fighting against the Nationalist Chinese government, thanks to the People's Liberation Army that he had built up, not by winning a provincial election. There was no way in which the Kerala Communists could take on the might of the Indian state or subvert the political process that had brought them to power. Moreover, far from being red-hot revolutionary, the programme they wanted to put across was moderately reformist.

Even so, there was deep distrust of their intentions which might explain the public outcry against two perfectly reasonable laws they passed in the state legislature. One was an agrarian reform bill, promised by previous ministries but never enacted, to give protection to tenant-farmers. The other was the Education Bill aimed at controlling and regulating the plethora of privately run schools and colleges which had become a byword for waywardness. The Christian Church, the Muslim League and the Nair Service Society, all controlling numerous educational institutions and landed estates, were in the forefront of the agitation which soon developed into a mass movement for the removal of the Communist ministry. The Congress party in the state immediately jumped on the bandwagon, despite its vow never to make common cause with the Muslim League.

Within the higher leadership of the Congress in New Delhi, opinion was divided. Nehru, as punctilious about proprieties as ever, argued that the central government's extraordinary powers should not be used to get rid of a duly elected ministry in a state. He favoured a policy of persuading the Communist ministry of Kerala voluntarily to accept the challenge of its opponents to put the two controversial bills to the test of a fresh vote by the people. But the Kerala chief minister, E. M. S. Namboodiripad, after protracted talks with the Prime Minister, refused to accept this advice.

Indira, backed by a powerful combination of Congress conservatives, had been arguing that talks with Namboodiripad were a waste of time. She now grew impatient and demanded that the Communists be sent packing without further delay. But the contrary view, fairly widespread among Congress ministers and MPs, was also being pressed equally hard. No one was doing it more vigorously than Feroze.

From their student days in London both Feroze and Indira had been friendly with a number of fellow Indians who were members of the Communist party then and by the time of the Kerala crisis were occupying important positions in the party. This did not prevent Indira from attacking the Communist party of India sharply, declaring that the 'major danger to India was from Communism' and even calling into question the patriotism of Communists. But Feroze's friendship with them was intact and all the more conspicuous in view of his wife's activities.

This, however, was not the only or even the main reason for Feroze's vehement opposition to Indira's plan to get Kerala's Communist ministry dismissed. Nor can it be said that Feroze was berating the contemplated dismissal of the Kerala ministry merely to spite his wife, though it is possible that had their relationship been better he might have expressed himself with some restraint.

As far as I could ascertain he firmly believed that drastic and unjustified action against the first non-Congress ministry would erode the democratic and liberal credentials of the ruling party and encourage even more 'undesirable tendencies' later.

Given this approach, Feroze would have opposed his wife's Kerala policy even if his relations with her had been cordial. But in that case, he would at least have talked things over with her and the two could have agreed to disagree. But now they were not even on talking terms. Marital discord had converted a political difference of opinion into intense personal bitterness. How had Indira and Feroze reached this pass? And why was his opposition so infuriating to her when she had the backing of very powerful people in the highest councils of the Congress?

Since the advent of freedom in 1947, as we have seen, Feroze was moping in Lucknow while his wife and two sons lived in the Prime Minister's house in New Delhi. In 1950, when some vacancies arose in the indirectly elected Parliament, he was nominated to one of these. If the objective was to enable him to live with his wife and children, it was fulfilled only partially and unsatisfactorily.

In order not to be completely cut off from his colleagues, friends and constituents, Feroze spent most of his day at a parliamentary quarter, to which he was entitled, and went to the Prime Minister's mansion for two meals and the night. The arrangement proved uneasy.

The thrice-a-day commuting was not much of a problem because the distance involved was short. But Feroze was vexed to find his father-in-law 'aloof' and his wife 'withdrawn'. Even more troubling was the reaction to this situation by his political colleagues and the public at large.

Feroze was generally and openly spoken of as the 'son-in-law of the nation'. This is a very wounding expression in India because of the paradox that while sons-in-law, because of their privileged position in the male-dominated Indian society, are a pampered lot, any son-in-law living under his father-in-law's roof is contemptuously called *ghar jamai* or no-good scrounger. Good-humoured bantering on this score to Feroze's face tended to turn into downright derision behind his back.

There must have been some masochistic streak in his make-up for he neither did anything to dispel the poor opinions of him nor seemed particularly to mind it. When India held its first General Election in 1952, Feroze comfortably won the Rae Bareli constituency in UP which his wife was to adopt as her own fifteen years later. But since most Congress candidates had sailed through equally easily, this was no great achievement. For four years since he first entered it, Feroze sat in Parliament without ever opening his mouth, confirming his detractors in their belief that he had nothing to say.

Those better acquainted with him knew him to be an intelligent, witty and engaging man, if at times a trifle loud. They found him to be warm-hearted and hospitable. They admired his flair for gardening and his skill in shaping lovely toys for his two sons. They also sadly shook their heads over the wanton waste of his time and talent.

In 1954, all of a sudden, Feroze surprised friends and foes alike by a magnificent maiden speech in Parliament in which he pitilessly and diligently exposed the misdeeds of a business house, particularly the gross misuse of insurance funds at its disposal. This led soon enough to the nationalisation of all life insurance companies and the arrest and imprisonment of the head of the business house, Ramakrishna Dalmia. Some of Feroze's expertise in the workings of the insurance business was obviously derived from his earlier association with it, apart from journalism.

Other such exposures followed and Feroze was hailed by an admiring public as a 'giant-killer'. He reached the peak of his glory in 1958 when he rose in Parliament to indict the Life Insurance Corporation he had helped set up. Its methods were no different from those of the private owners of insurance companies in the past, he thundered. In support of his charge, he cited the corporation's dubious investments in shares of questionable firms owned by an adventurer named Mundhra. His massive marshalling of the sensational details of the

Mundhra deal was spiced with biting wit. His prestige rose sky-high as the Finance Minister, T. T. Krishnamachari, resigned and some top officials also lost their jobs. But contrary to general belief, Feroze was far from being elated. He was supposed to be on top of the world. But he was not, as I had reason to know, having got to know him rather well since 1954.

Thereafter, whenever both of us were in Delhi we used to meet at least once every day, sometimes oftener. Slowly this developed into friendship which was, to me, personally stimulating and professionally rewarding. Feroze was exceedingly well informed about the inner goings-on in the government and was thus an excellent news source. His generous hospitality and our shared interest in good food was an additional bond between us.

Feroze's proclivity to gossip was well known. Scandal therefore formed part of our conversations which other friends would usually join. But from the first day I started seeing him until the day of his death I had observed a strict, self-imposed rule: never to pry into his own personal affairs though these were then much discussed in political Delhi. At times, Feroze dropped hints or made elliptical statements about his unhappiness; I listened to the information he volunteered but asked him no questions.

It was at Feroze's suggestion that I first met Indira in the winter of 1956. In the New Delhi Notebook of *The Statesman*, for which I then worked, I had written a short piece criticising Nehru for having invited the visiting Mexican artist, Siqueiros, to lunch. Siqueiros, I had argued, was doubtless a great painter. But he was also an accomplice in Trotsky's murder at Stalin's behest. Should the Prime Minister of India be seen to be honouring such a man?

Feroze told me that both 'Panditji', as Nehru was respectfully called by most Indians, and 'Indu' were intrigued by my criticism and wanted to know the basis for my charge against Siqueiros. The next day I gave him the book from which I had derived my information. A week later he said: 'Oh, I forgot. That book you gave me. Why don't you go and see my wife at the Prime Minister's house at four tomorrow? She will return your book and also give you tea.'

I got both tea and courtesy. Indira and I chatted pleasantly though desultorily. Siqueiros was not even mentioned although my book lay at the tea table. As I rose to leave, she handed the book to me, thanked me for 'lending it to us' and said: 'Even if someone did something wrong in his younger days, we should not refuse to recognise the good work that he might have done in later years.' This was my introduction to the style that was to become familiar, indeed famous, in later years.

Towards the end of 1957 I began to notice that Feroze was no longer dining at the Prime Minister's house as regularly as he used to. He would dine out more and more often, sometimes ringing me or other friends up to organise a short-notice dinner party. Stories about growing strains between him and Indira were now rife. Dinner guests at the Prime Minister's house had been reporting that Feroze, when present, would sit sullenly and finish his meal without taking part in the table talk his wife tried hard to keep up.

Tension did not seem confined to the dining room. Great hilarity was caused at a public function where Congressmen had brought their wives and children though they were supposed not to. Nehru chided them. From a back seat Feroze shouted: '*I* did not bring *my* wife here.' Indira was then sitting by her father's side.

There was no redeeming humour at another function, held in honour of some visiting dignitaries, where Feroze was dissatisfied with the seat allotted to him. He brought this to the attention of Tara Ali Baig, a friend of his who was the wife of the then Chief of Protocol and one of the function's organisers. Mrs Baig told Feroze that the seating plan had been 'finalised by Indu' who alone could change it. 'I am not going to talk to her,' he snarled.

However, why rely on such stray incidents as indicators of the state of the husband–wife relationship when revealing and incontrovertible evidence is available from the pen of Indira herself?

From 1950 until 1984, with a significant break during the Emergency years, Indira had kept up a continuous and lively correspondence with Dorothy Norman, an American social worker, scholar and author, whom she had met in 1949. Dorothy, twelve years senior to Indira, had initially befriended Nehru and had later published a two-volume biography of him. But a deep bond of friendship and trust seems to have developed between the two women rather fast. For not only did Indira write to Dorothy about her innermost thoughts and feelings with astonishing candour – 'I can tell you things which I wouldn't dream of telling anyone' – but also she seemed sure that her confidence would be kept and the letters would neither be published nor seen by anyone else. Obviously the trust was well placed. Until Dorothy published the letters a year after Indira's death, even the existence of the letters, let alone their content, was unknown.

Though they cover a wide range of subjects, the letters constitute a remarkable running commentary on the state of relations between Indira and Feroze. As early as 1950 Indira started writing about a 'sense of loneliness and isolation'. By 1954 she was so unhappy as to write: 'I am in the midst of a domestic crisis.' A year later she lamented: 'I have been and am deeply unhappy in my domestic life. Now the hurt and unpleasantness do not matter so much. I am sorry, though, to have missed the most wonderful thing in life, having a complete and perfect relationship with another human being . . .'

The theme recurred until the lowest point was apparently reached by the time the Kerala crisis came to a boil in July 1959. On the 21st of that month Indira poured out her heart in her letter to Dorothy, informing her that a 'veritable sea of troubles' was engulfing her.

On the domestic front, Feroze has always resented my very existence, but since I have become the President [of the Congress Party] he exudes such hostility that it seems to poison the air. Unfortunately, he and his friends are friendly with some of our ministers and an impossible situation is being created. The Kerala situation is worsening . . .

Herein lies a clue to Indira's bitterness about Feroze's opposition to what she was trying to do in Kerala, quite apart from her feeling of hurt that her most inveterate critic should turn out to be the man to whom she was married. Even earlier, as Congress President, she had had occasion gently to admonish her husband, though without naming him, for his outspoken criticism of the party to which he belonged. Now, however, she was fed up – and furious.

But if Indira was infuriated, so was Feroze. I had known him to be a deeply disturbed man since long before the Kerala crisis began. He did try to cover up his unhappiness with his bluff and boisterous manner. But it no longer worked. The adulation he received – and there was a lot of it – left him cold. He smoked incessantly and, despite the Congress taboo on alcohol, took to drinking, sometimes heavily. His friends were therefore pained but not surprised when, in September 1958, he had his first heart attack.

I remember that sad evening very well. It was warm and sticky. But Feroze insisted on being driven ten miles to dine at a café, started as a cooperative by waiters and other workers retrenched by the Indian Coffee Board after the closure of its coffee houses. Dev Kanta Borooah, later to become Congress President and an Indira worshipper and later still to turn against her, Subhadra Joshi, a woman MP and activist, and I comprised the foursome at the dinner. Feroze was in high spirits and seemed to be enjoying his food when the iron crab struck him.

At that time Indira and her father were traversing Tibet's Chumbi Valley on horseback – because there was no other mode of transport in the region then – on their way to Bhutan, a Himalayan kingdom which still is the closest thing to Shangri-La. After doctors pronounced Feroze to be out of danger a wireless message was sent to Nehru that neither he nor Indira need rush back.

By the time Indira returned, Feroze had recovered but was still confined to bed. From the airport, Indira drove straight to him and looked after him lovingly for several weeks. Some months later when Indira needed surgery for the removal of kidney stones, Feroze nursed her devotedly. Both seem to have been encouraged in the hope that their marriage could perhaps be salvaged. Along with their children, they even went for a holiday in Kashmir where they had honeymooned. But nothing seemed to help. The breach between them continued to widen.

'Look here,' Feroze said to me early in 1959, 'before you hear a doctored version of it, let me tell you that I have stopped going to the Prime Minister's house completely.' I was saddened but, in keeping with my resolve, did not ask him to elaborate. I noticed, however, that, for the first time in his talk with me, he referred to Indira very formally as 'Shrimati (Hindi for Mrs) Indira Gandhi', not as 'Indu' or 'my wife', as was his wont until then.

Over Kerala, Feroze was a man possessed. From early morning until late in the night he would lobby sympathetic ministers, such as Krishna Menon and K. D. Malaviya, about the 'folly' of dismissing the Kerala ministry. Because of his wide contacts with correspondents and commentators, he was also able to influence the press comment. His effectiveness fuelled his wife's anger. But he was fighting a losing battle.

Exactly ten days after Indira wrote her letter about Kerala and Feroze to Dorothy, Indira had her way. Despite Nehru's qualms, his government sacked the Communist ministry in Kerala and brought the state under President's rule, a euphemism for direct government by New Delhi.

The action, especially Indira's role in it, evoked strong criticism from the liberal opinion. But many more people praised her for her decisiveness. Cheers once again exceeded jeers when, in the subsequent elections, the Congress defeated the Communists though, in order to do so, it went back on its policy of never having an alliance with the Muslim League.

Feroze took his 'defeat' over Kerala very badly. He grew more and more morose and embittered. He also got very excited about a railway strike which he thought could have been avoided had he been allowed to mediate. In early September 1960, he had his second and fatal heart attack. On the day of his death he was four days short of his forty-eighth birthday.

His wife was then flying from Kerala to Delhi, unaware of what was happening. She was elated over the success of a women's conference she had presided over. She suddenly realised, as she claimed later, that whenever she was 'so pleased, something terrible usually took place'.

To write Feroze's obituary was one of the most painful tasks I have

70

ever had to undertake. I was in a state of shock but I could not allow this to come in the way of professional duty. One of the points I made in the obituary was that Feroze, in spite of being 'surrounded by friends and admirers' was 'essentially a lonely and unhappy man' and that 'to overcome his loneliness, he took to overwork which eventually killed him'. Quite a few friends and acquaintances, some of them claiming to speak on behalf of the Nehru family, remonstrated with me that I had 'needlessly raked up a politician's personal life'. The one person who never said a word about this matter was Indira.

In death Feroze seems to have succeeded in doing what he had failed to do during his lifetime. He suddenly endeared himself to Indira who found his death a 'heart-rending blow'. Her letters to Dorothy Norman about her benumbing grief and her realisation that, in spite of everything, 'at times of stress and difficulty, Feroze was always by my side' speak for themselves. Anyone who knew Indira even remotely could see at that time how shattered she was. A year before the death of her younger son, Sanjay, she told an author: 'The most important death in my life was my husband's . . .'

Several years after her husband's death, listening to some records of Beethoven, sent to her by Dorothy Norman, Indira remarked to friends: 'The Nehrus were very unmusical people. It was Feroze who introduced us to the joys of Western classical music.'

Great minds came to Nehru's mansion from far and near to seek his sage advice, to profit from his towering intellect, broad vision and deep insight into history or simply to listen to a 'voice of reason and sanity' in a world which seemed to have gone insane even in those 'good, old' days. Hardly anyone of them, however, bothered to probe the mind of his daughter or to take her seriously even after she had become Congress President. They were courteous to her, of course, but talked to her about trivialities.

Only close friends like Dorothy Norman and Pupul Jayakar, who had been Indira's friend from the days in Allahabad when both were teenagers, felt the injustice of it all. Some even believed that she would have been better off if she wasn't under her father's 'shadow'.

However, even after she came into her own, occupied her father's office for nearly as long as he had done and joined the ranks of world 'statespersons' in her own right, it was not for her penetrating intellect that she became known. Her forte was a quick grasp of the complexities of the global power politics, as affecting her country. She also had a gift for concentrating on the essential and a remarkable knack of producing, more often than not, the right response to whatever might be the problem. In short, she was a woman, not of ideas, but of instinct.

From the mid-Fifties onwards, both Norman and Jayakar saw to it that during her travels abroad Indira met men and women of distinction in the fields of arts, music, science and literature. This was entirely to her own liking; over the years she was to get to know a glittering array of eminent people like Buckminster Fuller and Charles Eames on the one hand and Barbara Cartland and Allen Ginsberg on the other. At a gathering of such glitterati at Dorothy Norman's home as late as in the Eighties she was to remark: 'I am an anti-establishment person required to run the establishment in my country.'

At her father's behest, Indira had started reading a great many books from early childhood. Some of them, such as those by Bernard Shaw and H. G. Wells, she could not fully comprehend. An impression has grown therefore that this perhaps put her off reading. Poet and author Dom Moraes spent some time in 1977 in the library of Anand Bhavan, the ancestral Nehru home in Allahabad, now a museum. He meticulously examined Indira's books as well as her father's and grandfather's. Motilal's books, according to him, seemed mainly to be legal. Jawaharlal's displayed an 'extraordinarily catholic taste . . . he seems to have wanted to know almost everything'. Indira's books 'were not numerous, and in some the leaves were uncut'.

There is no reason to disbelieve this statement, but it would be wrong to deduce from it that Indira lost interest in reading books from an early age. In fact, she remained a 'voracious and amazingly rapid reader' all her life. Her selection of books was eclectic and at times haphazard, as a visit to her personal library, still preserved at 1, Safdarjung Road, would show. Some books she read because they were recommended or sent to her by friends or acquaintances whose judgment she valued. Dorothy Norman sent her such books as William Thompson's *The Edge of History*, Ivan Illich's *The Deschooling of Society* and several others. She wrote back detailed comments on all these books. After reading the eminent Indian author, R. K. Narayan's version of Mahabharata she entered into a detailed discussion with him about her reasons for disagreeing with his interpretation of the Hindu epic.

Some books she read because they were relevant to business in hand. Before President Mitterrand arrived in New Delhi in 1982, she carefully read his *Wheat and Chaff*. Ten years earlier, before leaving for Stockholm to address the first UN Conference on Environment she read from cover to cover Alvin Tofler's *Future Shock*. When I mentioned this titbit in *The Times of India* Notebook, all major book-shops in Delhi and Bombay were virtually raided by an eager public and every single copy of the book was bought out. This was only a few months after India's magnificent victory in the war with Pakistan for the liberation of Bangladesh, and Indira was then at the zenith of her power and popularity.

During her years as her father's châtelaine and confidante, there were two men who could be called friends and allies of Indira. One was M. O. Mathai, Nehru's special assistant whose power was out of all proportion to his rank, and the other Krishna Menon, the Prime Minister's chief adviser on foreign policy.

Mathai has been rightly described as an 'adventurer from Kerala' who suddenly appeared at Nehru's door, shortly before independence, and offered his services practically in return for board and lodging. Thus it was that when Nehru moved to the Prime Minister's house, Mathai went with him. This propinquity, combined with his cunning and competence, enabled Mathai to build up his formidable power with remarkable speed. Cabinet ministers, senior bureaucrats and leading industrialists started vying with one another to curry favour with him.

It was Mathai, not Nehru, who first started 'pushing Indira into the limelight'. He urged her not to shy away from public service and discreetly nudged Nehru to appoint her on some official committee or other or to assign her responsibilities for the welfare of women and children for which, he would argue, she was most suited.

Perhaps inevitably, under the circumstances, Mathai's name was romantically linked with Indira's. That he was a bachelor and lived under the Prime Minister's roof was grist to the rumour mill. Far from discouraging the rumours, Mathai was only too happy to let the word spread that he was having a romance with the Prime Minister's pretty daughter. Much later, long after his far from glorious exit from the Prime Minister's house and, indeed, well after Indira herself had lost power in 1977, Mathai was to brag, as we shall see in a subsequent chapter, more or less openly that he was indeed Indira's lover.

In the Fifties, however, he knew better than to be boastful about his 'conquest', real or imaginary, though he was foolish enough to let power go to his head.

Whether Feroze, not at all unaware of the gossip about his wife and her father's special assistant, was jealous of Mathai he never indicated to anyone. But, as usual, he was the first to get wind of some sharp practices. Mathai was indulging in, exploiting his position as Nehru's aide. It transpired that he had collected huge donations for a trust he had started in his mother's memory and had bought from an industrialist an orchard at a ridiculously low price. Feroze collected the evidence of Mathai's wrong-doing with the thoroughness he was famous for. But, uncharacteristically, he did not raise this matter in

Parliament himself. This task he left to friendly MPs who were exceedingly well briefed. Mathai had no option but to resign and disappear into limbo as suddenly as he had appeared from nowhere, to surface again only in the late Seventies.

By contrast, not even a whiff of scandal attached to Indira's friendly relations with Krishna Menon though, like Mathai, he was a bachelor and, whenever in Delhi, lived at the Prime Minister's house. In 1957, when he was appointed Defence Minister, at Indira's suggestion, he set up house on his own, across the road from the Prime Minister's residence.

Menon was, in fact, something of a father figure to both Indira and Feroze whom he had taken under his wing when they were students in London and he was running the India League in Britain. Feroze's friendship with Menon was much the stronger and the more lasting. The two, as we have noted, had joined hands to oppose Indira over Kerala. But during the days Menon used to stay at the Prime Minister's house no one could have anticipated the Kerala crisis. Even so, Indira's relations with Menon were complex although both found it expedient to be allies, he to maintain his special position vis-à-vis Nehru and she to give a shine to her left-of-centre image, Menon being the darling of the Indian Left.

Indira was irritated with Menon, however, because of the embarrassment he caused her father through his bad manners and biting tongue. At the same time, she sprang to Menon's defence especially against the persistent attacks on him by Americans who once called him 'Hindu Vyshinsky', Vyshinsky being the acid-tongued prosecutor in the notorious Stalinist trials of the Thirties and later chief Soviet delegate to the UN, the position Menon held on behalf of India.

In 1966, after her first visit to the United States as Prime Minister, Indira told me, with evident relief, that mercifully and to her great surprise none of her American interlocutors had raised any questions about Menon, until then their favourite topic of discussion with her. In later years, Menon's relations with her were to see even sharper ups and downs.

In a class by itself was Indira's relationship with Lord and Lady Mountbatten. The Mountbattens had stayed in India for a very short time, from March 1947 to June 1948. Until August 15th, 1947, Lord Mountbatten was Britain's last Viceroy and thereafter free India's first Governor-General. But he, and even more Edwina Mountbatten, had instantly established a warm, cordial and lasting rapport with Nehru and, at one remove, with Indira. The widower and lonely Prime Minister was simply captivated by Edwina. In her company he could relax completely and be himself. The two started spending a great deal of time together by themselves. After the Mountbattens left India, Nehru and Edwina visited each other and also kept up a voluminous correspondence with each other. Hundreds of Nehru's letters to Edwina are in the Mountbatten Archives, while hers to him seem to have disappeared.

During the twelve years after she left India until her death in 1960, Lady Mountbatten came to Delhi at least twice a year and always stayed with Nehru. He visited her at the Mountbatten country home, Broadlands, whenever he passed through England. On one occasion at least, Edwina was seen 'clad in a housecoat, opening the door to Nehru.'

Mountbatten's official biographer, Philip Ziegler, insists that too much should not be read into the Nehru–Edwina–Lord Mountbatten 'triangle'. He also says that Mountbatten was not a 'complaisant husband'. Most Indians believe otherwise. They think that the Nehru–Edwina relationship was not just platonic and that, far from discouraging or resenting it, Mountbatten 'encouraged it, initially at least, because it served his purpose in India'. The forthcoming publication of Nehru's letters to Edwina might clinch or, at least, clarify the issue.

Whatever the truth about the Nehru–Edwina 'love affair', it does not seem to have affected the warm friendship between her and Indira. According to someone in a position to watch them, Edwina treated Indira as she would treat a daughter and Indira responded accordingly. On every visit Edwina brought her gifts, 'sometimes pieces of jewellery'. Indira gave her equally valuable presents, such as rare Indian shawls or exotic artefacts. The two talked cordially for hours. Edwina's death, four years before Nehru's, 'saddened' Indira.

At that time, cordiality was also the hallmark of Indira–Mountbatten relations. But over the years, this relationship cooled down and eventually soured.

The crunch came in 1971 when Indira 'deprived Indian princes of their privy purses'. To Mountbatten this was a terrible breach of faith. He protested to Indira and 'inveighed against the decision to every Indian he met'. For his part, Mountbatten became 'more and more concerned about Mrs Gandhi's behaviour'. In 1975 when her election to Parliament was set aside and she was disqualified from holding elective office for six years – a situation she overcame by declaring a State of Emergency – Lord Mountbatten confided to his diary: 'She has of course not been corrupt in the ordinary sense of the word, but she has certainly grown too big for her boots and is being tough and difficult with everybody.'

Mountbatten was indignant when Gayatri Devi, pretty and vivacious former Rajmata (dowager queen) of Jaipur, 'widow of his closest Indian friend' became a victim of Indira's Emergency powers and was put into prison. He tried his best to 'intercede' but to 'small effect'.

In 1966, after a visit to Delhi during which he had warmly welcomed Indira's elevation to the office that once belonged to her father, Mountbatten had stated: 'Every time I visit India, it tears at my heart-strings.' Ten years later he found the prospect 'so depressing' that he began to wonder 'whether he could bear to go there at all'. He also started complaining that Indira 'does not like me; indeed she does not like any of her father's friends'.

However, in 1976, despite the strain between him and Indira and despite the Emergency, Mountbatten did pass through India. From Bombay airport, where his plane halted, he made one phone call – to Gayatri Devi who had by then been released. He studiously refrained from ringing up Indira, something he had never done before.

Perhaps irked by Mountbatten's nagging criticism, Indira also did something petty. She leaked out to Indian newspapers, under the government's tight control because of the Emergency, details of Mountbatten's elaborate plan for his own funeral. He had sent the confidential document to the Indian government because he was keen on the participation in the ceremony by Indian troops, especially the Gurkhas he had commanded during the Second World War as Supreme Commander of the South-East Asia Command (SEAC). As Viceroy and later Governor-General he had grown even more fond of them.

However, when the IRA bomb, planted in his boat, blew up Mountbatten, Indira promptly sent the Indian army contingent he had asked to be present at his funeral.

While Indira was fighting and winning her battle in Kerala, seeds of a bigger and more disastrous war were being sown along the India–China frontier in the high Himalayas, at the other end of the country. Gone was the heady Hindi-Chini Bhai-Bhai (Indians and Chinese are brothers) era. Friendly Chinese embraces had been replaced by menacing claims and encroachments on territory Indians had always regarded as irrevocably theirs.

Even at the start of the India–China honeymoon, New Delhi had noticed that official Chinese maps were showing large chunks of Indian territory as parts of China. But Beijing had blandly replied that the People's government had not had time to 'revise the old Kuomintang maps'. Apparently reassured then, India felt cheated later. Not only did the Chinese insist that their maps delineated the India–China border accurately but also they had occupied some of the territory claimed by them. They had even built a road to link Tibet with Sinkiang through Indian Aksai Chin.

As India hurriedly set up 'penny-packet posts' to deter further

Chinese incursions, tension rose. It escalated further when the Dalai Lama, the spiritual and temporal leader of Tibet, fled Lhasa and was given asylum in India.

Nehru tried to resolve the crisis with China diplomatically. But the Chinese were intransigent and Indian public opinion became inflamed. Indira, as Congress President, supported her father and urged restraint. She wanted the country to be 'united firmly' against 'aggressive Chinese claims'. But she cautioned against 'hysteria'.

There was no let-up in China's aggressiveness and none in Indian outrage which began to border on the hysteria Indira had warned against. Nehru, his own wrong judgment reinforced by incompetent or craven advice, clung to the illusion that while there might be skirmishes between Indian and Chinese patrols, China would do 'nothing big'. For this he had to pay dearly. When, in October 1962, the Chinese struck in a big way, neither he, nor the Army, nor the country was prepared for it.

Military and political debacle followed. National morale disintegrated almost overnight. China's unilateral cease-fire and withdrawal turned the knife in the Indian wound. Nehru was attacked for 'credulity and negligence' by Radhakrishnan, the republic's President and somewhat estranged friend of the Prime Minister. Nehru, who admitted that India had lived a 'make-believe world', never really recovered from the trauma of 'China's perfidy'.

Indira knew that her father was broken in body and spirit. She looked after him with even greater diligence than before. He also started consulting her more often than in the past.

Her undefined but undoubted and extensive influence on the nation's affairs increased further when, in January 1964, Nehru suffered a stroke while attending the Congress party's annual session at Bhubaneswar in the eastern state of Orissa. He returned to Delhi in a wheelchair but did not give up the reins of government. Of course he needed much greater help than before. This was duly provided by two cabinet ministers and by Indira.

Of the three Indira was clearly the closest to the ailing Prime Minister. The extent of her power became a hot topic of discussion and controversy in the Indian capital. In order to take stock of the situation I asked to see her. I was given an appointment immediately.

Despite her worry about her father's health, she was calm and relaxed. She was at pains to point out that while she was helping her father, as always, it was 'absurd' to compare her position to that of President Woodrow Wilson's wife who practically ran the government during her husband's illness.

On return to my office I sent a detailed report of my talk with Indira to my then editor, G. E. Powell, who was in Calcutta, and now lives in retirement in Scotland. I concluded my confidential note to him with the remark that her disavowal notwithstanding, the lady seemed happy that the public and the press saw her to be the 'power behind the throne or, rather, the Prime Minister's sickbed'.

Jawaharlal Nehru, the greatest of all Indians after Gandhi and free India's first Prime Minister, died on May 27th, 1964. It was a hot and dusty day. It was also the anniversary of the birth, enlightenment and death of Lord Buddha. Indira was not the only one to be orphaned. All the six hundred million Indians felt the same way as she did. They poured out into the streets in staggering numbers to mourn the man they had hero-worshipped.

The funeral had to be delayed by a day because dignitaries were rushing to Delhi from all over the globe. Throughout this period Indira kept vigil by her father's body as it lay in state. She was numb with grief but dry-eyed.

In a revealing interlude on the morning of the funeral day, she gently told members of Nehru's personal staff, sitting around unshaven and unkempt, to go home, shave, bathe, change and then come back. 'My father,' she said, 'always liked neatness; there will be no slovenliness around him today.'

# 5   The Shastri Interlude

At the time of Nehru's death, it was a foregone conclusion that the man to step into his over-sized shoes would be Lal Bahadur Shastri, a diminutive, homespun and highly respected individual of fifty-eight, with a long ministerial and party career behind him. His main virtue was that he was seen to be a great conciliator. The contrast between him and the other contender for the top job, Morarji Desai, could not have been more striking.

Desai, then nearing seventy and now a sprightly ninety-three, was a senior party leader and a seasoned administrator. His credentials for becoming Prime Minister were impressive. But formidable opposition to him had built up because of his apparent inflexibility, intolerance and fads. His fanatical zeal for prohibition had earned him the sobriquet 'teetotalitarian'. An author was to describe him as a man 'physically resembling Cassius and spiritually Calvin'.

Until about two years before Nehru's death, Desai was generally regarded as his 'natural successor'. No one believed this more ardently than Desai himself. This was to prove to be a fact of critical importance to Indira: from the time she became Prime Minister until the moment of her death Desai, a single-minded and self-righteous man, opposed and harried her because of his firm belief that she had taken away the job which should, by right, have been his.

In 1964, however, Desai bowed to the inevitability that Shastri, rather than he, would succeed Nehru though he made no secret of his fury over being 'cheated out' of his due. He knew that he had been outmanoeuvred, and there was nothing he could do about it.

It was the handiwork of a collective of powerful Congress party bosses in the states, headed by Kumaraswamy Kamaraj, the rough-hewn but highly skilful chief minister of the southern state of Tamil Nadu. Other members of this group, quickly nicknamed 'the Syndicate', were men who would have been perfectly at home in those famous 'smoke-filled rooms' in the United States or even in Tammany Hall. They were Atulya Ghosh from West Bengal, Sanjiva Reddy from Andhra, Nijalingappa from Karnataka and S. K. Patil from booming Bombay.

Meeting in the temple town of Tirupati in South India in early 1963, the Syndicate had come to the conclusion that only a collective leadership, headed by Shastri, could fill the void that Nehru would leave behind and that Desai, with his penchant for laying down the law, should be kept out of the race. Towards this end the Syndicate made a shrewd move as early as August 1963. At a meeting of the Congress Working Committee, Kamaraj put forward a plan which has since been associated with his name. Offering to step down from the office of chief minister of Tamil Nadu and to devote all his time to 'strengthening the party', he proposed that others, serving as senior ministers in the central government or as chief ministers in states, should do likewise.

Nehru welcomed the idea and announced that he would be the first to follow Kamaraj's 'excellent example'. Predictably, there was a chorus of protest and he was persuaded to stay. At the same time, the essence of the Kamaraj Plan was accepted. All chief ministers and members of the central cabinet handed in their resignations to Nehru who accepted six in each of the two categories.

Desai, who was to allege later that the Kamaraj Plan was really Nehru's own 'brainchild', headed the list of central government ministers to go. Others to be sent out with him included Jagjivan Ram, a long-serving Harijan (former untouchable) minister, and Patil. A surprise inclusion in the list of the 'Kamarajed' ministers was Shastri. It was, in fact, a clever move.

Since the whole idea was to smooth the way for Shastri to succeed Nehru, it would have looked invidious if Desai alone had been sent away and Shastri remained in the cabinet. So why not send away Shastri, too, and get him back sooner or later on some pretext or other? Most people were convinced that Shastri would be brought back, and it happened much sooner than anyone thought.

In January 1964, as we have seen, Nehru suffered a stroke. He needed help in discharging his onerous responsibilities. Shastri was asked to rejoin the cabinet as minister without portfolio. Desai was deeply offended by the stratagem but maintained a dignified silence about it. He was far from silent, however, about his feeling that all the 'Machiavellian manouevring' by Nehru was for the sake of his own 'darling daughter', not of Shastri. How he came to this conclusion he never explained though he has always stuck to this belief.

Curiously, even Shastri, though firmly set on the succession course, was credited with the opinion that he was Nehru's second preference as a successor, the first being Indira. However, this opinion was attributed to him only after his death, not in his lifetime.

The idea that Indira could be her father's successor was not altogether fanciful. It was discussed constantly as much in Delhi's corridors of power as in coffee houses. Welles Hangen, an American TV journalist then based in Delhi, who later disappeared without trace in Vietnam, published a book in 1963. For its title, he used the question then haunting India: *After Nehru, Who?*

In this book Hangen listed, as Nehru's possible successors, Desai, Shastri and Indira, in that order. But he also included in his catalogue such improbable names as S. K. Patil, Krishna Menon, virtually sacked from the defence ministry because of the country's lack of preparedness at the time of the Chinese invasion in 1962, and Lieutenant-General B. M. Kaul, who had disgraced himself during the brief India–China war.

However, the issue in early 1964 was not whether Indira was a potential Prime Minister but whether Nehru was doing anything to ensure that she succeeded him. Since by that time the succession issue had been all but settled in Shastri's favour, the very idea that Nehru was still busy manipulating things on his daughter's behalf is preposterous.

Far from trying to foist Indira on the country as his successor, Nehru seems to have been unhappy that Welles Hangen had 'dragged in' her name in connection with succession. In fact, he asked Indira 'testily' why she had agreed to meet 'that American journalist' and answer his questions.

Nehru loved his daughter, of course, and had high ambitions for her future. But the limit of his ambition was reported to be that Indira would be a minister in Shastri's cabinet and thus an 'instrument of continuity'. He could not have foreseen, nor could have anyone else, that Shastri would die so soon. Moreover, whatever Indira might have done in her own time, Nehru was appalled by the very thought of dynastic succession. 'The concept of dynastic succession,' he declared publicly, 'is altogether foreign to a parliamentary democracy like ours, besides being repulsive to my own mind.'

In any case, as soon as official mourning for Nehru was over, Shastri was elected as his successor by the Congress Parliamentary Party unanimously and by acclamation. Desai was party to the Congress Working Committee's resolution demanding that the new Prime Minister be chosen not by contest but by consensus, to be ascertained by Kamaraj, who had by this time become Congress President. Since there was little doubt as to what the consensus was going to be, Desai was in no position to protest.

Indira was not in the race for the succession in June 1964. But what were her own feelings about her future at that time? A year or so earlier, Hangen had written about her: 'No public figure in India disclaims political ambition so insistently, and none is more disbelieved.' This was an accurate description of the situation then and this remained true of Indira all through her political career.

Just as Greta Garbo became the most publicised actress in the history of the cinema by the simple expedient of shunning publicity ostentatiously, so Indira perfected to a fine art the technique of accumulating more and more power in her hands while emphatically declaring that she had no power and that she wanted to be rid of whatever little power she did have. Nor was the gap between her words and deeds confined to the sole issue of winning power and holding it. As was to become clear later, the reality of her policies often had little to do with the rhetoric surrounding them.

It was not surprising therefore that even during her time of grief over her father's death, few believed her when she said that she was not interested in inheriting his political mantle or in holding any other political office. But unless her letters to Dorothy Norman are to be dismissed as a carefully planned fraud to be perpetrated on historians a quarter of a century afterwards, the conclusion is inescapable that the one thing Indira did not want in June 1964 was the tenancy of the room at the top in India's power structure.

Practically from the time of her husband's death in 1960 until that of her father's four years later, she had been writing to Dorothy Norman about her feelings of 'intense fatigue', 'dark despair', 'physical and emotional strain' and, above all, her need for 'privacy and anonymity . . . [which] I feel I cannot ignore without some kind of self-annihilation'.

Both her sons were then in England, Rajiv at Imperial College in London and Sanjay, obsessed with cars, learning his trade at a Rolls-Royce factory in Crewe. It was to London therefore that she wanted to go. She had in fact planned to buy a flat she had 'fallen in love with' there and when she discovered that it had already been bought by an acquaintance, she was 'terribly depressed for months'.

While repeatedly telling Dorothy that she wanted to live in London even if for only a year or so, Indira also stated: 'I am not running from anybody or anything. I can claim to have done my duty to my country and my family. I don't for an instant regret it. But now I want another life.'

Barely nineteen days before her father's death, she wrote: 'The desire to be out of India and the malice and jealousies and envy with which one is surrounded, is now overwhelming.'

No wonder then that when Shastri invited her to join his cabinet, Indira accepted reluctantly, asked for a month's time before being sworn in and opted for a 'light' portfolio, Information and Broadcasting, rather than Foreign Affairs, for which many thought she was more suited.

Shastri's motives in asking Indira to join the cabinet were mixed. His many qualities had undoubtedly earned him the office of Prime Minister but it was also a gift to him by Nehru. He did not want to appear to be ungrateful to the departed leader. He also knew that the presence in his government of Nehru's daughter would lend it strength. But while being a good man with a genuinely modest demeanour, Shastri was also a tough and wily politician who knew how to safeguard his own interests. He did not want a potential rival in his team. It was for this reason that he had excluded Desai from the new cabinet. While including Indira he was anxious to see to it that she did not become a rival centre of power.

Towards this end, Shastri adopted the policy of showing Indira all surface courtesies but allowing her no share or say in the making of policy. He did appoint her to the cabinet's major committees. But the meetings of these committees, even more than those of the cabinet itself, had become a mere formality though they never were as irrelevant as they were to become during the years of Indira's own supremacy.

Indira was quick to notice what Shastri was up to and started giving vent to her resentment quite openly. It was only a month after she had joined the cabinet that I first became aware of the depth of her feelings over being 'slighted and ignored' by the new Prime Minister.

Illness had prevented Shastri from attending the Commonwealth Prime Ministers' Conference in London in July 1964. He had sent T. T. Krishnamachari, Finance Minister, and Indira in his place. Krishnamachari did most of the talking at the conference and Indira was quite happy to be close to her children. She stayed on in London for a few days after the conference was over. After covering it, I also lingered on in London.

One Sunday morning I went to see her at Claridge's Hotel. She was talking to some personal friends, including Marie Seton, the writer on films, Freda Brilliant, the sculptress, and Ella Sen, an Indian journalist, and asked me to join them. Interrupting whatever they were talking about, Indira asked me if I had seen in the Sunday papers that Shastri had appointed Swaran Singh as Foreign Minister, a position held by Nehru all through his tenure and by Shastri until then. When I said that I had, she burst out: 'Should he not have consulted me and Krishnamachari? I do not want that job. But surely I should have been consulted.'

Things worsened after Indira's return home. A number of young junior ministers and MPs clustered around her. They started telling her that Shastri was slowly abandoning her father's policies. Some of the Prime Minister's own pronouncements 'strengthened this impression.'

Early in 1965 a major crisis broke out in Southern India. Under the Indian constitution, Hindi was to become the sole official language of the country in that year. Non-Hindi speaking states had become very agitated even during Nehru's time. But his assurance, that Hindi would never be forced on unwilling people and that English would continue to be an 'associate official language' for as long as non-Hindi states wanted it, had assuaged the ruffled feelings.

But some of Shastri's ministers, especially Home Minister G. L. Nanda, had given the impression of being Hindi zealots. People in South India had got alarmed and demanded that Nehru's assurance should be enshrined in the constitution by amending it. When Shastri pointed out that this would cause unrest in the Hindi states, a violent agitation in the southern state of Tamil Nadu began. Some opponents of Hindi immolated themselves.

Both Shastri and Kamaraj, the leader of Tamil Nadu, stayed in Delhi and did nothing, waiting for the situation to simmer down. Indira took the first available plane to Madras, rushed to the storm-centre of trouble and helped bring the situation under control.

Shastri was not amused. He felt, and told friends, that Indira was exceeding her brief and indeed 'jumping over' the Prime Minister's head. When I discussed this with her, she flared up. She said that she did not look upon herself as a 'mere Minister for Information and Broadcasting' but as one of the leaders of the country. 'Do you think this government can survive if I resign today? I am telling you it won't. Yes, I have jumped over the Prime Minister's head and I would do it again whenever the need arises.'

At my first meeting with Indira in 1956 I had noticed that her right eye blinked. Now I saw that because of her excitement her eyelid was flickering faster.

Indira was as good as her word. When, in August 1965, first reports came in of large-scale paramilitary infiltrations by Pakistan in Kashmir, she immediately flew to Kashmir, encouraged the security forces combating the infiltrators and addressed public meetings to maintain the public's morale. When actual hostilities began, she was at the battlefront, much to the nervousness of the generals. The troops, however, were enthused by her presence amongst them. This was the time when she was paid the left-handed compliment that she was the 'only man in a cabinet of old women'.

Back in Delhi she wrote out a short paper on how to prosecute the war with Pakistan and presented it at a meeting of the cabinet's emergency committee. In her words, 'Shastri took the paper from me, held it gingerly, as one would a dead rat by its tail, and asked: "*Is ka kaya karein?* (What should we do with it?)".' Dharma Vira, the cabinet secretary, she added, said that the paper should be given to him and 'this was the last I heard of it'.

The 1965 war between India and Pakistan ended the period when Indira could upstage the Prime Minister. The Indian victory on the battlefield was marginal. But the Indian objective of preventing Kashmir from being seized by Pakistan had been fulfilled. Moreover, this performance had contrasted sharply with the rout at the hands of the Chinese only three years earlier. Overnight Shastri had become a national hero. The little man, whose appearance on the cinema screen used to be a signal for audiences to laugh, started looking ten feet tall. He was applauded wherever he went. He started ignoring Indira and other senior colleagues more openly than before and running the government with the help of a few trusted officials. Indira was furious.

During this period I used to see her frequently and she never missed an opportunity to emphasise that she was being treated shabbily. Once or twice she even talked of resigning though, in my view, not very seriously. Sometimes, Pran Sabbharwal, a friend and journalist colleague who worked for the *Baltimore Sun*, and I went together to see Indira. She nicknamed us 'the twins'.

Shortly before the 1965 India–Pakistan war began, the Sikh agitation for a purely Punjabi-speaking state, in place of bilingual Punjab, had reached a peak. Sant Fateh Singh, a respected Akali leader, had threatened to burn himself to death if the demand was not conceded. He was persuaded to call off the agitation in return for the promise that the demand for a Punjabi-speaking state would be considered after the war was over.

In pursuance of this pledge, Shastri appointed a cabinet committee to examine the Sikh demand. He made Indira chairman of this committee but would not even see her, despite her repeated requests that before she could make any recommendation to the cabinet she must know the Prime Minister's views. Indira complained to everyone she met.

The last day of 1965 turned out to be a particularly unhappy one for her. She had once again conveyed to the Prime Minister that time was running out and that he must find time to discuss with her the issue of a Punjabi state. Shastri informed her that she should stay on after a cabinet committee meeting scheduled for that evening.

When Indira followed the Prime Minister's advice she was in for a shock. She was not the only minister to linger on. Krishnamachari did so, too. He was in an agitated mood and soon a squabble began between him and Shastri. Indira discreetly withdrew and went home in high dudgeon. An hour later Krishnamachari arrived at her house to inform her that, in sheer disgust with the Prime Minister's scant regard for him, he had resigned.

As the news of the resignation broke, I first went to see Krishnamachari and then Indira. 'I will be the next to be thrown out' was her opening remark, her right eye flickering. 'It is not a cabinet worth staying in.' She was particularly hurt by Krishnamachari's departure because he was a loyal Nehruite.

Indira was once again talking of leaving everything and going off to London to live there for a while at least. Both her sons were still there. Whether she knew or suspected or not, Shastri was also having the same idea. He confided to his advisers that Indira would be better off in London than in New Delhi. He was therefore planning to offer her the post of High Commissioner to Britain. He was holding back the offer for a while, however, because he had more pressing problems on his hands.

On January 2nd, 1966, he was to leave for Tashkent in Soviet Central Asia where the Russians had invited him and the Pakistani president, Field-Marshal Ayub Khan for peace talks under Soviet auspices.

From Tashkent Shastri returned in a coffin to a grieving Delhi. He had died at Tashkent barely hours after he and Ayub had signed a declaration ending the state of war between their two countries. The triumph had ended in tragedy. In less than twenty months India was confronted with a second succession. Indira's moment of destiny had arrived.

Welles Hangen, while discussing Indira's prospects of succeeding her father, had written, pertinently enough, that she could reach the 'room at the top' only with the help of the 'powerful parental key'. In the absence of that key he was not so sure. Nehru had been dead for more than a year and a half. And yet there seemed a certain inevitability about Indira becoming the next Prime Minister though it took a little time for the issue to be clinched.

Consensus was no longer a practical proposition, though it had prevailed when Shastri succeeded Nehru. Desai had made it clear that he would not give up his claim and the issue should therefore be settled by a contest in the Congress Parliamentary Party. Others said that this was fair but they immediately rejected his demand that the Congress MPs be left strictly alone to exercise their vote. Leaders who were not MPs must not try to influence anyone. In India's federal system, where the Congress Working Committee was the party's grand council and Congress chief ministers ruled areas larger than France or Britain, Desai's proposal was untenable.

Unlike Nehru's, Shastri's death was sudden and unforeseen. No prior agreement on his successor existed even within the Syndicate. Kamaraj, once again the kingpin of the decision-making structure, was credited with the view that Indira was the only answer to the situation. But others, while preferring her to Desai, had reservations about her. Patil tried hard to persuade Kamaraj to accept the mantle himself. The silent strong man from the South replied tersely: 'No English, no Hindi. How?'

On one point not only the Syndicate of party bosses but also many other Congress leaders were united: Desai had to be stopped. That being the case, Indira quickly emerged as the favourite though her performance as Information and Broadcasting Minister had been lacklustre and that as a parliamentarian extremely poor. Even after becoming Prime Minister she confessed that she was 'terrified' at the thought of having to answer parliamentary questions. Her only plus point as minister in charge of media was to have allowed a measure of free discussion and dissent on government-controlled radio, laid schemes for bringing television to India and relaxed censorship on films. She thus acquired a fairly large and influential constituency of liberal intellectuals and artists.

The Syndicate and the Congress chief ministers were not particularly concerned about what the intelligentsia was saying. They were thinking more about the next General Election, now only thirteen months away and the first to be held without the magic personality of Nehru. This is what clinched the issue in Indira's favour. Of all the Congress leaders she alone had something of her father's charisma and mass appeal, as had become evident during those whirlwind countrywide visits Shastri had so disliked. Like her father, she was popular among Muslims, Harijans and other minorities. And, like him, she was above all divisions of caste, religion, region and even faction.

She topped these winning qualities with one even her best friends hadn't suspected she possessed. While Desai staked his claim to prime ministership most stridently, Indira maintained a low profile and dignified silence. When pressed to define her position, she would coyly say that she would be 'guided by the wishes of the Congress and its President, Kamaraj'.

This paid her rich dividends in a society which values renunciation, but it was clearly a pose. At the time of her father's death she might have been uninterested in becoming Prime Minister. But the intervening Shastri interlude had changed things. She now wanted the job and was more or less convinced that it was hers.

However, she kept up the pretence of being a reluctant Prime Minister even after she had been duly elected. When one of her friends congratulated her, she quoted to him Robert Frost's famous poem about the man who did not want to be king and drew away his hand when offered by his father the kingdom he was sure he did not want.

'That's exactly how I feel,' she said cheerily. But the truth, as it became known only a few days later, was precisely the reverse of her claim. While the succession drama was on, her sons in England were naturally anxious to know what was happening. Three days before her conversation with her friend, she had written to Rajiv and quoted some other lines from the same poem by Frost which reflected her mood more accurately:

> To be king is within the situation
> and within me . . .

The Syndicate, however, had little time for poetry. It was busy with mundane calculations centring on the question of whether Indira would be a sufficiently pliable Prime Minister to do its bidding. Even Shastri had declared his independence of Kamaraj and other members of the collective. Would Indira behave like him? In the event, the party bosses concluded that they would be able to control Indira better than they had managed to do in the case of Shastri. How a cabal of hard-headed veterans of the power game came to this self-deluding conclusion – which they lived to regret later – is not clear. After all, they should have taken note of her repeated defiance of Shastri and indeed of her own father over Kerala in 1959.

Interestingly, the first move to make Indira the new Prime Minister came not from the Syndicate but from a group of Congress chief ministers, headed by D. P. Mishra, a man so clever and calculating that he was generally called Chanakaya, the Indian master of *realpolitik* who lived a thousand years before Machiavelli. Mishra also was to be Indira's trusted counsellor for some years though later, like all those too close to her, he was also to fall from grace.

As soon as Mishra and eight other Congress chief ministers issued a statement that in their view the interests of the country and the Congress would be best served by electing Indira as Shastri's successor, the Syndicate declared its powerful support for her. The Indira bandwagon turned into a juggernaut.

Desai was determined, however, not to give up without a fight. On January 19th, the contest took place at a meeting of the Congress Parliamentary Party in Parliament's domed Central Hall. The secret ballot was slow. Huge crowds assembled outside the circular building waited impatiently until Satya Narain Sinha, the party chief whip, appeared on the balcony. 'What is it?' the crowd shouted. 'Boy or girl?'

'It's a girl,' announced Sinha and the crowd went delirious with joy. Indira had won easily, securing 355 votes to Desai's 169.

Indira was mobbed as she came out of the building. There were deafening shouts of Indira Gandhi *Zindabad* (Long Live Indira Gandhi) and *Lal Gulab Zindabad* (Long Live the Red Rose). The latter slogan was significant and emotive. All through his adult life Nehru had sported a red rose in his buttonhole. Crowds were hailing Indira's victory as the 'return of the red rose'.

So great was the crush of the people that Indira could drive to Rashtrapati Bhavan, the presidential palace, only a quarter of a mile away, with great difficulty. There President Radhakrishnan invited her to form a new government.

A presidential limousine brought her to her home, 1, Safdarjung Road, where she had moved on becoming a minister in Shastri's cabinet and which was to be the Prime Minister's house until the melancholy morning on which she was gunned down. Vast crowds, including the representatives of the world media, had preceded her. I stood in a corner of the verandah as she came in. She gave me a smile and waved at some others.

Her fine, chiselled features bore just a trace of fatigue. Her large, dark eyes wandered from one side to the other as she surveyed the exuberant scene. For the first time I realised the meaning of the expression 'lonely in a crowd'. For at the greatest moment of her life, surrounded by countless supporters and admirers, Indira seemed as lonely as she must have been during her childhood at Anand Bhavan.

Both her sons were away in England. No other member of the family was around. Even her devoted personal staff and domestic retainers had merged with the happy, humming throng.

Somewhat helplessly and in a faint voice, she said: 'Will someone, please, give me a glass of water?'

# 6   The Dumb Doll

Indira Gandhi's rise to power had been swift and spectacular. At forty-eight she was ten years younger than either her father or Shastri had been on first becoming Prime Minister. But this honour could not have come to her at a more difficult time. It was perhaps an omen of the trials ahead that her swearing-in coincided with the death on a plane crash in the snow-bound Swiss Alps of Homi J. Bhaba, the father of Indian nuclear science and a family friend.

Two wars in less than three years and two leadership successions over half that period would have been strain enough on a vast and diverse land still in the formative stages of becoming a nation-state. The strain was magnified by the almost complete failure of the rains over two successive years, 1965 and 1966. The impact on agriculture, the mainstay of the national economy and, despite many irrigation projects, still a gamble in the monsoons, was catastrophic. The spectre of famine haunted large parts of the country. Chronic shortage of foreign exchange made commercial imports of grain practically impossible. India's already considerable dependence on concessional imports of wheat from the US under Public Law 480 became critical.

As prices shot up, economic hardship led to mass discontent which was promptly compounded by political turmoil born of the approaching General Election. Groups, such as engineers, doctors and teachers which had previously stayed aloof from agitation, now came out in the streets demanding higher pay and allowances. Student agitation, usually confined to a few trouble-spots, spread to the entire country like a contagious rash. Food riots in West Bengal, a particularly volatile state, necessitated the calling out of the Army.

In the sensitive north-eastern region, bordering China and inhabited by a tribal population, to the ongoing Naga revolt was added the insurgency by the Mizo tribe. The language issue continued to simmer in the South. The moment of decision on the Sikh demand for a Punjabi-speaking province, opposed by some Hindus, had also arrived. Previously, as chairman of a cabinet committee, Indira had been required only to make a recommendation to Shastri. Now the difficult decision was hers.

The outlook on international relations was only a little less dismal than the domestic scene. The high prestige India had enjoyed in the world during the Nehru era was badly eroded after the 1962 war with China and now looked like a thing of the past. Relations with the US,

90

whose help was vital to tide over the food crisis, were strained as much by the use of American arms by Pakistan in its war with India in 1965 as by sharp differences between New Delhi and Washington over the vexed Vietnam war. Harold Wilson's factually wrong and palpably partisan comments on the origin of the 1965 India–Pakistan war had brought Indo-British relations to a new low. In the Non-Aligned Movement, Indonesia and Ghana were busy trying to undermine Indian leadership of the movement. Most alarmingly, the Soviet Union, India's staunch supporter against Pakistan, was gradually moving towards a more even-handed policy in relation to the two neighbours.

In the face of such adverse circumstances, Indira's complete inexperience of government and administration became a much stronger handicap than it might otherwise have been. She was being hampered also by a growing split in the Congress. In the euphoria of her victory over Desai in the contest for the prime ministership it had been overlooked by her and her supporters that he had taken away a third of the Congress Parliamentary Party's votes even though every single Congress leader of note had backed Indira. The alienated one-third became even more vehement in their opposition to her. She was therefore seen to be at the mercy of the Syndicate.

Partly for this reason, she started distancing herself from the Syndicate and relying on a rival group of advisers, consisting of those who had gathered round her during the short-lived Shastri era which was also the period when she was most discontented. The most important member of this coterie, collectively nicknamed the 'Kitchen Cabinet', was Dinesh Singh, a junior minister at the Foreign Office, whose family had known the Nehrus since the days of Indira's grandfather, Motilal. The Kitchen Cabinet's, particularly Dinesh's, influence on her was much resented, and not by the Syndicate alone. The situation was made worse because the members of the Kitchen Cabinet tended to be more clever than wise, and their advice more glib than sound. To complicate matters further, none of those with a seat in the Kitchen Cabinet could resist the temptation of flaunting his newly acquired influence and power. Moreover Dinesh did nothing later, to discourage the impression, as we shall discuss, that his relationship with the Prime Minister was one of both political and personal intimacy.

The more the Kitchen Cabinet showed off, the angrier other sections of the Congress became, including powerful chief ministers who had backed Indira against Desai. It was against this dispiriting background that Indira had to face her first session of the All India Congress Committee (AICC) as Prime Minister, at Jaipur in Rajasthan barely a month after taking over the top job.

Even Congressmen had become critical of the Tashkent declaration that Shastri had signed with President Ayub of Pakistan. This was because, contrary to Shastri's repeated declarations before going to the talks under Soviet auspices, the agreement provided for the return to Pakistan of the strategic Haji Pir pass in Kashmir, captured by Indian troops at a very heavy price in human blood. Even so, Indira managed to get the Tashkent accord endorsed by the AICC.

With the food crisis – the burning issue before the AICC, as before the country – she was at sea, however. Kerala, the hardest-hit state, was traditionally averse to eating anything other than rice, now practically unavailable. Appealing to the people of Kerala temporarily to change their food habits, Indira announced that she herself would neither eat nor serve rice until rice supplies to Kerala were adequate. This may have been a nice symbolic gesture, but it was no substitute for a coherent and effective policy on food procurement and distribution for which the grim situation cried out.

To prevent rapacious grain traders from rushing scarce food supplies to prosperous areas where people had plenty of purchasing power, practically since independence India had operated a deliberate policy of dividing the country into half a dozen food zones, each consisting of a surplus state and a couple of deficit ones. While the grain could move freely within a food zone, inter-zonal movement was strictly prohibited.

Over the years, chief ministers of surplus states, usually drawing their strength from the rich peasantry, had grown hostile to food zones. They wanted grain to move wherever it would fetch the highest price. But they lacked the courage to press their point on Nehru who was apt to fly into a rage at any suggestion that his government should follow policies favouring the rich rather than the poor. However, with Indira, as with Shastri, they were in a much stronger position.

They therefore pressed hard their demand for the immediate abolition of the food zones. Though some of their colleagues, heading the governments in deficit states, demurred, the public seemed to be against the food zones because people were getting tired of controls. The central government, however, could not take such a complacent view of the situation. It knew that the abolition of food zones would necessitate massive compulsory procurement of grain in surplus states and rigorous rationing in deficit ones, neither of which could be enforced because the Congress party lacked the requisite political will while the administration was bereft of the necessary skill.

Shastri had died without being able to persuade the chief ministers to agree on a viable policy. It was now Indira's task to evolve the elusive consensus, but she did not seem to know how.

At the Jaipur AICC she was confronted by rare unity between

the Congress Left and the Congress Right behind the demand for
scrapping the food zones forthwith. Despite appeals from the rostrum,
a demand to this effect was pressed to the vote. It was clear from the
show of hands that the amendment had been carried. But T. Manean,
a party functionary who was taking the count, panicked and announced
that the amendment had been rejected. Hundreds of delegates rose
to protest; pandemonium prevailed. A visibly shaken Indira was
practically pushed to the microphone to cope with the situation as
best she could. In a brief and halting intervention, she promised to
review the 'entire food policy', appealing to the delegates to withdraw
the amendment. Saying this, she hastily made her exit. Kamaraj,
who had been squabbling with her over her government's decision to
invite the multi-national corporation, Bechtel, to set up fertiliser plants
in India, now intervened on her behalf. He announced, amidst great
tumult and confusion, that the amendment had been withdrawn
following the Prime Minister's assurance. Never before had the top
leadership of the Congress cut such a sorry figure at an AICC meeting.
But worse was yet to follow in Parliament which met soon after Indira
returned to Delhi, somewhat shaken by her experience at Jaipur.

In Parliament she was now even more inarticulate and nervous than
as Information and Broadcasting Minister. Later she was to become
a fluent, even fiery, debater. But in the initial months of her prime
ministership she was tongue-tied and apparently unable to think on
her feet. Things might not have been so bad, had the opposition
shown her the kind of indulgence usually extended to a new Prime
Minister. But far from doing so, the motley collection of opposition
parties and groups seemed united in barracking and harassing her.
Ram Manohar Lohia, an able but eccentric socialist leader who was
also a habitual Nehru-hater, was her main tormentor. It was he who
gave her the nickname 'goongi gudiya', the Dumb Doll. The epithet
was to stick to her for some years until she struck her opponents dumb
themselves by the sheer fury of her counter-attack.

The churlishness and downright discourtesy with which she was
treated in Parliament – the Speaker's attempts to come to her aid
were of little avail and protests by Congress MPs inevitably led to
unruly scenes – were to leave a lasting impression on both Indira and
Parliament. Her father had wallowed in Parliament. He used it as
both a sounding board and a forum for educating the country in
democracy and egalitarianism. Indira developed for Parliament the
'kind of disdain it had shown her'. She started absenting herself even
from important debates and, in the years of her supremacy, treated it
with scant respect. During the Emergency she reduced Parliament to
a mere rubber stamp. The foremost democratic institution thus got
distressingly devalued in the world's largest democracy.

Indira's discomfiture during the initial months of her prime ministership was accentuated by her failure to keep her promise, made at the Jaipur AICC, to work out a comprehensive food policy by reviewing the food zones. She just could not get an agreement among the chief ministers of surplus and deficit states although all of them belonged to her party. Even more tragic was her reneging on a promise to an all-party opposition delegation that she would lift the Emergency imposed at the time of the Chinese invasion in 1962 and needlessly kept going long after the danger on the frontier was over. The chief ministers were naturally reluctant to part with the Emergency powers they had acquired. But they alone cannot be blamed for the continuation of the Emergency. Indira was also more unwilling than unable to end the State of Emergency. The author was constrained to write at that time that it would be 'easier for a conclave of cardinals to make a collective declaration of atheism than for the Congress governments, at the centre and in the states, to give up the powers given to them by the Emergency'.

Ironically, faced with a grim food situation which made the need for American aid desperately necessary, Indira was forced to follow the economic policies of Shastri she had denounced only a few months earlier as an 'unacceptable departure' from the course charted out by her father. Her leftist image had contributed to her rise to the top. Now it was becoming a thing of the past. She had abandoned the socialist rhetoric she used to be so fond of as Congress President. 'Pragmatism' was her new watchword.

Her first budget acquired the dubious distinction of 'lowering, for the first time since the start of the planning process in India', the annual plan outlay from that provided for in the preceding year. Even the truncated plan could go through, however, only if adequate foreign aid was available, and this was a big if. At the time of the 1965 war between India and Pakistan, the United States had suspended aid to both countries. Now the World Bank and the International Monetary Fund were insisting on some preconditions for the restoration of aid. These included a higher priority to agriculture, a downgrading of public sector industries and provision of ample scope for both indigenous private enterprise and private foreign investment.

This much was public knowledge. Secretly, the World Bank, the IMF and the US administration were also demanding a substantial devaluation of the Indian rupee. Shastri was prepared to accept this 'advice' but was obstructed by his Finance Minister, Krishnamachari, whom he could get rid of only just before leaving for Tashkent. Indira, whose knowledge of economics was even more limited than that of other subjects, was relying for advice on some members of her Kitchen Cabinet, especially C. Subramaniam and Asoka Mehta, and on L. K.

Jha, whom she had inherited as her chief adviser from Shastri. They all were enthusiastically for devaluation. Further weight was added to their stand by the support of her cousin, B. K. Nehru, then serving as Ambassador to the United States.

Before taking the final plunge, however, Indira decided to visit the United States, the first country to have the 'honour' of welcoming her as India's new Prime Minister.

She made it a point loudly to proclaim that she was going to Washington only on a 'goodwill visit' and not to seek food or financial aid. But the truth was precisely the opposite. In fact, in a private talk with me a day before I left for the US and a week before she did, she candidly stated: 'Don't publish this, but my main mission is to get both food and foreign exchange without appearing to be asking for them.'

Indira also chose to get the issue of Punjabi Suba, an ostensibly Punjabi-speaking but actually Sikh-majority state, out of the way before catching the plane for the United States. She decided to accept the Sikh demand for reorganising Punjab in such a way as to exclude Hindi-speaking areas and leave the Sikhs in a majority in the smaller Punjab. She was hailed for her 'boldness' and 'maturity', and when some Hindus rioted against the Sikhs she came down heavily on them. The task of reorganising Punjab could not be completed, however, because of an interesting snag. After the original Punjab was partitioned between India and Pakistan, Lahore, the undivided province's capital, went to Pakistan. For the Indian Punjab, a beautiful new capital, indeed a dream city called Chandigarh, was planned and built by the famous French architect, Le Corbusier. Both the new Punjabi-speaking state and Haryana, the residuary Hindi-speaking state, claimed Chandigarh uncompromisingly. Indira ruled that Chandigarh would go to neither but, as a city under direct central rule, serve as the joint capital of both Punjab and Haryana. This, too, was welcomed as a 'shrewd move'. In fact, it became an explosive ingredient in the Sikh problem in Punjab which was to erupt in the Eighties and take Indira's life.

On the way to the US, Indira broke her journey in Paris, giving London a miss and asking her sons to cross the Channel and meet her in the French capital. She was signalling not only her displeasure with Wilson's pro-Pakistani stance but also her admiration for de Gaulle. Her message, which was to become clear much later, was that whatever her current difficulties, her ambition for her country was rather like de Gaulle's for his. Throughout her talks with the French leader she spoke in impeccable French and *Le Grand Charles* made no secret of being charmed. Minoo Masani, a former socialist who became an arch Conservative MP and an inveterate critic of Indira's, was quick to remark, somewhat prophetically, that Madame 'would be our *Mon Général*'.

On the face of it, Indira's visit to the US was a tremendous success. In fact, it was a major disaster though it took reality some time to overtake the illusion. The unprecedented media build-up given to her was indication enough of the host country's feeling. It was excelled, however, by President Lyndon Johnson's gushing praise for 'this proud, able, gracious lady'. At a party in her honour at the residence of Ambassador B. K. Nehru, Johnson surprised the guests by announcing loudly that he would see to it that 'no harm comes to this girl'. He caused even greater consternation later that evening when, brushing aside protocol, he decided to stay for the Ambassador's dinner in Indira's honour instead of returning to the White House after the cocktail party. The hostess was in a panic because changing the table plan was not easy. P. N. Haksar, a member of the Prime Minister's entourage, saved her a great deal of bother by withdrawing from the dinner. Then serving as Deputy High Commissioner in London, Haksar was soon to be picked by Indira to head her secretariat, replacing L. K. Jha, who had attracted criticism from Indira's Left-leaning supporters.

Haksar's leftist reputation was well established since the Thirties when he was a student in England. He proved to be the ablest and most upright adviser Indira ever had, though he did become controversial. He was criticised for making the Prime Minister's secretariat much too powerful, thus enabling Indira to 'concentrate almost all the powers of government in her hands'. Ironically, Haksar, like almost everyone very close to her, was also discarded in course of time. During the Emergency he came to grief. Though Indira had recalled him from retirement two years earlier and made him Deputy Chairman of the Planning Commission, his octogenarian uncle was arrested on the flimsy charge of not displaying the price of some items in his shop – simply because Haksar had incurred the anger of Indira's younger son, Sanjay.

During Indira's US visit, however, Haksar's role was relatively minor and largely behind the scenes.

There is little doubt that, partly at least, Johnson was responding, with true Texan warmth, to Indira's charm and candour. But his exuberance had clearly a great deal more to do with the success the American side had had in getting from the visiting Indian Prime Minister most of what it wanted. Indira had promptly agreed to a substantial devaluation of the rupee. She also accepted an American proposal to use the huge rupee funds the US had accumulated in India, because of massive shipments of PL480 wheat, to set up an Indo-American Educational Foundation, modelled on the Ford Foundation. Both Nehru and Shastri had rejected this suggestion on the understandable grounds that it would give America undue and undesirable influence on higher education and research in India. But Indira evidently was in dire need of American goodwill.

This should also explain the quick acceptance by her and her advisers of changes in Indian economic policies in order to shift the emphasis from the public sector to private and from multilateral aid to private foreign investment. What delighted Johnson the most was a sudden toning down of Indian criticism of America's role in the Vietnam war – a subject of great sensitivity to him. Just before Indira was leaving for a one-to-one meeting with Johnson, she was strongly advised by Jha, B. K. Nehru and others to tell the US President that India 'shared America's agony over Vietnam'. Haksar protested, whereupon Indira decided to amend her statement to the effect that 'India understood America's agony over Vietnam'. The semantic change was immaterial. What mattered was that for several months there was hardly any criticism by India of the Vietnam war although earlier it had been routine.

Johnson's quid for Indira's quo was a promise of over three million tons of sorely needed food and of nine hundred million dollars as aid. He also indicated that the US would persuade the World Bank to be more responsive to Indian needs than it had been. On top of it, there was his personal promise 'not to let any harm' come to her. Evidently, it was not just a rhetorical flourish. After she had left in the first week of April, Johnson called in Ambassador B. K. Nehru to tell him, 'We must get her elected [in the General Election due a year hence]. You tell me what to do. Send her food? Attack her? I'll do whatever you say.'

During her visit to the US, as during all her subsequent travels abroad, Indira was extremely well turned out. Her natural beauty was greatly enhanced by her impeccable taste in dress and the dignity of her bearing. On her travels, she used subtle make-up and wore just the right amount of jewellery, though she avoided both at home. The Nehrus tended to go grey from an early age. Indira had therefore started dyeing her hair even while her father was alive. But she always kept a white streak at the crown of her superbly coiffured hair. This, some were to say in later years, was symbolic of the 'steel in her spine'.

With all that, however, at a White House dinner in her honour, Indira courteously declined to join Johnson on the dance floor when he invited her to do so. She explained that though she had enjoyed Western-style dancing during her student days, 'her countrymen wouldn't approve of their Prime Minister dancing in a ballroom'. It is not known whether it occurred to her that some of the decisions she had taken at Johnson's behest would displease her countrymen a great deal more than a whirl round the White House dance floor would have done.

Apparently pleased with what she had achieved, Indira left for London to do a little plain speaking to Harold Wilson about the 1965 India–Pakistan war and his 'unacceptable' attitude towards it. This done, she flew off, as scheduled, to Moscow where she was well known, having been there frequently both with her father and on her own. In October 1964, she had been the first Indian minister to be in the Soviet capital after the fall of Nikita Khrushchev, when she was assured by her hosts that there would be no change in Russia's policy of friendship with India despite the change of leadership in the Kremlin. Now, as Prime Minister, she was received by her Soviet opposite number, Alexei Kosygin, no stranger to her.

Evidently, the impact of her talks in Washington was still strong in her mind because, after the usual pleasantries, she asked Kosygin: 'How can you expect the Americans to pull out of Vietnam until they can find a way to save face?'

'And how many Asian lives will be lost while the Americans are thinking of a way to save face?' retorted the Russian premier.

Back home the reaction to what Indira had agreed to during her talks in Washington was even sharper than Kosygin's retort. Criticism of her within her own party was as widespread as without. She was charged with a 'sell-out' over Vietnam as well as over economic policy. The Indo-American Educational Foundation was denounced by all political parties and every single eminent educationist. Irked by the virtual tirade against her, and especially by Krishna Menon's virulent attack on her policies, she dismissed the charge of a sell-out as 'absurd' and accused Menon of 'rank misrepresentation and distortion of facts'. She told her critics that no country could do without foreign aid, the acceptance of which did 'not mean foreign domination'. 'Even Lenin,' she thundered, 'had taken American aid after the Russian revolution'.

Her new-found eloquence did not, however, check the rising tide of criticism. Indeed, people, including important members of the Congress party, started accusing her of 'deviating' from her father's policies. Vehemently denying this, she declared:

If it is necessary to deviate from past policies, I would not hesitate to do so. I must pursue policies which are in the best interests of the country as a whole. If you do not like these policies, you have every right to remove me and have your own leader ... The Congress is big, but India is bigger.

Here was the first hint of her strategy to appeal to the country over the head of her party, which she was effectively to adopt later, but no one caught the hint partly because her fortunes were so low that no one expected any defiance from her.

On June 5th, 1966, Indira announced a thirty-five per cent devaluation of the rupee and immediately got into much deeper trouble than she had been until then. Her own knowledge of economics was rudimentary. At a press conference she had once allowed herself to remark that the greatest economic problems facing the country then were 'inflation and rising prices'. Journalists had laughed indulgently. On devaluation, she was being guided, apart from American pressure, by her chosen advisers. They were so busy devising for her a strategy of 'adventurous pragmatism' that they completely ignored the political consequences of devaluing the currency clearly at the behest of the US, the World Bank and the IMF.

Since the decision had to be taken in great secrecy, Indira got the first warning about the dangers of devaluation well after the eleventh hour. This happened when she decided belatedly to consult Kamaraj. He hit the ceiling. She was sufficiently alarmed to consider a 'postponement of the decision on devaluation'. But the second thoughts were too late. The IMF had already been notified. Indira took the plunge and announced the devaluation. All hell broke loose. Public opinion was aroused as never before except against the Chinese invasion four years earlier. The entire opposition, from the extreme Left to the extreme Right, condemned devaluation unequivocally.

An incensed Kamaraj started blaming himself for having put Indira in power in the first place, muttering: 'A big man's daughter, a small man's mistake.' At his instance, the Congress Working Committee made history of sorts by passing a resolution denouncing the government for its decision on devaluation. If he did not follow this up with a move to dislodge Indira from the prime ministership, it was because Kamaraj knew that such a course just before the General Election would be disastrous for the party as a whole.

It was well known, however, that Indira's continuance as Prime Minister after the election could no longer be taken for granted as far as the Syndicate was concerned. Then there was Desai waiting to reclaim what he firmly believed was his due.

Publicly, Indira defended devaluation as best she could. But privately she admitted that she had been taken for a ride. The unpopularity of the decision apart, the discipline required to derive the expected advantage from devaluation was found to be lacking in both the government and private trade. The Americans also let her down. The aid they had promised did not materialise. Indira had taken pride in accepting only aid without strings. Now, people jeered, she was stuck with 'strings without aid'.

All this was to have a powerful and lasting effect on Indira and her style of leadership. Paranoia and a deep sense of insecurity were ingrained in her character since early childhood. Now these became principal traits of her complex personality. She came to believe that she could 'trust no one' because everyone, no matter how close or beholden to her, was 'capable of betraying her'. Asoka Mehta and C. Subramaniam, principal advocates of devaluation, were the first to feel the cold blast of her distrust and disdain. In due course, both were eased out. Others, too numerous to be kept count of, were to meet the same fate in later years.

At this time Indira also came to the conclusion that she had to destroy the Syndicate before it destroyed her. But she was realistic enough to realise that she could not do so just then. She had to bide her time. The other decision that she took, more or less simultaneously, required to be put through at once.

Led up the garden path by the Kitchen Cabinet, constantly lambasted and menaced by the Syndicate and let down by the US and other aid-givers, Indira concluded that her political survival depended on a reversion to Left-leaning policies and a revival of her mildly radical image so badly tarnished in recent months.

It was on Vietnam that she first made the policy switch. After three months of total silence on the subject and three weeks of storm over devaluation, on July 1st, 1966, her government issued a statement 'deploring' American bombings of Hanoi and Haiphong. The timing of the statement was dictated partly by her visits some days later to Egypt, Yugoslavia and the Soviet Union. Though she had been furious with Krishna Menon because of his 'wild attacks' on her foreign policy, she consulted him while drafting the statement on Vietnam. By the time she left for Cairo on the first leg of her journey, the statement had been expanded and amplified into an Indian 'initiative' to bring peace to war-torn Vietnam.

Originally the Indian proposals on Vietnam were vague enough not to cause offence to Washington. But as Indira's three-nation journey progressed, her statements became sharper until, in Moscow, she signed a joint statement with Kosygin which not only called for an immediate and unconditional halt to the bombing of Hanoi and Haiphong but also 'condemned' the 'imperialist aggression' in Vietnam.

The reaction in Washington was instant and predictably indignant. Even so, nobody could have foreseen the extent of Johnson's fury. He required each shipment of food to India to carry his personal authorisation which was always late in coming. India lived from ship to mouth and, with every morsel of American food, swallowed a measure of humiliation. Sensitive Americans were appalled. But the irascible Texan in the White House was impervious to their appeals for compassion. When the US Ambassador in Delhi, Chester Bowles, pointed out that Indira wasn't saying anything that was not being said by the UN Secretary-General, U Thant, and the Pope, he was curtly told that the Pope and U Thant 'do not want our wheat'.

As was only to be expected, Johnson's crude attempt to use food as a political weapon proved self-defeating. Indira became even more outspoken in her criticism of the US over Vietnam and sent Ho Chi Minh a very warm message of congratulations on his seventy-seventh birthday. Her countrymen, who had earlier denounced her for bowing to American pressure, now applauded her assertion of national independence. Even so, she refused to accept the advice of some who urged her to say no to American food given under humiliating circumstances. 'If food supplies stop,' she told me, 'these ladies and gentlemen who are talking tall will not starve, but millions of poor people will.'

Having undone some of the rightward 'tilt' in economic policy, Indira also announced the cancellation of her earlier agreement with President Johnson on the setting up of a joint Indo-American Educational Foundation. Both Left-leaning Congressmen and the wider Left outside warmed to Indira again.

Not everyone was impressed, however. Some saw her policy switch to be opportunist. One opposition MP lampooned her for 'behaving like a capitalist in Washington and a socialist in Moscow'. She only smiled. It was to take Indians some years to discover that everything Indira did was dictated by a keen instinct for self-preservation and that every position she took, whether radical or rightist, was always flexible.

In early November 1966, when Indira had been in power for barely ten months, Hindu chauvinists, hoping to exploit the emotive cow-slaughter issue in the coming elections, brought their struggle to Parliament's doorstep. A huge procession, led by trident-wielding naked *sadhus* (ascetics), quickly degenerated into a riot in which a policeman was killed, government property and private cars burnt and shops looted. Six people lost their lives in police firing on the rampaging mob.

The demand of the protesters was not at all new. Indira's father, way back in 1956, had rejected it firmly. He was not insensitive to the religious feelings of the cow's protectors. But, backed by secular opinion, he was of the opinion that in a multi-religious country where beef was the only inexpensive source of protein for the poor, a total ban on the killing of cows would be wrong. When pressed by a senior member of his party, Govind Das, to impose a blanket ban on cow-slaughter, Nehru reacted angrily and declared that he would rather resign than give in to 'this futile, silly and ridiculous demand'. Indira was equally firm in refusing to be 'cowed down by the cow-savers'.

Indeed, she used the mayhem created by cow-protectors to ease out sickly, ineffectual and *sadhu*-loving Home Minister, G. L. Nanda. His main claim to fame was that he had been caretaker Prime Minister after the deaths of both Nehru and Shastri. On the second occasion, he had even had the temerity to suggest that since Desai was determined to contest Indira, unanimity in the party could be restored by adopting him as the 'compromise' candidate. No one had taken him seriously, but Indira was furious. She had wanted to divest him of the home portfolio while forming her first cabinet but was advised by Kamaraj to desist. Now she demanded Nanda's resignation. He went flailing his skinny arms and protesting that he was being made a 'scapegoat'. Even at the moment of her success in getting rid of Nanda, Indira was rudely reminded of the limits of her power. The Syndicate simply vetoed her plan also to drop from the cabinet Finance Minister Sachin Chaudhuri and Foreign Trade Minister Manubhai Shah. Worse was yet to come.

In December, the Congress Parliamentary Board started choosing the party's candidates for the General Election due in early March. Indira discovered to her dismay that the Syndicate was calling the shots, and she herself had little say in a matter of supreme importance to her. How could she be sure of her continuance as Prime Minister after the poll if she could not get enough of her supporters accommodated in the Congress list? Over her protests, the Syndicate denied the party ticket even to Krishna Menon. Her plaintive plea that a decision in this case be postponed was also disregarded. Indira pocketed the rebuff. Menon did not. He resigned from the Congress and stood in his constituency, North Bombay, as an Independent. He lost but at least made his point.

Many other important and honest Congressmen not to the liking of party bosses were treated like Menon. Like Menon, they left the party to seek new pastures and, in many cases, were welcomed by parties opposed to the Congress which were enthused by the thought that the ruling party was embarked on a self-destructive course. Opposition parties were still too numerous and too seriously divided by political ideology and personal ambitions of their leaders to be considered a serious threat. But egged on by Ram Manohar Lohia, the peppery socialist leader who had nicknamed Indira the 'dumb doll', all opposition parties, from the extreme Left to the extreme

Right, agreed to subordinate all their differences, no matter how serious, to the paramount objective of breaking the Congress Party's monopoly on power since independence.

Firing the first shot in the election battle, Lohia appealed to the country to 'throw the Congress out' so that 'this pretty woman' did not have to 'suffer pain and trouble beyond her endurance'. But, unlike his earlier jibes, this one had little effect on Indira. As she told interviewers around that time, she had developed a 'degree of detachment' that took the edge off the strains and pressures of high office in trying circumstances.

On Christmas Day 1966, with the General Election less than three months away, she gave the public the first glimpse of her strategy to turn the tables on those who were apparently confident of removing her from office after the poll. She told the press: 'Here is a question of whom the party wants and whom the people want. My position among the people is uncontested.'

It was to this strategy of appealing to the people over the heads of the party bosses, of pitting her mass appeal against their skill in manipulating the party machine, that her entire election campaign was geared. She was no stranger to electioneering, having canvassed for Congress candidates in all the three previous General Elections. But helping her father in those days was one thing and going to the polls as Prime Minister quite another. She was conscious of some of her deficiencies, now more noticeable than before. Her voice was squeaky and she was no great orator. She lacked her father's breadth of vision and wide range of ideas. She decided to overcome these handicaps by giving philosophical themes a wide berth, concentrating on practical issues and people's daily problems and trying to speak with as much poise as she possibly could.

Above all, however, it was her objective to project her personality to as many of her countrymen as possible and to make them feel that no other leader cared for them half as much as she did. She travelled from one end of the country to the other like a hurricane.

More often than not her defence of her government's failings was simplistic, even inane. But when provoked or bullied, she fought back with impressive vigour. At Jaipur, the capital of a former princely state a hundred miles from Delhi, where the opposition candidate was the Gayatri Devi, Jaipur's Rajmata or dowager queen, an attempt was made to disturb her meeting. She was roused into launching a blistering attack on the entire princely system, asking her audience to 'go and ask the Maharajas how many wells they had dug for the poor in their states when they ruled them, how many roads had they built and what had they done to fight the slavery of the British?'

At Bhubaneswar in Orissa she refused to interrupt her spirited

election speech even after she had been hit by a stone. Her nose was
badly hurt, but she went on speaking while using a handkerchief to
staunch the bleeding. The next day her fractured nose had to be
operated on in Delhi. She had always been conscious of her nose
being too large. She therefore told the doctors to treat the accident
as an opportunity for much-needed plastic surgery on her nose. They
dodged the request. Over seventeen years later, on the day of her
funeral, mourners noticed that, in death as in life, the nose was the
most prominent feature of her face.

Before going to Bhubaneswar, Indira had campaigned in her own
constituency, Rae Bareli in UP, once represented by her late husband,
Feroze. Here, in a virtuoso performance, she neatly sidestepped all
the problems of hunger and poverty and concentrated on delivering
the message that she was above political parties, indeed above politics,
and interested only in serving the Indian people, all of whom she
considered to be 'members of my family'.

'Your burdens,' she told the simple villagers, 'are relatively light
because your families are limited and viable.'

> But [she added] my burden is manifold because *crores* [a *crore* equals
> ten million] of my family members are poverty stricken and I have
> to look after them. Since they belong to different castes and creeds,
> they sometimes fight among themselves, and I have to intervene,
> especially to look after the weaker members of my family, so that
> the stronger ones do not take advantage of them.

At the end of her speech she was lustily cheered and hailed, for the
first time, as 'Mother Indira' even though she was then only fifty.
However, another legend that was to surround her until the end of
her days was born.

The affectionate outpouring of the admiring crowds was not reflected in the election results when they came in. They came, in fact,
as something of a shock to Indira. The Congress vote was down to
forty-one per cent from forty-five per cent polled in 1962 when the
party had last gone to the hustings under her father's leadership. But
this relatively small shrinkage of four points had led to a disastrous
loss of twenty-one per cent in seats, thanks to the first-past-the-post
system borrowed from Britain by independent India which until then
had worked to the Congress party's advantage. In a house of 520
seats, the Congress share plummeted to 283. The Congress majority
was thus dangerously narrow, especially considering the strife between
Indira on the one hand and Desai and the Syndicate on the other.
'After the broken nose, a slap in the face,' was the verdict of *The
Times*, London.

It was in the states that the true extent of the setback to the Congress became evident. The party lost power in eight major North Indian states, driving the author to record that one could travel all across the Indo-Gangetic plains 'from Calcutta to Amritsar without having to traverse an inch of Congress-run territory'. The impression that the mighty Congress was tottering was magnified, perhaps unduly, by a succession of dramatic defeats of Congress leaders, especially those of Syndicate stalwarts such as S. K. Patil and Atulya Ghosh. In a class by itself was the 'fantastic fall' of Kamaraj. Besides being a king-maker in New Delhi, he was virtually the uncrowned king of his state, Tamil Nadu. It was now lost to DMK, a militantly regional party which had once espoused the cause of Tamil Nadu's secession from India. To complete his humiliation, Kamaraj had also lost his own parliamentary seat.

Paradoxically, the sensational electoral setback to the Congress strengthened, rather than weakened, Indira's position though she could not have her way entirely. A party badly mauled at the polls could hardly afford a renewed and recriminatory struggle for leadership. The Syndicate itself, which could have made a bid to dislodge Indira, lay shattered. The argument for Indira's re-election as Prime Minister was strengthened also by the feeling that she would be more acceptable than any other Congress leader to the non-Congress state governments that were being formed in areas where the Congress had lost. But none of this impressed Morarji Desai. Convinced that he was 'better suited and better qualified to lead the Congress and the country', he was determined to stake his claim yet again.

Not only had he won handsomely, like Indira, but also he was free from any blame for the Congress government's failures during the previous three years because he had stayed totally aloof from it. The Syndicate had given up its earlier hostility to him but its own influence had now dwindled. Indira and her camp reacted to Desai's daily declarations sharply. She was heard saying that where the office of Prime Minister was concerned, she would not 'tolerate any fun and games'. A bitter battle for leadership therefore seemed unavoidable.

It was firmly avoided, however, by a group of Congress leaders who intervened to say that there would be no 'damaging contest' for leadership at a time when the party's 'crying need' was for the 'closing of ranks'. Interestingly, supporters of both Desai and Indira were represented in the mediatory group almost equally. Kamaraj, though cut down to size by the debacle at the polls, managed to seize the leadership of the mediatory efforts and practically to impose a compromise on the two contestants.

Under it, Desai became Deputy Prime Minister and Finance

Minister in Indira's cabinet and she was elected Prime Minister unanimously. But so petty and wounding was the bargaining over Desai's role as DPM and so great the distrust between the two sides that the unity between them was, right from the start, sullen, negative and spurious. Indira and her supporters saw Desai as the 'Syndicate's Trojan Horse', while he and his friends resented Indira's distrust of him.

Having had to accept Desai as Deputy Prime Minister, Indira displayed her strength and independence in the composition of the cabinet that took office on March 14th, 1967. She excluded from it Sanjiva Reddy, the only member of the Syndicate who had managed to be re-elected, though she mollified him by making him Speaker of the Lok Sabha, the lower house of Parliament, the counterpart of the British House of Commons. In 1966, she had had to choose her ministerial team in consultation with Kamaraj. Now she showed the list to him at the last minute only as a matter of courtesy. Chavan, a close ally at that time, stayed in Home Affairs, allotted to him when Nanda was eased out. Jagjivan Ram, a leader of Harijans, former untouchables, and antagonistic to Desai, was shifted from Labour to the vital portfolio of Food and Agriculture. Dinesh Singh was promoted to cabinet rank and made Commerce Minister. Only the discerning noticed that while the Syndicate's favourites were dropped or downgraded, some of the new ministers were nominees of those chief ministers who had been steadfast in their support of Indira.

# 7   Short-cut to Supremacy

So tenuous and phoney was the compromise under which Desai became Deputy Prime Minister in Indira's cabinet that the struggle between them, far from being mitigated, was aggravated.

On the day the compromise took effect Desai was asked at a press conference whether he still regarded himself 'more competent' than Indira Gandhi.

'How can the Deputy Prime Minister be more competent than the Prime Minister?' he countered.

'But yesterday you said you were,' persisted the questioner.

'Yesterday,' said Desai airily, 'was yesterday. Today is different.'

The assembled journalists laughed.

But the way Desai behaved in the inner councils of the government was no laughing matter for Indira. At a meeting of the Planning Commission in May 1967, at which the problem was how to find enough resources belatedly to launch the fourth five-year plan, held in abeyance since the 1965 war, Indira had barely started speaking when Desai interrupted her, addressing her as 'Indiraben', or Sister Indira, as every woman is addressed by every man in his home state, Gujarat.

'Indiraben,' said Desai, 'you don't understand this matter. Let me deal with it.' She was 'livid with anger but let him have his say'. Desai and the Syndicate were by now allies. But while the Syndicate was plotting to overthrow Indira, Morarji was following a dual policy. He was telling his supporters to do what they liked or thought feasible to undermine Indira's position but 'never to discuss their plans with him'. As a 'man of principle', in his own way, he did not want to invite a charge of 'disloyalty'.

Indira, fully aware of what was going on, knew that she would have to take on the Syndicate and Desai. But she also realised that a head-on clash with them would not suit her. She had to consolidate her position first and this could be done by slowly winning her points on issue after issue.

The first tussle between Indira and her adversaries within her party took place over the choice of the next President, the constitutional Head of State.

Though modelled on the British monarchy, the office of President in India can exercise, especially at times of political uncertainty and instability, considerable discretion. In the circumstances of 1967, the choice naturally was invested with much delicacy.

Indira wanted the party to opt for Dr Zakir Husain, a highly respected educationist and freedom fighter who was unlikely to be arbitrary or even controversial. He was also a Muslim which meant that his elevation to the highest office in the land would be welcome to the largest religious minority in the country as well as to others anxious to strengthen Indian secularism. Husain was then serving as Vice-President just as the outgoing President, Dr Radhakrishnan, had done before moving into the presidential palace. But the Syndicate, with Desai's tacit backing, demurred. It wanted Radhakrishnan to be given a second term. Its unstated but clearly implied argument was that, given the dissensions in the party, in the secret ballot for the presidential poll Congress MPs and members of state legislatures might not vote for the party nominee.

Encouraged by the same thought, the opposition parties persuaded the Chief Justice of the Supreme Court, K. Subba Rao, to be their candidate. He agreed and relinquished his office a few months before he was due to retire. The significance of his candidature was not lost on the country. Only a few days earlier, Subba Rao had presided over a bench that had, by a narrow majority of four to three, deprived Parliament of its right, enjoyed by it during the preceding seventeen years, to amend the fundamental rights enshrined in the constitution. This verdict was unacceptable to Indira who felt that the sovereign will of the people, as expressed through their elected representatives, should be supreme and therefore Parliament's right to amend all parts of the constitution, including the chapter on fundamental rights, should remain untrammelled.

She could not do anything about Subba Rao's candidature. But on the choice of the Congress nominee she had her way. She shamed her opponents into silence by asking: 'When people want to know why was Zakir Sahib bypassed, what answer will you give?'

Husain was elected with a comfortable majority. This was seen as a triumph of both Indian secularism and Indira. Some of her aides and acolytes used the occasion, however, to sling mud on the Syndicate and Desai, needlessly aggravating already inflamed feelings. This was a prelude to the smear campaigns both sides were to run against each other as their struggle for power hotted up in subsequent months.

Soon after her disastrous decision on the devaluation of the Indian rupee, as we have noted, Indira had lurched leftward, most notably on the Vietnam issue. Now, faced with the prospect of having to fight both the Syndicate and Desai, she strengthened her resolve to appeal to her 'natural constituency', the Left, both within the Congress and without. She did so by having a second look at the economic policies she had followed during the preceding fifteen months. This was a shrewd and timely move, for the election setback had put economic policy on top of the agenda in the agonising debate within the party. The issue came to a head at an AICC meeting in Delhi in May.

Shaken by the poll reverses, the party ranks, especially the radical ones, promptly nicknamed 'Young Turks', compelled the leadership to recognise that not only young people, exercising their franchise for the first time, had voted against the Congress but also there had been a disturbing erosion of the party's traditional support base among Harijans or former untouchables, religious minorities and the poor in both urban and rural areas. The only way the party could recover the lost ground, the angry ranks insisted, was to rededicate itself to its old objectives and the socialistic programmes that had been downgraded during the 'pragmatic era'.

This did not cause much bickering but the radicals' demand for the replacement of the 'old, discredited' leaders did. Desai protested against the attempt to 'malign' the elder leadership. Patil backed him. Indira mildly disapproved of attacks on older leaders but endorsed the demand for a shift to economic leftism, in preference to the policies she herself had been pursuing.

Despite the noise and din, however, neither side, and least of all Indira, wanted to force the issue. A compromise, ten-point programme was drafted on which both the radicals and the conservatives could agree. It was basically a reaffirmation of such traditional Congress policies as land to the tiller, protection of the rights of former untouchables and tribal people, a national minimum wage for both industrial and farm labour, housing sites for rural homeless and so on, which had been honoured more in the breach than the observance.

The key issue before the AICC was the future of the banking industry. Since as far back as 1950 some voices had been raised in favour of nationalising major banks but even Nehru had not encouraged the demand. In the changed atmosphere in 1967, the Congress leadership settled for 'social control' of banking, which meant appointment of watchdog committees to monitor credit policies and other operations of privately owned banks. The 'Young Turks' suffered a setback when their attempt to change social control of banks into outright nationalisation failed. Desai, as Finance Minister, was totally opposed to it and, for once, he was supported by Indira. However, just when it seemed that the compromise resolution would sail through, the radicals sprang a surprise and won what was later to become a 'landmark victory' and have far-reaching consequences.

One of the ten points in the compromise resolution concerned the former rulers of princely states of which there were as many as six hundred in British India. A few of these states were as large as France, while some were pathetic principalities whose 'princes' were

109

perpetually in debt. The revenue of the smallest state did not exceed the income of a goat-herd.

All the princes had been, in theory, sovereign in their territories which meant that they had been free to plunder and oppress their subjects as much as they liked provided that neither this nor any other activity of theirs jeopardised British interests in any way. Whenever this limit was crossed, the ruler was instantly deposed by the British. In every major state and in a group of smaller ones, a British resident kept a close watch on the activities of the luxury-loving rulers, the decadence of many of whom was beyond belief. This arrangement, called subsidiary alliance, came to an end with independence and partition.

Most rulers of the states falling within India acceded to the Indian Union without much fuss; a few who created problems were later forced to fall in line. In return for their cooperation, the rulers of major states, numbering about 250, were given generous privy purses (these were to be in perpetuity though the amount could be, and was, reduced at the time of succession from one generation to the next) and allowed to keep their titles as well as such other privileges as flying their personal flags and standards, having personal number plates for their cars, gun-salutes on ceremonial occasions and so on.

Though considered just and fair in the aftermath of independence and partition when it was entered into, this arrangement attracted criticism with the passage of years. But the Congress leadership was able to convince the country that promises made by the government must be kept. With the rise of radicalism, however, the mood in the Congress party was bound to change. The feelings of Congressmen were ruffled moreover because a fairly large number of former princes had contested the 1967 General Election on the ticket of a newly-formed rightist party called the Swatantra, and had won.

Against this background, the Congress leadership included in the ten-point programme the demand that the privileges enjoyed by the former princely order be abolished. But the privy purses were left strictly alone.

This apparently gave the 'Young Turks' the idea of avenging their defeat over bank nationalisation. Late in the night when attendance at the AICC was thin and senior leaders, including Indira and Desai, had left, the radicals moved an amendment insisting that both the privy purses and the privileges of princes be abolished. The amendment was carried by precisely seventeen votes to four. But it became a decision of the AICC and therefore of the post-election Congress programme.

The disunity and dissensions within the top leadership of the party were clearly reflected in the varied reactions to the extraordinary situation. To nobody's surprise, Kamaraj remained silent though it was generally known that he favoured the amendment, as he endorsed all radical demands. This, incidentally, was to cause Indira some difficulty in the subsequent power struggle because she could not denounce him as a 'right-wing reactionary', an epithet she routinely used against the rest of the Syndicate. Atulya Ghosh made no secret of his happiness because he had always been opposed to the privy purses. Chavan (who, as Home Minister, would have to deal with the problem) also indicated he had no objection to the amendment. But S. K. Patil was furious; he denounced the move as 'stark madness'. Desai also repudiated it as a 'breach of faith' with the princes. Indira, enigmatic as always, expressed concern only at the 'manner in which the amendment was passed'.

After this, as was only to be expected, divisions within the party became sharper. Desai was constantly under attack by Indira's supporters in Parliament as well as outside. He retaliated by winning a majority on the executive of the Congress Parliamentary Party. His friends and collaborators, led by a lively and articulate woman, Tarakeswari Sinha, skilfully used this forum to keep the Prime Minister at bay.

No wonder Indira's government was virtually paralysed in the face of the radicals' demand that the ten-point programme be implemented forthwith. Tempers rose and led to a clash in October 1967 when the AICC met at Jabalpur in Central India. The 'Young Turks' demanded the immediate nationalisation of banks. Desai flatly refused. To the surprise of many delegates, the leadership closed ranks. Indira took the floor to support Desai. She announced that nationalisation would be considered only after social control had been given a 'fair trial for at least two years'.

But the unity of the leadership was too good to last. There was no let-up in intra-party bickering. A major conflict arose over the choice of the new Congress President to replace Kamaraj who had held the post for more than four years. The Jabalpur AICC had laid down that the new party chief be chosen by Indira and Kamaraj jointly. This was easier said than done because the two, though often agreeing on economic policy, were implacably hostile to each other. After a great deal of haggling, their choice fell on S. Nijalingappa, then chief minister of Karnataka. He was an original member of the Syndicate but there was no personal animus between him and Indira. Even the agreed choice of Nijalingappa became a source of discord between Kamaraj and Indira because news management had by now become a major pastime of her Kitchen Cabinet. Despite Nijalingappa's clear request that nothing should be said to the press about his willingness to accept the party President's post until he had seen Kamaraj the next day, the Prime Minister's men leaked a distorted version of the developments, making out as if Nijalingappa had done a deal with

Indira. This technique of making tendentious leaks to the press at night was to flower to the fullest some eighteen months later at the time of the Congress split that was to leave Indira supreme and the Syndicate as well as Desai on the scrap heap.

Presumably to establish his neutrality between Indira and Kamaraj, Nijalingappa gave equal representation in his Working Committee to the two sides. The relationship between them varied from bitter conflict to armed truce. Mutual recrimination was endless. No one heeded the new Congress President's appeal for discipline. The Desai camp was incensed by the charges of corruption against Morarji's son, Kanti Desai, which also impugned the Deputy Prime Minister's own integrity, levelled on the floor of Parliament by the most prominent 'Young Turk', Chandra Shekhar. The Congress Parliamentary Party 'authorised' Indira to censure him. She conspicuously refrained from doing so. Desai and his friends were furious. Incidentally, six years later Indira was to imprison Chandra Shekhar and later still he was to head the Janata party that was first to defeat her at the polls and then to put her in jail.

By early 1968, Kamaraj and Desai had come to the conclusion that Indira had to be removed from office. But they were unable to act. For one thing, Nijalingappa, as Congress President, was refusing to go along with them. He was saying, as he confided to his diary, that the Prime Minister's enforced resignation would 'break the party and the whole country would be in chaos'. For another, many Congressmen, even though bitterly opposed to Indira, felt that no move should be made against her until the Congress as a whole had overcome wider external challenges in states where non-Congress parties had come to power a year earlier. The Congress, they argued, must wrest power from the all-inclusive combinations of opposition parties from the extreme Right to the extreme Left.

To nobody's surprise, these comprehensive and cacophonic coalitions had proved short-lived. The various parties comprising them were constantly at odds with one another. The situation was worsened by implacable personal antagonisms among important non-Congress leaders, caste conflicts and factional disputes. Consequently, in state after state, ministries would collapse and be replaced by other combinations, equally opportunistic and transitory. Ministerial office and even financial inducements were being offered to legislators to cross the floor. Legislators were, in fact, changing their loyalties faster than their underwear. In Haryana, legislators began to be called *Aya Rams* and *Gaya Rams* or 'Messrs Come' and 'Messrs Go'. The whole political process was being brought into disrepute.

Only the DMK government in Tamil Nadu was stable and coherent.

West Bengal's was a case apart. Here the core of the United Left Front Ministry was formed by the Communist Party Marxist (CPM), the more militant of the two Communist parties which came into being in 1965 when the Communist Party of India (CPI) split. Unlike the CPI which remained staunchly pro-Soviet, the CPM at first leaned towards China in the Sino-Soviet cleavage and later adopted a neutral attitude. In the two Communist strongholds in India, West Bengal and Kerala, the CPM was much the stronger. Consequently, in the Left Front government in West Bengal, the CPI and other largely local Left parties had to play a second fiddle to the CPM 'Big Brother'.

On the other hand, the CPM, considered dangerously radical for many years, needed a veneer of respectability to be acceptable to the Bengali *bhadralok* (middle-class gentlefolk). This was provided for it by Ajoy Mukherjee, the West Bengal Congress leader hounded out by the Syndicate, who had formed a party of his own called the Bangla Congress which joined hands with the Left Front. Although the Bangla Congress won only a fraction of the seats won by the CPM, Mukherjee was elected chief minister.

However, Mukherjee's power was notional rather than real. The CPM and other constituents of the Left Front acted as they pleased. He was in no position to restrain them. The leftist parties had problems of their own, both with one another, especially with the CPM, and internally. Smaller parties did not want to be gobbled up by the CPM, so each took an extreme position to safeguard itself and thus a competition in radicalism followed. The Marxist leaders faced a dilemma. They wanted to consolidate their power and for this purpose were willing to respect the sensitivities of the middle class that required them to behave responsibly. But their impatient ranks demanded that they make good their revolutionary promises. Compelled to do something dramatic, they settled for coercing industrial owners and managers into making heavy concessions to labour through a novel method called *gherao*. Thousands of angry and screaming workers would encircle the luckless industrialist manager and prevent him from moving about, eating or even making use of the bathroom for hours on end until he succumbed. The police were expressly forbidden to intervene except under the orders of the Labour Minister. Several such nasty *gheraoes* took place. Industrialists and managers in Calcutta panicked. The rest of the country was outraged. An outcry for the immediate dismissal of the CPM-led ministry followed.

There was widespread and acute unrest in the countryside also, and not in West Bengal alone. Land-grab movements began in several states. Nor was it a coincidence that India's first Maoist party, the Communist Party Marxist–Leninist (CPML), was formed immediately after the 1967 General Election. The Maoists were called the

113

Naxalites, after Naxabari, the village in West Bengal where they had held their first convention.

Ironically, the agrarian unrest was stoked at least partly by the success of the Green Revolution, unquestionably one of Indira's major achievements. Determined never again to expose her country to the kind of humiliation Lyndon Johnson had heaped on it during the years of terrible food shortage, she had embarked on the agricultural strategy geared to achieving maximum results in minimum time. This meant concentration on areas with assured irrigation and on large farms that could afford imported hybrid seeds and other costly inputs. The results in terms of a spurt in production were impressive. But both regional and class disparities were widened. In the first place, the Green Revolution succeeded only in the fertile wheat belt, leaving a large number of states untouched. Secondly, the rich farmers became richer, some incredibly so, and the poor farmers were further impoverished to the point of having to sell their small farms to those already reaping the benefits of the new agricultural strategy. An official study found it necessary to warn that the 'Green Revolution might turn red'.

The cumulative strain of having to cope with disturbed conditions in large parts of the country and uninterrupted attempts within her party to dislodge her from power began to tell on Indira. For the first time since becoming Prime Minister, she complained that she was having disturbed sleep and sometimes found it difficult to sleep at all. Ironically, it was Desai who warned her against taking sleeping tablets and advised her to overcome insomnia through 'sheer will power'. Little did he realise how seriously she would take his advice to fight both sleeplessness and him.

Before taking on Desai and the Syndicate, however, she had to do something about the Marxist-led ministry in West Bengal whose excesses were eroding the confidence of some people in her own government's capacity to curb lawlessness. In a move which was to become a precedent for similar high-handedness in future, she allowed the Governor of West Bengal to dismiss the Left Front ministry and install in its place a ministry of a small group which had chosen to leave the Front and join hands with the Congress. The Marxists took to the streets to protest against the central government's 'constitutional coup' but were quickly subdued. In the legislature, however, they made it impossible for the new ministry to function. President's rule was imposed in West Bengal. It was also decided that fresh elections would be held there in February 1969. Indira took the opportunity to impose President's rule in several other states, including UP, Bihar and Punjab, where ministries formed by opportunistic alliances had been falling in quick succession.

Fresh elections were duly held in all these states in February 1969. They did not solve the problem of instability anywhere except in West Bengal where, to the Congress party's dismay, the Marxist-led coalition was returned with an even bigger majority than before. The Congress was reduced to a rump. The Marxists, on the other hand, were in a position to form a ministry entirely on their own. But they preferred to share power with their allies and even retained Ajoy Mukherjee as figurehead chief minister.

Within the Congress party, the continuing in-fighting reached a high point soon after the Left Front was back in power in West Bengal. By April 1969, even Nijalingappa, 'irked by Indira's failure or refusal to consult him even on matters which concerned him as the party chief', had come round to the view that 'she did not deserve to continue in office and had to be removed'. His change of heart coincided with the return to Parliament of Kamaraj and S. K. Patil, strengthening the Syndicate's hands.

Nijalingappa wasted no time in striking at Indira. The annual session of the Congress – a much larger gathering of delegates than the meeting of the AICC – was held at Faridabad, an industrial township on the outskirts of Delhi but falling within the Haryana state then ruled by a wily, dynamic and authoritarian chief minister named Bansi Lal, who was to earn great notoriety in later years as one of Indira's hatchet men.

In his presidential address, Nijalingappa made a blistering attack on Indira's economic policies, especially on the public sector for its 'inefficiency and failure to make profits'. Delegates were stunned. D. P. Mishra and Uma Shankar Dikshit walked out 'in disgust'. The 'Young Turks' immediately tabled two motions to censure Nijalingappa; he ruled them out of order on the grounds that the Congress President's address could not be debated. Indira, in high dudgeon, was bound by no procedural niceties. In a spirited rejoinder, lustily cheered, she declared that the 'primary motive' of the public sector was not profit but promotion and the preservation of 'national self-reliance'. Her economic policies, she added amidst renewed applause, would always be dictated by the 'need to preserve the paramountcy of India's political and economic interests'.

In choosing the point of contention with Indira, Nijalingappa had been singularly inept, as he was also to be when the fight between the two sides was to reach the point of decision in subsequent months. If he had not known it earlier, the reaction of the delegates to Indira's defence of her economic policies should have alerted him to the danger of attacking her on this score. Moreover, he could not have been unaware that at a closed-door meeting of a small committee of

115

Congress leaders, Desai had found himself 'hopelessly isolated', with Chavan, Jagjivan Ram, C. Subramaniam and even Kamaraj pressing him to accept bank nationalisation. He had refused nonetheless.

What might have happened at the Faridabad Congress after battle had been joined between Nijalingappa and Indira would never be known. For the vast marquee under which the Congress had met caught fire immediately after Indira's fighting speech. The stormy session ended literally in smoke. Many doubted the claim that the fire was 'accidental'.

Within a week of the fiery fiasco at Faridabad, providence provided the Syndicate with the opportunity it had been looking for. On May 3rd, 1969, President Zakir Husain, who had maintained a dignified detachment from the Congress power struggle, died suddenly. The vacant presidency became the focus of a renewed test of strength between the two sides. If past practice was to be followed, Vice-President V. V. Giri should automatically have been adopted as the Congress candidate. But neither side wanted him. The Syndicate's mind was made up. It wanted to nominate one of its own members, Sanjiva Reddy, then Speaker of Parliament. Though a formal decision was left to a meeting of the Congress Parliamentary Board at Bangalore in July, when the AICC was scheduled to meet there, Reddy's name was mentioned in informal discussions among Congress leaders. Indira remained 'totally non-committal', nor did she mention any other name. Instead, she left for an official visit to Japan.

In Tokyo she got word that the Syndicate's purpose in installing Reddy in the presidential palace was to remove her from her office and elect Desai instead. The paranoia, so deeply ingrained in her personality since early childhood, was now at its peak. Even so, on returning home she remained silent and open to all ideas. She knew that she could not get a person of her own choice accepted by the Parliamentary Board because the Syndicate had a majority in it. A defeat at the Board would make her vulnerable. She therefore chose silence and delay, hoping that a last-minute compromise with the Syndicate might yet be possible. But the Syndicate was determined on a show-down and she had to pick up the gauntlet. Even so, right until the moment she was outvoted at the Bangalore meeting of the Parliamentary Board, she tried hard to find a meeting ground with the Syndicate. Contrary to the reputation for being incorrigibly combative and confrontationist that she was soon to acquire, she seemed genuinely reluctant to reach the parting of the ways with the Syndicate and thus bring about a split in the Congress, a claim she repeated as late as three and a half months before her assassination.

Just before the delegates started assembling at Bangalore, she was advised by P. N. Haksar, now her principal official counsellor, that

116

the best way to vanquish the Syndicate would be to convert the struggle for personal power into an ideological one. The advice was sound and timely. Indira acted on it at once.

The leftist critics of the Syndicate and Desai had gained further strength since the irruption of economic policy differences at the Faridabad AICC. They were, in fact, raring to confront the 'bunch of reactionaries' who were 'thwarting' the people's urges for socio-economic reform. The stage was thus set for Indira to give an ideological twist to her quarrel with the Syndicate.

Indira's technique of doing so was entirely typical of her emerging style. It relied heavily on the element of surprise. Pleading 'indisposition' (no important Indian is ever ill, only indisposed), she absented herself from the Congress Working Committee's meeting at Bangalore on the first day. But she sent to the Committee, through Fakhruddin Ali Ahmed, a loyal cabinet colleague who later became the country's President, a note on economic policy. Remarking that hers were 'some stray thoughts, hurriedly dictated', she wanted the Committee to consider these for 'full or partial acceptance'. Some of her ideas were old and familiar ones to which the Congress had often paid lip service without doing much to implement them. But the key point in her document, as in all Congress discussions, related to bank nationalisation. In an adroit stroke, she did not endorse the demand for immediate nationalisation of commercial banks, once again being pressed by the 'Young Turks'. But she indicated, with delightful ambiguity, that she was willing to reconsider the bank nationalisation issue even though the two-year period allowed to social control by herself was not yet over.

Her message, despite her elliptical style, was clear. She had no great interest in bank nationalisation as such. But she was using this issue to safeguard her position on the question of selecting the party nominee for the presidential poll. If her wishes were accommodated, she would allow social control on banks to go on. Otherwise she would insist on outright nationalisation.

The Syndicate, believing her to be cynical, decided to counter her cynicism by its own. Under its guidance, the Working Committee endorsed the Prime Minister's note in 'its entirety' and stated that it was for her government to implement it. The next day Desai, of all people, commended the resolution incorporating Indira's thoughts to the AICC, which also adopted it unanimously.

Everyone then got busy with the really important event at Bangalore, the Parliamentary Board's meeting to consider the presidential nomination, treating the economic policy resolution as a sideshow. Once again Indira tried to see if confrontation could be avoided even at this late stage. She suggested that Jagjivan Ram be made President, fulfilling Mahatma Gandhi's dream of putting an untouchable in Rashtrapati Bhavan, the presidential palace that was formerly the residence of British Viceroys. But the Syndicate did not budge from its support for Sanjiva Reddy who was chosen by a majority. What shocked Indira was not the Syndicate's attitude but the fact that her Home Minister, Chavan, had sided with it. She had believed that Chavan would support her, if not out of loyalty to her, at least to preserve his own 'progressive image'.

Indira's father, too, had been similarly outvoted in the Congress Parliamentary Board on the issue of the presidential nomination in 1957. But his position being secure, indeed impregnable, he took the majority decision in his stride. Indira could not afford to do so because the Syndicate's whole purpose in making Reddy the President was to oust her.

She came out of the meeting of the Board in great fury, making no attempt to maintain her normal appearance of calm imperturbability. At a hurriedly summoned press conference she declared that the party bosses would have to 'face the consequences' of their action. And, giving a glimpse of her strategy to fight them, she added that their decision to 'force' a presidential candidate that she disliked on her was really an 'assault' on her 'views and attitudes and . . . social and foreign policies. When one holds certain views one expects to be attacked.'

Journalists attending the press conference got the impression that Indira was behaving like a 'wounded tigress'. Some of them speculated that she was about to strike at Chavan for his 'disloyalty'. But having given vent to her hurt feelings, she reverted to her technique of maintaining total, in this case ominous, silence about her next move.

Even before Indira had left Bangalore, Vice-President V. V. Giri announced that he was going to contest the presidential election as an independent candidate anyhow. The possibility that Indira might 'ditch' Reddy and support Giri – something she eventually did – now opened up. But before it could be seriously discussed, other climactic events took place.

Realising that any action against Chavan would smack of 'personal vendetta' and detract from the ideological crusade she was claiming to lead, Indira decided to act against Desai. In a lightning strike, she divested Desai of the finance portfolio on the plea that in view of his 'strong reservations' on basic issues, it would be 'unfair' to 'burden' him with the responsibility of implementing the economic programme. To take this responsibility upon herself, she assumed the finance portfolio. Desai was taken totally by surprise. Her letter to him was polite enough, but it simply announced a *fait accompli*. The proclamation announcing the change had already been issued by the Acting President. Appalled at having been treated as a *chaprasi*, an office peon, Desai accused Indira of discourtesy, rejected her request for him to stay on as Deputy Prime Minister without portfolio and resigned.

Having seized the initiative, Indira did not give her adversaries time to recover from the shock of Desai's sudden dismissal but made another sensational move by nationalising fourteen leading commercial banks. She did so by ordinance though Parliament was due to meet in twenty-four hours. This was intended to underscore that nationalisation was a 'personal act' of the Prime Minister. There was substance in the Syndicate's scream that her action was politically motivated and had little to do with economic reform. But it was drowned in the delirious welcome the people at large gave the nationalisation ordinance. Low-paid government and private employees, taxi and auto-rickshaw drivers, educated unemployed and others who had never seen the interior of a bank were so enthused that they danced in the streets with joy. They also joined massive rallies at the Prime Minister's residence, the like of which had never before been held or encouraged. There was doubtless some organisation behind this show of popular support but the 'public enthusiasm was genuine and largely spontaneous'.

The phenomenal outpouring of public sentiment scared the Syndicate away from its resolve to 'censure' Indira in the Congress Working Committee for her 'shabby treatment' of Desai. But its members joined right-wing opposition parties such as the Jana Sangh and Swatantra as well as major English language newspapers in expressing alarm over Indira's propensity to take politics to the streets and, above all, over her tactical alliance with the Communist Party of India (CPI) whose cadres were gleefully swelling the rallies at the gate of the Prime Minister's house.

When accused of being a 'Communist fellow-traveller', Indira asked angrily how she could have become a Communist simply by 'implementing Congress programmes' for which her 'hypocritical' critics within the Congress party had been 'voting year after year'. The section of the press critical of her she dismissed as the 'mouthpiece' of 'monied individuals owning newspapers', and she added spiritedly that if she had wanted to be a Communist 'nothing could have prevented me from doing so'.

The political battle over Indira's populist measures was, predictably, accompanied by a legal one. Both the ordinance nationalising the banks and the law to replace it which Indira got enacted – 'in indecent haste', according to her critics – were challenged in the Supreme Court and declared invalid by it. She overcame the problem by taking over the managements of the banks without disturbing their shareholding and then completed the process of nationalising leisurely, by enacting a law that met the objections raised by the Supreme Court in its earlier judgments. She thus had her way but the uphill struggle with the Supreme Court sowed the seeds of a conflict between her government and the highest judiciary which was to exacerbate the already inflamed atmosphere in the country.

Indira's close friend, Pupul Jayakar, complimented her on the excellent timing of her decision to nationalise the banks. In a revealing reply, Indira said that the timing was not chosen by her but by her adversaries. 'They drove me to the wall and left me with no other option'.

For the present, however, the main issue was the President's election. Awed by the rolling juggernaut of popular support for Indira, totally uncertain about what she might do and anxious to ensure that Reddy got enough votes to win, Nijalingappa, acting on behalf of the Syndicate, made a big mistake. He established contact with the Jana Sangh and Swatantra – the two opposition parties sympathetic to the Syndicate but identified by Indira and her supporters as archsymbols of total negation of the Congress policies of socialism and secularism – and persuaded them to cast their second preference votes in favour of Reddy, their first preference votes going, of course, to C. D. Deshmukh, an elder statesman and the joint candidate of all organised opposition parties.

This not only damned the Syndicate in the eyes of many Congressmen and a large number of people but also enabled Indira to get out of the corner she had painted herself into. Despite her opposition to Reddy, she had signed his nomination papers on behalf of the ruling party though she was dragging her feet on Nijalingappa's request that she should also issue a whip calling upon party MPs and members of state legislatures to vote for Reddy.

Nijalingappa's blunder enabled Indira to repudiate Reddy's candidature though she refrained from publicly supporting Giri for a while. Instead, her followers started clamouring that they be allowed to vote according to their 'conscience' because Reddy's candidature had been vitiated by Nijalingappa's 'unholy alliance' with 'communal and reactionary' parties of the opposition. Nijalingappa angrily denied this charge and pointed to Indira's own hobnobbing with Communists and other 'dangerous' elements. Thereafter, the battle for the 'conscience votes' was fought through what came to be known as the 'War of Midnight Missives'. Both sides wrote acrimonious letters to each other, usually delivered as close to the newspapers' midnight deadline as possible. Their contents were usually leaked to the press well before their delivery to the addressee. The Prime Minister's propaganda machine saw to it that the last word in the morning was hers.

It was late on the night of August 20th that the presidential election results were declared. The suspense had lasted till the very end because the race was neck and neck. In the end, Giri won, though by a very narrow margin. But this did not matter. In love, war and Indian elections, the winner takes all, irrespective of the margin of victory. The Syndicate's rout was complete. Indira's victory was greeted by the people with exuberance similar to that over bank nationalisation.

Even in the midst of euphoria and the victory parades it was clear to Indira that her fight was far from over. A careful look at the voting figures showed that Giri had scraped through with a minority of Congress votes and a majority of votes by an odd combination of diverse opposition groups. Two-thirds of Congress MPs and nearly three-quarters of Congress members of state legislatures had stood by Reddy, the party's official nominee disowned by Indira.

It was equally clear that the relations between Indira and the Syndicate had reached breaking point. But such was the mystique of Congress unity that neither side wanted to take the blame for the split that was in fact unavoidable. Intricate manoeuvres, wild rumours, high excitement and slanging matches were the order of the day from August 25th, when the Congress Working Committee met for the first time since Giri's election as President and tried to let bygones be bygones, and November 7th, when the Congress split at last became a reality. There was also a succession of mediatory efforts, some of them thoroughly bizarre. Taking a leading part in these was Chavan. Immediately after Giri's victory he had switched sides from the Syndicate to Indira. She was happy to have his support but made it clear to him that she no longer trusted him. Kamaraj was to tell me more than a year later that if he had had the slightest suspicion about Chavan's 'slipperiness', he would not have allowed his colleagues in the Syndicate to force Reddy's candidature on Indira.

Despite mediatory efforts and several surface courtesies – Indira drove to Nijalingappa's house to enquire after his health when he fell ill under the stress of events and later invited him to lunch to discuss Congress unity – the ugly reality asserted itself fast enough. Midnight correspondence between the two sides was resumed and became increasingly vitriolic.

Indira sprang another surprise on the Syndicate when, in the midst of unity talks, she made her followers submit a requisition for a special meeting of the AICC to 'elect a new Congress President'. Even though more than enough AICC members had signed the requisition, some of the Prime Minister's supporters added to them 'a few forged signatures, too'. This was symptomatic of the unethical standards to which her supporters were prepared to descend for a cause they believed to be just.

Nijalingappa fixed November 1st for the consideration of the requisition but brought matters to a head much earlier. On October 28th, he wrote a lengthy and bitter open letter to Indira, accusing her of having started a 'personality cult' around herself that was 'threatening democracy in the organisation'. He reminded her that the 'handful of people' whom she was blaming for having 'arrogated' to themselves undue powers were the very people who had made her Prime Minister in the first place. He also alleged, not without basis, that 'baits and threats' were being freely used by the government to 'secure regimentation and personal loyalty'. His punch line was: 'You seem to have made personal loyalty to you the test of loyalty to the Congress and the country.' These were prophetic words. But at that time they evoked only derision. The mass sentiment in favour of 'progressive' Indira and against the 'reactionary' Syndicate, of which Nijalingappa had by now become a symbol, was much too strong.

A part of Nijalingappa's fury and frustration arose from the weakness of his position. Chavan having gone over to Indira's side, he was no longer sure of a majority in his own Working Committee. He tried to get over this difficulty by dropping from the Committee two close associates of Indira, Fakhruddin Ali Ahmed and C. Subramaniam. Calling the manoeuvre shabby, she sacked several junior ministers sympathetic to the Syndicate, announced a boycott of the meeting called by Nijalingappa and her decision to hold a parallel meeting of the Working Committee at her residence.

On the morning of November 1st, a tense Delhi witnessed the strange spectacle of two meetings of the Congress Working Committee taking place at one and the same time at two different places, the Prime Minister's house and the AICC headquarters in Jantar Mantar Road. Each meeting was attended by ten of the Committee's twenty-one members. The solitary uncommitted member, K. C. Abraham, underlined his neutrality by briefly attending both the meetings. He was warmly welcomed at both gatherings. At Jantar Mantar Road, he was the only Working Committee member to be left unscathed by a wild and ugly mob of the Prime Minister's supporters who had roughed up all members of the Nijalingappa faction while the Delhi police 'looked on'.

Despite this dismal drama both sides were still coy about taking the final step of making the Congress split formal. Instead each accused the other of 'unconstitutional behaviour' aimed at 'disrupting Congress unity'!

Ultimately, it was Nijalingappa who ended the charade and made the Congress split final and irrevocable. He announced Indira's expulsion from the primary membership of the Congress on the grounds that she had 'rebelled' against the Working Committee and directed the Congress Parliamentary Party to elect a 'new leader in her place'. Indira was entering Rashtrapati Bhavan for an official lunch in honour of a visiting foreign dignitary when she first heard of Nijalingappa's decision. She remained perfectly calm and showed not the slightest sign of strain. All through the meal her smile remained radiant and conversation lively.

Later in the day she called a meeting of her cabinet at which senior ministers reaffirmed their loyalty to her. A few waverers were asked to resign which they promptly did.

The critical question, however, was how many Congress MPs would be on each side. Intense lobbying went on all night. When it appeared that a majority of the party was with Indira, the herd mentality took over. Of the 429 Congress members of both houses of Parliament, 310 attended the meeting called by Indira. Of them 220 belonged to the Lok Sabha, the lower house of Parliament, with a total membership of 530 at that time. The remaining ninety belonged to the 250-member Rajya Sabha, the upper house. Of the MPs who went with the Syndicate and Desai, sixty-eight belonged to the Lok Sabha. They elected Ram Subhag Singh, not Desai, as their leader though the former Deputy Prime Minister was named Chairman of the Party in both houses.

Each side claimed to be the real Congress party but Indira's supporters became known as the Congress (R) or Requisitionist and the Syndicate's camp as the Congress (O), the letter in parenthesis standing for Organisation, though Indira's propaganda machine liked to call the rival body 'Congress Zero'.

As a result of the Congress split, Indira had lost her majority in both houses of her Parliament. But this did not worry her at all because her government was in no danger. It was being supported by the Communist Party of India, several regional parties and a number of independents. A Congress (O)-sponsored motion of no-confidence in her was decisively defeated. Huge rallies continued to be held outside the Prime Minister's house as a demonstration of mass support for her. The other side did not even try to organise similar rallies or meetings.

It was in this atmosphere that the AICC meeting requisitioned by Indira took place in New Delhi on November 22nd. Of the 705 members of the AICC, 446 attended. Having demonstrated that the majority of the Congress ranks were with her, Indira exhibited emotion for the first time in public. Speaking from the chair she traced her family's and her own long association with the Congress and burst into tears at the thought that some party bosses should have had the 'temerity' to have 'expelled' her from the Congress. Beyond this she said nothing about her opponents. But her supporters spared no invective or abuse in lambasting the Syndicate. She did nothing to restrain them.

There could be no doubt that Indira had emerged much the stronger from the Congress split. The 'dumb doll' had been suddenly transformed into a confident, assertive and dominant leader to whom the appellation 'ruthless' had also begun to be attached. Her mass appeal was never in doubt. A large section of the intelligentsia now warmly rallied round her, believing the forty-eight-year-old Indira to be a young, bright-eyed symbol of hope and change, especially when compared with her elderly rivals. The remarkable courage and tactical skill she had displayed in her conflict with the Syndicate also won her new adherents. Only a few were disturbed by the questionable methods she had sometimes employed or condoned.

Indicative of the mood prevailing at that time was the case of Jagjivan Ram's unpaid taxes. Ram, then one of Indira's principal lieutenants, was a Harijan leader and an able minister of long standing. Allegations that he had used his long innings in high office to amass vast wealth need not concern us here. But it was an irrefutable fact, though not generally known, that for as long as ten years he had failed even to file his tax returns. Desai, as Finance Minister, was privy to this fact practically all through this period. But he kept quiet about it until the Congress split loomed on the horizon, when he made the scandal public.

Instead of asking Ram to resign or at least remonstrating with him, Indira made light of the serious lapse on the part of her senior colleague. Ram, she said nonchalantly, was a busy man and had 'obviously forgotten' to file his tax returns. Surprisingly, the country, by and large, accepted this specious explanation.

On the other hand, Indira's opponents, through their wild and often absurd charges against her, were helping her to consolidate her power and popularity. For instance, Nijalingappa went so far as to allege that in order to gain Communist support for her survival in power, Indira had 'not hesitated to subordinate some of India's policies to the Soviet Union'. Even those who did not like her alliance with the CPI would not believe him for the simple reason that a woman who had revolted against the Syndicate's overlordship was unlikely to submit to the dominance of anyone else.

Indira knew that sooner or later, indeed sooner rather than later, she would have to go to the polls to win power on her own rather than run a minority government with the support of others. But, having become adept in the power game, she decided to wait until she had wrested control of the states still ruled by Congress ministries owing allegiance to the Syndicate. To achieve this result all scruples were once again thrown to the winds and Indira's men went on a spree to buy over Congress (O) legislators in states. This dubious technique did not succeed in all cases though it did in some.

Meanwhile, Indira took several steps to disprove that her radical rhetoric was only a cover for her personal power struggle with the Syndicate. She abolished the managing agency system which had dominated the Indian mercantile scene from the days of Clive. The trend towards decentralised economy was halted and a Monopolies and Restrictive Trade Practices (MRTP) Commission was appointed to regulate the future expansion of private industry and trade. At the same time, Indira turned down the demand of some of her radical supporters for the nationalisation of foreign trade and the cancellation of all concessions given to foreign investors in previous years. If this significant nuance went practically unnoticed, it was because of the Syndicate's mindless propaganda that she was either a Communist or a Communist dupe.

Barely six months after the Congress split, Indira felt strong enough to undertake a sweeping reshuffle of her cabinet. She shifted Chavan to the Finance Ministry and took over his powerful portfolio of the Home Ministry herself. She used this opportunity to make even more far-reaching changes. Until then the Home Ministry controlled the Intelligence Bureau, a powerful monolith that ran both internal and external intelligence. Indira divided the IB into two, leaving the original bureau in charge of internal intelligence and counter-espionage and entrusting external intelligence to the newly formed Research and Analysis Wing, better known by its delightful and perhaps appropriate acronym, RAW. She then brought IB and RAW – together with Revenue Intelligence, until then a part of the Finance Ministry – under the Prime Minister's direct control.

Another notable feature of the reshuffle was the demotion of Dinesh Singh, once the second most powerful person in the government. Moved to the coveted Foreign Office only fifteen months earlier, he was shifted, over his protests, to a less glamorous ministry. Soon he was dropped from the cabinet altogether and later still suspended from the party on the charge of 'hobnobbing' with the opposition.

Other members of the Kitchen Cabinet who had dreamed of inheriting the power once wielded by the discredited and defeated Syndicate were also to meet a fate similar, though not identical, to Dinesh Singh's.

Delhi's politics almost always had a flavour of the Mughal Court.

As Indira's power grew, the political culture got increasingly transformed into the 'courtier culture'. The phenomenon was to reach its
apogee years later but its deleterious consequences were becoming
apparent even then. Ministers anxious to ingratiate themselves with
Indira started 'passing the buck to the boss' through the Prime
Minister's secretariat instead of discharging their own assigned responsibilities. Bureaucrats took their cue from their political masters.
The power centre in the world's largest democracy was slowly turning
into a *durbar*. But so upbeat was the country's mood that warnings
against excessive concentration of power and indeed against 'creeping
dictatorial designs' made little impression. For her part, Indira pooh-
poohed the allegation and jauntily declared that the Prime Minister's
secretariat had not been 'invented' by her but had existed since the
days of Shastri.

The most exciting item on the political agenda still was the abolition
of the princes' privy purses and privileges. Curiously, no one was
paying much attention to the unfulfilled promises to implement land
reforms, protect the economically weak and enforce the laws on
minimum wages in both factories and farms.

Indira failed to get the privy purses abolished through negotiations
with the trade union of former rulers, called the Concord of Princes,
which was her preference. She then tried to do so by enacting a law
to amend the constitution. On September 2nd, 1970, in the Lok
Sabha it got the requisite two-thirds majority of those present and
voting as well as a clear majority of the total membership of the house.
But in the Rajya Sabha, the upper house of Parliament, three days
later, the measure failed by a single vote. Indira's frustration was
accentuated by the jubilation of her opponents. The same evening,
after an emergency meeting of the cabinet, she got a presidential
proclamation issued 'derecognising' the princes and with this withdrawal of recognition their claims to privy purses vanished into thin
air.

The next morning a triumphant Indira left for Lusaka, the Zambian
capital, for the summit of the Non-Aligned Movement (NAM). There
she was treated with special respect and heard with attention.

On her return home, she got busy with state assembly elections in
Kerala. It was a carefully devised experiment which was to determine
her political strategy for quite some time to come. It also represented
an exquisite twist of irony.

As we have already noted, in 1959 Indira was primarily responsible
for throwing the then undivided Communist Party of India (CPI) out
of power. Now, eleven years later, she entered into an open and direct
alliance with the CPI in order to defeat a Left United Front, led by the

more militant Communist Party Marxist (CPM). The circumstances which had made the Kerala election possible were both interesting and indicative of the wider power play in the country in the wake of the Congress split.

In the 1967 General Election, the CPM-led Front had come to power in Kerala, as in West Bengal. But the CPM's position in Kerala was less dominant than in West Bengal and its quarrels with its coalition partners, especially the CPI, fiercer. As Indira broke with the Congress Old Guard and radicalised the policies of her government, the CPI decided to support her warmly while the CPM, to say nothing of the Maoist groups, treated her with suspicion and antipathy. The Marxists had good reason to do so because her party, the Congress (R), also called the Indira Congress, was waging a relentless struggle against them in both Kerala and West Bengal, their two strongholds.

In June 1970, the CPM-led ministry, of which the CPI was a part, fell because of dissensions. The Congress supported a minority CPI ministry. Its leader, Achutha Menon, proved to be a man of great ability, with integrity to match. The Congress-led coalition comfortably won the mid-term election ordered by Indira in September. However, the ministry that was formed was led by Menon. Some CPI leaders started dreaming of replicating the 'Kerala pattern' at the federal centre in New Delhi, though admittedly under Indira's leadership. Within a few years the dream was to turn into a nightmare.

For the present, however, Indira was happy to extend her alliance with the CPI in Kerala to the rest of the country. She was planning to hold early elections to Parliament though she was keeping everyone guessing about the date on which these would be held. She was convinced that cooperation with the Communists would do her good, especially in states like UP and Bihar where the Congress (O), led by the Syndicate and Desai, and right-wing parties were busy forming a 'grand alliance' to defeat her. Unlike the CPM, the CPI did not have a major stronghold in any state. But it had fairly widespread pockets of influence in areas where Indira needed its support the most.

On December 27th, 1970, Indira went on the air to announce that the Lok Sabha had been dissolved and that elections to the house would be held in mid-February. This announcement was bound to come some time or the other. But what seems to have influenced Indira's timing was a Supreme Court verdict, delivered only twelve days earlier, invalidating the presidential proclamation that had abolished the privy purses of the princes by derecognising the former rulers.

This judgment, coming on top of the earlier ones throwing out a succession of laws concerning bank nationalisation, became the proverbial last straw on the backs of a large number of Indira's radical supporters who had been clamouring that the higher judiciary, 'determined to protect private property and vested interests', had become an 'obstacle to social justice' and therefore 'something had to be done about it'. The struggle preceding the Congress split had given rise to shrill slogans in favour of a 'committed bureaucracy' and a 'committed press'. Now there was a demand for a 'committed judiciary'.

The more radical followers of Indira, including many 'Young Turks', demanded the convening of a new constituent assembly to undertake a 'comprehensive and radical' review of the 'entire constitution' with a view to setting up a 'Second Republic'. Indira refused to countenance it. When the radicals persisted in pressing their demand she rebuked them and warned them against methods that 'bypass democracy'. 'I am against certain attitudes of mind, certain methods of functioning,' she declared. 'If Communists use them, I am against them. If Congress uses them, I am afraid I am against such Congressmen also.'

She was clearly indicating that even while using populist measures to preserve her pre-eminent position, she would have no truck with extremist methods. But once again her preference for working within the given framework and refraining from turning the system upside down went unnoticed because the level of contention was much too high, especially in view of the approaching parliamentary election.

On the other hand, whether Indira then realised it or not, the stage was being set for a confrontation between the executive and the judiciary which would begin sooner than her admonition to radicals might have indicated.

The 1971 parliamentary poll quickly turned into a referendum on Indira's leadership. She relished this. When *Newsweek* asked her what the main issues in the election were, she replied gleefully: 'I am the issue.'

As if to endorse her claim, the 'grand alliance' of her opponents coined the slogan 'Indira *Hatao*' (Remove Indira). In an inspired response, she declared that she was not opposed to any individual and was interested only in freeing her people from the scourge of poverty, her battle-cry would be '*Garibi Hatao*' (Remove Poverty). The impact on the country was instant and electric. The poor, a vast majority of the population, were overwhelmed by the belief that they had at last found their redeemer.

Her party's election campaign was run almost exclusively by her. Since there was no party machine worth the name and hardly any leader to question her, Indira was the sole selector of the candidates and also the sole campaigner. She plunged into electioneering with the ferocious energy she had become famous for, travelling faster and further than during any previous poll. Often she would stand in an open car for hours so that crowds lining the roads could see her easily. She invoked radical rhetoric for all it was worth to rouse the masses. At the same time, she took good care to reassure the classes that she was no hot-head revolutionary and would be mindful of their interests. She repeatedly declared that she had 'absolutely no intention of abolishing the institution of private property' and used a meeting of industrial tycoons to explain that her scheme of 'gradual and peaceful' change had no room for violent elimination of 'whole classes'.

The popular enthusiasm for Indira was manifest. Even so, not only the 'grand alliance' but also many independent observers believed that the election would be a 'damned close run thing'. One reason for this was that the Congress (O) was supposed to have a better machine at its disposal. Congress (O) leaders also felt that their persistent 'exposure' of Indira's 'political immorality' would have the desired result. Moreover, several of the major English-language newspapers which used to applaud her had turned against her, a few of them virulently.

However, the election resulted in a sensational victory for Indira. The anti-Congress trend revealed by the 1967 General Election was reversed. The Congress (R) won 352 seats or seventy more than the undivided Congress had captured four years earlier. The Congress (O) and its allies were practically wiped out. One of the candidates to be trounced was Indira's opponent at Rae Bareli, Raj Narain, a burly and buffoonish socialist who had the dubious distinction of coining the slogan 'Indira *Hatao*'. However, he lived to fight another day and to turn the tables on Indira.

Indira's Communist allies were in an even worse quandary than her opponents who had bitten the dust. The CPI had hoped to acquire from the elections even greater leverage than it had enjoyed during the last months of 1969 and throughout 1970. But precisely the reverse had happened. Indira no longer needed its support not only for a majority in Parliament but also for the magic two-thirds majority required to amend the constitution – an item high on her agenda in view of the Supreme Court's judgment on privy purses.

# 8   Her Finest Hour

After her tremendous triumph in the parliamentary elections, Indira tried to redeem her radical pledges. She nationalised general insurance in May 1971. A few months later the constitution was amended to restore to Parliament the authority to amend the fundamental rights, negating the four-to-three judgment of the Supreme Court delivered by Subba Rao. Interestingly, the Congress (O), reversing its earlier stand, supported the measure. A second constitutional amendment made Parliament, rather than the Supreme Court, the arbiter of the amount to be paid to those whose properties might be taken over for public purposes. It also made laws intended to give effect to the directive principles of state policy enumerated in the constitution immune from judicial challenge of any kind.

These were important, even exciting, changes. But neither the country's nor the Prime Minister's mind was on them. Both were preoccupied throughout 1971 with a terrible tragedy on India's door-step.

Exactly eight days after Indira was elected leader of the Congress Parliamentary Party on March 17th, this time without a whiff of dissent, a major crisis, brewing for a long time, suddenly erupted in what was then East Pakistan and is now the Republic of Bangladesh. The fury of the crisis was reminiscent of the cyclones that periodically devastate this luckless land, a particularly nasty one having struck it only a few months earlier.

Since its creation in 1947, Pakistan had been a geographical monstrosity. More than a thousand miles of Indian territory separated its eastern and more populous wing from the western one where political power resided. The largely Punjabi élite dominating the all-Pakistan government made no secret of its disdain for the distant Bengalis. Even in Dacca, the capital of East Pakistan, top bureaucratic positions were held by Punjabis or other West Pakistanis. In the Army, the eastern wing had no representation worth the name, an East Bengal Regiment having been raised only a few years before the two wings parted company.

Almost immediately after Pakistan's birth, it became clear that its two wings had no bond except the Muslim religion. The lack of links was aggravated by a bitter dispute over language. The new state of Pakistan declared Urdu to be its sole official language. The Bengalis, deeply attached to their beautiful and highly developed language, fiercely resisted this. Bengali students, killed during the anti-Urdu riots before the unwise decision was amended, became the first martyrs whom Bangladesh reveres every year. The seeds of future conflict were thus sown. The breach between the two wings widened because of glaring and growing disparities of economic development and political power.

Perhaps the wrongs done to East Pakistan could have been mitigated, if not righted, had democracy taken root in Pakistan. The eastern wing's numerical superiority and traditional, if volatile, commitment to the political process and electoral politics might have provided a corrective to the imbalance in governmental power. But that was not to be. From 1958 onwards, Pakistan had been under military rule, and the Army's contempt for the Bengalis far exceeded that of West Pakistani civilians.

Unsurprisingly, a movement for greater autonomy for East Pakistan began. Its leader was the charismatic and somewhat demagogic Sheikh Mujibur Rahman, generally known as Sheikh Mujib, later to be called the Father of Bangladesh and later still to be slain by some of his disgruntled followers. He argued that the long neglected and exploited people of East Bengal should be able to 'use the fruits of their labour for their welfare' rather than 'helplessly watch them being carried away to the west'. His movement received a big boost from the 1965 India–Pakistan war, during which East Pakistan discovered, to its mortification, that it was defenceless against India. If it escaped Indian occupation, it was because of New Delhi's fears of 'possible Chinese intervention' in the event of Indian troops marching into East Pakistan.

Vague at first, the Sheikh's campaign for autonomy eventually crystallised into a six-point charter of demands which, if accepted, would have made East Pakistan all but independent except for a loose confederation with the western wing. Mujib had originally conceded only foreign relations and communications to the federal government in Rawalpindi where it had been moved from Karachi by the military dictator, Field-Marshal Ayub. Subsequently, he agreed to add defence to this list but strictly on the condition that the east and the west would have equal representation in the Army. The military rulers were infuriated. They arrested him and charged him with sedition 'in collusion with India'.

His trial, which came to be known as the Agartala Conspiracy Case (Agartala is an Indian town close to the border) was abruptly terminated, however, when, in early 1969, Field-Marshal Ayub was swept out of power by a powerful movement for his overthrow and the restoration of democracy. But, instead of democracy returning to Pakistan, martial law came back with a vengeance.

The bluff, blustering and often incredibly crude General Yahya Khan, who took over from Ayub, lacked his predecessor's political skills. Moreover, over-indulgence in drink and dissolute living had dulled his senses. But he had one redeeming feature. He was committed to holding free and fair elections, the first in his country's chequered history. His decision to postpone the poll because of a cyclone created misgivings about his intentions, but the elections were duly held in December 1970. Their results came as a big surprise, indeed sensation. They also created a deadlock that would eventually break Pakistan into two, a fate that has befallen no other country since the end of the Second World War.

Having campaigned fiercely on the basis of the famous six-point programme for regional autonomy, Mujib and his party, the Awami League, swept the polls, winning 160 of the 162 seats allotted to East Pakistan in the National Assembly. Besides making his supremacy in the eastern wing absolute, this gave Mujib a clear majority also in the National Assembly although his party had not contested a single seat in West Pakistan, entitling him to be Prime Minister of the whole of Pakistan.

This was resisted not only by Yahya but also Zulfiqar Ali Bhutto, Ayub's Foreign Minister who had revolted against his mentor and had emerged, from the 1970 elections, as the leading personality in the western wing though his dominance was in no way comparable to Mujib's in East Pakistan. Bhutto's party, the Pakistan People's Party (PPP), won eighty-one National Assembly seats out of the 138 allotted to the western wing. But the power of this Sindhi politician of great ability which was exceeded only by his ambition was in fact greater than the voting figures suggested. This was because Bhutto had managed to win over Punjab, Pakistan's heart in every sense of the word. His relations with the Army, though not of the best, were close enough, while Mujib was deeply distrusted by the Generals.

In next to no time Bhutto became the Army's main collaborator in keeping Mujib at bay. He even refused to allow the National Assembly to meet in Dacca until there was an agreement between him and Mujib on the future power structure in Pakistan. From this deadlock was born the most powerful nationalist movement of our times which triumphed after a brief but bloody war.

Yahya, whose calculation that the elections would result in a hung Parliament and he would therefore continue to be the arbiter among a gaggle of squabbling politicians had been disproved, lighted the fuse when, on March 25th, he ordered a comprehensive crack-down on East Pakistan. His and the Army's bad faith was clear from the sheer brutality of the obviously preplanned repression. Within the first few hours, student leaders, university teachers, writers, poets and other intellectuals in their hundreds were pulled out of their beds and slaughtered in cold blood. Anyone protesting on the streets was shot at sight. Mujib was arrested and whisked away to West Pakistan. A rash of local and largely spontaneous uprisings threw up new and previously unknown leaders. Soon the entire East Bengali population was in revolt.

Not only the East Bengal Police but also the East Pakistan Rifles, a paramilitary organisation and the East Bengal Regiment, the only Bengali formation in a predominantly Punjabi Army, mutinied. Forty-eight hours after Yahya's cruel crack-down Major (later General and President of Bangladesh) Ziaur Rahman declared independence. Several Awami League leaders who had escaped to Calcutta in India announced the formation of a government in exile, with Tajuddin Ahmed at its head. As killings by the Pakistani Army turned into genocide, Tajuddin declared: 'Pakistan is now dead and buried under a mountain of corpses.' The fight for a free Bangladesh had begun.

Strange though it may seem, India was taken by surprise by these grim developments. Doubtless the country had been preoccupied with internal problems but this could not explain, let alone excuse, the lack of even a contingency plan. Among the people at large there was a tidal wave of sympathy for the people of Bangladesh being butchered by the Pakistani Army.

Nearly two months before the Bangladesh crisis had burst with elemental fury, an Indian Airline plane had been hijacked from Srinagar, the capital of Kashmir, to Lahore in Pakistan where it was blown up amidst anti-Indian hysteria in the presence of Bhutto and with the apparent acquiescence of the Pakistani authorities. India retaliated by banning Pakistani overflights over Indian territory. This handicapped the Pakistani Army in its campaign of suppression and murder in East Pakistan. But the military rulers overcame the problem by flying around the Indian peninsula and securing refuelling rights in Sri Lanka, then called Ceylon.

As Pakistani atrocities in East Pakistan mounted, so did the dismay of the Indian people who started clamouring for 'action', a polite euphemism for Indian military intervention. Humanitarian feelings were the main motivating force behind this outcry. But many Indians also saw in the heart-rending situation an opportunity to cut Pakistan down to size. Indira, more clear-eyed than most of her countrymen, was not at all oblivious of this opportunity. But she was 'determined not to be stampeded into doing anything' that might lay India open to the charge of violating international law or enable the Pakistani military junta to discredit the liberation struggle in Bangladesh as an offshoot of a 'conspiracy by Hindu India'. For the first few months of the Bangladesh crisis she had repeatedly to calm her countrymen, including Members of Parliament, who were becoming increasingly critical of her government's inaction. She gently told them that a 'wrong step or even a wrong word' would have an 'effect different from the desired one'.

This was the first indication of the superb qualities of leadership Indira was to display, to the joy and pride of most Indians, all through the Bangladesh crisis and the fourteen-day India–Pakistan war. She won admiration for the skill with which she harmonised the military, political and diplomatic strands of the Indian response to the crisis next door. Deftly she mastered the situation rather than allow it to overwhelm her. Before making any major move she tried to build up national consensus behind it, keeping in almost continuous touch with opposition leaders. Her sense of timing turned out to be even more remarkable than during her struggle with the Syndicate.

Refusing to make any warlike noises, even while realising that war with Pakistan was becoming unavoidable, Indira gave primacy to the issue of the terrified refugees from East Pakistan who were pouring into India in a torrential flood. In a matter of months their number rose to a staggering ten million. Declaring that what was 'claimed to be an internal problem in Pakistan has also become an internal problem in India' and emphasising the 'unbearable' financial and other burdens the refugee problem imposed on India, she appealed to the world community to 'stop Pakistan's brutal repression' and promote a political settlement in Bangladesh so that the refugees who had become such a drain on India could return home 'in safety and honour'.

At the same time, she took good care to see to it that the refugees, indistinguishable from the people of West Bengal, did not wander and disappear into hovels and slums as so many migrants from East Pakistan had done in preceding years. Through a virtual administrative miracle and at colossal cost, the refugees were isolated from the indigenous population, housed in camps, clothed adequately and medically looked after so that no epidemic could break out. The objective, eventually fulfilled, was that when the time came for them to go home they would actually do so.

Indira's strategy of dealing with the Bangladesh crisis had the full backing of the Indian Army commanders, headed by General (later Field-Marshal) Sam Manekshaw, who had argued at the start of the crisis that India should not get involved in it militarily until after the end of the rainy season. Heavy rains in that part of the subcontinent made movement extremely difficult and, in any case, Manekshaw believed that no military move should be made without thorough preparation. An even more powerful reason for caution was the fear of Chinese intervention in hostilities between India and Pakistan. In the winter months, the Army chief argued, the mountain passes would be snowbound, making it difficult for the Chinese troops to roll down the Himalayas.

India's concern about possible Chinese moves was magnified after the visit to New Delhi in July 1971 of Henry Kissinger, President Nixon's national security adviser. He did not drop any hint of his famous secret trip to China that was still a few days away. But he said enough to leave his Indian hosts in no doubt that should China intervene in an India–Pakistan conflict arising from the Bangladesh crisis, the Indians should expect no help from the United States.

Coming on top of the Nixon administration's self-admitted 'tilt' towards Pakistan, this was a major shock to India. When it was announced later that month that Kissinger had been to China and that the country which the Americans did not even recognise had invited Nixon, India, aware that it might have to intervene in Bangladesh sooner rather than later, felt very exposed to the Chinese threat. Memories of 1962 were still fresh in the Indians' mind although the country had come a long way from those despairing days. From this situation arose the Indo-Soviet Treaty of Peace, Friendship and Cooperation, signed in New Delhi on August 9th, and made public the same day at a mass rally.

The treaty, first offered to India by the Soviet Union in 1969, when Russia had started supplying arms to Pakistan also, had not evoked much response from New Delhi initially. In the new situation, Indira felt the treaty to be in the Indian interest. She saw to it that it was negotiated with great speed and in remarkable secrecy.

Contrary to the scare raised by some foreign countries and a few of Indira's Indian critics, the Indo-Soviet treaty took care of the Chinese threat without in any way compromising India's policy of non-alignment, either then or in later years.

Even before the Indo-Soviet treaty was signed Indira had ensured that the *Mukti Bahini* (Liberation Army) formed by the Bangladeshi people was given sanctuary in Indian territory and the necessary training and equipment. This task was assigned not to the Army but to the Border Security Force which performed it efficiently. Indira personally supervised coordination between a multiplicity of governmental organisations which would normally have been at loggerheads with one another.

Having done all this at home, she turned her attention to international opinion and tried to harness it to India's purpose. She had been writing to world leaders about the Bangladesh issue for some time, especially drawing their attention to Sheikh Mujib's secret trial in a Pakistani jail. She appealed to them to prevent any harm coming to the imprisoned Bangladesh leader at the hands of the Pakistani Army.

In September she visited the Soviet Union where she was listened to with attention and respect when she explained that the raging conflict in Bangladesh and the resultant refugee problem were threatening India's security and indeed its 'very existence'. The outstanding event of the Moscow visit, however, was her refusal to start negotiations with any lesser Soviet leader, until Leonid Brezhnev, then out of the Soviet capital, was back to talk to her.

A month later, she left on a twenty-one-day tour that took her to Belgium, Austria, West Germany, Britain, France and the United States. Everywhere she displayed statesmanship in defending the Indian position, and in all these countries, except the US, she encountered sympathy for the plight of the Bangladeshi people and understanding for the Indian predicament. This was accompanied by plentiful advice to India to show 'restraint' and enter into negotiations with Pakistan, instead of seeking a military solution to the problem. Indira turned it down courteously but firmly, pointing that there was 'no India–Pakistan dispute involved'. If negotiations were to take place, she added, these were to be held between the Yahya regime and the duly elected leadership of the Awami League in Bangladesh.

Typical of her style in private negotiations was an exchange with the British Foreign Secretary, Sir Alec Douglas-Home.

'Our fear,' said the soft-spoken Sir Alec, 'is that there would be war.'

'We won't start it,' was Indira's laconic reply. The two moved to some other subject.

Since the public and media opinion on Bangladesh in most Western countries was way ahead of the stand taken by their governments, Indira put her public appearances in Britain to good use to hammer home the message that the appeals for restraint addressed to her were meaningless. No government, she told the BBC in an interview, could have shown the restraint that hers had done despite 'such tremendous provocation and threat to our safety and stability'. When the word restraint was used yet again by the interviewer, she shot back: 'When Hitler was on the rampage, why didn't you say, "Let's keep quiet and let's have peace with Germany and let the Jews die"?'

All this was not without effect. When the crunch came and the Bangladesh war became a subject of heated discussion and hectic diplomatic activity at the UN Security Council, Britain and France abstained from voting on resolutions unacceptable to India. Later, in January 1972, they were quick to recognise Bangladesh.

\*     \*     \*

The story in the US was starkly different, as much during the Security Council debates in December 1971 as during Indira's visit to Washington more than a month earlier. In Kissinger's words, the Nixon–Gandhi conversation 'turned into a classic dialogue of the deaf'. We also have it on his authority that Indira and Nixon 'were not intended by fate to be personally congenial'. Nixon's comments, after meetings with her, he adds, 'were not always printable'. Indira expressed herself more graciously but she amply reciprocated Nixon's feelings about her. During the 1971 encounter between the two, personal dislikes seem to have exacerbated policy differences. Indira, the leader of the world's most populous democracy, got nowhere with Nixon, the head of the most powerful one. But she more than made up for it by addressing the American public, already critical of the Nixon–Kissinger tilt towards Pakistan, over the US President's head.

When the question of a meeting between her and Yahya was raised at the National Press Club, she replied that she could not possibly 'shake hands with a clenched fist'. She also pointed out that while she had never said a 'rude word' about anybody, Yahya had been making offensive statements about her and about things in general which precluded a 'friendly conversation'.

There was loud laughter and prolonged applause for her audience knew what she was alluding to without specifically referring to it. Only a few days earlier Yahya, in a drunken outburst at a banquet in honour of a Chinese dignitary visiting Pakistan, had bawled: 'If that woman thinks she is going to cow me down, I refuse to take it.' Soon enough 'That Woman' became the title of one of Indira's many biographies.

Despite the seriousness of Indira's mission to West Europe and America, there was once again a lot of comment on her personal charm, 'feminine mystique', impeccable taste and elegant turn-out. It also did not go unnoticed that amidst all her worries and preoccupation she had found time to watch Nureyev at the Royal Ballet in London and to attend a Beethoven concert in Vienna.

During her stay in London Indira had told a meeting of the India League, 'I am sitting on top of a volcano and I honestly do not know when it is going to erupt.' Shortly after returning home she knew that the flashpoint had been reached. The brutality of the Pakistani Army had reached its crescendo. The India-backed *Mukti Bahini* was fighting back with equal ferocity. The hot pursuit of the Bangladeshi guerrillas by the Pakistani troops was leading to clashes between them and the Indian armed forces. To allow this situation to go on and let the civil war in Bangladesh rage indefinitely would be an invitation to disaster in India. If the moderate and secular Awami League could not win a sufficiently early victory over the murderous Pakistani Army of occupation, it was bound to be replaced by more radical, sectarian or even extremist groups hostile to India. Such a development close to India's highly volatile eastern region and insurgency-prone north-eastern states was fraught with the gravest consequences. There was also the danger that an indefinite stalemate in the Bangladesh conflict would make the area a happy hunting-ground for outside powers.

Indian public opinion was by now inflamed. The demand that the Indian armed forces be directed to 'clinch' the issue of Bangladesh was heard everywhere. In the forefront of this campaign was a highly respected leader who had retired from active politics many years earlier, Jayaprakash Narayan – better known as J.P. – who was to turn into Indira's Nemesis only a few years later though on the issue of Bangladesh the two were in broad agreement.

With all this, however, Indira was reluctant to be the first to start full-scale hostilities. Her dilemma was resolved for her by the Pakistani military dictator, Yahya.

On the late afternoon of December 3rd, 1971, just before sunset, General Yahya Khan launched what later came to be known as his 'unlucky strike'. Bombers of the Pakistan Air Force attacked a number of Indian advanced air bases. It was a clumsy and unproductive effort which achieved little besides starting the war for the liberation of Bangladesh. Had Yahya waited another twenty-four hours, the responsibility for starting the war might well have been India's. Military planners had decided that in the absence of any action by Pakistan, they themselves would have to act on December 4th because the 'full-moon fortnight starting on December 3rd could not be allowed to slip by'.

Indira was in Calcutta when the war began. She flew back to Delhi late at night, conferred with her cabinet, secured the concurrence of the opposition leaders with her plans and in a midnight broadcast appealed to the people vigorously and valiantly to pursue the 'war forced on us'. That night she worked practically until sunrise, giving directives to military chiefs and reviewing the execution of the plans she had approved in preceding weeks. Early that morning, her personal physician, Dr K. P. Mathur, went to see her; he found her utterly relaxed and busy with the onerous problem of choosing a bedspread for the divan in her study!

All through the period since March 25th, she had resisted the strident demand for recognising an independent Bangladesh. On December 6th, however, she announced this recognition to a wildly cheering Parliament. She also told Parliament that the *Mukti Bahini*, the 100,000-strong Bangladeshi guerrilla formation, was fighting along with the Indian forces and that the war on the eastern front was being waged under the joint Indo-Bangladesh command.

The well-oiled Indian war machine performed brilliantly, thanks largely to Indira's skill in overall direction, and the lightning campaign to free Bangladesh was over in exactly fourteen days. In the west, India was following basically a holding strategy. Even so, the Indian Navy shot into prominence for the first time by bombarding Karachi, West Pakistan's only port, and then blockading it.

For all his addiction to drink, Yahya had not acted foolishly in opting for war on December 3rd. He was either encouraged to believe or took it for granted that full-scale hostilities would invite intervention by China or the US or both and that while the Indians would thus be contained, the UN Security Council would enforce a cease-fire and thus the eastern wing's separation from Pakistan would be prevented.

Chinese help never came. The US did order a task force of its Seventh Fleet to the Bay of Bengal. But before the *Enterprise* and other US warships, followed at a discreet distance by a Russian armada, reached anywhere near Indian waters, it was all over in Bangladesh. In any case, Indira and her advisers, on hearing of the US decision to make at least a show of intervention on the side of those who were morally in the wrong and militarily losing, decided to ignore the American attempt to 'browbeat' India.

On December 16th, the defeated and demoralised Pakistani Army in Bangladesh surrendered. Over 93,000 officers and men laid down their arms. Never since the Second World War had such a large-scale surrender taken place. Nor has anything like it been repeated since 1971.

Pakistani generals had in fact been offering to surrender for two or three days but initially there was some disagreement about the terms of capitulation. On the day of the Pakistani surrender Indira waited patiently in her office in Parliament House, having been told that the surrender document would be signed before lunchtime in Dacca. Anticipating this she had given an appointment to a Swedish TV team to interview her at half past two in the afternoon. But there was a last-minute delay in the surrender ceremonies.

At two thirty sharp Indira asked her Information Adviser, H. Y. Sharada Prasad, to call in the Swedish TV crew. Surprisingly, the interviewer was not interested in the momentous developments taking place in the subcontinent. He wanted to talk to Indira about her childhood and preference in clothes and colours. She answered his questions with good humour until an hour or so later a red telephone on her desk rang.

She uttered only four words, spaced by two short pauses: 'Yes', 'yes', 'Thank you'. General Manekshaw was on the line giving her the good news that the Bangladesh war had been won. Though understandably excited, she showed no signs of it. She told the Swedes to wait for her in the anteroom because she was briefly required in Parliament and briskly headed for the House.

There her excitement showed as she announced to the tense and expectant MPs: 'Dacca is now the free capital of a free country . . .' The rest of her statement was drowned in wild cheering and had to be repeated later.

During the short walk between her office and the Parliament chamber, Indira had told Sharada Prasad: 'I must order a cease-fire on the western front also. For if I don't do so today, I shall not be able to do it tomorrow.' This was a clear reference to the feeling in the country that West Pakistan should be taught a 'proper lesson' before ending the war and her own awareness that any such attempt, after the achievement of Indian objectives in the east, would be both unpopular with world opinion and perhaps dangerous. In the draft of her statement, prepared by P. N. Haksar, her principal adviser, a clear announcement of a cease-fire in the west had in fact been included.

And yet, to Haksar's surprise and dismay, Indira left it out and confined herself to announcing the victory in Bangladesh. When Haksar asked for the reasons for the omission she only told him to ask General Manekshaw to see her and call a meeting of the cabinet's Political Affairs Committee.

A jubilant Manekshaw arrived and smartly saluted the Prime Minister. She asked him what the Army felt about a cease-fire in the west. He replied that, as always, the Army would 'obey the government's orders whatever they be' but he believed that to announce a unilateral cease-fire would be the 'right thing to do'.

Hardly had the Army chief gone back when the members of the Political Affairs Committee of the cabinet trooped in. Manekshaw came back, along with Admiral Nanda and Air Chief Marshal P. C. Lal, because the three service chiefs were required to be in attendance.

Indira raised the question of what to do on the western front. Only Jagjivan Ram responded to her poser. He had been, as we have noted, one of her two main lieutenants at the time of the Congress split. She had rewarded him with the Defence portfolio and by ignoring his tax evasion. But of late she had become distrustful of him, had taken to making fun of his propensity to amass wealth by methods that would not bear scrutiny and had totally ignored and bypassed him all through the Bangladesh war. She had dealt with the military chiefs directly or through a trusted aide, D. P. Dhar, a former Ambassador to the Soviet Union who was to become a cabinet minister later and then go back to Moscow as Ambassador.

A disgruntled Jagjivan Ram suggested that the Army's views ought to be ascertained. 'Well,' remarked a smiling Indira, 'let's ask your chief of the Army staff.' Manekshaw repeated to the meeting what he had said privately to Indira only a few minutes earlier. The meeting dispersed and Indira proclaimed an immediate cease-fire in the west.

The people of India knew nothing about this little drama behind the scenes. They were too busy lustily cheering and lionising Indira.

In far-away Washington Nixon and Kissinger were also busy – spreading the canard that Indira wanted to 'dismember' whatever was left of Pakistan but was deterred and compelled to order a cease-fire only because of American pressure, applied through the Soviet Union. A certain plausibility to this was lent by the coincidence that after the US decision to despatch the Seventh Fleet to the Bay of Bengal D. P. Dhar had gone to Moscow and on his return was accompanied by the Soviet Deputy Foreign Minister, V. V. Kuznetsov, who stayed in Delhi from December 12th until the end of the war.

When questioned by *Time* news magazine about all this, Indira retorted: 'I am not a person to be pressured – by anybody or any nations.'

For weeks the country was delirious with joy over the outcome of the Bangladesh war. It had liberated the people of Bangladesh, cut Pakistan down to size and made India the pre-eminent power in the region. The credit for all this was given, appropriately enough, to Indira.

Her victory over the Syndicate had won her much admiration. That over Pakistan in Bangladesh turned the admiration into adoration. In India the dividing line between political process and religious ritual tends to be blurred. Her countrymen – led, interestingly, by sophisticated leaders of opposition parties – hailed her as Durga, the eight-armed, tiger-riding, invincible goddess in the Hindu pantheon. The 'dumb doll' of yesteryear had come a very, very long way. Women, especially in villages, started worshipping her also as an incarnation of *Shakti* or female energy. Most men above a certain age fell in love with her in a platonic sort of way. On behalf of a 'grateful nation', President Giri awarded her Bharat Ratna, the highest honour the country can confer on its sons and daughters.

It was in this heady atmosphere that the ten million refugees from Bangladesh were sent back home with remarkable speed and smoothness. Elections were held in a number of states whose legislatures had reached the end of their tenure. In all these, including the Marxist citadel, West Bengal, the Prime Minister's party won hands down.

Indira was now at the pinnacle of her power and glory. *The Economist*'s description of her as the 'Empress of India' seemed apt. But from this Olympian peak, she had nowhere to go except down. No one, however, could have foreseen that the downhill slide would be so swift and so cruel, indeed so searing.

# 9   Down the Hill, Dismally

The afterglow of the victory in Bangladesh faded rather fast, and Indira soon ran into a very rough patch in her hitherto ascendant career. But before that happened, she managed to do one more thing right.

Having won the war she had to attend to the more arduous task of restoring peace to the subcontinent, hopefully a durable one. This she did by signing an agreement at Simla, an Indian hill station that had served as the summer capital during the Raj, with Zulfiqar Ali Bhutto, Pakistan's new ruler and the first to have been duly elected to his office. His party, as we have seen, had won eighty-one of 138 seats in the National Assembly from what was left of Pakistan. The discredited Yahya regime had no option but to transfer power to this able, articulate, arrogant and at times insufferable man.

Inordinately proud of his academic record at Oxford and Berkeley, Bhutto was contemptuous of Indira's intellectual attainments and made no secret of his opinion that the only things that made her 'look great' were her 'throne' and the 'name she carries'. Indira's opinion of him was even poorer than his of her. She 'distrusted' him completely and it took her some effort to overcome her reluctance to shake hands with him at Simla.

Even so, the two managed to hammer out a mutually acceptable accord. Bhutto even changed his opinion of Indira and told Indian journalists that she was 'really her father's daughter in every sense of the word; and when I say this I wish to add that I have always held Mr Nehru in the highest admiration'.

Indira did not want to humiliate Bhutto or Pakistan. But she wanted to use the opportunity to resolve the Kashmir issue once and for all. Bhutto's objective was to get back the 93,000 Pakistani POWs and the nearly 5,000 square miles of Pakistani territory occupied by India. Indira readily returned the bulk of the Pakistani territory except that in Kashmir, all of which India claimed as her own although Pakistan was in occupation of nearly a third of the state. But she told Bhutto that the prisoners-of-war could not be sent back without the concurrence of Bangladesh which, still unrecognised by Pakistan, was insisting on trying at least 195 Pakistani military personnel on well-documented charges of war crimes.

For his part, Bhutto said he could not formally declare the Kashmir issue as closed. But he did agree to the Indian demand that both countries undertake not to resort to force or threaten to use force in Kashmir and agree to settle the issue only bilaterally. In other words, foreign interference, mediation or arbitration was to be precluded. The 1949 cease-fire line in Jammu and Kashmir was redrawn into a new Line of Control which meant that the UN observers posted along the previous line no longer had any role to play.

Bhutto promised Indira – this later became a subject of controversy in both India and Pakistan about allegedly 'secret' clauses of the Simla agreement – that he would quickly recognise Bangladesh to facilitate the return of the POWs and also work for permanently settling the Kashmir dispute on the basis of the status quo. But he later dragged his feet on both his verbal commitments. It took another year to work out a trilateral agreement under which the Pakistani prisoners could go home with Bangladeshi consent and without any war crimes trials taking place.

Diplomatic, telecommunications, travel and trade links between India and Pakistan could not be re-established until 1976 and became possible largely because of Indira's initiative.

Indira's troubles began even before the ink on the Simla agreement was dry. Several of these, as we shall see, were the consequences of her own actions or inactions. Some arose from factors beyond her control. The worst of these was the renewed failure of rains after six successive good monsoons which, combined with the success of the Green Revolution, had virtually obliterated the memories of the savage drought during the first two years of Indira's prime ministership.

The weather gods could not have chosen a more difficult moment to turn hostile to Indira and her country. The overflowing government granaries had been all but emptied to feed the ten million refugees from Bangladesh. Other expenditure on the refugees and the heavier outlay on the war had also caused a budgetary deficit and a drain on the foreign exchange reserves. As food became scarce, prices soared. So did economic discontent. People enthused by Indira's radical and populist rhetoric were dismayed to find that she could not even deliver enough food, let alone keep her promise of banishing poverty and ensuring economic growth with social justice. Those who used to join exuberant rallies in support of her now started demonstrating against her government.

Indira's capacity to deal with the economic crisis, which acquired major dimensions within months, would have been greater had her party, advertised as the New Congress, not got into an awful mess and had Indira, even more damagingly, not allowed her own credibility and shining image to be eroded. The erosion resulted from mounting and increasingly plausible charges of corruption against the Prime Minister's henchmen. Critics said that these men were able to collect 'tons of black money', that is to say, money that never appeared in account books and on which no tax was paid, only because of 'her protection'.

Corruption was nothing new in India. It had been a part of the country's life from time immemorial, as testified by the ancient sage Kautilya in his masterpiece on statecraft, *Arthashastra*. Over the years, it had grown steadily. The heavy regulation of the economy by the state since independence had opened up new possibilities of graft for both politicians and civil servants. The amounts involved here were huge compared with which the petty corruption – pervasive at every level because palms had to be greased to get an electricity connection, buy a rail or bus ticket or secure other routine facilities – paled into insignificance.

However, people expected Indira Gandhi's party, committed to bringing socialism to the country, to be more honest and cleaner than the old undivided Congress. But this turned out to be a vain hope. On the contrary, compared with the amassing of wealth by some of her close associates, the misdeeds of the discarded Syndicate leaders, once looked upon as godfathers of corrupt Congressmen, began to appear trivial. Those shocked by the brazen loot and, even more, by Indira's apparent inability or unwillingness to do anything about it, were fobbed off with the explanation that funds had to be collected for the party or else it would be difficult to defeat the 'forces of reaction, backed by big money' in elections. Persistent critics of 'burgeoning' corruption were glibly denounced as 'spokesmen of vested interests' indulging in 'character assassination'.

There was a certain background to the frenzied fund-collection by Indira's party managers though it could not, of course, excuse their blatant excesses. During the 1967 General Election she had found, to her great annoyance, that though she was Prime Minister and the undivided Congress party's chief campaigner, the purse strings were 'tightly controlled' by the Syndicate which was 'denying' funds to her supporters while being 'generous' with its own nominees. Determined never again to be in the same predicament, Indira not only tended to exaggerate the importance of money in winning elections but also made a series of other mistakes.

One of these – born apparently of the fear that big business houses would donate liberally to the 'grand alliance' opposed to her and especially to the Swatantra party they themselves had promoted – was the imposition of a ban on political donations by joint stock companies. The immediate result of this was that, legal and straightforward contributions having been banned, illegal, under-the-table dealings started between political parties on the one hand and industrialists and businessmen on the other. A dangerous nexus between politics and black money came to be established. Collections in cash rather than cheques made it possible for fund collectors to siphon off a part of the collected hoard to their own pockets.

From this situation arose Indira's second error. Her father had taken care never to soil his own fingers with fund collection for the party. The task was usually assigned to an outstanding leader – Sardar Patel, Nehru's Deputy Prime Minister, Morarji Desai, and S. K. Patil, in that order – and he himself had nothing to do with it, except to ensure that there was no scandal. Indira decided to keep a tight control over the collection and disbursement of funds. Inevitably, it became a talk of the town that 'suitcases full of currency notes' were being routinely taken to the Prime Minister's house. S. K. Patil was quoted as having said that she 'did not return even the suitcases'.

Bitter contention accompanying the Congress split, the consequent breakdown of consensus in the country and the renewed polarisation of politics once the euphoria over the liberation of Bangladesh had evaporated and economic hardship had spread combined together to introduce two other damaging distortions in the collection of party funds.

In the old days of stability, donors contributed to the Congress as a general investment in the ruling party's goodwill; there was no direct link between a donation and official favours. In the changed atmosphere, the pattern of *quid pro quo* took over. Those expected to cough up huge amounts of cash wanted favours done for them there and then. The Prime Minister's principal fund collector, Lalit Narayan Mishra, who was made Minister of Foreign Trade just when funds were needed, was only too willing to do cosy deals with all comers. As if this was not enough, Mishra – whose name soon became a byword for financial hanky-panky and political skulduggery – also started threatening those unenthusiastic about filling the Congress (R) coffers with action under various economic laws. In a country where black money is estimated to be 'nearly half of the total currency in circulation', there are few businesses capable of withstanding strict legal scrutiny. In any case, there was no dearth of young entrepreneurs and even adventurers who were willing to give Mishra or his nominees any amount of money as long as they were given licences or other opportunities to enrich themselves. No wonder then that a great many 'new stars' appeared on India's industrial firmament soon after the 1971 General Election.

While angry charges and counter-charges about 'unlimited corruption' were being exchanged between Indira's party and its opponents, some strange happenings gave additional ammunition to those questioning her credibility and the probity of her government. Of these, the Nagarwala case was the most important and also the most bizarre.

On May 24th, 1971, Ved Prakash Malhotra (no relation of the author), chief cashier of the State Bank of India, received a phone call purporting to come from the Prime Minister. It instructed him to pay Rs sixty lakhs (roughly thirty-three thousand pounds those days) to a man waiting on a road who would identify himself as *Bangladesh ka Babu* (gentleman from Bangladesh). Malhotra took a taxi to the appointed spot and handed over the money to the man who turned out to be Rustom Sohrab Nagarwala, a former army captain who had also worked for Indian Intelligence.

Malhotra discovered that he had been taken for a ride only after he had rushed to the Prime Minister's house to report the completion of his 'mission' and to ask for a receipt.

Nagarwala, who had curiously left a tell-tale trail of his movements, was arrested the same day. It turned out that he was also an impersonator, for, as he confessed to the police, he had imitated Indira on the phone.

Parliament was understandably in an uproar. But no answers were forthcoming to some very pertinent questions: had the Prime Minister rung up Malhotra earlier? If not, how was he familiar with her voice? Could the cashier have drawn a large sum from the bank vaults unless there was a precedent for the transaction? And whose money was it, anyway?

In three days flat – a record in a country notorious for the law's unconscionable delays – Nagarwala was tried, convicted and sentenced to four years' rigorous imprisonment.

The mystery behind the Nagarwala case was never solved. Having confessed that he had 'fooled' Malhotra to collect money for the cause of Bangladesh and manfully accepted his sentence, Nagarwala developed second thoughts in jail. He started asking for a retrial and might have pressed his demand but for his death in jail in March 1972. He was known to be a heart patient, but this did not prevent the speculation that his death was unnatural. Tongues wagged even more furiously six months later when the police officer who had investigated the Nagarwala case with astonishing speed also died, in a car crash.

After Indira's defeat in the 1977 General Election, the Janata government appointed a number of commissions of inquiry against her and her second son, Sanjay. One of these was asked to unravel the Nagarwala mystery. It failed to find anything that might have compromised Indira. Two years after her death, New Delhi's *Hindustan Times* published detailed reports alleging that the CIA, with which Nagarwala had had close links, had used him to 'smear' and 'embarrass' Indira at a time when her policies on Bangladesh were proving inconvenient to the Nixon administration.

However, at the time it took place, the Nagarwala affair did a great deal of damage to Indira. Rumours were rife that she had stashed an 'enormous' amount of ill-gotten money and was using it as well as her complete control on the intelligence agencies for her purposes. Many believed that she was maintaining intelligence dossiers on her cabinet colleagues and state chief ministers to keep them in line.

The state of Indira's party was no better and perhaps a great deal worse than the image of her government. Instead of being reinvigorated, as she had promised it would be, the Congress (R) was sliding into decay. One of the reasons for this was that, having made sure that in the fight between Indira and the Syndicate they were on the winning side, most of the Prime Minister's supporters had no interest in changing their mental outlook, working methods, lifestyle, factional functioning and addiction to self-advancement by hook or by crook. The New Congress was indistinguishable from the Old. Members of the new party were discovering, however, that the only way to get on and get ahead was to gain and retain the goodwill of 'The Leader', as Indira was called now, and they happily resorted to every form of flattery and fawning to achieve this objective.

The process was accelerated by Indira's own preference to establish her unshakable supremacy in the ruling party and to cut down to size anyone in her ranks who could even remotely become a rival centre of power. Having seen twice that chief ministers had played an important role in the making of the Prime Minister, she wanted to make sure that in future the Prime Minister alone would make or unmake chief ministers. Nijalingappa's derided prophecy that she would make loyalty to her person the test of loyalty to the Congress and the country was coming true. Her followers seemed quite happy with this, and started vying with one another in proving to her that they were more loyal than the rest.

Indira used the 1972 state assembly elections to ease out four chief ministers – Mohan Lal Sukhadia of Rajasthan, Brahmananda Reddy of Andhra Pradesh, not to be confused with Sanjiva Reddy the defeated Presidential candidate, M. M. Chaudhury of Assam and S. C. Shukla of Madhya Pradesh – each of whom had a power base of his own. In their place and in other states, she installed her own trusted nominees who could not possibly have got elected in an unfettered poll in the legislature parties. Such party meetings were now mere formalities. On a famous occasion, all the 280 Congress members of the Legislative Assembly or provincial parliament of

Madhya Pradesh were asked to come to Delhi and hold a meeting on the lawns of the Prime Minister's house to elect a new leader.

While choosing state chief ministers in 1972, Indira tried a novel and bold experiment which won her some credit. She appointed a Muslim, Barkatullah Khan, as chief minister of Rajasthan, a state with an overwhelming Hindu majority. She then repeated this performance in Bihar where Abdul Ghafoor was made chief minister. Indira was to tell close associates that this was something 'even her father had never been able to do' and she was 'proud of it'.

Unfortunately, her pride was not vindicated by her two protégés. Though both were good and courtly men, they were also political lightweights and sadly bereft of administrative talent. Before long they had to be replaced. Thereafter, quick replacement of hand-picked chief ministers in states ruled by Indira's party became an established pattern.

Around the same time, Indira made an attempt to put some spirit into her followers by holding party elections which were expected to let the rank and file have a say in shaping the future power structure. But these elections had to be cancelled in midstream because she was inundated with complaints, verified by independent sources, of voting by legions of 'bogus' members, 'gross intimidation', 'mass bribery' and 'rank manipulation'. Party elections were never again held or even attempted for as long as Indira lived, and this legacy of hers persists to this day.

Another factor which was complicating life in the Congress (R) was the steadily heightening conflict between various factions of the more radical of Indira's followers. There were three separate strands among those wanting her and the Congress to take a pronouncedly leftist position. The first consisted of traditional Congressmen who genuinely felt for the poor and the downtrodden. Some of these were socially conservative while others were wedded to Nehru's modern outlook. But all were agreed that the party should follow economic policies tailored to the needs of the poor and the weak. The second, somewhat better organised, group comprised those who had joined the Congress in the Sixties after leaving a social democratic party, the Praja socialist party. Chandra Shekhar, Mohan Dharia and several other 'Young Turks' belonged to this group. It was jealous of and constantly at odds with the third and the most well-knit combination which consisted of former Communists. These were men and women who had drifted into the Congress after allowing their membership of the Communist Party of India (CPI) to lapse or because of expulsion from it. To the dismay of former socialists, the former Communists in the Congress (R) got a boost when, after the 1971 election, Indira made Mohan Kumaramangalam, a former CPI leader and a friend of

148

hers since her days in England where he was then a fellow student, her Minister for Steel and Mines. The nationalisation of the coal industry was one of his first acts.

Because of Indira's countrywide alliance with the CPI, the ex-Communists within the ruling party became even more powerful and influential. Around this time it was discovered, or at least alleged, that they had in fact joined the ruling party in pursuance of a 'thesis' propounded by Kumaramangalam. The essence of the 'Kumaramangalam thesis' was that since the Communist party by itself could not establish a socialist order, as many CPI members and sympathisers as possible should join the Congress, make common cause with 'progressive' Congressmen and compel the party leadership to implement its own socialistic policies.

This disclosure did not make much difference to the former Communists' position. On the contrary, they organised themselves into a Congress Forum for Socialist Action which acquired quite a clout. Former socialists and traditional Congressmen, disturbed by this development, formed a rival Nehru Forum. Indira, at first inclined to lean towards the Socialist Forum, started maintaining a balance between the two forums and later ordered that both be disbanded. This was duly done but in no way diminished the underlying and increasing hostility between the two sides.

Under the umbrella of Indira's 'undisputed and indisputable' leadership, a multiple power struggle went on among her followers. Lalit Narayan Mishra had set himself up as a centre of power and he had been joined by Bansi Lal, chief minister of Haryana, who had first attracted notice at the Faridabad session of the AICC that went up in smoke. Jagjivan Ram, who belonged to Bihar, as did Mishra, was most resentful of the latter's influence which had eclipsed his own. He was not the only one to be unhappy. D. P. Mishra, Indira's counsellor of a longer standing than his namesake, also advised her to 'clip the wings' of both the Communists and Lalit Mishra. This advice was endorsed by Uma Shankar Dikshit, another elderly confidant of Indira who was then her Home Minister. On the ex-socialists' demand that the alliance with the CPI be terminated, the two counsellors were divided. Indira accepted Dikshit's advice to reject the demand and ignored D. P. Mishra's plea for bidding farewell to the CPI.

Conflicting pressures and pulls, combined with the compulsion of harsh circumstances, led to confusion in both policy and personnel. Once again Indira was seen to be pursuing contradictory goals. The economic crisis and the consequent need for foreign aid, especially a standby credit from the IMF, required the abandonment of radical

149

policies and reversion to economic liberalisation and concessions to foreign investors. When radical ranks protested against this 'retreat from socialism' she felt obliged to make some radical gesture. One such was the imposition of ceilings on urban land ownership. Unexceptionable and even commendable in theory, in practice it impeded new construction of houses and thus pushed up house rents!

It was in this confused and confusing situation that some developments which were to have far-reaching repercussions in years to come took place. One of these was particularly fateful.

Lalit Mishra and Bansi Lal, playing upon Sanjay's ambition to be India's Henry Ford, brought the stain of corruption to the Prime Minister's own doorstep. They were working to a design aimed at pleasing Indira as a fond mother and at making her and her favourite son beholden to them.

In 1969, when Sanjay was in his early twenties he became one of a dozen applicants for a licence to manufacture what was grandiosely called the 'people's car' or an inexpensive vehicle for the masses. He claimed that this car would be wholly Indian without any imported components at all. His credentials to undertake such an ambitious venture were at best debatable. He was a drop-out from the Doon School, an élite institution in the Himalayan foothills, though his passion for cars was undoubted. Presumably for this reason his mother had sent him to Rolls-Royce in England to learn his chosen trade. But there also he had failed to complete the course.

No wonder then that there was an uproar in the country when Sanjay turned out to be the only applicant to get the coveted licence to set up his Maruti factory to produce 50,000 cars a year. Indira dismissed charges of nepotism and favouritism with a shrug of her slender shoulders. She told parliamentary questioners that licences were awarded not by her but by 'concerned ministries and committees'. She also said that a young man should not be 'prevented from doing something he was keenly interested in merely because he was the Prime Minister's son.'

Criticism of Sanjay and Maruti became even more strident when it became known that Bansi Lal had acquired three hundred acres of prime farm land in Haryana territory on Delhi's outskirts and given it to Sanjay as his factory site at 'artificially low prices and in violation of a regulation that prohibited plant construction within a thousand metres of a defence installation'.

Soon rumours began to circulate that Sanjay, exploiting his mother's name and helped by Lalit Mishra, had amassed vast sums of money by 'persuading' businessmen to invest in Maruti dealerships long before there was any hope of the first car rolling off the assembly line or even of the assembly line being set up. It was alleged that some big industrialists had set up *benami* or fictitious firms of investors to please Sanjay and, through him, his mother.

This was only the beginning of the troubles Sanjay and his pet project were to cause Indira. But any friend, well-wisher or adviser who drew Indira's attention to this or pointed out that Sanjay should refrain from taking up commercial activity while he stayed under the Prime Minister's roof immediately fell from grace. P. N. Haksar was the first to suffer this fate.

As 1972 drew to a close the heady days of Indira's victory in the 1971 General Election and the even more intoxicating triumph in the Bangladesh war were all but forgotten. Opposition parties, routed less than two years earlier, were getting ready to exploit the major slump in Indira's prestige even while her personal power within the ruling party and the country grew to the extent that she was already attracting the charge of being 'authoritarian'. The people's minds were on food which was becoming more and more scarce and when available steadily costlier.

Inevitably, food was also on top of the agenda of Indira's party when it met for its annual session at a temporary township built near Calcutta for this purpose and much criticised for its opulence and lavishness at a time of such widespread hunger.

Indira's usually reliable instinct for smelling danger must have deserted her at Bidhan Nagar, as the venue of the Congress session was called, or she must have felt some compelling need to refurbish her radical image, for she agreed to a decision to nationalise the wholesale trade in foodgrains, making government the sole buyer of wheat, beginning with the harvest of April 1973 and of rice starting with the crop of the subsequent October. Doubts and misgivings about embarking on this dangerous course, especially in a year of acute food shortage, were expressed by several delegates obviously familiar with the complexities of the food market but were brushed aside. Eventually the disastrous decision was scuttled, but not before it had caused havoc.

Food stocks began to disappear as soon as the decision was announced. Consumers unable to lay hands on grain panicked. The government was unable to help them. Food riots the country was spared even in 1966 now took place in Nagpur, Bombay and Mysore. In Kerala all schools and colleges were closed after students looted food trucks.

By the start of 1973, the magic slogan *Garibi Hatao* (Remove Poverty) had become an object of ridicule. While Indira gingerly explained that poverty could not be banished 'overnight', her critics declared poverty was not being removed, only the poor.

151

It was in this dismal atmosphere that the long-feared confrontation between Indira's government and the highest judiciary became a reality. At issue this time was the law that Indira had got enacted in 1971 restoring to Parliament untrammelled rights to amend the fundamental rights enshrined in the constitution – which really meant the power to abridge property rights. It was immediately challenged in the Supreme Court.

So strong were passions in the country both for and against the new constitutional amendment that the Chief Justice, S. M. Sikri, appointed a special bench consisting of all thirteen judges to consider it. They could not have been more divided among themselves and the majority with which they delivered their judgment in February 1973 could not have been narrower.

Six judges, headed by Chief Justice Sikri, pronounced against the government all the way. Six others, of whom A. N. Ray was the most senior, upheld the government almost fully. The deadlock was broken by Justice H. R. Khanna's verdict, though he agreed with the first six on some issues and with the other six on other points.

The net result of this terribly complex seven-to-six judgment was that Parliament was allowed to amend all parts of the constitution, subject to the restriction that its 'essential features' – such as its democratic, republican and federal character – were not destroyed. The examples cited in the judgment were illustrative, not exhaustive. What was or was not an essential feature of the constitution was left to the courts to decide.

The judgment was generally seen as Indira's defeat and she seemed to agree. Her supporters condemned it as an 'attack on Parliament and the Prime Minister'. Her 'enemies', they said, having been routed in elections, were now acting though the judiciary which had become a 'handmaiden of vested interests'. Opposition parties, now spear-headed by the Congress (O), and many newspapers and a large section of the legal profession, hailed the verdict as a 'necessary brake' on Indira's 'capriciousness'. Once again the rhetoric on both sides was heated. The atmosphere became as surcharged as before the Congress split.

By an interesting coincidence, the judgment was delivered just a day before Sikri's retirement. This enabled Indira to take dramatic retaliatory action which enraged her opponents, alarmed many who were not particularly hostile to her and delighted her supporters. The level of contention in the country rose fast.

From the days of Nehru the government had strictly followed the convention of appointing the most senior member of the bench as the Chief Justice whenever a vacancy arose. The idea was to avoid even the slightest suspicion of politics or the personal preference of the head of government affecting the choice of the Chief Justice who, though only the first among equals, plays a crucial role in guiding the courts and appointing the benches to hear particular cases.

If the established convention was to be followed, Sikri's successor would have been J. M. Shelat. But he was one of the six judges who had given a more restrictive interpretation of Parliament's powers and ruled against Indira's government. The next two judges on the seniority list, K. S. Hegde and A. N. Grover, had also joined Sikri and Shelat in rejecting the government's case.

Indira, egged on by her counsellors and confidants, decided to bypass all three senior judges and appoint as Sikri's successor A. N. Ray, most senior of the six judges who had ruled in favour of the government. The announcement hit the country like a thunderbolt. The Prime Minister's critics screamed that she had thrown to the winds a healthy convention in order to 'suborn' judges through the instrument of 'supersessions'. The large and traditionally influential legal community also condemned her for 'trying to destroy the judiciary's independence'. All three superseded judges resigned, and this added to the outcry.

The public's mood became fiercer when, during Parliament's angry debates, the government's view was put forward by Kumaramangalam, with his Communist past, rather than by the Law Minister, H. R. Gokhale.

In all this excitement and contention over the judiciary, some judicial proceedings in a dingy room at the Allahabad High Court, India's second oldest, went almost unnoticed.

Raj Narain, the grand alliance candidate defeated by Indira at Rae Bareli, had filed a petition challenging her election. It was being heard at a snail's pace entirely typical of the Indian judicial system – so much so, that two high court judges had retired one after another while still hearing the petition. The third, Jagmohan Lal Sinha, was still recording evidence.

Narain was a socialist and a stormy petrel. Sporting a shaggy beard and a ludicrous bandana as headgear, he was often dismissed as something of a buffoon. He had indeed been nicknamed the 'Clown Prince of India'. But, for all his exhibitionist and laughable ways, he was also a politician of unusual tenacity and persistence. He used to boast that he would see Indira out of office and power. Most people dismissed it as a wild dream, but his faith in his capacity to make good his boast was unshaken.

Indira, however, had other things to worry about than the excruciatingly slow-moving hearing of the election petition at Allahabad. The economic crisis had become very grave. Drought, affecting 180 million people, entered its second year in 1973 and would persist, in some areas, in 1974 and 1975 as well. Prices continued to rise. In mid-1973 they were twenty-two per cent higher than on the day Indira had accepted Bharat Ratna, the highest national award, at a glittering ceremony in Parliament House in January 1972. By August 1973 it was clear that the budgetary deficit, the trade gap and the drain on foreign reserves had all reached alarming proportions. Indira had to pocket her pride, forget all her brave declarations about self-reliance and appeal to the World Bank and the International Monetary Fund (IMF) for emergency help. It was available, but only on condition that economic policies were changed to the IMF's liking.

This meant backtracking on the economic strategy pursued since 1971. But Indira stoically swallowed the bitter pill. Manmohan Singh, one of her top economic advisers, said after her death that he was 'struck by the courage' with which Indira tied up an 'anti-inflationary policy package' in 1973–4. When told that almost all the elements in her policy would be 'politically unpopular', she commented: 'What is required to be done, must be done.'

Courage, however, was no antidote to the mounting wave of industrial unrest and political turmoil caused as much by economic hardship as by the spreading belief that Indira's regime was becoming synonymous with 'unbridled corruption' and 'creeping authoritarianism'. In Bombay alone, where I then lived, there were no fewer than 12,000 strikes and sit-in protests during 1972–3. There were strikes, protest marches and clashes with the police in most parts of the country. Students, in the forefront of the turmoil, went on the rampage in place after place. In the key state of UP in May 1973 there was a mutiny by the Provincial Armed Constabulary. The Army, called out to control the situation, could do so only after thirteen Army soldiers and twenty-two rebellious PAC men had been killed and over a hundred injured.

One of the anti-inflationary measures Indira had taken was to slash government expenditure. This meant increased unemployment and greater discontent. A part of the wages of almost all salaried employees was immobilised through a scheme of compulsory deposits. Those unable to make ends meet at the best of times cried 'foul'. To placate them and to enforce 'equality of sacrifices' she also placed a ceiling on dividends. But, as her critics pointed out, slimmer dividends did not affect the lavish lifestyle of the rich, while the cut in the already paltry wages of the poor was very unkind indeed.

A major upheaval, brewing in the western state of Gujarat, the home state of both Mahatma Gandhi, the Father of the Nation, and Morarji Desai, Indira's principal rival, erupted early in January 1974. It brought into sharp focus all that was going wrong in Indira's India.

It was also to change the entire tone of Indian politics and perhaps change the course of modern India's history.

Indira was being denounced as a 'dictator' by her opponents and deified as the 'supreme leader' by her fawning supporters. And yet her writ often did not run in her own party. In Gujarat, as in other states, she had given the office of chief minister to an estimable but inconsequential party man, Ghanshyam Oza, whose main claim to fame was total loyalty to her. He could not hold down his job and was toppled by a wily rival, Chimanbhai Patel.

Though she disliked Patel, Indira not only resigned herself to his manoeuvre but also sought his help to raise funds for state assembly elections in UP and Orissa which were due in February 1974. Patel was delighted to oblige. His method of collecting funds was typical of ruling party politicians. He asked 'oil kings' in a state where the cooking oil industry has a commanding position to make the necessary donations in return for a virtual licence to push up as much as they liked the price of cooking oil, in very short supply because of continuing drought.

The issue of corruption and Indira's party's links with 'hoarders and profiteers' thus came to the fore. Parliament in the meantime was unable to transact any business because of daily disruption of proceedings for nearly a year over a scandal called the 'Tulmohan Ram affair'. Ram was an inarticulate MP from Bihar, a state which Lalit Narayan Mishra, Indira's main fund-raiser and Foreign Trade Minister, was running like a fiefdom. Mishra persuaded him and some other MPs from his state to sponsor an application for industrial licences to some dubious parties in distant Pondicherry with which these MPs had nothing whatever to do. After much resistance and reluctance Indira referred the matter to the Central Bureau of Investigation and shifted Mishra from Foreign Trade to Railways. But she refused to make public the Central Bureau of Investigation's findings, fuelling the suspicion that she had something to hide.

In Gujarat, unlike in Parliament, popular anger could not be controlled. For more than ten weeks the state was in virtual anarchy. At one time a curfew had to be imposed in Ahmedabad and 105 other cities and towns. Looting of shops, burning of buses and government property and attacks on the police became routine. Before the dust finally settled, 103 people had been killed, 300 injured and more than 8,000 arrested.

Its intensity was not, however, the most distinctive feature of the Gujarat agitation, though this by itself was an important enough cause for concern. There were two other really ominous implications of the Gujarat uprising which were to have lasting and far-reaching consequences for the country.

In the first place, what had begun as a movement against high prices and corrupt practices in the ruling party soon turned into a vigorous campaign for a wider transformation under the banner 'Nav Nirman' or movement for regeneration. In other words, the challenge to the legitimacy of Indira's leadership turned into a challenge to the 'legitimacy of the entire system she presided over'.

It was no coincidence that the Nav Nirman movement zeroed in on the objective of securing Chimanbhai Patel's resignation and the dissolution of the Gujarat state assembly or provincial Parliament. Since several Congress leaders of Gujarat were also against his continuance in office Indira was quite happy to let him go. But she baulked at the demand for the legislature's dissolution. She kept it in suspended animation in the hope that another Congress (R) ministry would soon take over. The popular sentiment against her was much too strong, however. She was compelled to dissolve the assembly even though her party had a two-thirds majority in it.

While conceding this demand Indira insisted that she and her party had become targets of a 'powerful conspiracy' backed by hostile foreign elements. Shankar Dayal Sharma, the President of her party, had been saying openly that the CIA was behind Indian vested interests wanting to defeat the 'progressive forces in India'. At the height of the Gujarat agitation, reports appeared in Ahmedabad newspapers that political officers of the US Consulate-General in Bombay had been meeting 'certain elements in the Gujarat ministry' in an attempt to cause a 'political setback to Mrs Gandhi'.

The second feature of the Gujarat episode was even more damaging. Independent India was no stranger to street violence by the government's opponents and its repression of them, often with excessive force. But all through the preceding quarter of a century neither side had transgressed certain self-imposed limits. In Gujarat, for the first time, this mutual restraint broke down. The underlying reason was a total collapse of belief in each other's good faith. 'Each side,' wrote Francine Frankel, an astute American political scientist and specialist in South Asia, 'became convinced that the other would no longer abide by the rules of democratic politics. Each justified its excesses in the interest of safeguarding democracy from the assaults mounted on it by the other.'

It was against this grim background that the much-respected Jayaprakash Narayan or J.P. emerged from self-exile to canalise stray and often directionless protests against Indira and her style of government into a powerful and unified, though not necessarily coherent, movement which soon became national, in both scope and significance.

\*     \*     \*

The country, it seemed, was waiting for J.P. to ascend the stage and swing into action. In his younger days he had been an ardent socialist but later he preferred to be a Gandhian. He was the last lingering link with the stalwarts of the freedom struggle. Not even a whiff of scandal had ever attached itself to him. And although he could sometimes be naive – as, for instance, in welcoming and commending to his countrymen the 'basic democracy' of the Pakistani military dictator, Field-Marshal Ayub – he had won a saintly halo by renouncing power and even active politics.

It was his great moral authority, at a time when Indira's moral authority had been heavily compromised, to say the least, that enabled J.P. to become a rallying point for all the national sentiment directed against her and effectively to challenge her formidable power.

A year earlier, at the time of the supersession of the three Supreme Court judges, J.P. had irritated Indira by writing to her to criticise her action and to express his fear that the 'very foundations' of Indian democracy might be 'destroyed'. In a curt reply she had stated that J.P.'s letter was part of a 'concerted attempt to decry me and the very policies for which Jawaharlal Nehru stood'.

Earlier still, when J.P. had displayed no antipathy to her, at any rate not publicly, Indira, in a letter to Dorothy Norman, had described him as a 'frustrated man', and added: 'Right now his theme is that I am the "world's great dictator". This is Morarji Desai's bandwagon with the Jana Sangh on one hand and Communist extremists on the other.'

But however great her dislike of J.P., Indira had to contend with the power and the sweep of the agitation he was leading. What came to be known as the J.P. Movement began in Bihar and was, at first, confined to this state. Like Gujarat's Nav Nirman movement, the Bihar agitation was aimed at securing the resignation of the state's Congress (R) government and dissolution of the assembly although the overwhelming majority Indira's party enjoyed in it was intact. But there the similarity between the two situations ended.

In Gujarat, there was spontaneity behind the agitation which had begun as a protest by students' committees without any political affiliations. Opposition parties had got into the act later. In Bihar, the movement was organised and the cadres of opposition parties – particularly the youth wing of the right-wing Hindu party, the Jana Sangh – provided it with muscle.

The opposition parties had good reason to be in the forefront of J.P.'s movement. In February 1974, when the Nav Nirman agitation in Gujarat was still on and all over the country disenchantment with Indira was widespread, her party had won the state assembly elections in UP and Orissa. This showed that Indira's hold on the former untouchables, Muslims and other minorities and the poor in general was still unshaken. But another reason for her victory at the polls was the chronic disunity within the opposition parties and groups. In the crucial state of UP, the congress (O) had won a working majority of seats with only thirty-four per cent vote. All the resources at the government's disposal were unabashedly used to further the Congress (R)'s chances.

J.P. was denouncing all this and the opposition parties hoped that his towering leadership and the common struggle would forge the bonds of opposition unity which had so far remained an unattainable goal.

This time Indira, having been forewarned by the events in Gujarat, was forearmed in Bihar. She dug in her heels against J.P.'s demands and mobilised the Bihar armed police as well as the central government's paramilitary organisations, such as the Border Security Force and the Central Reserve Police, to suppress the agitation. Militant students started an orgy of violence; they were met with even stronger counter-violence by the state. Their plans to intimidate Congress members of the state assembly to resign were thwarted. Visitors to Bihar noted that the whole state looked like a 'vast armed camp' at an approximate daily cost of 'a lakh of rupees (nearly five thousand pounds) a day', a large sum by Indian standards.

As the J.P. Movement gathered momentum, Indira's belief that she was the victim of a 'well-laid conspiracy' was strengthened by a countryside railway strike, hurriedly organised by a maverick socialist trade unionist and former Jesuit priest, George Fernandes. The country was still in the midst of the economic crisis and food continued to be scarce. Convinced that the railway strike, if allowed to succeed, would lead to mass starvation and open up the floodgates for demands for wage increases, Indira decided to put it down at all costs.

Accordingly, the strike, which began early in May 1974, was crushed with a degree of brutality India had never before witnessed. More than 20,000 railwaymen were arrested. Families of those absenting themselves from work were thrown out of railway quarters and many strikers were beaten up. According to Tariq Ali, by no means unsympathetic to Indira though his commitment to the working class is more pronounced, the campaign against the strikers was 'personally conducted by Indira Gandhi, who was reported as telling a cabinet colleague in favour of mediation that once this strike had been crushed, there would not be another for fifty years. The whole operation was, in fact, conducted like a war.'

There were Indians who were appalled by the brutality with which the railwaymen had been treated. But most of her middle-class countrymen, including those who accused her of authoritarianism, applauded Indira for her 'firmness' in dealing with the railway strike.

Their dichotomy was easily explicable. They did not want their own rights and privileges to be touched. Many, if not most, of them were also sticklers for all the Westminster norms being observed in Delhi, and were angry when Indira failed to do so. But they also wanted the trains to run regularly and did not want aggressive trade unionists to hold the country, or any business for that matter, to ransom.

The country applauded Indira even more enthusiastically in September 1974 when she cracked down heavily on smugglers, foreign exchange manipulators and other economic offenders. The smuggling of gold, consumer durables unavailable in India, Scotch and foreign cigarettes and narcotics had become one of the biggest businesses in India. It was also the most blatant. Smuggled goods were openly sold and eagerly bought. Leading smugglers were not only well known and fabulously rich but had also become legendary figures, rather like the Mafia godfathers. Most of them had the best of relations with politicians in power whose elections they funded and were also on excellent terms with police and customs officials.

On September 17th, the situation changed radically. In a pre-dawn swoop, 134 leading smugglers in the country were arrested and detained for two years.

This had been made possible by an ordinance signed earlier that morning by the new President, Fakhruddin Ali Ahmed, one of Indira's loyal lieutenants, who was elected to his exalted office in August after the rather reluctant retirement of V. V. Giri, who was much hurt by Indira's refusal to let him have a second term.

The round-up of the dons of the smuggling business was not the only popular and beneficial measure taken by Indira during a period when she was besieged by turmoil aimed at overthrowing her. She was able to achieve a great deal else, especially in the fields of technology and foreign policy in which she was specially interested.

On May 18th, 1974, the country temporarily forgot the railway strike, then still on, and the J.P. Movement, to hail a landmark in its history. Early that morning, India became the sixth member of the Nuclear Club, the world's most exclusive. At a place called Pokharan in the Rajasthan desert, scientists of the Atomic Energy Commission had successfully detonated a nuclear device underground and thus made India the sixth nuclear nation. Though several countries called it a nuclear test, Indira and her government insisted that it was a peaceful nuclear experiment (PNE). Indira was given credit for this development and she deserved it because without her support the project would not have been feasible. But the joy and gloating over the PNE was even more short-lived than that over the victory in Bangladesh.

Indeed, many of her critics started saying that Indira had ordered the nuclear test simply to divert attention from her 'misdeeds' and the mass agitation they had engendered. This was clearly unfair criticism. In order for it to be conducted in May 1974, the PNE had to be ordered early in January 1972 when Indira was at the peak of her popularity and therefore in no need of a diversionary move. To make India self-reliant in nuclear technology was an important element in her policy and she always acted in pursuit of it. At the same time, she emphatically maintained that her nuclear policy was entirely peaceful and that she did not want the country to go in for nuclear weapons. As we shall see later, this remained her policy until the end.

Like the euphoria over the nuclear explosion, satisfaction over the arrests of smugglers also subsided rapidly. Before long smuggled goods were back on the pavements of Bombay, the main centre of smuggling, and in other cities. It was business as usual in the underworld even though the godfathers were still in jail where they were in a position to secure every luxury they wanted.

In the cruel world of Indian politics, however, the Maintenance of Internal Security Act, made more Draconian than before by the presidential ordinance of September 17th, was now being used against Indira's political opponents who had nothing whatever to do with smuggling. Few foresaw that this was only a prelude to worse things.

In the area of foreign policy Indira brought off a virtual coup by dramatically improving India's relations with Iran which, under the leadership of the Shah, had become an important regional power. After the 1971 war, the Shah had taken up cudgels on behalf of Iran's ally, Pakistan. He had warned India that any attempt to dismember what was left of Pakistan would be resisted by Iran. Indians watched unhappily as the Shah proclaimed himself Pakistan's 'armourer and protector'.

Through painstaking and largely secret diplomacy – in which she was helped by P. N. Haksar and her very able Foreign Minister, Swaran Singh – Indira convinced the Shah of India's total lack of interest in promoting chaos or instability in Pakistan or any other country in India's neighbourhood. For his part, the Shah saw the advantage to his own country of close economic and political co-operation with India. In October 1974, during a state visit to India that caused much heartache in Pakistan, he praised Indira and signed several agreements for large-scale Indo-Iranian collaboration.

Shortly after the Shah had returned to Teheran, Indira also brought to an end a nagging problem that was causing her government some concern. Sikkim, a tiny Himalayan kingdom wedged between India and China, adjacent to the strategic Chumbi Valley, had been a British protectorate until 1947 and an Indian one since then. By the Seventies

The Nehru clan into which Indira was born. Her grandfather, Motilal, standing in the
middle of the back row is flanked by his son and her father, Jawaharlal (left), and
R. S. Pandit, husband of Indira's elder aunt, Vijayalakshmi Pandit. Indira herself is in the
arms of her grandmother, Swarup Rani.

Indira's own family of which she became 'as protective and possessive a matriarch as her
grandfather was the patriarch of the larger Nehru clan'. From left to right, standing,
sons Rajiv and Sanjay; seated, Rajiv's wife Sonia, Indira and Sanjay's wife Maneka.
Rajiv's and Sonia's two children, son Rahul and daughter Priyanka, are also in the .
picture.

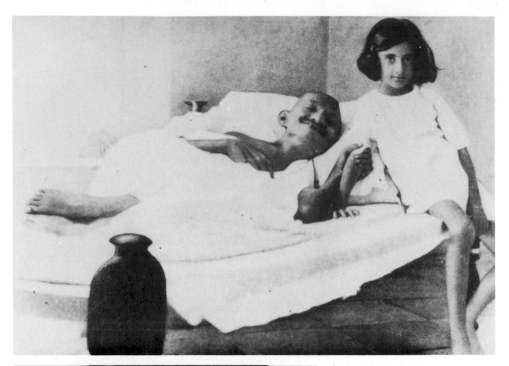

Indira, then six years old, with Mahatma Gandhi, Father of the Nation, and no kinsman of Feroze Gandhi whom she was to marry eighteen years later.

Indira at fourteen with her parents. Her unconventional dress gave her a boyish look and led many to the mistaken belief that she was Jawaharlal Nehru's son.

Indira and her husband, Feroze Gandhi, at their wedding on March 26th, 1942. Special vedic hymns had to be chosen for the ceremony because the bride, a Hindu, and the bridegroom, a Parsi, belonged to different religions and neither would think of conversion to the religion of the other.

Indira with Edwina Mountbatten, her father and her son Rajiv. Nehru and Edwina were very close to each other and many believed them to be lovers.

Indira being sworn in as Minister for Information and Broadcasting in the cabinet of Lal Bahadur Shastri, her father's successor and her own predecessor as Prime Minister.

Outside Parliament House on January 19th, 1966, immediately after being elected Prime Minister.

With President Lyndon
Johnson in the White
House, April 1966.

The two Iron Ladies: Indira
and Margaret Thatcher, who
developed an easy rapport,
had both gone to Somerville
College, Oxford, though at
different times.

With the troops at the time of the Bangladesh War.

At the site of the underground nuclear explosion at Pokharan in Rajasthan, western India, on May 18th, 1974.

Empress of India, the sobriquet earned by Indira after India's spectacular victory in the war with Pakistan in 1971 which led to the liberation of Bangladesh, formerly East Pakistan. The caricature is by India's most famous cartoonist, R. K. Laxman.

Indira, a doting grandmother, with her first grandson, Rahul.

its ambitious ruler, the Chogyal, married to an American, started claiming sovereign status in the hope of being able to play off India and China against each other. With a whole Indian Army corps in Sikkimese territory, vital for Indian defence, Indira just could not tolerate a Sikkimese regime hostile to India.

After brief agitation in Gangtok, the Sikkimese capital, by the local population, which was almost certainly encouraged by New Delhi, the Chogyal agreed to make his kingdom an 'associate state' of India. Early in 1975 Indira completed the process of Sikkim's merger with India and made it Indian territory.

While the country generally welcomed this, it was also criticised by some. Morarji Desai protested against this 'annexation'. But as Prime Minister only two years later he refused to undo what he had considered to be wrong.

Apart from these few achievements, there was little to cheer Indira. The national scene could not have been gloomier. J.P.'s Movement had reached its height and he, breaking out of the confines of Bihar, had made it a countrywide crusade against Indira and the 'widespread corruption' and 'distortion of the democratic process' bred by her.

There were chinks in J.P.'s own shining armour also. For instance, this lifelong Gandhian was now 'justifying violence'. Taunted by Indira that he had found himself such 'communal' allies as the cadres of the Rashtriya Swayamsevak Sangh (RSS), the storm-troopers of the Jana Sangh, he had started saying that if the RSS was communal, then so was he himself. He had also gone back on his earlier promise to take on Indira in the elections due to be held in 1976. But he had done so on the grounds that Indira was 'destroying' democracy so fast that the elections might not be held. Through his movement, he added, he did want to drive Indira out of power, but his real objective was wider – to usher in 'total revolution'.

This was a vague, even woolly, concept that was never fully defined. Some thinking Indians, not necessarily out of sympathy with J.P., pointed out that the concept could even be dangerous. For instance, Sham Lal, Editor of *The Times of India* at that time, after inquiring: 'What kind of revolution can it be which can dispense with a strategy, a vanguard and even cadres?' pointed out that the only thing J.P. and the opposition parties rallied round him were agreed on was to 'oust' Indira and the Congress from power. This, he added pertinently, would 'replace a comparatively well-knit coalition of interests with a loose federation of interests' thus creating a 'political climate propitious not for a revolution but for anarchy'. But his was a voice in the wilderness.

So hostile was the articulate public opinion to Indira and so much in favour of J.P. that he was being viewed as a saviour. Not only was his talk of 'total revolution' lapped up but also his meaningless concept of a 'partyless democracy'. He was travelling at a fast and furious pace all through the country and was drawing large, enthusiastic crowds wherever he went. Indira, by contrast, stayed in Delhi.

This was not the only reversal of roles. In the past, the political initiative was usually Indira's. Now it had passed into J.P.'s hands. Most of the time she only reacted to what he said or did.

A significant outcome of J.P.'s Movement was a change of mood among a substantial number of Congress MPs. Many of them held J.P. in high esteem and felt that instead of confronting him, Indira should try to conciliate him. Some of them plucked up enough courage to say so to her. Under their pressure she reluctantly agreed to meet J.P. The meeting that took place at the Prime Minister's house in November 1974 was a disaster.

On arrival, J.P. was infuriated to find that Indira was flanked by Chavan and Jagjivan Ram. He was under the impression that he and she would talk by themselves. Indira, aware that J.P. was 'banking' on Ram and Chavan to 'revolt against her', had chosen to put all three in a tight corner.

Ram and Chavan remained silent. Exchanges between Indira and J.P. were sharp and acrimonious. She alleged that his movement was being 'financed' by his 'wealthy friends under the influence of Americans'. He retorted that she was leading India towards a 'Soviet-backed dictatorship'.

The two were not to meet again until after Indira's defeat in the 1977 General Election. But, unknown to most people, including Ram and Chavan, there was a poignant aside to the painfully futile meeting between Indira and J.P. Asking to see her alone, J.P. handed Indira a bundle of yellowing but carefully preserved papers, neatly wrapped in a folder. These were letters written by her mother, Kamala Nehru, during the Twenties and the early Thirties, to J.P.'s wife, Prabha Devi, who had died a year earlier.

Kamala and Prabha, both neglected by their husbands absorbed in the freedom struggle, had become good friends though Prabha was much younger, just as J.P. was a good twelve years younger than Nehru. The letters were full of Kamala's account of the humiliation she had to suffer at the hands of the Nehru women which, if made public, would have been most embarrassing to the Prime Minister. J.P. had first become aware of the existence and contents of these letters only when he started putting together his wife's effects after her death. He took the 'first opportunity to hand the letters over to Indira'.

This noble gesture did nothing to arrest the steady descent of the Indira–J.P. confrontation into a no-holds-barred fight to the finish.

From this time onwards, J.P. started calling upon the armed forces and the police to disobey her 'illegal orders' and appealing to Jagjivan Ram and Chavan to ditch her and join the struggle to overthrow her.

If 1974 had been for Indira more turbulent and troublesome than the preceding year, 1975 began on an even more traumatic note. On the third day of the new year, Lalit Narayan Mishra was killed at the Samastipur railway station by a timebomb buried under the rostrum from which he was addressing a meeting. He was the first Indian cabinet minister to be assassinated.

Indira and her supporters immediately blamed the murder on the 'cult of violence and hatred' spread by J.P. and his flock of opposition parties. They hit back in kind, alleging that her own government had got rid of Mishra because he had become an 'embarrassment to her'. Mishra's own family complained about 'apparently deliberate delay' in giving him medical aid and the 'laxity' of security at the Samastipur meeting. The suspicion that some government agency might have been behind the assassination spread fast.

There came a stage when Indira publicly protested that 'even Congressmen' were 'being misled by the blatant lies' linking her to the crime. Vigorously denying the charge, she declared that the Mishra murder was only a 'rehearsal' of things to come of which she was the 'real target'. And she added with some emotion: 'When I am murdered, they will say I arranged it for myself.'

Mohan Dharia, a 'Young Turk' and a junior minister, infuriated Indira further by condemning 'police brutality' on those agitating under J.P.'s leadership and declaring that Indira should negotiate with J.P. again. She asked for Dharia's resignation within the hour, which he submitted. But she must have noticed that exclusion from the council of ministers had 'suddenly boosted his popularity, even among Congressmen'.

Indira also watched helplessly when a march on Parliament, led by J.P., turned out to be one of the biggest demonstrations the Indian capital had ever seen. But a bigger blow was to hit her a few days later.

On April 2nd, Morarji Desai, then seventy-nine, protesting that Indira was unfairly delaying elections in his home state of Gujarat where the assembly had been dissolved in January 1974, announced that he would fast unto death unless the elections were conceded immediately. Indira argued that elections could be held only after the drought was over, otherwise relief to the suffering people would be hindered. Desai described this as a specious argument and claimed that Indira's real reason was her fear that she would lose, as she had lost a number of by-elections in various parts of the country.

Backed enthusiastically by J.P., who accused Indira of 'rape of democracy', Desai duly went on an indefinite fast. For a week Indira weighed the pros and cons of allowing a respected and elderly leader to die and accepted Desai's demand on the seventh day. Her opponents went wild with delight over her 'capitulation'.

The Gujarat elections were fixed for early June. Indira, having spent the bulk of May electioneering in that state, was getting ready to go to Mexico City at the end of June to be a star speaker at the first-ever UN Conference on Women. Pupul Jayakar, designated one of the members of her delegation, was leaving for New York a month earlier. She came to bid the Prime Minister goodbye, and before leaving said: 'See you in Mexico.'

Indira gave her a dazzling smile but added: 'You know, there is that judgment yet to come.' Jayakar thought the remark to be odd but paid it no attention.

June is the hottest, dustiest and the most trying month in India. Temperatures can be as high as 110 in the shade. Tempers can be very short. In the midst of a bitterly fought election in Gujarat and the even more bitter Indira–J.P. conflict, they were shorter than usual. Everyone was on edge.

On June 12th, the votes cast in the Gujarat poll a day earlier were to be counted. At the Allahabad High Court, Justice Jagmohan Lal Sinha chose this day to deliver his momentous judgment on Raj Narain's election petition against Indira. To prevent its leakage, he had written the operative part of his lengthy judgment in his own hand.

Though not entirely unexpected, his verdict stunned the country. He not only set aside her election from Rae Bareli in 1971 but also debarred her from elective office for six years. The 'corrupt electoral practices' she had been convicted of were minor and technical. Government officers and engineers had built the rostrums at her election meetings and her private secretary, Yashpal Kapoor, had become her election agent before his resignation from government service had become effective.

J.P. and all others tirelessly working to overthrow Indira were jubilant. Justice Sinha had suspended the operation of his judgment for twenty days to enable the ruling party to 'make alternative arrangements'. But Indira's moral as well as legal position had now collapsed completely. She had no option but go. Or so her opponents thought. She, however, seemed to be having other ideas. No one yet expected it, but within a fortnight she would be ready with a counter-stroke that would make her beaming tormentors wonder what exactly had hit them.

# 10    Emergency: The Cardinal Sin

Within hours of the Allahabad High Court's judgment, election results in Gujarat started coming in. Immediately, it was clear that Indira's party had lost to a hurriedly cobbled-up combination of opposition parties, masterminded by J.P. and called the Janata Front. Her cup of misery was full to the brim.

It is arguable, to say the least, that had the judgment against Indira come during the heyday of her popularity – say, immediately after the Bangladesh war – it would have been shrugged off by the country. But during the intervening three years the national mood had changed completely. Few were prepared even to concede that the charges she had been convicted of were trivial. It was left to foreigners like James Cameron to point out that it was 'as though a head of government should go to the block for a parking ticket'. The cry from one end of India to the other was that 'Indira Must Go'. J.P. declared that her continuation in office would be 'incompatible with the survival of democracy in India'.

Justice Sinha's judgment was, of course, subject to appeal in the Supreme Court, and there was more than an even chance that Indira would win the appeal. The real and agonising question was what was to happen during the four to six months the Supreme Court was likely to take to hear and decide the appeal. Her legal claim to stay in office would be strengthened if the Supreme Court would give her an unconditional stay of the Allahabad verdict. But all precedent went against this expectation. In all such cases in the past the stay had been conditional. A disqualified minister or MP could, while his or her appeal was pending, take part in Parliament's proceedings but could not vote. A Prime Minister placed in this awkward position could hardly be effective though it is a safe bet that even in the event of an unconditional stay, J.P. and other opponents of Indira would have raised the most strenuous objections to her continuing as Prime Minister.

It was on this point that hectic consultations were taking place at the Prime Minister's house. Almost all her cabinet colleagues had trooped there on getting the first word from Allahabad. But their role was largely peripheral. Indira, while keeping her own counsel, was listening only to a handful of confidants.

For a while on the fateful day of June 12th, 1975, it seemed that Indira was inclined to step down temporarily, put into her office the

165

able and unambitious Swaran Singh who was unlikely to behave like the proverbial cuckoo in the nest, and return to power after her appeal was upheld by the Supreme Court and her prestige restored. But this turned out to be a feint. And, in retrospect, it became abundantly clear that she never had any intention of laying down office even for a minute.

The most conclusive evidence for this came from herself, though several years later when she was out of power. Breaking her habitual silence on this subject, she told Dom Moraes, one of her many biographers, that she had no option but to stay in office after the Allahabad judgment because the country was 'in peril from both internal and external enemies' and that there was 'no one else' around who could cope with the 'grave threat'. Evidently, her faith in her indispensability was never shaken.

On the day of the Allahabad verdict, however, she did keep the option of temporary withdrawal from office open to discussion. There were several among Indira's friends and well-wishers who were convinced that stepping down from office until the Supreme Court had pronounced on her appeal would be in the best interests of both · herself and the country. But they either kept quiet or expressed themselves most gingerly.

Unusually strident, by contrast, were the hordes of those who argued that stepping down from office should not even be contemplated. This, they maintained, was precisely what the country's 'enemies' wanted. Most cabinet ministers, almost all Congress chief ministers and a large number of MPs joined this chorus. They were anxious to display their loyalty to Indira, of course. But their main concern was to preserve their own positions in the Indira-built power structure the whole of which, they feared, might collapse if she was out of office even temporarily.

The kind of dangers that might arise if Indira did step down also became apparent during the short few hours when the option was considered and rejected. Jagjivan Ram, the alienated Defence Minister, let it be known that, under Indira, he would serve loyally and happily. But if she thought of making Swaran Singh Prime Minister even temporarily, he would assert his 'superior' claim. The Intelligence Bureau reported to her – inaccurately, as it later turned out – that some elements were demanding that Chavan should be the temporary Prime Minister. A month earlier, forty Congress MPs had met at the residence of Mohan Dharia, the dismissed junior minister. Chandra Shekhar, a leading 'Young Turk', had presided. The consensus at the meeting was that efforts should be renewed to persuade Indira to seek a settlement with J.P. The meeting was held in great secrecy, so the country did not know anything about it. But Indira knew exactly what had gone on. She had begun to feel that she was faced with not only an external conspiracy but also one within her own ranks.

It was the Prime Minister's second and favourite son, Sanjay, who put an end to the 'nonsensical' talk of his mother's temporary withdrawal from office. He had doubtless the most to lose by any such development because, after the award of the Maruti car licence to him, he had become one of her influential advisers. Indeed, he now had the most to gain from the decision to disregard the legal and moral implications of the Allahabad judgment. In a matter of months, he would become the second most powerful person in India.

Sanjay's edict, ruling out all talk in his mother's party about her temporary withdrawal from office, at once became the signal for an outbreak of mass hysteria on both sides of the great divide. The Prime Minister's camp, reverting to its favourite technique of holding rallies at her doorstep, diverted buses from Delhi's notoriously inadequate transport service to neighbouring states to bring in villagers mobilised by faithful chief ministers.

J.P. and his supporters were outraged. To demand Indira's resignation, they resorted not only to mass rallies and protest marches but also to a daily sit-in at Rashtrapati Bhavan, the presidential palace, by leading opposition MPs. One of the protesters, a Falstaffian character named Piloo Moody, carried around his neck a medallion proclaiming 'I am a CIA Agent'. This was his way of ridiculing Indira's claim that her opponents were being 'manipulated' by the American intelligence agency and other foreign elements hostile to India.

On the other hand, Indira's determination to stay on in office received powerful – and, to her, extremely useful – support from an unexpected quarter. Nani Palkhivala was then, as he continues to be, one of the most eminent constitutional lawyers of India. He was also a top executive in the country's largest industrial conglomerate, the Tatas. His sympathies had traditionally been with the political parties of the right opposed to Indira, though he was not an active politician himself. It was he who had successfully argued in the Supreme Court against Indira on the issues of bank nationalisation and the abolition of the privy purses of former princes. Early in 1975, he had published a book, *The Constitution, Defaced and Defiled*, generally critical of the amendments to the constitution enacted by her.

Some time before the Allahabad verdict, however, he appeared to have become less critical of Indira. On the day of the judgment, he was in Delhi, rather than Bombay where he normally lived. When others rushed to the Prime Minister's house on their own, he was the only one to be sent for. He not only agreed to argue her appeal in the Supreme Court but also said that there was no legal or political reason for her to step down during the hearing of her appeal. His admirers were aghast and criticised him sharply. He was not deflected, however, from arguing before V. R. Krishna Iyer, the Supreme Court's Vacation Judge (the court is sensible enough to take a six-week vacation during Delhi's scorching heat), Indira's appeal against Justice Sinha's verdict and her plea for an unconditional stay of it.

All eyes were now on Justice Krishna Iyer. He gave his ruling on the prayer for a stay order on the afternoon of June 24th. It was an overlong order, full of avoidable verbiage, mixed metaphor and eccentric syntax. Its purport, however, was that Indira could have only a conditional stay of the Allahabad verdict. She could stay in office and speak in Parliament. But, until the appeal was decided, she could not vote in Parliament.

With a whoop of delight J.P. announced, on behalf of all the opposition parties, the decision to launch a 'countrywide movement' to secure Indira's resignation. He unfolded the details of the plan at a huge rally the next evening at New Delhi's Ramlila Grounds, a favoured venue for important political public meetings and for the annual Hindu festival of Dussehra at which effigies of demons symbolising evil are ceremonially burnt. The plan called for daily demonstrations not only in Delhi and the state capitals but also in every single one of the country's three hundred and fifty-six district headquarters. The rally's high point was J.P.'s renewed and impassioned appeal to the Army, the police and the bureaucracy to 'refuse to obey' Indira and 'abide by the constitution instead'.

Morarji Desai was even more explicit later that evening. 'We intend to overthrow her, to force her to resign. For good,' he told a foreign journalist. 'The lady won't survive our movement . . . Thousands of us will surround her house to prevent her from going out . . . We shall camp there night and day.'

But just as Desai and J.P. were conjuring up joyous visions of a beleaguered Indira throwing in the towel, she was setting into motion the counter-stroke she had planned in utmost secrecy with the help of only a few totally trusted advisers and aides. An important and somewhat unexpected one of them at that time was Siddhartha Shankar Ray, chief minister of West Bengal and prominent lawyer who had known Indira since their childhood, as his maternal grandfather, C. R. Das, and Motilal Nehru, Indira's doting grandfather, were friends and comrades in the freedom struggle.

At about eleven at night on June 25th, Indira, accompanied by Ray, went to Rashtrapati Bhavan to inform President Ahmed that her government had decided to impose a State of internal Emergency (an external Emergency had been on since the 1971 war with Pakistan) and to assume sweeping powers under it.

Normally, she should have carried with her a resolution of her cabinet to this effect. But Ray explained to the President that under the rules of the government's business, it was not necessary for the cabinet to endorse the decision in advance. This could be done later, as the Prime Minister's word was enough. The President asked no questions and signed the proclamation.

Almost immediately, India went under Emergency rule and the world's largest democracy was turned into a virtual dictatorship. J.P. and Desai were roused from sleep and told that they were under arrest. Chandra Shekhar, Dharia and several other prominent members of the ruling party were also hauled to jail. Mass arrests were simultaneously taking place all over the country. All this had evidently required elaborate preparations, but not a word about them had leaked out.

At midnight the lights went out in Delhi's Bahadurshah Zafar Marg, India's Fleet Street, where most of the capital's newspapers are located. Power breakdowns are routine in India and no one gave much thought to the failure of the lights. When the breakdown lasted longer than usual, editors became alarmed. Eventually, they had to abandon their plans to bring out the morning paper. Later they were to learn that the power had been deliberately switched off so that the news of the arrests of J.P., Desai and thousands of others could not be reported.

Most Indians, who were asleep, like J.P. and Desai, when Indira struck, first learnt about what had happened in their country from a BBC World Service broadcast at seven-thirty on the morning of June 26th. Half an hour later the Prime Minister spoke on All India Radio. Her brief statement was vintage Indira. 'The President,' she said, 'has declared a state of Emergency. There is no need to panic.' She went on to say that some 'precautionary arrests' had been made but refrained from mentioning the names of those taken into custody. Nor were these names allowed to be published by newspapers which were immediately subjected to censorship far more stringent than they had ever had to suffer during the British Raj.

Many people said then and some continue to say to this day that Indira imposed the Emergency because she was 'authoritarian by nature', was fed up with dissent and vigorous opposition and was happy to have dictatorial powers. This is not a fair assessment even though it must be conceded that Indira, at times, behaved imperiously. But she disproved this charge by the one simple act of calling for fresh elections entirely on her own and apparently without being under any pressure to do so, barely nineteen months after the imposition of the Emergency.

That apart, Mary Carras, the only biographer of Indira to have attempted a political psycho-analysis of her, came to the conclusion that not only was she 'democratic' in 'temperament and personal style' but her 'self-image had been that of a democrat', and indeed 'her self-respect' derived 'in good part from this self-image'. Carras also noted, most perceptively, that Indira's commitment to a democratic way of life was combined with a certain 'ambivalence regarding the proper use of authority' which was further complicated by her conviction that her 'personal worth was tied up with her desire to do great things for her country'. Indeed, as we have already noted, she tended to identify herself with the nation completely and therefore to look upon personal threats to her as threats to the nation.

Looking back at the two decades of Indira's domination of India's public life, there can be no doubt that the imposition of the Emergency was her worst and most catastrophic mistake, indeed her cardinal sin. For it destroyed whatever little chance there was before June 25th, 1975, of normal politics returning to India and of the democratic consensus, smashed to smithereens, being slowly rebuilt. Because of the Emergency, the intensely inflamed polarisation of Indian society, centring largely on Indira's personality, became irreversible. Unfortunately, the situation did not change with her decisive defeat at the polls in the 1977 General Election she had herself ordered, and by the consequent rise to power of the Janata government, headed by Desai and deeply committed to 'restoring democratic decencies and norms.' The Janata's collapse and Indira's own return to power in 1980 also made no difference to the bitter political divide.

Nor was there any diminution in the hatreds that had displaced mutual tolerance, the lifeblood of democracy. On the contrary, these grew. For this shocking state of affairs Indira's responsibility was no less, and perhaps a little more, than that of her inveterate and often shrieking opponents. But, in the end, it was she, not any one of them, who fell victim to a mixture of mounting political hatred and monstrous religious fanaticism.

However, to revert to the imposition of the Emergency, the point must be stressed that Indira had acted not because she was dictatorial by nature and wanted to establish a permanent dictatorship but because, having convinced herself that both she and the country were targets of a malign conspiracy, she was determined to stay in office by fair means or foul to fight her 'enemies'.

Although I had refused to concede this at the time, cool reflection does show that once Indira had decided to stick to office after the Allahabad High Court's judgment and the Supreme Court's conditional stay of it, the imposition of the Emergency had become unavoidable.

For nearly a year and a half she had watched helplessly as J.P.'s Movement, vigorously supported by a large section of the press which

170

also reported in detail all that was being said against her from the public platform, practically paralysed her government. This was so when she did not have the stigma of having been convicted of corrupt election practices attached to her name. If she had to continue in office with a modicum of credibility, J.P., Desai, other opposition leaders and perhaps some of the more troublesome dissenters in her own party had to be immobilised and the press, which she believed to be virulently hostile to her, silenced.

The first objective was easy to achieve. The government had in its legal armoury any number of repressive laws, including the Defence of India Rules and MISA, the Maintenance of Internal Security Act, only recently made more stringent by a presidential ordinance. But what was the use of locking up the opposition leaders if the press was free to be in full cry? And there were no laws on the statute book under which it could be muzzled.

That is where Siddhartha Shankar Ray's legal expertise came in. He advised Indira that the only way was to proclaim a State of internal Emergency and acquire Draconian powers to impose press censorship. Indira plumped for this advice. In succeeding years many were to ask her – I did, too – why she had failed to perceive the catch in Ray's advice and overlooked the fact that something which might be technically legal could rob her of legitimacy in a trice. When I said this to her in September 1979, she only smiled. Several others I know drew the same response. But P. Shiv Shankar, who defended her in various courts of law during the Janata rule, later became her Law Minister and is a member of her son's cabinet now, told me in 1986 that Indira had confided to him that her utter unfamiliarity with law was responsible for her inability to realise the pitfalls in Ray's advice. This explanation cannot be dismissed as self-serving.

Indira's father and grandfather were both lawyers, Motilal greatly more eminent than his son. So were most other leaders of the freedom movement, including the greatest of them all, Mahatma Gandhi. She, however, was totally innocent of matters legal and constitutional and usually 'went by the advice of trusted experts'. 'What do I know of the constitution and its Emergency provisions?' she was reported by Shiv Shankar to have told him.

A bigger blunder than to opt for the Emergency was Indira's decision to bypass her cabinet before taking the momentous step and securing its endorsement only after the deed was done. This one point became her strongest indictment after she fell from power and was held accountable by the Janata government. This is also one issue on which, to the best of my knowledge and belief, she never broke her silence. Her reasons can therefore only be conjectured.

It is doubtful if she expected any strong opposition to her plans from a group of men who had, astonishingly, allowed themselves to cease to be her colleagues and became her minions. It is more likely therefore that her main anxiety was to prevent the leakage of her elaborate plans for a countrywide crackdown which she and a small coterie, now headed by Sanjay, were putting through behind a thick blanket of secrecy. So much so, that P. N. Dhar, who had replaced P. N. Haksar as her principal official adviser, first learnt of what was afoot just before Zero Hour when he was shown the draft of the brief broadcast Indira was to make the next morning.

The secrecy of the Emergency operations could be easily preserved even after the cabinet had approved them by the simple expedient of keeping the meeting going until after the President had signed the proclamation. But that was not to be.

It was at the unusual hour of six in the morning of June 26th that a meeting of the cabinet was summoned. The Emergency proclamation, presented to it as a *fait accompli*, was endorsed in a matter of minutes. There was no discussion worth the name. Only Swaran Singh asked some question of a largely procedural nature.

Later in the day he told some close friends: '*Yeh thanedari nahin chalegi*' (This resort to crude police powers will not work). Such was the prevailing atmosphere, which would persist during the Emergency and beyond, that, in next to no time, Swaran Singh's caustic remark was conveyed to Indira. Shortly afterwards he lost his position as Defence Minister and was dropped from the cabinet. His job was entrusted to the rough and rude Bansi Lal, the Haryana chief minister, who had gone out of his way to help Sanjay's Maruti car project.

J.P.'s hope that either Jagjivan Ram or Chavan or both would revolt against Indira was belied to the point of being turned into a cruel joke on him. Ram, in fact, piloted in Parliament the official resolution to seek its approval for the Emergency proclamation. His speech was little short of a paean of praise for both Indira and the Emergency. With most opposition leaders behind bars and Indira's overwhelming majority, the resolution was easily passed.

Chavan chose total silence. Months later, when the initial shock of the Emergency had begun to subside and, privately at least, people had begun raising embarrassing questions about those who had pusil-lanimously acquiesced in its imposition, Chavan asked P. N. Haksar, then Deputy Chairman of the Planning Commission but at the receiving end of much harassment by the Emergency regime: 'When, do you think, I should have started opposing the Emergency?'

'From the first day,' replied Haksar, reminding Chavan of the latter's 'valiant role' during the Quit India movement in 1942.

*    *    *

172

However, why blame Chavan alone? Almost literally no one raised his or her voice when Indira hit the country with the hammer-blow of the Emergency proclamation. Indeed, the apparently instant and complete acceptance of the Emergency was as stunning as its sudden imposition.

For over a year the country had reverberated with the war cries of those who said that she was busy 'destroying democracy' and were determined to fight her to the finish. But when the blow actually fell and democracy looked as if it had been destroyed for good by a single stroke of the President's pen, there was not even a squeak. In Bombay, judging by what had been happening and was being said in preceding months, I had expected massive demonstrations against Indira's out-rageous act. There was not even a ripple. People going about their jobs as usual were, of course, angry. In private conversations with friends, they gave expression to their fury and frustration. But publicly they thought silence to be the better part of valour. Expectations that other cities and towns must be showing greater life and courage were shattered by the evening when it turned out that there had not been a mass rally, a protest march or a sit-in anywhere in the country. J.P.'s mighty Movement, it seemed, had vanished into thin air.

Most newspapers also fell in line with remarkable speed, abandoning their stridency and meekly following rigorous censorship rules which would not allow them even to say how many had been arrested and who they were. Any comment that could even remotely be considered critical of the government was taboo. Some newspapers, on the first day of the Emergency and censorship, left blank spaces from where material had been censored out. Told that this would not be tolerated, they resorted to publishing quotations in defence of freedom of expression from Gandhi, Tagore and Indira's own father, Nehru. This, too, was forbid-den firmly by a Goebbels-like V. C. Shukla who now headed the Minis-try of Information and Broadcasting.

After the end of the Emergency, Shukla's successor in the Janata government, L. K. Advani, a former journalist and a mild-mannered man, was to taunt the Indian press with the words: 'You were asked only to bend, but you chose to crawl.'

Not only was there no resistance or even visible opposition to the Emergency, it was also rather popular with the people at large, in the initial months at least, underscoring once again that the Indian people are both anarchy-loving and authority-loving. The return of normal and orderly life, after relentless disruption by strikes, protest marches, sit-ins and clashes with the police, was applauded by most people. Government officials, high and low, unsure of what might happen to them otherwise, started arriving for work on time and taking fewer tea breaks.

All these 'achievements' of the Emergency and more were duly publicised by the government's propaganda machine, presided over by Shukla. Some of its moronic functionaries even started crowing that the trains had started running on time.

There was a surprising spurt in the number of people who suddenly discovered great merit in Indira and Sanjay. Some of their new cheer leaders used to play the same role at J.P.'s rallies in preceding days. Typical was the case of M. F. Husain, one of the most famous Indian modern painters. His works fetch the highest prices in the Indian art market. He is also a colourful character. With his flowing grey beard, a mane to match and addiction to walking barefoot he is conspicuous in any gathering. So he was in J.P.'s famous march on Parliament on March 6th, 1975. Within a few days of the proclamation of the Emergency he painted a huge triptych which, drawing heavily on Hindu mythology, depicted Indira as the goddess Durga, emerging triumphant from a baptism of fire and riding away on a tiger after vanquishing her foes and traducers. It was not one of Husain's best works, but it was the most publicised because the Prime Minister's image-builders seized upon it at once. Support for the Emergency by an artist of Husain's stature was very important to them.

The trouble was, however, that although hordes were trying to clamber on the bandwagon of the Emergency – out of sheer opportunism or because of the propensity of most people in a feudal society to be on the winning side – very few people of Husain's distinction were a part of this stampede. That is where one of the many paradoxes in Indira's life came in.

Her father had been the darling of the Indian intelligentsia which constituted his battalions throughout his life. Along with much else, Indira inherited this affection of the intellectuals, scientists, artists, authors, poets, film-makers and so on. Their support was a source of great strength to her. When she started splitting the Congress, there was a division in the ranks of the intelligentsia whose role in Indian public life is out of all proportion to its numbers simply because of its dominance of the media, academia, bureaucracy and business management. However, a very large section of journalists, writers and opinion-makers, if not a majority of them, was enthusiastically on her side.

These were men and women, brought up in the Nehruvian school of thought, itself an Indian version of British Fabianism born in the 'pink Thirties'. They believed in state control of the 'commanding heights of the economy', in a welfare state and in narrowing of disparities between the rich and the poor. Attractive and apparently left-leaning Indira was a leader after their hearts. Her opponents, headed by the Syndicate, were seen by them as conservatives and reactionaries deserving anathema. On the other hand, very vocal editors, educationists, publicists and intellectuals had come to the conclusion that ideology was for Indira nothing more than a convenient camouflage; that in her search for unfettered personal power, she was throwing to the winds all norms of democracy; and that she had to be fought and defeated.

With the advent of the Emergency this situation changed radically. The bulk of the intelligentsia began to believe that her critics and detractors were right. Even those who did not fully agree with this view were no longer prepared to speak up for her. They retreated into sullen silence. There was no dearth of 'intellectuals' happy to turn into Indira's drum-beaters, but most of them were of little substance and less influence.

Indira dealt with this state of affairs by publicly decrying the intellectuals as 'dupes of foreign elements and ideas hostile to us' and privately trying to win over their support. As there was an outburst of shock over, and criticism of, the suspension of democracy by Indira the world over, her emissaries tried hard to get a statement signed by Satyajit Ray, the famous film director, and other eminent authors, professors and scientists to the effect that the Emergency was necessary, that Indira was right in claiming that Indian democracy had 'gone off the rails' and she was only trying to put it 'back on the track'. No one with a reputation to lose was prepared to sign it.

A major change came over Indira herself as soon as she had imposed the State of Emergency. Even during the turbulent months preceding June 25th, she used to travel a great deal and speak about conditions in the country quite freely and frankly. On March 9th, 1975, I myself had had a long talk with her – my last until 1978 – in Bombay. She was there for the annual naval exercises which meant spending a whole day at sea. This gave her plenty of time to converse with others on board.

It was she who brought up the subject of the turmoil in the country and went on to repeat the standard formula that J.P. and other 'enemies' of hers were 'part of a deep-laid conspiracy' against her and the country.

I pointed out that the situation was more complex than that and drew attention to the many causes of economic and political discontent. Above all, I said, the moral authority of her government had suffered grievously because of mounting corruption and the widespread belief that links between her party and 'black money' had become 'so close as to be unbreakable'. She was unruffled and commented that such talk originated from those who 'themselves owned hoards of black money'. She then mentioned the name of the editor of a leading newspaper, then as well as later very hostile to her, and said that he had come to see her with the message that if the legal proceedings against the paper's proprietor, then taking place before appropriate bodies, were 'withdrawn', she would face 'no more problems' from them.

We discussed a number of other issues including Sikkim. I expressed unhappiness that this rather small problem should have been solved in two rather clumsy phases, separated by several months. 'Ah,' she said, 'you don't know my ministers. They don't understand these things and some of them are happy to work against me.'

After the imposition of the Emergency this kind of candour and sociability on her part came to an end. She withdrew into her shell and, as time went by, became more and more isolated. Even 'Dorothy Dear' got a very cold shoulder. The regular exchange of letters with her abruptly stopped. Shattered by the news from Delhi, Dorothy at first refused to believe it. But when unpleasant facts could not be brushed away, she wrote Indira an impassioned letter asking her to rescind her decision. It remained unanswered. So did frantic messages sent through 'common friends'.

The visit to the UN Conference on Women that was to have been a high point in Indira's career as a woman Prime Minister had to be cancelled. Indeed, throughout the period of the Emergency she was in no position to show her face anywhere except in Moscow.

Indira's attempt to make out that the Emergency was, in fact, an opportunity to make good the promises of social and economic change which had remained unfulfilled failed to make headway. She did come forward with a Twenty-Point Programme which was largely a rehash and elaboration of the old, forgotten Ten-Point Programme of 1967. But it had at least two new elements which, in normal times, could have enthused the country. One was the blanket cancellation of all small debts owed by the poorest of the rural poor to the usurious money-lenders in the villages and the other a phased plan to set free labourers condemned to 'bondage' because of their inability to repay their own or ancestral debts to their 'employers'.

But times were not normal and the country generally saw the Twenty-Point Programme as a cynical ploy to divert attention from the outrage Indira had perpetrated on it. In any case, the new programme lost momentum even faster than the old one had. This was so because the vested interests against whom the reforms were directed were now entrenched even more securely than before. They had jumped on the bandwagon of the Emergency. Indira was happy to welcome whatever support she could get.

However, if Indira's Twenty-Point Programme failed, her plan to build up her son, Sanjay, as her political heir succeeded beyond all expectations, hers or his. Her party welcomed the move as if this was the most natural thing to happen in the world's largest democracy. A brash and extremely tactless young man, Sanjay often treated his mother's colleagues and other elders churlishly. They meekly pocketed his insults. Chief ministers engaged themselves in a fierce competition to invite him to their states and arrange big welcomes for him as if he were a conquering hero. Ministers, MPs and even many officials vied with one another in doing Sanjay's behest or anticipating his wishes. Like his mother's, his word was their command. Government-owned radio and television were publicising him day and night. Newspapers were lending a helping hand. India was becoming the 'Land of the Rising Son'.

Sanjay even added five points of his own to Indira's Twenty-Point Programme. None of these was without merit. By advocating adult literacy ('each one teach one'), family planning, slum clearance, tree plantation and the eradication of dowry, he was surely catering for some of India's pressing needs. But as the sum total of the personal credo of a young man hoping to rule India into the twenty-first century, it was rather fatuous.

Another attribute of the by now all-powerful Sanjay produced its own problems. From the time he had returned from England, without completing the course at Rolls-Royce, and started tinkering with cars at a neighbourhood garage, Sanjay had displayed a remarkable knack of attracting 'dropouts, drifters and roughnecks' to him. Youngsters of this kind flocked to him in large numbers in the hour of his power and glory. They indeed took over the ruling party's youth wing of which Sanjay was the supremo. Innocent of even elementary norms of political behaviour and with their eye on the main chance, they had only two interests: to use their muscle power to prove their loyalty to Sanjay and to grab whatever material gain they could. The Prime Minister, though she should have been embarrassed at one remove, did not seem to care.

Under the circumstances, it was no surprise, though it surely was ironic, that Sanjay became the principal architect of his mother's misfortunes.

Fear, like all other human emotions, began to subside. After about six to eight months, the 'excesses' of the Emergency began to become known. Anger started spilling out from the privacy of people's homes into public places. The press was still in chains. Radio and TV continued to be the government's megaphones. Rumour and reporting through word of mouth therefore took over. The government's mis-deeds, substantial enough, thus tended to get magnified as word travelled from one person or place to another.

The number of arrests, by itself, was shocking. According to Amnesty International, 140,000 Indians were detained without trial in 1975–6, as against just under half that number put into jail by the British during the Quit India movement in 1942 in the entire subcontinent. However, the Amnesty figure needs to be examined a little more carefully, for the Janata government, after it came to power, computed, on the basis of information received from the states, that the detainees numbered 100,000. What seems to have happened is that while 140,000 persons must have been taken to prison at one time or another during the Emergency, releases were also taking place all the time. Consequently, the highest number of prisoners at any given time might well have been around 100,000, and no more.

The treatment of ordinary prisoners, as in normal times, was appalling, but opposition leaders were treated with consideration. Desai was confined to a Dak bungalow throughout his nineteen-month detention. J.P. was also taken to a similar rest house to begin with but, because of his illness, was transferred to hospital, first in Delhi and then in Chandigarh. In November 1975, he was released but only after his brother, Rajeswar Prasad, wrote to Indira about his 'declining health' and asked her whether it would be in her government's interest 'if J.P. died in jail'. During the rest of the Emergency J.P. was confined to bed in Bombay's Jaslok Hospital and it was in a wheelchair that he took part in 'victory rallies' after Indira's fall from power.

At the time of J.P.'s release it was alleged by his friends and supporters that 'something had been done to him' during his detention which had aggravated his kidney ailment. Indira, like medieval queens of India, was being accused of 'slow poisoning of her adversaries in her captivity'. The Janata government took this charge seriously enough to appoint a commission of inquiry to investigate it. The commission found no evidence to support the allegation.

Twenty-two Emergency prisoners did die in jail. Of one, Rajan, an engineering student in Kerala, 'no trace could be found'. If this did not give rise to the shock and protest that it might have done, the reason was that deaths in custody have never been unknown in India even in normal times.

Much greater indignation was aroused by the treatment meted out to George Fernandes, the maverick socialist and leader of the crushed railway strike, who had organised an underground resistance movement against the Emergency. Having secured sufficient quantities of dynamite from Baroda in Gujarat, he was busy launching a campaign of blowing up bridges, derailing trains and burning government property. It took the police a long time to arrest him. In their frustration over this failure, the police tortured George's brother, Lawrence, until he was 'broken in body and spirit'. Their mother, Alice Fernandes, repeatedly wrote to Indira about what was being done to her son but she 'did not even get an acknowledgment'.

Lawrence Fernandes at least lived to tell the tale. Snehlata Reddy, a pretty and talented actress suspected of running errands for George, died soon after being released from prison. A chronic sufferer from asthma, she could not survive the ill-treatment to which she was subjected in the hot, humid prison cell where she was kept 'along with prostitutes and criminals'.

George Fernandes and his collaborators were the only Emergency prisoners to be put on trial. But their prosecution, still incomplete when elections were held and Indira was defeated, was withdrawn by the Janata government. George had stood in the elections as a Janata candidate. He could not canvass because, as a maximum security prisoner, he was constantly kept in chains. But he won hands down and became Industries Minister.

More than all this, indeed more than anything else, what turned India against the Emergency and Indira were the excesses of her darling son and duly designated successor, Sanjay. These stemmed from his passionate devotion to the cult of contraception and his craze for 'beautifying' Indian cities by clearing 'away' not only the slums but also their dwellers.

Now, population in India does need to be controlled. Some of the festering slums also need to be replaced by something worthy of human habitation. But there is a decent, democratic way of pursuing these goals and there is a haughty, ham-fisted method of doing the same thing. Sanjay, anxious to be known in Indian history as the man who 'got things done', opted for the latter. The revulsion against his ways became obvious only when, in March 1977, it blew his mother out of office and power. But the signs of the coming upheaval were visible even at the time when Indian reality was being effectively obscured by censorship.

The first known resistance to Sanjay's capriciousness took place in Delhi's Turkman Gate, a historic landmark in the Indian capital, like the magnificent Jama Masjid, not far away. The entire area between the great mosque and the Turkman Gate is full of narrow and dark lanes and bylanes, and this maze is inhabited largely by Muslim families. These people had watched angrily but silently when centuries-old shops around Jama Masjid, including some of the legendary stalls that had sold delectable kebabs to successive gener-ations, were knocked down. And then, in April 1976, demolition squads arrived to raze to the ground the slums which were home to these tens of thousands of people. Outraged, they resisted the demolishers. They were met by a hail of police bullets. Six people were killed on the spot. But Sanjay would not relent. The Turkman

Gate area was reduced to rubble and its inhabitants moved to a new township across the River Yamuna, about twenty miles from their places of work.

Sheikh Abdullah, the towering Kashmiri leader who had again become chief minister of his state as a result of his accord with Indira only in February 1975, was in Delhi on the day of the Turkman Gate firing. He went to the spot and was disgusted by what he saw. President Fakhruddin Ali Ahmed, who had meekly signed the Emergency proclamation, was as appalled as the Sheikh. Both were Muslims. Both protested to Indira, but she was not prepared to hear a word of criticism of her beloved son.

From then on until after Sanjay's death in June 1980 while stunt-flying an aerobatic aircraft, the secret of his extraordinary hold on his mother never ceased to be a subject of avid discussion in India and continued to arouse interest overseas. Some of the answers the debate produced were absurd. For instance, as sober a British journalist as Ian Jack allowed himself to suggest that 'incest' might have been at the back of it all. One of the many Indian friends of Indira who turned into bitter foes claimed that Sanjay would 'slap' his mother. However, he never produced a shred of evidence to support his assertion.

The most widely believed explanation was that Sanjay was able 'emotionally to blackmail' Indira because of her 'feeling of guilt' over her 'neglect' that 'contributed' to her husband's 'premature' death. However, it is necessary to add that author Salman Rushdie and his publishers, Jonathan Cape and Pan Books, who made precisely this assertion had to tender, shortly before her death, an 'apology' to Indira in a libel case in the High Court at London's Old Bailey.

K. D. Malaviya, Oil Minister in the cabinets of both Nehru and Indira, who did not particularly like Sanjay and whose commitment to socialism was both deeper and more sincere than Indira's, was nearer the point perhaps. He told me that, to the best of his knowledge and belief, Indira was convinced that in her 'darkest hours' – after the Allahabad High Court judgment in June 1975 and after her fall from power two years later – Sanjay alone 'saved' her from being ruined politically and perhaps liquidated physically.

After the Turkman Gate outrage, gunfire was heard at Muzaffar Nagar, a Muslim-majority town a hundred miles to the north of Delhi, and at some other places. Once again people were revolting against supposedly voluntary but, in fact, forced vasectomies. Indira explained away these minor insurrections as 'stray incidents of no great consequence'. Only after she called for elections did she realise that these stray incidents were really harbingers of a political hurricane that would sweep her out of power.

During her days in the wilderness, Indira used to complain that though she and her son had been relentlessly maligned for having ordered forced sterilisations on a massive scale, no one had been able to cite more than a handful of such incidents. She had a point. But she conveniently tried to slur over the fact that while actual incidents of young and not so young men being dragged out of cinema halls or bus queues and taken to the operating table might have been few, the air of fear and panic they created was pervasive. The people, especially in North India where Sanjay's writ ran, concluded that the essence of the Emergency was an attack on their very manhood and dignity. It should also be mentioned that to most unlettered Indian males there is no difference between sterilisation and castration.

Force, moreover, has many different manifestations. A system of incentives for birth control and disincentives for large families is entirely understandable. But in an authoritarian atmosphere, with an overbearing Crown Prince in charge, incentives and disincentives also assumed a grotesque form.

Under Sanjay's dictates, all petty government employees, including policemen, municipal inspectors, doctors, nurses, teachers and so on, were told that they would not get their monthly pay unless they 'motivated' a prescribed number of people to undergo vasectomy. If this edict to mini-Czars of the administration was not an open invitation to coercion on a large scale, what else was it? Inevitably, the brunt of bureaucratic high-handedness fell primarily on the poor, including Harijans, Muslims and others who had been Indira's traditional vote banks.

No wonder then that as soon as fresh elections were announced, the dam of pent-up public fury burst. The pains of the Emergency were now exposed to the light of day. The gains of the Emergency, such as they might have been, were forgotten. Indira and her son were about to get their come-uppance.

181

# 11   The Matriarch at Home

In its initial months at least, the Emergency restored to India a kind of calm it had not known for years. Spared the almost daily, and often violent challenge to her authority, Indira now had more time than before to devote to her family which lived, in the time-honoured Indian tradition, jointly, under her roof. As the family grew, it became necessary to add more rooms to the Prime Minister's official residence. Her government was happy to do so.

Indira's attachment to her two sons had been strong from the start. In later years, she used to say proudly that, unlike Delhi's society ladies, she had 'always bathed and fed' her little children herself, never leaving these tasks to nannies or other domestic help. When her sons were very young she also managed to find time to tell them bedside stories.

There were, of course, long stretches of separation when Rajiv and Sanjay first went to boarding school and then to England for their studies. Brief reunions, during Indira's visits to London, used to be, in her words, 'heavenly'.

By the end of 1967, both the boys were back home and the family was reunited. The first parental problem Indira then faced was her elder son Rajiv's decision to marry his Italian sweetheart, Sonia Maino, whom he had met at Cambridge. Though she had defied the 'whole world' at the time of her own marriage to Feroze, Indira did not like the idea of her son marrying a foreigner. But when Rajiv seemed firm in his resolve she gave in gracefully. Rajiv and Sonia were married in December 1968. Hundreds of guests were invited to the wedding reception. I lived in Calcutta at that time but travelled to Delhi for the occasion because Indira wanted all the 'friends of my husband' to be present. Sanjay's wedding, six years later, to Maneka Anand, daughter of a Sikh colonel, was a private and very small affair.

Relations beween mothers-in-law and daughters-in-law are usually strained in India, more than elsewhere in the world, largely because of the joint family system and the overwhelming attachment of Indian mothers to their sons. Almost everyone who saw it was pleasantly surprised therefore that from the moment Sonia stepped into Indira's home, the two women became extremely fond of each other. Over the years, the bond between them became strong. Indeed, Indira delegated to Sonia much of the responsibility for running the household.

The contrast between this affectionate and mutually supportive relationship and that between Indira and her younger daughter-in-law, Maneka, could not have been greater. The Indira–Maneka relations were at first ambiguous, then troubled and finally implacably hostile, as we shall discuss presently.

Indira was overjoyed when Rajiv's and Sonia's two children, son Rahul and daughter Priyanka, were born in quick succession. She simply adored her grandchildren and overwhelmed them with love and affection, rather in the manner that her own grandfather, Motilal, had done in her case. In this respect, at least, her demonstrative grandfather's influence on her had proved to be stronger than that of her father's, known for his reserve and restraint.

As a toddler, Rahul would accompany his *dadi* (paternal grandma) to her office and would be brought back home. She tried to avoid as many official lunches as she could so that she could rush home at lunchtime to be with the family, especially the grandchildren. Towards the end of her life she had begun to say that the only regret she had about her gruelling work schedule was that usually by the time she could get back home the 'children were asleep'. Around this time, Indira also started inviting foreign dignitaries and eminent Indians to family, rather than official, meals. She laid the table and supervised the menu personally and took even greater pains with the flower arrangement.

Sanjay's and Maneka's son was born in March 1979 and named Feroze Varun. To the child of her favourite son, named after her late husband, Indira became devoted even more than to the older grandchildren. She was heartbroken when, in the wake of their bitter estrangement, Maneka understandably took Feroze Varun with her and repeatedly refused to let Indira see him as often as she wished to.

It is no exaggeration to say that long before Feroze Varun's birth and even before Sanjay's marriage Indira had become as possessive and protective a matriarch of the Gandhi family as Motilal had been the patriarch of the larger Nehru clan.

Some tried to invoke this to justify Indira's frantic and often crude attempts to build up Sanjay as her successor. They even linked her exertions on behalf of her younger son to Motilal's success in 1929 in ensuring that he passed the Congress presidentship to his son, Jawaharlal. Hadn't even Mahatma Gandhi acknowledged, they asked, that Motilal saw the country 'through Jawaharlal'? Couldn't Indira be feeling the same way about Sanjay?

The comparisons were untenable and the arguments specious. Sanjay was no Jawaharlal, not by any stretch of the imagination. In the Twenties, Jawaharlal was established as a young and idealistic leader with a broad vision and a great future. Sanjay's contribution to public life in the Seventies was symbolised by the scandals surrounding the Maruti car project and the shenanigans of the goons who had become his devotees. Moreover, it was not Motilal who made Jawaharlal the Congress President but Mahatma Gandhi, but for whose support Motilal would have got nowhere and who was later to name the younger Nehru his own 'political heir'. Above all, Motilal and the Mahatma were offering Jawaharlal a crown of thorns and the leadership of a long and arduous fight for independence, not the government of a sixth of mankind. But this made no difference to the multitude of Indira's *chamchas* – literally 'spoons' but figuratively meaning, in India's colourful political lexicon, sycophants – who went on proclaiming loudly that Sanjay was the true and legitimate successor of 'Madam', as Indira was now called by one and all.

Questions about Indira's personal and private life were constantly asked and incessantly discussed, especially on New Delhi's overbusy grapevine, but never satisfactorily answered. She was a woman of beauty and elegance, with a zest for life and a capacity for enjoying it, as the twinkle in her large, dark eyes as well as her laughter in rare moments of relaxation showed. She had been widowed at only forty-three, and before that for several years she had been estranged from her husband. Did this mean that she had condemned herself to a life of loneliness? Or was she, like so many women rulers in history, having romantic attachments or even affairs on the quiet?

Most of those in a position to know – either because they enjoyed her confidence or because it was their job to maintain a close and continuous watch on her for, among others, security reasons – maintain that, given the fish-bowl existence that Indira had to lead through most of her adult life, she could not have had a liaison on the quiet, even if she had wanted to. And, according to them, she didn't want to. Moreover, as we have noted, one of the reasons for her estrangement from Feroze was his reputation for a roving eye and philandering. It followed, therefore, that during his lifetime at least she would give him no cause for complaint that her behaviour was no better than his.

However, nothing ever prevented perfervid gossip and speculation about Indira's love life, either before Feroze's death or afterwards. Fairly early after she had become her father's châtelaine, her name was romantically linked, as indicated earlier, with M. O. Mathai, Nehru's trusted aide who lived at the Prime Minister's house. He was not an attractive man to look at but he had a certain charm. Moreover, he was devoted to Indira's two sons, especially to Sanjay. His far from glorious exit from the Prime Minister's house in 1959, instead of ending rumours of a romance between him and Indira, fuelled them.

For, as we have noted, Feroze had played an active part behind the scenes in unearthing Mathai's malfeasance which had made his resignation unavoidable. Feroze, many said, had acted because of 'jealousy'.

In his hour of disgrace, such talk was music to the otherwise deflated Mathai. Even during his heyday he had not been averse to discreetly encouraging gossip about a love affair between him and Indira. It was a great disappointment to him therefore that some time after he ceased to be in the limelight, discussion about an Indira–Mathai romance also ceased. But he bided his time and, in 1978, after Indira had fallen from power and was being harried by the Janata government, he publicly boasted about having been Indira's lover though he did so more by innuendo than by explicit statement.

In two separate books, Mathai maligned not only Indira but her father, whose alleged philandering he described in great detail, naming names and, in one case, mentioning even the size of the lady's bust. In writing about Indira, however, he was more careful. He did not name her directly in some of his pornographic passages but left little doubt about who he was referring to. For instance, he darkly hinted that the 'person concerned' should be grateful that a video film of her escapades 'in the Dwarka suite in Rashtrapati Bhavan', the luxurious rooms in the presidential palace where foreign dignitaries stay, was in his 'possession' and not in anyone else's.

Mathai climaxed his boasts with the declaration that one chapter of his book, entitled simply 'She', had been withheld at the last minute and would be published as a separate booklet later. It never was. It is doubtful if the chapter ever existed – no trace of it was found after Mathai's death.

Although Mathai's book came out at a time when maligning Indira had become a highly profitable cottage industry – a flood of Emergency books depicting the former goddess Durga as the worst figure in the entire Indian demonology were being published and selling like hot cakes – he must have been disappointed by the country's reaction to his outpourings. Few books in India have got such bad reviews as Mathai's did. Typical was the reaction of Khushwant Singh, then Editor of *Illustrated Weekly*, who called Mathai's work 'Diary of a *Namak Haram*'. Literally the expression means a person who is untrue and ungrateful to the person whose salt he or she eats. But metaphorically Indians use it for treachery of the worst kind. In my review, in *The Times of India*, I described Mathai as a 'double-distilled combination of a braggart and a blackguard if ever there was one'. There was not a squeak of protest from him.

Interestingly, it was Mathai who, besides pretending to be Romeo to Indira's Juliet, was the first to put into print what many had been saying for years: that there had been a fairly prolonged love affair between Indira and Dinesh Singh, the most important and influential member of her Kitchen Cabinet from 1966, when she first came to power, until he fell from grace over two years later.

Unfamiliar with the complexities of political and administrative procedures and unwilling to trust ministers senior to her in age and experience though now serving under her, Indira was indeed greatly dependent on Dinesh's advice and grateful for his help. But rumours were immediately rife that the relationship beween the two was more intimate than that between a boss and a trusted aide. Dinesh Singh's own demeanour in those heady days strengthened the rumour and gossip.

Both power and romantic conquest have one thing in common. More than half of the joy and intoxication of either is lost if one cannot show off. Dinesh was sensible enough never to say anything that would amount to a verification of the belief that he was Indira's lover. But he never said or did anything to dispel or discourage the spreading impression. On the contrary, whenever and wherever Dinesh might be dining out those days, the host's phone used to ring at around ten or ten thirty; the message, from one of Dinesh's aides, would be that the Prime Minister wanted to see him at once. Some or even most of these calls might have been perfectly genuine and equally innocent. Indira always worked late into the night and, in her house, bustling with personal and security staff, sent for colleagues and advisers, individually and in groups, regardless of what time it was.

Nevertheless, the prevailing impression, by no means confined to the salons of the rich in Delhi usually obsessed with politics and political gossip, was that there was more to the Indira–Dinesh relationship than met the eye. K. C. Pant, now Defence Minister and then a junior minister, was waiting for Indira in his constituency in the Kumaon Hills of UP at the head of a large crowd. To his embarrassment and anger, he overheard the ribald talk among some local Congress leaders standing behind him, accompanied by winks and nudges, as Indira's helicopter landed and Dinesh alighted close on her heels.

From a distance, Mathai was keeping a closer watch on the kind of talk Pant had chosen contemptuously to ignore. Indeed, only a few months after Indira had become Prime Minister, Mathai wrote to her about the 'loose and unfortunate' talk about Dinesh that was going on. The letter went on to ask her why she was 'inviting' such talk by allowing Dinesh 'access' to her bedroom. Indira had replied almost immediately that at home she did most of her work at a desk in her bedroom, which had 'always been there', and that any number of men besides Dinesh, including ministers and officials, were in and out of the room while she was working.

No one heard of this exchange of letters for full twelve years. Then, in his book, Mathai published the correspondence. Indira's reply, scribbled over three or four short slips of paper in her own hand, was printed in facsimile.

Another six years later, in March 1984, Donald Trelford, Editor of *The Observer*, sent a despatch to his paper from New Delhi in which he described Dinesh Singh, 'now greying', as Indira's 'former lover'. There was no particular reason for Trelford to write about Dinesh except that the two had run into each other at a musical soirée. But he went on to inform his readers that Dinesh had been 'dropped unceremoniously' when Indira 'discovered' that 'she had a rival'.

The sheer absurdity of Trelford's second statement discredits his entire theory. In any case, neither he nor anyone else produced even an iota of evidence to support his claim.

Long before Dinesh's fall from grace, indeed even before he began to be talked of as the 'Prince Consort', there appeared on the Delhi scene a man, both mysterious and mystical, who was to be talked of as Indira's lover more incessantly and for a longer period than either Dinesh or Mathai. His name, Dhirendra Brahmachari, was rather ironic. For the surname, clearly adopted and not inherited, means a man who takes a vow of celibacy for life.

Brahmachari was careful never to boast of being a celibate. But he assiduously advertised himself as a swami or man of God and a guru in the ancient Indian science of mental concentration and physical exercise called Yoga. A man of obscure, indeed mysterious, origins – despite his craving for publicity and penchant for giving long interviews, he refused to discuss his age or parentage – Brahmachari had arrived in Delhi a little before his time, for no one had yet foreseen that godmanship would become international big business in only a decade or so. But he did not do badly at all. On a local scale, at least, he quickly converted meditation and mysticism into profitable merchandise.

What first brought Brahmachari to the attention of Delhi society were his exceptionally good looks and his ability cheerfully to withstand Delhi's winter in a thin, virtually see-through *dhoti* (a loose sheet wrapped round one's waist and down to the ankles) with which he also sometimes covered his otherwise bare torso. He became something of a sensation when it became known that he had been teaching both Nehru and Indira Yoga. Soon thereafter he was given prime land in the heart of New Delhi at a highly concessional price by the government and, with the help of generous donations, Brahmachari set up a Yoga school to which riches and beauty flocked with alacrity. Years later it transpired that Indira had told Lal Bahadur Shastri, then Nehru's Home Minister, to help Brahmachari set up the Yoga *ashram*.

On April 17th, 1958, she had written to Dorothy Norman informing her that she had started getting up early to do a 'special set of Yoga exercises . . . taught us by an exceedingly good-looking Yogi'. Indira added: 'In fact, it was his looks, especially his magnificent body, which attracted everybody to his system which is easy and practical. He is, however, exasperating to talk to – so full of superstition.'

The last part of her statement was not without a quirk of irony, for, Indira seemed to have no difficulty in talking to Brahmachari as he became one of the more important members of her close circle with free access to the Prime Minister. More importantly, whether because of his influence or due to life's woes and vicissitudes, she herself became superstitious, frequently visiting places of worship, organising special prayers or rites of propitiation on various occasions and constantly consulting astrologers and soothsayers.

As Brahmachari's proximity to Indira grew, so did his power and wealth. He soon became notorious for his high-flying and hedonistic lifestyle. He drove a Toyota and flew his own private aircraft which, he insisted, had been donated to him by his foreign devotees. The Customs and tax authorities 'accepted his claim uncritically' and allowed him to import the plane into the country without any questions being asked. He even set up a gun factory in the foothills of Jammu and Kashmir, and a second *ashram* not far away. With the rise of Sanjay, Brahmachari's power and influence increased even further. The two men became close collaborators and virtually inseparable. D. P. Mishra, Indira's one-time counsellor, was among the very few people to rush to her support after her shattering defeat in the 1977 General Election. But he said to me that he found it 'impossible to talk to her alone because Sanjay and Brahmachari would come into the room again and again'.

The Janata government started a number of cases against Brahmachari, as against Indira and Sanjay, to say nothing of many of her other associates and supporters. But nothing came of these. Most were unconcluded when Indira returned to power and all legal proceedings started by the Janata were dropped. Brahmachari happily reverted to the role of a power-broker he had played in earlier years. Angry questions about his influence-peddling were asked in Parliament. The government gave evasive replies. People nicknamed Brahmachari 'Rasputin' but Indira seemed not to care. No minister or official was powerful enough to say no to Brahmachari's requests.

In the course of time, Brahmachari also became a glamorous TV star, giving a bi-weekly lecture on Yoga. Surrounded by eye-catching

188

models to demonstrate each Yoga exercise, he would answer viewers' questions put to him by a particularly flirtatious woman. Neither the authorities of the usually staid and often prudish Indian TV nor the protesting public could do anything about Brahmachari's blatant sexual allusions and even homilies on the merits of masturbation.

Even after Sanjay's death and Rajiv's reluctant acceptance of his mantle, when other Sanjay loyalists, headed by his widow, Maneka, were being shunted away, Brahmachari remained unscathed.

Then one evening early in 1984 Brahmachari's programme was taken off TV without any warning or explanation. In rumour-saturated Delhi this was taken as the beginning of his end. The speculation was accurate, for the next morning, to his mortification, Brahmachari was denied entry into the Prime Minister's house. Word spread fast that Rajiv, rather than his mother, had taken the initiative to show Brahmachari the door. He saw no reason why she should get a bad name for the sake of the likes of Dhirendra Brahmachari.

Denied access to Indira during the last months of her life, Brahmachari tried to get close to her bier after her death. (He had practically presided over Sanjay's funeral.) When Indira was being paid the last obsequies, he sidled up to the raised platform where her pyre was about to be lit. Reportedly at Rajiv's instructions, he was quietly led away and not again allowed to come anywhere near the cremation ceremony.

There is nothing more to be said about Brahmachari, Dinesh Singh or Mathai. The only question is: what does all that has been said and pieced together amount to? Clearly, not much, and certainly not to a confirmation of a succession of torrid romances on the part of Indira. There is something to be said about the theory of the Indian Prime Minister's fish-bowl existence and its unavoidable consequences. Whatever attraction Indira might have felt towards some men, known or unknown, and whatever her normal craving for male companionship, she apparently had no escape from the overwhelming constraints her public position placed on her private life. The utter lack of 'that most wonderful thing in life, having a complete and perfect relationship with another human being', of which she had complained, was the price she had to pay for the absolute power she cherished no less.

It is only fair and proper to note that the persistent and prurient prying into Indira's love life, real or imaginary, had a lot to do with the fact that she was a woman who had risen to the top in a male-dominated society and milieu. A man in her place, especially if he were a widower, could have indulged in his peccadilloes without inviting anything more than some sniggering at cocktail parties or thigh-slapping in the locker-rooms of clubs.

After all, her own illustrious father was generally believed to have had a fairly long and satisfying relationship with Edwina Mountbatten, as we have discussed earlier. Even Desai, for all his claims to asceticism, used to chuckle, rather than explode in anger, whenever gossip, printed or otherwise, linked his name to some comely woman, as happened quite a few times.

Indira or any other woman in the same position could never have reacted in similar circumstances equally nonchalantly which negates her claim – made from the moment of being elected Prime Minister until the last – that the fact of her being a woman was irrelevant to her responsibilities. 'I am a person with a job to do,' was her terse reply to those who asked how it felt to be a woman Prime Minister. Of course, she was not the first woman to rise to that office. That distinction belonged to Srimavo Bandaranaike, in neighbouring Ceylon, now Sri Lanka. Golda Meir became Prime Minister of Israel also before Indira was chosen for the same office in India. But the size and importance of her country invested the event with a significance the previous two cases had lacked.

Another point Indira liked making was that a head of state or government should never think of himself or herself as belonging to any particular group 'whether it is sex, religion or caste'. She had a point but between her brave words and reality there was a chasm.

For instance, in January 1966, several Indians despaired about the country because its 'destiny' had been entrusted to a 'woman'. The more superstitious ones added that the woman happened, 'inauspiciously' to be a widow. That apart, there were practical difficulties she could not wish away. Since all her senior cabinet and party colleagues were men – surprisingly, no woman held a high rank in her government though several were appointed as junior ministers – she could not deal with any of them at the level of intimacy which was quite common in the cases of Nehru and Shastri and their colleagues.

Even in small matters, being a woman made a difference. While travelling overseas, Indira could indulge in the latest fashions. Travelling in the conservative countryside in India she would cover her head and wear a full-sleeve blouse. Most Indian women wear blouses that leave the midriff bare; Indira never did.

On one occasion, a complete stranger, an elderly Muslim, wrote to her that it was 'not right' on her part to 'shake hands' with foreign men. She patiently replied to him that, as Prime Minister, she had to follow the customs of her foreign guests, not those of her own country which she 'preferred'.

Some of the problems arising from the fact of her being a woman were hilarious. One arose during her first visit to the United States in March-April 1966. She had arrived at Williamsburg in Virginia one evening, rather angry with something or the other, thus causing much anxiety to her cousin, B. K. Nehru, then Ambassador to the US. The next morning she was to fly to the White House by helicopter to be accorded a formal welcome by President Johnson.

B. K. Nehru, a late sleeper, was aroused from slumber at a very early hour by a phone call from the White House. Johnson was on the line. He had read in *The New York Times*, the US President said, that Indira did not like to be addressed as 'Madam Prime Minister'. How was he to address her on arrival at the White House?

The Ambassador, saying that he would answer the question after seeking instructions, rushed to Indira's suite. She told him that Johnson should feel free to address her as he liked. As soon as B. K. Nehru was about to leave, she added: 'You can also tell him that some of my cabinet ministers call me "Sir". He can do so, too, if he likes.'

On the other hand, it was never lost on Indira that the much quoted compliment to her, that she was the 'only man in a cabinet of old women', was a back-handed one and really centred on women's handicaps in politics.

Interestingly, writing on the same subject, a sober and serious journal, *Economic and Political Weekly*, went so far as to refer to the 'fate of Sultana Raziya', a thirteenth-century queen and the only woman ruler of India to precede Indira. Raziya, as history records, was a competent ruler. But within three years she was first deposed and then killed by 'factious nobles, jealous of her romance with one of her commanders, an Abyssinian Master of Horse'.

Maybe Indira had read Raziya's story carefully and avoided the kind of entanglement that had cost the Sultana her life. In the end, however, Indira too was slain, though for entirely different reasons.

Incidentally and poignantly, shortly before his death, during a discussion on Indian history with me, Feroze also dwelt at some length on Raziya's tragic end.

The most remarkable comment on Indira, in the context of women and power, came a year after her death from Helmut Schmidt. Indira, wrote the former West German chancellor, was '*zoon politikon*', political animal without gender.

# 12   The Empress Overthrown

Indira's decision to hold a fresh General Election, announced on January 18th, 1977, was even more sudden and unexpected than the proclamation of the State of Emergency nineteen months earlier. No one was more surprised than her political enemies. Some of them had not heard of her radio broadcast when the doors of their prison cells opened and they were released. No less startled were most of her friends and supporters, for only a handful of them had been taken into her confidence about what was afoot.

One of the ruling party members to know of the impending announcement passed through Bombay and gave me vague hints that the General Election was in the offing. I thought of sending a cautiously worded despatch to this effect to *The Guardian* but, before doing so, decided to consult Bhagwan Sahay, a distinguished retired civil servant who had served both Nehru and Indira in many sensitive posts. He was usually very well informed and I had great faith in his judgment.

'Have you taken leave of your senses?' he exclaimed when I told him what was on my mind. 'She cannot afford to hold elections because she would never win them. So forget your despatch.'

In the circumstances, it was no surprise that Indira's motives behind her otherwise welcome decision were viewed with the deepest suspicion. Since nothing good was expected from her, it was assumed that she had some trick up her sleeve.

More than a decade after the event, it is easy to see why Indira opted for elections and risked loss of power, to say the least, rather than hang on to power for some more years under Emergency regulations which she could have done. Evidently, she wanted to regain her credentials as a democratic leader which she had lost. She was also concerned about her 'place in history'. She did not want to be known to future generations as the leader who destroyed democracy in India, so lovingly nurtured by her own father. Probably she hoped – or was encouraged to hope by her Intelligence agencies and craven advisers – that she could restore democracy and yet remain in power by winning the election scheduled to be held in March. But she was prepared to lose the poll and power, if necessary, to bring democracy back – a claim she was emphatically to repeat in August 1984, just over two months before her death.

In the early months of 1977, however, hardly anyone was prepared

192

to believe any of this. Most people's thoughts were summed up by S. K. Patil, a pillar of the Syndicate and himself a master tactician. On coming out of jail, along with other opposition leaders, he told them that Indira was holding the poll without giving them any time to catch their breath, let alone organise themselves and collect the necessary funds, so that she could win the snap election and then reimpose the Emergency. He called Indira's plan a 'trap' and advised his colleagues not to fall into it. They shared his misgivings but politely rejected his advice to boycott the poll.

Far from laying a trap for her opponents, it seems, in retrospect at least, that Indira was trying frantically to get out of one she had landed herself in. At the end of November 1976, Fory Nehru, the Hungarian-born wife of Indira's cousin, B. K. Nehru, went to see her. The Nehrus then lived in London where B.K. was High Commissioner of India. Fory, who speaks Hindi fluently, spoke to Indira at length about what she had seen and heard about the excesses of the Emergency – the coercion about vasectomies, the brazen behaviour of the Sanjay loyalists, the high-handedness of police officials who extorted money from innocent citizens by threatening them with arrests under the Emergency's blanket powers and so on.

Instead of getting angry or even contradicting Fory, Indira held her head in her hands and said thrice: '*Mein kya karoon* (what should I do?), *mein kya karoon, mein kya karoon.*'

Pupul Jayakar has written about an even more emotional conversation at her New Delhi residence between Indira and the great sage and savant, J. Krishnamurthi, who normally lived and preached in Los Angeles but visited India once a year to deliver a series of sermons. In 1975, he refused to come in protest against the proclamation of the State of Emergency. The next year Indira asked Jayakar to persuade 'Krishnaji' to resume his annual visits and say in his lectures exactly what he liked, regardless of the Emergency. Indira saw him whenever he was in India and went to meet him in December 1976.

According to Jayakar, at this meeting with Krishnamurthi, Indira wept and told him that she was 'riding a tiger' and did not know how to dismount. He did not give her any 'specific' advice but told her: 'Since you are more intelligent than the tiger, you will find a way.'

As soon as electioneering began, it became clear that the tide of public opinion had turned, perhaps decisively, against Indira. The earliest indication came at the very first rally the opposition parties held at New Delhi's Ramlila Grounds where no public meeting had taken place since the fateful day when J.P. had appealed to the Army and the police to disobey Indira's illegal orders. Once again J.P., flanked by Desai and other leaders, was the star speaker. The rally itself was the largest and the most exuberant ever held in the capital. J.P.'s appeal to the people to use their 'precious vote' to throw Indira out of power was greeted with thunderous applause. The huge crowd went delirious with joy when he announced that the hitherto squabbling groups had all agreed to merge into the Janata party and fight Indira unitedly. An impromptu collection was made and handed to the leaders as the first contribution to the Janata's election chest. From then onwards, crowds at every Janata meeting would chant that the new party deserved both 'votes' and 'currency notes'. People contributed most generously.

Indira, by no means unaware of the tremendous response evoked by the newly-formed Janata party, had more unpleasant surprises awaiting her. On February 2nd, Jagjivan Ram, who had meekly piloted the resolution seeking Parliament's approval for the Emergency proclamation, resigned from both the cabinet and the Congress party. In doing so, he was joined by H. N. Bahuguna, an astute and able politician and former chief minister of the key state of UP, whom Indira had sacked unceremoniously in November 1975, and Nandini Satpathy, former chief minister of Orissa. Unlike Bahuguna, Satpathy was at one time a great favourite of Indira's. She, however, had a Communist past and was therefore eased out when, largely at Sanjay's behest, the Prime Minister decided to downgrade both her alliance with the Communist party and the ex-Communist members of her own party.

Mohan Kumaramangalam had died in a plane crash in 1973. After him the most important former Communist in the Indira camp was Rajni Patel, boss of the Congress in Bombay and the party's principal fund-raiser. He had a brief moment of glory but was soon discarded along with his comrades.

The irony of it all was that nobody was supporting the Emergency more stridently than the Communists and the ex-Communist Congressmen. They received their first major shock in December 1975 when Sanjay, in an interview with Uma Vasudev, for her magazine *Surge*, went so far as to condemn the Communists as 'anti-national' and 'traitors' because of their opposition to the 1942 Quit India movement launched by Mahatma Gandhi against the British. At the start of the Second World War, the Indian Communists had denounced it as an 'imperialist war'. But as soon as Russia was invaded by Hitler, it became 'a people's war' for them. Since the Quit India movement disrupted the war effort, they opposed it and earned the gratitude of the British government as well as the ire of Indian nationalists.

Not content with this, Sanjay had also denounced the public sector as inefficient and called for privatisation of state-owned industries.

The word about the contents of Sanjay's sensational interview spread like wildfire before the magazine was ready for circulation. CPI leaders frantically rang up the Prime Minister's office. She was away in Orissa and, in her absence, no one else could do anything about the Sanjay interview. When she arrived late at night, a delegation of Communists was waiting for her with their complaint. She told them that she would ask the chief censor to prohibit the circulation of the magazine carrying the interview but refused to disown Sanjay's views. Like the Syndicate and the Kitchen Cabinet, the Communists were now being dumped.

The circulation of the Sanjay interview may have been proscribed, but his message spread across the country. It was welcomed by Indian big business which hailed him as a new Messiah. The US embassy in New Delhi was also pleased. Although the governments of the two countries continued to bicker over Indira's charge of the CIA's malign interference in India's internal affairs, some Delhi-based American diplomats established 'close and cordial relations with Sanjay'.

Immediately after resigning from Indira's party, Jagjivan Ram, Bahuguna and Satpathy announced the formation of a new party, the Congress for Democracy, which promptly entered into an alliance with the Janata.

By now the entire country was electrified. To gauge the national mood and to cover the election campaign I travelled extensively in UP and Bihar, the two Hindi-speaking states which elect a fourth of Parliament's total membership. Within the first forty-eight hours, it was clear to me that Indira had reached the end of the road. The election had turned into a referendum on the Emergency and there was little doubt that the people were determined to reject it.

Indira jumped into the electoral fray with her usual vigour and was more mobile than her adversaries because of the use of Air Force aircraft and helicopters. She lampooned the Janata as 'khichri', which means both a hotch-potch and a rice-and-lentil dish normally given to those with impaired digestion. She also asked the people to choose between the 'stability and progress' she was offering them and the 'confusion and instability' represented by the Janata.

Janata leaders hit back hard. They said that despite having assumed dictatorial powers, Indira had failed to help the poor and the hungry. The Janata would give the country both 'bread and freedom'. They asked whether the Indian people would entrust power yet again to the two pairs of hands that had 'misused and abused it so grossly'. Their audiences would reply with resounding cries of 'No, never'.

While the Janata's election meetings were full of exuberance and even excitement, those addressed by Indira, even when well attended, were dull and listless. For the first time since her début in politics in the Fifties, Indian people were in no mood to listen to her.

When she taunted the Janata that it did not even have an identifiable leader acceptable to all its constituents as the future Prime Minister, Charan Singh replied on its behalf: 'Our leader will be elected by the parliamentary party; theirs is born from the mother's womb.'

In next to no time forced vasectomies became the main election issue, in North India at least, and on this Indira was most vulnerable. In Lucknow, the capital of UP, a fellow journalist and old friend who was a Muslim and a lifelong supporter of both Nehru and Indira, said to me, with tears in his eyes: 'These vasectomies have become for us the greased cartridges of 1857.' He was referring to the Indian Mutiny a hundred and twenty years earlier which was triggered by rumours that the cartridges given to soldiers of the British Indian Army were greased with the fat of cows (holy to Hindus) and pigs (forbidden to Muslims).

At hundreds of meetings I attended, and thousands of others I could not, Sanjay was described as the arch-villain of the Emergency and attacked more savagely than Indira was. But in his mother's party he continued to be the second most important person. He had a great deal of say in who would get the party ticket and who would not. He used this authority to get a number of his henchmen included in the party's list of candidates. He himself decided to contest for Parliament from Amethi, next door to Indira's constituency of Rae Bareli in UP.

Maneka, Sanjay's wife, was always by his side as he campaigned in Amethi, and she attacked the Janata leaders more vehemently than either her husband or her mother-in-law did.

Two days before polling day, All India Radio announced that some shots were fired at Sanjay's jeep but luckily he had escaped unhurt. Surprisingly, the country, including most newspapers, dismissed the incident as an 'engineered' one, designed to win sympathy for Sanjay.

First election results started coming in on the afternoon of March 20th. Within an hour it was clear that Indira and her party had suffered a debacle. In the South the Congress support held remarkably. But in North India her party was wiped out. It could not win even a single seat in the region, giving rise to the gleeful quip that a drunken lorry driver could go on a rampage from the India–Pakistan border to the frontier between India and Bangladesh without incurring the risk of running over a single Congress MP.

Indira and Sanjay headed the long list of ruling party stalwarts to have been defeated ignominiously. She lost to Raj Narain whose election petition had led to the Allahabad High Court's judgment against her and her son lost to a totally unknown wrestler.

The Prime Minister's election agent, M. L. Fotedar, now a minister in the Indian cabinet, using his clout, tried to get the counting of votes in her constituency suspended. But the young returning officer refused to oblige. The hassle had continued, however, for some hours before the verdict could be given. Consequently, the official announcement of Indira's defeat, followed almost immediately by that of Sanjay's, came in the early hours of a very cold morning.

However, despite the late hour and the freezing cold, tens of thousands of people were still outside newspaper offices, watching the latest news displayed on specially installed boards and celebrating the succession of Congress defeats. As news of Indira's and Sanjay's defeat was flashed, the crowds started dancing with joy. Some at least of those rejoicing over her defeat had danced also eight years earlier when she had nationalised major commercial banks.

The scene at the Prime Minister's house was described to me by Pupul Jayakar who had dropped in there just before dinner time. She found the atmosphere 'gloomy', though a staff member present at that time described it as 'funereal'.

'I have lost, Pupul, I have,' were the only words Indira uttered. She then asked for dinner to be served. Sanjay and Maneka had not yet returned from Amethi. Rajiv and Sonia were red-eyed and said they were not hungry at all. Indira calmly asked them to stay at the table anyhow and herself 'ate a full meal'.

As Jayakar left 1, Safdarjung Road, cabinet ministers of the defeated government were driving in for a midnight meeting at which they made their last recommendation to the Acting President, B. D. Jatti, (President Ahmed having died in February, 1977) that the Emergency be formally lifted. This was done immediately.

The nerve-centre of the Janata jubilation was Jagjivan Ram's residence, a ministerial bungalow he was entitled to keep for six months after resigning from the cabinet, just over a mile away from the Prime Minister's house. There, amidst scenes of wild excitement and cheering, some sombre consultations were going on behind the scenes.

Janata leaders had received word that rather than accept the people's verdict, Indira was planning to involve the armed forces to prop up her rejected regime. The rumour was wrong. But it had started because some precautionary arrangements were being made to forestall any breakdown of law and order, should it occur.

The reports were now revised to the effect that not the Army but the Border Security Force was being used 'to stage a coup'. Jagjivan Ram used his contacts to ascertain that this rumour, too, was baseless.

Indira waited until March 22nd, presumably for the last election result to be declared, before tendering her resignation. In a short statement she declared that she accepted the people's verdict with 'due humility'. She also owned up to 'full responsibility' for her party's 'serious reverses'.

The Acting President accepted her resignation but asked her to stay on until the new government could take over. This was necessary because the victorious Janata party was having trouble over the choice of the new Prime Minister. Desai, Charan Singh and Jagjivan Ram were all claimants to the top job. None had a clear majority in the newly formed party but any two could block the third.

Ultimately, J.P. and another opposition elder above the dust and din of active politics, J. B. Kripalani, were asked to adjudicate the leadership issue. They decided in Desai's favour, and thereafter all the Janata MPs, three-quarters of whom had never before seen the doors of any legislature, trooped to Rajghat, the final resting place of Mahatma Gandhi, to take a vow that they would remain united.

On March 23rd Desai was sworn in as Prime Minister. But it took him another twenty-four hours to complete the formation of his government. It was on the evening of March 24th that the leaders of the Janata government returned to the Ramlila Grounds to thank the people for electing them. The gathering was once again mammoth. Desai was, of course, the main speaker, but the star performer was Atal Bihari Vajpayee, leader of the Jana Sangh constituent of the Janata, now Foreign Minister and always a spell-binding orator. He began by congratulating the Indian people on their wisdom in 'consigning Indira to the dustbin of history'. The phrase, which sounds much harsher in Hindi, was cheered by the large gathering for several minutes.

That night I went to dine with a couple, both friends of mine, who had suddenly found themselves in the doghouse because they had supported the Emergency a trifle too ostentatiously. For this reason, conversation with them remained rather stilted. But things suddenly brightened up because of what their maidservant said while serving the meal.

'Vajpayeeji,' she remarked, 'should not have used such bad language about Indiraji.'

'Why not?' I decided to needle her. 'Hasn't Indiraji done very bad things to a large number of people?' But the elderly, unlettered and visibly distressed woman held her ground.

'Yes, Indiraji did bad things and she did good things in the past. The people have dethroned her. Isn't that enough?'

I ought to have been more alert to the significance of this exchange, especially in view of what came to pass later, but regrettably I was not. What did the opinion of an ignorant woman matter when the whole country was reverberating with the cry that Indira and Sanjay must be given their just deserts and the Janata government was responding to the demand with alacrity?

Indeed, Desai and his colleagues lost no time in appointing a number of commissions of inquiry to unearth Indira's and Sanjay's misdeeds. The most important of these was the one-man commission, consisting of a former chief justice of the Supreme Court, Mr J. C. Shah, to inquire into the imposition of the Emergency and all the excesses that followed. In Sanjay's case some criminal cases were also filed. Several of them related to the affairs of the Maruti company and other allegedly fraudulent business practices and one to the burning of all available prints of a film, critical of his mother's government, which was made just before the proclamation of the State of Emergency by, of all people, an MP named Amrit Nahata belonging to Indira's own party. The film was called *Kissa Kursi Ka* or 'A Tale of A Chair', the chair symbolising power in all Indian languages.

Having humbly 'bowed' to the people's verdict, Indira at first tried to put a brave face on her shattering defeat. 'I feel as if tons of weight have been lifted from my shoulders,' she announced soon after her resignation. Nobody believed her. That did not matter, but what did matter was that her once exemplary self-control broke down almost completely under the accumulating stress.

She started breaking into tears frequently and openly and often 'crying bitterly' not so much over the loss of power which undoubtedly hurt as because of her gnawing worry over her own physical safety and even more about that of her beloved son, Sanjay.

On the morrow of her defeat at Rae Bareli she had gone to Pupul Jayakar's house. Those who saw her reported that she was on the 'verge of hysteria'. She had received word that the people of Turkman Gate, brutally evicted from their homes a year earlier, had joyfully returned there and were threatening to give Sanjay a taste of his own medicine by 'sterilising him in public'. Some friends of Jayakar conveyed this to J.P. who reportedly advised Janata leaders of the area to put a stop to such talk.

J.P., a man of old-world charm, also called on Indira, for whose overthrow he had striven so hard despite his indifferent health. Desai was furious over this gesture. So were a large number of Janata MPs who renewed their clamour that Indira be awarded 'exemplary punishment without delay'. Most newspapers joined this outcry.

At the same time, many leaders of her party who had slavishly obeyed her every wish and whim, now distanced themselves from her. Some openly disowned her leadership. Among them was Dev Kanta Barooah who had coined the stupid slogan 'Indira is India, and India is Indira'. She was no longer in Parliament, so the leadership of the

199

150-strong Congress party, elected mostly from the South, went to Chavan. One of his first acts, without any consultation with Indira, was to agree to Desai's proposal to elect as President of the republic Sanjiva Reddy whose candidature for this post in 1969 had driven Indira to splitting her party. Reddy was elected unopposed. Indira felt 'betrayed' by her friends and followers and hemmed in by enemies 'determined' to 'destroy' her.

Though it might have seemed a small matter compared with self-preservation, she had to worry also about where to live. Had she been elected to Parliament, she would have been entitled to decent enough accommodation even after ceasing to be Prime Minister. But she had lost her seat.

Mohammed Yunus, a family friend and former Ambassador, immediately vacated his bungalow, 12, Willingdon Crescent, and the Janata government, in a rare gesture of magnanimity, agreed to allot it to Indira provided she paid 'market rent', several times higher than the usual one. The Willingdon Crescent house was naturally smaller than the Prime Minister's official residence but it was elegant enough and had nice gardens around it. Indira and her family moved there to start a new, uncertain life.

The tables were turned on Indira in more ways than one. Formerly she used to order her intelligence agencies to maintain surveillance on her foes. Now she was constantly under watch by the usually crude gumshoes of the Intelligence Bureau, whose efforts to merge into their surroundings were more comic than successful.

Under the eyes of the government's spies Indira withdrew into silence and inactivity. For days she did not even come out of her new habitat. This confirmed many in their belief that, politically at least, they had heard the last of her. They were to be proved grievously wrong.

# 13　Return of Mother Indira

Indira's defeat in the 1977 General Election and the consequent rise to power of the Janata party were hailed by many Indians as a 'revolution by the ballot box'. If this was indeed an accurate description of what had happened, then it must have been the only revolution in history to have been devoured by its children.

Not only did the Janata government destroy itself with astonishing rapidity but also it did something which was far removed from its original intentions: it helped and hastened Indira's return to power. This it did in more ways than one. Its crass incompetence and constant infighting – despite the vow of unity taken at Mahatma Gandhi's mausoleum – shocked those who had voted for it with so much enthusiasm. But it is doubtful whether these by themselves could have endeared Indira to the people. What clinched the issue in her favour was the Janata's relentless vendetta against her. The 'prosecution' of Indira turned into 'persecution' and this appalled many even among those who had earlier insisted that she be held accountable for all her 'crimes'.

On the other hand, there was a relatively small but extremely vocal section of the intelligentsia, with great influence in the media, which berated the Janata government for being lax or lenient in its investigations of the charges against her and her son. Within the silent majority, however, there was now greater inclination to agree with Indira that the Janata had 'nothing else' to do except to 'persecute a lone and defenceless woman'. The story is best told from the beginning.

Soon after March 1977, when Indira was shellshocked and isolated, the Janata government was receiving enormous applause simply by restoring civil liberties and democratic freedoms which had been denied during the Emergency. It also got great credit when it repealed some of the sweeping changes made in the constitution by Indira and restored the earlier balance between the judiciary and the executive which she had altered in the latter's favour. The people cheered even more when some disgraceful laws Indira had passed under the amended constitution to protect her own position were also removed from the statute book.

For instance, she would have won her appeal against the Allahabad judgment anyhow. But she took no chances, and amended the election

201

law in such a way as to make it obligatory on the Supreme Court to uphold her election to Parliament and to remove the disqualification ordered by Justice Sinha. Not content with this she had two other laws passed to make the election of the President, the Vice-President, the Prime Minister and the Speaker of Parliament wholly immune from judicial scrutiny and to make any newspaper criticism of these four dignitaries an offence. As a perceptive writer was to comment later, the inclusion of the other three holders of high office in the various laws 'resembled light musical accompaniment to the sombre theme of prime ministerial power'. Indira had, in fact, sponsored an even more shocking bill to confer on herself a 'lifelong immunity' from civil or criminal action. But it was later dropped.

At the same time, daily and highly publicised hearings by the Shah Commission were giving Indira a very bad name. To make matters worse, a number of coincidental developments were also proving embarrassing to her.

Within two months of her fall from power, for instance, Sanjay's father-in-law, T. S. Anand, was found dead at his farm not far from Delhi. He had a history of depression and of one attempted suicide. He had also left a note stating that he could no longer 'bear to see Sanjay's suffering'. Even so, the cry went up that the colonel had been 'eliminated' because he was the 'weakest link' in the attempt to cover up Sanjay's egregious excesses. Soon thereafter, Delhi's Lieutenant-Governor, Kishan Chand, removed by the Janata government and grilled by the Shah Commission, also committed suicide by jumping into a well. He too had left a note to say that death was better than a 'life of humiliation'. But it was again alleged that he was pushed into the well.

In the circumstances, it was no surprise that few were prepared to believe that Indira might be back in power some day. She herself was apparently sceptical about this. For when, on the morrow of her defeat, Aruna Asaf Ali, a heroine of the freedom struggle and since then a respected leftist leader, assured her that the people would 'surely bring her back', she replied: 'When? After I am dead?' Soon, however, the unthinkable became not only possible but also probable.

What changed the people's attitude towards her was that the Janata's attempt to call her to account for her acts of omission and commission during the Emergency had degenerated into a campaign of 'hatred and harassment'.

The Shah Commission turned into something of a cross between a US congressional inquiry and a Chinese people's court. In the overflowing commission chamber the atmosphere was overwhelmingly hostile to Indira. Everything said against her and her family was lustily cheered; the slightest attempt to defend her was booed. Indira refused to testify before the Shah Commission on the grounds that she could neither violate the oath of secrecy she had taken nor 'incriminate' herself. For this she was prosecuted. But Sanjay responded to the commission's summons and turned up there accompanied by a claque of aggressive supporters. Their appearance became a signal for a free-for-all exchange of abuse and blows which culminated in the hurling of chairs. But before this happened a great deal of water had flowed down through the Yamuna.

As part of the Janata's campaign to arraign Indira both before the courts of law and at the bar of public opinion, the Home Minister, Charan Singh made a statement in Parliament on May 23rd, 1977 alleging that Indira Gandhi had 'planned or thought of killing all opposition leaders in jail during the Emergency'. This gave Indira her first chance to bounce back into the political activity from which she was supposed to have been banished.

Describing Charan Singh's statement as 'shocking and preposterous' Indira refuted his charge. She said that J. P. Vajpayee, now Foreign Minister, and Charan Singh himself had been released from prison at the 'first intimation of ill-health'. This would hardly have been done by someone out to liquidate them.

Indira ended her statement by asking the Janata that, instead of pursuing its 'smear campaign and character assassination' directed against her, it might 'at least now' pay some attention to 'atrocities on Harijans' and to other pressing problems of the people such as 'increasing lawlessness' and 'spiralling prices'. She had not only picked on the weakest spots of the Janata administration but also was indicating her plan of action to return to the public gaze.

Ironically, with the restoration of civil liberties to the law-abiding citizens, lawless elements had also been emboldened. Smugglers, hoarders, profiteers and even 'bad characters' had all been released as a result of the Janata's decision to repeal Indira's Draconian laws. Crime rose fast even in the heart of the Indian capital. Some people at least started longing for the discipline of the Emergency. The situation was gravely complicated by disarray and disaffection within the police force. During the Emergency many police officers had enforced repressive measures with excessive zeal. The Janata started legal and disciplinary action against them. This divided the force. There were places where half the force would be busy 'investigating the conduct of the other half' rather than doing its normal job of apprehending criminals and law-breakers. There were several strikes and mutinies by policemen.

Prices rose unduly, partly because unscrupulous traders felt free to act as they pleased and partly because the rains had started to fail again.

The most heart-rending problem during the first few months of the Janata rule, however, was the sudden spurt in the atrocities on Harijans, the former untouchables. By no means unknown during Indira's regime, such horrors had now become both more frequent and more gruesome. This was not without reason. The power base of the Janata, especially of its wing led by Charan Singh, included several intermediate castes, such as Jats, Yadavs, Ahirs and Rajputs, who were even more aggressively anti-Harijan than the highest of high castes which had traditionally supported the Congress. Power went to the heads of these castes in the vanguard of the Janata ranks. They became a law unto themselves in the countryside, and brutally put down anything they saw as a sign of Harijan self-assertion.

No wonder then that immediately after contradicting Charan Singh, Indira, who had until then been immobilised in Delhi, set out on a journey to Belchi, a remote village in Bihar, where a particularly revolting outrage on the Harijans had taken place. Scores had been burnt alive. Harijan women were raped. It was the rainy season and Belchi, surrounded by knee-deep mud and slush, was inaccessible. Indira was unfazed. She saw a villager walk ahead of his elephant, asked for a lift and clambered up to the animal's back. Prathiba Singh, a party member from Bihar who had accompanied Indira on the journey, was asked to join her. She said later that while she herself was 'terrified', Indira seemed to be enjoying the elephant-ride.

What Indira enjoyed vastly more was the reception the Harijans and other poor people of Belchi and of villages *en route* gave her. She was elated and felt reassured that all was not lost and that she could regain the support and affection of the alienated people if only she tried.

On returning to Delhi the first thing she did was to decide to go to Rae Bareli, her constituency which had rejected her so completely. She went by train because, she said, she could not 'afford the air fare'. At Lucknow railway station, where she alighted before motoring to Rae Bareli, and all through her journey across her constituency, she was given a rousing reception by her supporters. Simon Winchester of *The Guardian*, who was with her all through, reported that the clear message of this journey was that Indira's constituents had 'forgiven her in ten minutes flat'. But almost all Indian newspapers published long despatches claiming that she had been greeted with black flags, a sign of disapproval in India. This was a measure not only of the media's bias against her but also of the climate of opinion in which few protested against such blatant lack of objectivity.

However, her visits to Belchi and her constituency enraged the Janata ranks into demanding that instead of being left free to stride across the country, Indira should be arrested and put on a

'Nuremberg-type' trial. Rumours that she would be taken into custody went on day after day but nothing happened. Among those deeply unhappy with this 'indecision' of the Janata government was Home Minister Charan Singh, a staunch advocate of the 'most stringent action' against her.

Indira was concerned about the possibility of being imprisoned, but she put a brave face on it. She made her first public appearance in Delhi after her fall from power at a meeting in a large hall. The subject of her lecture was planning. The Janata government, altering the established pattern of five-year plans, had introduced the concept of a 'rolling' plan. Indira told a capacity and cheering audience that the planning process was being 'rolled up' by the Janata. Her real message was, however, different.

Arriving late for the meeting, Indira found every seat taken, many people standing in the aisles and the podium surrounded by a battery of TV cameras, newspaper reporters and photographers. 'I already feel imprisoned,' she declared, amidst loud cheers and laughter. Janata leaders, however, were not laughing.

It was on October 3rd, 1977, a day after Mahatma Gandhi's birth anniversary, that the much-talked-of arrest of Indira turned into reality. The police arrived at 12, Willingdon Crescent in the afternoon. What followed was pure theatre from which Indira was to derive tremendous political advantage.

She took her time to get ready. In the interval, her devoted staff made a few phone calls. Within minutes, a multitude of her supporters swarmed round her residence like angry bees. She then demanded of the police officers: 'Where are the handcuffs?' Without being man-acled, she added, she would not leave. Badly shaken, the police officers begged her not to embarrass them. She then got into the police van, amidst the shouting of slogans by her infuriated supporters. As the police van drove off so did a procession of the cars of the faithful, headed by Sanjay's Matador.

When it looked as if the police were planning to take Indira out of Delhi's administrative jurisdiction into the Haryana state, the Black Maria was surrounded by vehicles carrying Indira supporters. During the heated argument that followed, she quietly got out of the van and sat calmly on a culvert, as if the surrounding excitement had nothing to do with her. The police officers had no choice but to bring her back to Delhi where she was lodged in the Police Lines. She sat up all night reading a book she had carried with her.

At ten the next morning she was to be produced before a magistrate at Tees Hazari Courts. But this was easier said than done. All the streets leading to the court house were blocked by seething mobs, divided more or less equally into two. One section was condemning Indira's arrest and pronouncing anathema on the 'vindictive' Janata government. The other was carrying black flags and shouting 'Indira Gandhi *Murdabad*' or 'Death to Indira Gandhi'. Inevitably, the two sides clashed. The police used tear gas and batons to disperse them.

The scene inside the court room was no less exciting, but lasted for just two minutes. The magistrate released Indira 'unconditionally' because there was 'no charge against her'. The court room resounded with cheers and slogans in her favour.

This fiasco of Indira's arrest not only meant a serious loss of face for the Janata but also put her firmly on the come-back trail. Later, when she was briefly imprisoned, tens of thousands of people were to court arrest in protest against the action. This was to startle the Janata leaders who were somehow convinced that she had forfeited the people's sympathy for good. Two young supporters of Indira from UP, the Pandey brothers, went so far as to hijack an aircraft of the domestic airline by threatening the crew with a toy pistol. They were quickly overpowered and were jailed. In 1980 when Indira returned to power both the brothers were rewarded with membership of the UP legislature. This was to cause Indira serious embarrassment when, two years later, Sikhs agitating for an independent state of their own hijacked an aircraft to Pakistan. The supporters of the accused men argued that they were also making a political point, like the Pandey brothers.

From the time Indira had gone to Belchi, people who had stayed away from her immediately after her defeat in the elections started flocking to her new residence, as they had done when she lived in the Prime Minister's house. But what was a trickle to begin with turned into a torrent after her arrest in October 1977. Prime Minister Desai also gave audience to the public every morning. But crowds at his official residence were greatly outnumbered by those going to Indira's house to greet her. She had nothing to give them but the poor people brought her small gifts, often inexpensive religious books. An American girl visiting her became so emotional that she took off her ring and refused to leave until Indira agreed to accept it.

Another American visitor, witnessing the manifestly admiring crowds of poverty-stricken people surrounding her, said to her that something must have been done for them if they still kept coming. 'No,' Indira replied, 'those for whom something was done are nowhere to be seen.'

This biting remark was at least partly directed against senior leaders of her party who had turned their backs on her. Some of them had joined hands with the Janata. Most explained their compliance with

206

her wishes during the Emergency as an outcome of 'sheer fear'. Brahmananda Reddy, who had replaced Borooah as Congress President, treated her with indifference. Criticism of Sanjay's continuing influence on her was a regular feature of Congress conclaves. Though he had announced his decision to withdraw from the Youth Congress, it was known that his mother relied on his advice on party affairs and indeed regarded him as her 'main protector' at a time when she was being 'persecuted' by the Janata and 'betrayed' by her own party colleagues.

It was becoming clear that she and the rest of the Congress leadership could no longer coexist. On New Year's Day 1978, the breach became formal when Indira split the Congress for a second time in a decade. This time there was no recourse to euphemism in naming the new party. It was called simply the Congress (Indira) or the Congress (I), for short. The other half of the party called itself the Congress (S), the letter in parenthesis standing for Swaran Singh who had become its President.

Even some of those who had gone along with her felt that she had 'made a mistake'. But in the elections to several state legislatures, held in February 1978, her decision to go it alone appeared to have been vindicated. The southern states, Karnataka and Andhra, which had stood by the Congress during the preceding year's debacle, now opted for her, defeating both the Janata and the rival Congress. Even more impressive was the Congress (I)'s performance in Maharashtra, the citadel of Chavan, now regarded by Indira as the captain of the 'Janata's B team'. Ironically, neither side being able to form a ministry in Maharashtra, the two Congresses had to form an uneasy coalition. It did not last long because the Janata was able to 'win over' enough of its members to bring it down.

But, from the Maharashtra experiment, stemmed a clamour that the two Congresses must reunite for the greater good of both and of the country. Swaran Singh was quoted as having said that he was left with the 'party files while the ranks had gone over to Mrs Gandhi'. Unity talks went on endlessly and unproductively until both sides got tired of them. Indira had no interest in unity. She seemed determined to have a party 'completely under her and her son's control'.

In this resolve she was evidently strengthened by a great many things, the most important of which was the popular response to her wherever she went. She had again started travelling extensively and now she went about as an ordinary citizen, without any panoply of power, and yet people, including those who had forsaken her during the 1977 General Election, welcomed her enthusiastically.

The Janata government and Indira's critics among the intelligentsia were dismayed. What was wrong with the people, rallying round the 'deposed dictator'? Did they not read the Shah Commission's report, submitted in March and April 1978, clearly holding that the proclamation of the State of Emergency by Indira was 'fraudulent'? The Commission had, in fact, held that no valid reason existed for the declaration of a State of Emergency and Indira's decision was taken in a 'desperate endeavour to save herself from the legitimate compulsion of a judicial verdict against her'. 'Thousands were detained,' the Commission went on to say, 'and a series of totally illegal and unwarranted actions followed involving untold human misery and suffering.'

Indira was travelling in Karnataka, visiting temples and monasteries, and finally settling down in a lovely rest house in the hills of Mercara to do some writing and to indulge in her passion for walking barefoot in the mountains or on the seashore. It was in these sylvan surroundings that she got word that Sanjay was in deep trouble.

In one of the many cases against him, he was accused of trying to 'intimidate and suborn' prosecution witnesses. The trial judge did not want to deal with this issue. It therefore reached the Supreme Court which decided, on May 5th, 1978, that Sanjay be placed in 'judicial custody for a month'. Indira took the first available plane to Delhi but before her arrival he had been hauled to the Tihar jail where many of the Emergency prisoners had been lodged, often in appalling conditions.

From the airport Indira drove straight to the prison where, in front of TV cameras and a horde of reporters, she embraced her son and exclaimed: 'Don't lose heart. This is going to be your political birth.' For a woman excessively careful about her choice of words, as if even a stray remark might betray her, this was a strange and unexpected lapse. For in just eleven words, she had contradicted her elaborate and transparently false claim, built up over the preceding fourteen months, that Sanjay was 'never in politics'. Emotional stress had obviously got the better of her habitual caution.

By the time Sanjay came out of jail, two important developments had taken place. Indira had made up her mind to overcome an irritating political disability by re-entering Parliament. More importantly, the infighting within the Janata had intensified and this hurriedly cobbled-together coalition was showing signs of falling apart.

As we have seen, the only thing that had brought together the four disparate parties comprising the Janata was their common desire to throw Indira out of power. Now that she was showing signs of regaining her lost popularity, it would have stood to reason that the ruling party would close ranks, if only to keep her at bay. But this was far from being the case.

What to do with Indira was, of course, one of the issues in the sordid dissensions at the highest levels of the Janata leadership in full public view. But, by now, this was a sideshow. The real point at issue was the leadership of the Janata government. A no-holds-barred power struggle was on. The three old men expected jointly to lead the Janata were at loggerheads with one another. J.P.'s unifying influence was no longer available because he, 'feeling neglected by Desai', had retired to Patna.

Charan Singh, the Home Minister, was no longer reconciled to Desai being the Prime Minister and made no bones about wanting the job for himself. It was he who shouted the loudest about the need to lock up Indira at once. In demanding this he was providing leadership to the large number of Janata men who were saying that the Shah Commission having established 'Indira's guilt', her punishment should follow without delay.

This was a clear misrepresentation of reality. Justice Shah had taken care to point out that, under the Indian law, commissions of inquiry were only fact-finding bodies without any judicial powers and therefore 'could not pronounce anyone guilty of anything'. As for the 'illegal and unwarranted' acts the commission had spoken of, each specific charge would have to be formulated separately and then launched in a court of law. Given the notorious legal delays, this could take years. Desai, having been embarrassed by Indira's previous arrest without any cause, was insisting that any further action against her should be taken only after collecting foolproof evidence.

But Charan Singh had no time for such sophistry. Early in June he wrote an angry letter to Desai describing the cabinet as a 'collection of impotent men' incapable of bringing Indira to justice. Desai retaliated by asking Charan Singh to resign which he did promptly. The Prime Minister took the opportunity also to ease out Raj Narain, the buffoonish socialist who had defeated Indira and was appointed Health Minister. He had immediately become a loyal lieutenant of Charan Singh and was masterminding the Home Minister's attempt to displace Desai.

The seeds of the Janata's destruction were thus sown. Charan Singh was too important and too powerful to be kept out of the cabinet and Raj Narain too vengeful to forgive or forget a slight. No wonder then that efforts to bring back Charan Singh into the cabinet began even before the ink on his resignation letter was dry. These efforts were pursued most vigorously by the Jana Sangh section of the Janata which was under great pressure because one of the issues Raj Narain had raised was that the Jana Sangh's continued association with the RSS, a militia-like Hindu organisation, was driving Janata's Muslim supporters back to Indira. The charge had some validity because – like the atrocities on Harijans – Hindu–Muslim riots, in which the Muslim minority was usually at the receiving end, had increased.

However, it was not until the end of the year that a compromise could be hammered out under which Charan Singh could return to the cabinet, this time as Finance Minister because Desai would not give him back the Home portfolio. As a compensation, he was made Deputy Prime Minister, but he had to share this honour with Jagjivan Ram, another aspirant to prime ministership. In the meantime, several momentous events had taken place in the country.

One of these was Indira's return to Parliament on November 7th, 1978, in a by-election at Chikmagalur, a rural constituency in the southern state of Karnataka, where her party was in power. The campaign for this crucial by-election turned out to be the most acrimonious the country had witnessed until then. Determined to keep her out of Parliament, the Janata had deputed her arch-enemy, George Fernandes, to take charge of the contest. His fulminations against Indira were matched by the state chief minister, Devaraj Urs, then perhaps her most vociferous supporter and a skilful politician. Almost the entire Indian press was hostile to her and predicted that she would lose. The reality on the ground was that wherever Indira went she was welcomed by the people, especially the women, as 'Indira Amma' or Mother Indira. When the votes were counted she had won by a massive majority.

What happened after her election to Parliament was both far more bizarre and far more fateful than anything that had preceded it.

Soon after becoming an MP again, Indira embarked on a journey to Britain. She had been invited by several associations of Indians settled there. But by the time she reached the British shores, rival organisations of Indians had appeared on the scene to show her black flags and to condemn her for her 'dictatorial ambitions so blatantly displayed during the Emergency'. This was an exact reflection of the political polarisation, centred on her personality, that had already taken place back home and was to become more and more inflamed with the passage of time.

On the way to London, Indira's plane had stopped in Moscow. The Russians, who had once lionised her, gave her the cold shoulder – they sent only a relatively junior functionary to greet her – which enraged her. The Russians were of course responding to the Janata government's request that she be treated as a pariah, as she 'richly deserved' to be. A similar request was sent to London, too. But both Prime Minister Callaghan and Margaret Thatcher, the Leader of the

Opposition, disregarded it. The two Iron Ladies had met before in New Delhi and later a great personal rapport was to develop between them.

Even so, in January 1979 when Callaghan, as British Prime Minister, paid an official visit to India, the Janata repeated to him its petty proposal that he should not receive her. But he told the Janata leaders that, as a Leader of the Opposition, she was entitled to all 'courtesies' which visiting heads of government in Britain 'accorded to the Leader of Her Majesty's Opposition'.

During the interval between Indira's visit to Callaghan at Downing Street and his invitation to her to tea at Rashtrapati Bhavan in Delhi Indira had not only been deprived of her seat in Parliament but had also been imprisoned.

While she was still in England, the Privileges Committee of Parliament had held her 'guilty' of contempt of Parliament for 'obstructing four officials' who were collecting information for a parliamentary question on Sanjay's Maruti car project. The committee had said that an apology by her would meet the ends of justice. But if she refused to apologise, the House should decide what punishment to award her.

It would have been out of character for Indira to offer an apology or even to express regret. The Janata's 'hawkish majority' therefore insisted that she should both be expelled from Parliament and imprisoned until the prorogation of the House. This was done by a resolution passed late in the evening of December 19th, after a very heated debate.

Before Indira was taken to Tihar jail, she was virtually mobbed by her party members and others. Some Congress women started crying. She consoled them and recited to them a slightly garbled version of a song she must have read many years earlier. For she said:

> Wish me well as you bid me goodbye,
> With a cheer, not a tear in your eye,
> Leave me a smile,
> I can keep all the while,
> That I am away.

Indira was still in jail when, on December 23rd, Charan Singh made a show of his strength by holding a huge rally of rich and middle class farmers, his main power base, on his birthday. Through an intermediary, Indira sent him a bouquet of flowers.

Desai and his complacent counsellors failed to notice the clear sign that contact had been established between Charan Singh and the woman he had wanted to destroy. His lieutenant, Raj Narain, had in fact, been holding long meetings with Sanjay, plotting how to install Charan Singh in Desai's place. These confabulations were to bear fruit some seven months later.

On being released from prison after a week, Indira went straight to Chikmagalur to tell her constituents that their verdict had been nullified by the Janata 'illegally and wilfully'. Her next port of call was Madras where she met J. Krishnamurti, the sage who had told her two years earlier that she was more intelligent than the tiger she was riding.

This time his advice to her was to 'leave politics'. Indira, as she later recounted to Pupul Jayakar, told him that the Janata government had levelled a hundred charges against her, including one of the 'theft of two chickens'. 'I told Krishnaji,' she added, 'that I have only two alternatives, to fight or let them destroy me like a sitting duck.'

Indira's decision to fight the Janata was superfluous, for, by now, the Janata leaders seemed hell-bent on destroying one another. Led by Charan Singh, many were charging Desai's son, Kantibhai, with misusing his father's position for 'personal gain' through 'dubious business deals'. Desai reacted by saying that there were charges against Charan Singh's wife. The latter retorted that he would welcome an inquiry against his wife provided one was held against Desai's son as well. This was not acceptable to the Prime Minister.

Jagjivan Ram, the Defence Minister, found himself in a very embarrassing position because of his son's waywardness. The young man was photographed copulating with a woman not his wife. His claim that he had been 'drugged' and forced to 'pose in the nude' was belied by the photographs which were published in *Surya*, the magazine edited by Sanjay's wife, Maneka.

Charan Singh was not content with attacking Desai. In a letter to the Prime Minister, he described Bahuguna, Minister for Petroleum, as a 'KGB agent'. Bahuguna said, also in writing, that Charan Singh was a 'mad man'. And yet this did not prevent the two men from making common cause against Desai.

At the end of February, when Charan Singh presented his first and last budget, Desai realised the folly of giving him the sensitive Finance portfolio. For Charan Singh's proposals gave a bounty to farmers and imposed punitive taxes and other levies on Desai's and the Jana Sangh's supporters in urban areas who were duly annoyed.

Immediately after the budget, Desai at last got legislation passed to set up special courts to try Indira and Sanjay summarily and for offences specially created under the new law. But it was now too late; in mid-July the Janata government fell because Charan Singh's supporters ratted on it. He was invited by President Reddy to form a

212

new government and 'secure a vote of confidence from the lower house of Parliament within a month'.

Charan Singh never faced the House. Indira had supported his claim to the prime ministership. Now she was demanding the price for this support: withdrawal of the Special Courts Act. This he was in no position to do. On August 22nd the President dissolved Parliament, asked Charan Singh to stay on as caretaker Prime Minister but 'without taking any major policy decision' and ordered an election in the first week of January 1980.

By now the people who had danced with joy at Indira's defeat were fed up with both the fallen Janata and the comical Charan Singh who had not faced Parliament even for a day. Moreover, because of raging drought for a second year running, there was great economic hardship in the country. During the four months preceding the poll prices 'registered the highest increase in any comparable period since independence'.

Indira made the prices of potatoes and onions a major election issue. But her main battlecry was that she would give the country a 'Government that Works'. This was rather pallid compared with the magic slogan *Garibi Hatao* (Remove Poverty) but probably it was what the people were looking forward to.

On January 6th, 1980, during the first hour of the counting of votes it was clear that the woman who was supposed to have been 'thrown into the dustbin of history' was India's chosen leader once again. A banner headline in *The Times of India* – 'It's Indira All the Way' – said it all.

# 14 Triumph into Tragedy

Over her triumphant return to power, Indira rejoiced doubly, for herself and, even more so, for Sanjay. The election had lent some legitimacy to his enormous power and title to the throne, both blighted in the past for having been built up behind the protective ramparts of the Emergency. He was no longer dismissed as an imposition on the country by a loving and wilful mother determined to establish dynastic rule. Instead he was seen to have won his political spurs. He had gone through a grim struggle and the Janata government's persecution had failed to cow him. Moreover, he had been elected to Parliament, in his own right and with a big majority, from Amethi where he had been trounced only three years earlier.

Consequently there was a much greater acceptance of him as the Crown Prince, even though his manners and style had improved only marginally. From being a wielder of authority delegated to him by his mother, he had now become her partner in power. By now the Congress (I) – the letter in parenthesis standing for Indira – had turned into a combination of a praetorian guard and a feudal court. It not only accepted Sanjay's pre-eminence but applauded it, heaping on him praises so extravagant as to be beyond belief. But neither the flatterers nor Sanjay nor his mother seemed embarrassed. Party men, used to swearing allegiance and loyalty to Indira, often several times a day, amended their litany suitably. They now genuflected to both Indira and 'her family'.

While choosing Congress (I) candidates for the parliamentary poll Sanjay had taken care to strengthen his own power base. No fewer than 234 of the 541 successful party men were new not only to Parliament but also to politics itself. Of them close to 150 were hard-core Sanjay supporters, hand-picked by him from among Youth Congress activists. Most of them, as has been noted, were lumpen young men. They had flocked round him when he first became his mother's heir-apparent, in the hope of riding to power and prosperity on the tails of his *kurta*, a loose, collarless shirt. But they had stayed by his side even after he had fallen on lean days. Their fierce loyalty to him, even in the darkest hour, had impressed him as well as his mother. It was typified by the declaration of one of the youngsters who, after becoming an MP declared: 'If Sanjay tells me to do so, I will even put my head into an oilseed crusher.' But however commendable their loyalty to their leader, their sense of responsibility or probity left a great deal to be desired.

214

Innocent of the Congress culture, such as it was, and even of minimum parliamentary proprieties, unencumbered by ideology or idealism, short on cerebration and long on the exercise of muscle power, Sanjay's acolytes looked upon their membership of Parliament and proximity to the centre of power as a short-cut to making the 'maximum possible money in the shortest possible time'. Any criticism of this proclivity by a shaken and enfeebled parliamentary opposition, or indeed any criticism of Indira or Sanjay, became a signal for the youthful hordes to start barracking and thus making Parliament's functioning virtually impossible, except on Sanjay's terms. Indira looked silently on.

At this time Sanjay's power was at its zenith and practically irresistible. Ministers and top civil servants vied with one another to do his bidding, however arbitrary. Those having qualms about this soon found themselves in trouble; politicians were sidelined and 'recalcitrant' bureaucrats were summarily removed from their positions, humiliated and often kept waiting for months for alternative, usually inconsequential, postings.

No one would have batted an eyelid if Indira had chosen to induct Sanjay into her cabinet. But she shrewdly refrained from doing so in order to create the impression that the impetus to propel Sanjay into high office came from others, rather than her. Sure enough, a move to draft him for the job of chief minister of UP, the most populous and politically the key state of India, duly began. The motives behind it were mixed. Those who had hitched their wagons to the Sanjay star – and they included many who had earlier denounced him vehemently – were confident that even a short stint as UP chief minister would put on Sanjay the stamp of approval as his mother's successor. Others, apprehensive about what the abrasive and impulsive young man might do but afraid to oppose him, took recourse to praising his qualities of leadership and demanding that he be given a 'suitable opportunity to prove himself'. They felt they would be better off with Sanjay away in Lucknow, the capital of UP, than if he remained in Delhi. But neither side was able to further its objectives. The move to make Sanjay the chief minister of UP failed to get off the ground largely because of his reluctance to leave the centre of power. Presumably to meet the demand that there should be some formal focus of Sanjay's vast but amorphous power, Indira made him General Secretary of the All India Congress Committee, now called AICC(I).

The opportunity for appointing a new chief minister in UP and eight other states had arisen because Indira had chosen to repeat in reverse a dubious precedent set by the Janata government in 1977 which had, however, been upheld by the Supreme Court. The Janata had then argued that in the states where the Congress had been

215

routed in the parliamentary poll, it had forfeited the right to rule even at the state, or provincial, level though the tenure of the state legislatures was not yet over. When the Congress ministries in these nine states refused to resign, they were summarily dismissed. In the fresh elections that followed, the Janata and its allies won in all nine states. Three years later, in early June 1980, Indira retaliated against the Janata and in all nine states; Janata and Janata-supported ministries were sacked. In the ensuing elections, the Congress (I) emerged triumphant.

One of the states where the wheel of political fortune turned a full circle a second time was Punjab. Here the majority of the population belongs to the Sikh religion, though countrywide the Sikhs form only a tiny, two per cent minority. The Akali party, claiming to represent all the Sikhs in Punjab, had traditionally felt frustrated because the Congress usually won the elections by gaining a substantial number of Sikh votes (especially of the deprived castes which resented the aggressiveness of the prosperous Jats dominating the Sikhs) and the bulk of Hindu votes, the Sikh majority over the Hindus in Punjab being rather narrow. Twice the Akalis managed to scrape to power but only in uneasy coalition with the Jana Sangh, the right-wing Hindu Party, later to merge with the Janata and now styling itself the BJP or the Bharatiya Janata party. On both occasions the coalitions were shortlived. In 1977, for the first time, the Akalis won a thin majority in the Punjab assembly on their own, but they chose to form a government in the state in partnership with the Janata and shared power with the Janata at the federal centre in New Delhi. They were pleased with the stability of their ministry in Punjab which hoped to run its full term until 1982 and perhaps return to power in the elections due that year. But all these comforting calculations were belied by harsh realities of life.

In the 1980 parliamentary poll, the Akali party was in for a shock. It won only one parliamentary seat out of sixteen. In the subsequent state assembly elections that Indira ordered after dissolving the nine state legislatures, it suffered an equally shattering defeat. The Congress was back in power in Punjab. The resultant Akali anger and Sikh frustration fuelled the agitation that was later to set Punjab ablaze and eventually to lead to Indira's assassination.

Seeds of Indira's other misfortunes were also being sown at the same time, ironically or perhaps inevitably, by Sanjay. To nobody's surprise he had had the final say in the choice of chief ministers in the states where fresh elections had been held. Some of the selections he made proved embarrassing and came unstuck before long. That of Abdul Rahman Antulay as chief minister of Maharashtra, the state which includes the city of Bombay, the country's financial and commercial capital, turned out to be particularly disastrous. All this, however, lay in the future.

At the beginning of her second innings as Prime Minister the item at the top of Indira's agenda was a foreign policy problem of great importance and complexity. Its handling suffered both because of her personal foibles and the public exuberance of her supporters.

On December 26th, 1979, the Soviet tanks and troops had rolled into Afghanistan, the traditional buffer between the Indian subcontinent and Russia, over which the 'Great Game' had been played every so often during the British Raj. India was then in the throes of a hard-fought election with little time to worry about this admittedly grave development. The world, outraged by the Soviet invasion of a small neighbour, poured out its anger at the United Nations. A debate on Afghanistan was scheduled for early January. Instructions had to be sent to the Indian delegation to the UN, but, incredible though it may seem, India was virtually without a government.

Charan Singh's caretaker government, which had not faced Parliament for a single day and had been defeated in the elections, nevertheless continued to be in office technically. The reason for this was bizarre. The last of the election results having been announced on the night of January 6th, Indira was in a position to form her government the next morning. But she refused to be sworn in until January 14th, a very auspicious day, according to the Hindu calendar, and therefore much recommended by her astrologers. This curious behaviour was entirely characteristic of Indira. She was vehement in denying that she either believed in superstition or had faith in astrology. In 1971 she had gone so far as to declare that she did 'not even believe in God'. But her reliance on astrologers, soothsayers and holy men was well known. During the thirty-three months in the political wilderness this dependence had clearly increased. So superstitious had she become that 'priests specially invited from the holy city of Varanasi conducted purifying rituals for eight days' before she moved house again to 1, Safdarjung Road, which had been her own home from the time of her father's death in 1964 until her defeat in the General Election in 1977.

In the confused situation, the Foreign Office disregarded Charan Singh and sought instructions on Afghan policy, to be conveyed to the delegation in New York, from Indira. Two senior officials who carried the papers to her house in Willingdon Crescent found their way blocked by massive crowds celebrating her victory by beating drums and sounding bugles. Helped by security men, they managed to get inside the house only to find that Indira was surrounded by the more prominent of her supporters and smothered under garlands.

217

They said their piece as best they could and returned to their offices to await her directive.

During her eleven years of power until 1977, Indira had not only continued but also strengthened her father's policy of maintaining close and friendly relations with the Soviet Union. It was in her time that the Indo-Soviet Treaty of Peace, Friendship and Cooperation was signed in 1971. But after her fall from power the Soviets had treated her shabbily, presumably because they did not wish to offend the Janata which wanted foreign governments not to have anything to do with her. She therefore had no great reason to rush to the Russians' rescue. But she seldom allowed personal feelings to interfere with the pursuit of India's national interests as she saw them.

Looking at the Afghan problem accordingly, she felt that while opposing the presence of any foreign troops on the soil of any country, India must not antagonise the Soviet Union over the Afghan issue. She also said that the Soviet military intervention in Afghanistan was not the start of the problem but a culmination, albeit an undesirable one, of a whole series of actions by the Shah of Iran, the US and others to wean Afghanistan away from its close relationship with the Soviet Union, in being since the Twenties. She therefore ruled that New Delhi should call for a political, rather than military, solution of the problem so that conditions could be created for an early withdrawal of the Soviet troops from Afghanistan.

From the Indian standpoint it was an unexceptionable position to take though it was bound to be unpopular with the West. But thanks to the raucously noisy atmosphere in Indira's house, the lack of an efficient secretariat at her disposal and the high spirits of some of her pronouncedly pro-Soviet associates, the instructions sent to the Foreign Office were considerably at variance with Indira's own reaction. The speech that the Indian spokesman made at the UN showed 'excessive understanding' to the Soviet Union and understandably attracted sharp criticism both at home and abroad.

Indira was quick to correct the distortion. Thereafter, she held fast to the policy framework she had outlined in the first instance. Lord Carrington, then British Foreign Secretary, was in New Delhi within a few days of the UN debate. He did not agree fully with what Indira had to say on the Afghan issue, but, according to one of his aides who sat through the discussions, Carrington was 'much impressed' by the logic of Mrs Gandhi's presentation. President Giscard d'Estaing of France, who followed a week later, publicly endorsed Indira's Afghan policy. The joint communiqué issued by them later became the basis of the consensus on Afghanistan at a meeting of the Non-Aligned Foreign Ministers in New Delhi, to which both Pakistan and Afghanistan were parties.

If in her talks with Western and Non-Aligned leaders Indira stressed the inadvisability of joining the 'chorus of condemnation of the Soviet Union', orchestrated by the US and China, to the Russians she spoke sharply about the need for an early Soviet withdrawal from Afghanistan. Andrei Gromyko, the veteran Soviet Foreign Minister (later President of the Soviet Union), rushed to Delhi as soon as Giscard left. Indira heard him patiently but told him tersely: 'On this I cannot help you.' Later she became the first and, so far, only head of government to demand the Soviet withdrawal from Afghanistan from a public platform in Moscow.

The Afghan conflict almost immediately spawned a threat to India's own security which was to remain one of Indira's major worries until her death. Since independence India had had to fight four and a half wars, only one of them with its bigger neighbour, China. The remaining three and a half were with Pakistan. Though smaller than India, Pakistan had felt emboldened to attack it in 1965 because of American weaponry, generously given to it by successive US administrations since 1954, under a mutual security pact. The 1965 war had led to a US arms embargo on both countries but ways were found to get round it in the case of Pakistan. American arms were therefore also much in evidence during the 1971 war which led, nevertheless, to Pakistan being cut into two and the creation of the independent republic of Bangladesh.

Hopes that Pakistan would not pose a threat to India again were given a boost when Pakistan's military regime, headed by General Zia-ul-Haq, became the world's pariah because of the execution on April 4th, 1979, of Zulfiqar Ali Bhutto, Pakistan's only duly elected Prime Minister since partition, and her pursuit of nuclear capability, initiated, ironically, by Bhutto himself. The US had stopped all aid to Pakistan two days after Bhutto was sent to the gallows. But as Russian troops poured into Afghanistan, almost overnight Pakistan became a 'frontline state' in US strategy in the region. The US resumed not merely economic aid but massive arms supplies to Pakistan. These included the highly sophisticated F-16 aircraft capable of delivering nuclear bombs. History seemed to be repeating itself menacingly. Indira was gravely concerned. At the very least, she argued, her country would have to spend a great deal of money – diverting scarce resources from development to defence – to maintain a power balance sufficient to cope with a two-front defence against both Pakistan and much larger China.

Even as concerns grew about India's deteriorating strategic environment, Indira knew that her greatest difficulties lay at home. The problems were both political and economic. They were also old and familiar, except that over a relatively short period they had become

219

more intractable than before. The Indian unity that her father and she had striven to preserve and consolidate was coming under increasing strain. Differences between various religious groups were becoming more acute. Communal riots – as Hindu–Muslim killings are called – were becoming more frequent and more vicious. Atrocities on Harijans (former untouchables), tribals and other weaker sections of society were also on the increase. This endemic tragedy of India had been aggravated by the rise to power in the Janata period of the economically strong but socially backward intermediate castes.

The economic scene was no less dismal. Indira, as we have noted, had won the election by promising to keep prices within check and giving the country a 'government that works'. But her new government proved to be helpless against further price rises. Discontent grew and took some surprisingly new forms. For instance, instead of landless labourers and poor peasants coming out to agitate in the streets, the lead was taken by rich farmers who had already benefited the most from development plans and now clamoured for more.

Meanwhile in distant Assam in the country's north-eastern region a timebomb was ticking away in the shape of student agitation to expel from the state millions of settlers who had come in from what is now Bangladesh. This, as we shall see, was to explode when Indira could have done without the problem.

In the early months of her second 'innings', however, Indira and Sanjay seemed to have little awareness of the challenges that lay ahead. They were busy with mundane and relatively minor matters. They had given undue priority, for instance, to weeding out government officials holding important positions who were considered insufficiently 'loyal'. In the process, many civil servants known for their competence and integrity were also given short shrift. On the other hand, several officers of 'proven incompetence but unquestioned loyalty to Indira and Sanjay', some of whom had earned notoriety during the Emergency and were later pilloried by the Janata, were ostentatiously reappointed to crucial and sensitive posts.

At the same time, a bizarre drama was being enacted in the law courts where Indira and Sanjay only a short while earlier had been in the dock on charges too numerous to be catalogued. From the moment of her dramatic defeat in the 1977 General Election there had been a clamour for the establishment of special courts so that Indira could be summarily punished for excesses during the Emergency. Ordinary courts were infamous for their delays. However, two special courts were appointed only in May, 1979, barely ten weeks before the Janata government itself collapsed. Charan Singh, who then became Prime Minister, could do so only with the backing of, among others, the

Congress (I). It endorsed the President's decision to invite him to form a government but soon withdrew its support to him because of his refusal to wind up the special courts. The two special courts were thus in business on January 14th, 1980, when Indira was sworn in as Prime Minister for the fourth and, as it turned out, final time.

The very next day, one of the special judges, Justice Jain, 'dissolved the special court', declaring loftily that he really had no jurisdiction to try the cases because 'the creation and establishment of this court and declarations and designations to try the said cases were not made in accordance with the provisions of the constitution'. Why he had failed to perceive this illegality during the preceding six months he did not care to say. But his example proved contagious and was quickly followed by the second special judge, Justice Joshi.

There were protests against this by newspapers and political leaders opposed to Mrs Gandhi. But nobody seemed to listen. Certainly the judiciary did not. For, thereafter, cases against mother and son were dropped with speed that was far from seemly. Nothing illustrated the situation better than the fate of the famous *Kissa Kursi Ka* case in which, as we have seen, Sanjay and the former Information and Broadcasting Minister, V. C. Shukla, had in fact been sentenced to two years' imprisonment each. The sentences had been suspended until the disposal of their appeals by the Supreme Court which was still hearing the arguments when Indira returned to power.

Ram Jethamalani, a leading lawyer, prominent Janata MP and an intemperate critic of Indira and Sanjay, had prosecuted the *Kissa Kursi Ka* case and it was he who was appearing in the Supreme Court to argue against the appeals. But since prosecution in India is a function of the executive, not of an independent law officer, the counsel representing the state was also changed with the change of government. The new man took precisely 'fifteen minutes to dispose of a record that ran into 6,500 pages, filling twenty volumes'. The highest court in India took no notice and wrote a 300-page judgment quashing the convictions of Sanjay and Shukla.

Nor did the Supreme Court take notice of another revealing development appertaining to this case. Amrit Nahata, the maker of the film, which could never again be traced after its seizure by the government, and the original complainant against Sanjay and Shukla, had doggedly pursued his allegations that they had burnt his film in Sanjay's Maruti car factory. But as soon as Indira won the January 1980 election, Nahata did a volte-face that baffled his friends and delighted his foes. He filed a sworn affidavit in the original court claiming that he had instituted a false case against Sanjay and Shukla in a fit of vengeful anger, and that he was making a clean breast of his misdemeanour because his 'conscience' had of late been 'troubling' him! Sanjay's supporters welcomed all this as the belated triumph of truth and justice over the Janata's campaign of calumny against him.

Despite the country's daunting problems, to which she was no stranger even in the past, things seemed to be going exactly as Indira would have liked them to. But then Sanjay's sudden death on the morning of June 23rd, 1980, dealt her the cruellest blow of her life from which she never really recovered. He was then just over thirty-three and had left behind, apart from his inconsolable mother, his young widow, Maneka, and their baby son, Feroze Varun, then just three months old. Only ten days earlier, Indira and Sanjay had driven in a ceremonial procession to the headquarters of her party in Akbar Road, not far from her residence, where she had formally installed him as the Party General Secretary. Evidently, this was to be the first step in her grand design for him – a dream that now lay shattered on the wooded escarpment where the aerobatic plane that Sanjay was stunt flying had crashed.

Sanjay's death helped turn the spotlight on all that had gone wrong in his mother's reign largely under his influence. The aircraft that plunged him to his doom had been brought into the country under dubious circumstances. It was supposed to be a 'gift' by a foreign 'disciple' to Dhirendra Brahmachari, the 'holy man' with so great an influence over Indira and Sanjay as to earn the nickname 'Rasputin'. Contrary to government regulations, Brahmachari was allowed to import the plane free of duty. Doubts about its airworthiness, expressed by some after the accident, were never substantiated. But there was little doubt that Sanjay, whose flying style was not of the best in any case, did not have enough experience to handle this particular aircraft.

In fact, a month before the disaster, Air Marshal J. Zaheer, Director-General of Civil Aviation, had informed his superiors in writing that Sanjay was violating safety regulations and thus endangering his own life as well as the lives of others. Since it was difficult to issue written instructions in Sanjay's case, the air marshal had recorded, the best course would be for the Minister for Civil Aviation to have a quiet word on the subject with Mrs Gandhi. Whether because of preoccupation with state assembly elections or for some other reason, the minister did not get round to talking to the Prime Minister for quite some time. Meanwhile, the file started by Zaheer was seen by Sanjay. What followed was entirely typical. Within hours the air marshal was asked to go on compulsory leave. His deputy, G. R. Kathpalia, 'who used to be dutifully in attendance on several of Sanjay's flights', was asked to take charge.

When Air Marshal Zaheer's fears were so sadly vindicated, the cabinet met, in the absence of Indira who was too stunned to attend, to pay tribute to Sanjay and place on record its appreciation of his services to the nation. It also took the opportunity to resolve that an open judicial inquiry into the disaster be held. Almost immediately this decision was rescinded, at Indira's behest. She evidently realised that Sanjay's shenanigans would not bear scrutiny. The departmental probe then ordered, produced a predictably anodyne report.

All this was damaging. But it could hardly make any difference to a mother benumbed by the loss of a beloved son in the prime of his life. Indira's grief knew no bounds. On June 23rd, 1980 she broke down completely and cried uninhibitedly in public. But she controlled herself fast, indeed with astonishing speed. Her stoicism had always been famous; now it appeared awesome. On the morning of June 27th, she was back at her office desk, 'straight-backed, dry-eyed, business-like and utterly composed'. A fortnight later she laughed for the first time since Sanjay's death, when told that the US-based eminent Indian music conductor, Zubin Mehta, after having protested repeatedly against an Indian ban on the Israel Symphony Orchestra, had at last been officially assured that he could bring ISO to India provided that 'no member of the orchestra is a Jew'. But the elaborate composure and self-possession were only on the surface. Deep within, Indira was badly, perhaps irremediably, wounded. In the privacy of her home she would often wake up at night and go looking for Sanjay or start crying for him. The strain told on her fine physique. In the words of her friend, Pupul Jayakar, Indira's 'face aged, the eyes became stark, the hair was pushed back carelessly, the footsteps heavy'.

By March 1981, however, Mrs Jayakar felt confident that Indira had regained her old energy and zest and was 'no longer old in mind or body'. But she was being too optimistic. For as late as on July 7th, Indira wrote to her:

> You let fall a phrase about my overcoming sorrow. One can over-come hate, envy, greed and other such negative and self-destroying emotions. But sorrow is something else. It can be neither forgotten nor overcome. One has to learn to live with it, to absorb it into one's being, as a part of life.

And yet life and work had to go on. Even overwhelming personal grief could not be allowed to come in the way of public duty. The Herculean task of governing India could not be abdicated or neglected. Indira did revert to business as usual. She even managed to look as elegant and brisk as in the good old days. She smiled and laughed. But something seemed to be lacking. It was perhaps her dogged will to win, combined with a sureness of touch for which she had been

223

acclaimed in the past. Now she seemed to be fumbling and faltering, virtually advertising her inability to cope with the challenges crowding in on her.

The burden of sorrow over Sanjay's death had grown much the heavier because she had to carry also the cross of his less than savoury legacy. Embarrassment had begun almost at the beginning of the grim tragedy. Indira visited the site of the crash not once but twice. She searched the wreckage for Sanjay's wristwatch and keys. This could have been a bereaved mother's legitimate longing for mementos of her lost son, but the legions of her critics thought otherwise. The country was swept by rumours that the watch and the keys were essential to Indira 'for access to Sanjay's finances and documents' so that the 'control over these would be hers and not pass to Sanjay's widow, Maneka, and Maneka's family, with the unforeseen political implications this might involve'. The gossip could have been wholly baseless and malicious, but it was widely believed then and continues to be believed today.

Most of those who readily believed, and even helped spread, stories about Indira's anxiety to get hold of Sanjay's 'vast wealth', allegedly stashed away at home and abroad, did not feel that they were being hypocritical in sympathising with her or in sending her their condolences. In India any parent, including one's worst enemy, is entitled to commiseration at the loss of a child, especially a son. But this does not mean that he or she necessarily deserves any other consideration.

A similar dichotomy was reflected in the behaviour of people who even while claiming to share Indira's grief made no effort to conceal their relief over the cause of it: elimination from the Indian scene of Sanjay whom they considered 'the most sinister and menacing figure' of their time. Nor was this feeling confined to Indira's opponents.

On June 23rd I was visiting Bombay, where are located the headquarters of *The Times of India*, the newspaper of which I was then the Delhi Editor. I was browsing through some papers when a peon came running to my cubicle to say that the Chief Editor wanted me to go and see him immediately. He added that it seemed that Sanjay Gandhi was dead. I expressed my disbelief. But at that very moment a colleague came rushing with a news-agency flash announcing the fatal crash. By now quite a few people had assembled. 'Providence,' exclaimed someone, 'has come to the country's rescue.' No one remonstrated with him for his insensitivity.

I was back in Delhi by that evening. After passing the early edition of the paper, I joined two friends, both high officials in Indira's government, for a late supper. 'India's history has changed today,' commented one. 'For the better,' added the other.

Nor was the situation improved by the extravagance of Sanjay's funeral at the taxpayer's expense. His elder brother, Rajiv, who was overseas at the time of the fatal crash and had rushed back home, was alone in urging restraint and suggesting a private cremation. But Sanjay loyalists were adamant on a public funeral and on making it a 'memorable' one. Many eyebrows were raised when it was announced that the cremation would take place at a specially erected platform only a few yards from the spot where Sanjay's illustrious grandfather, Jawaharlal Nehru, had been consigned to the flames and which has since become a hallowed place of pilgrimage for millions. No one was, however, able to do anything about it.

Enough people would have joined Sanjay's funeral procession anyhow. He had a large following of his own, curiosity about him was immense and his untimely death had caused widespread shock. But those out to advertise their loyalty to their 'departed leader' were unwilling to leave things well alone. They found it expedient crudely to mobilise mourners through the time-honoured technique of 'rent-a-crowd'. 'Sycophancy,' as Tariq Ali noted pertinently, 'tended to drown genuine emotion.'

An orgy of building plaster pyramids in Sanjay's honour followed. From one end of the country to the other, statues of him, often hideously crafted, were put up. Plans to start Sanjay schools, hospitals and gymnasia were breezily announced. Rare was the city or town where a road or street was not named after him. A huge and costly pictorial exhibition on his life, called 'Son of India', was put up at Pragati Maidan, Delhi's officially run permanent exhibition ground. State-controlled radio and television worked overtime to 'perpetuate' his memory.

Rhetoric at memorial meetings ran so wild as to fly in the face of rationality, to say nothing of propriety. Ruling party leaders, some of them more than twice Sanjay's age, compared him to Jesus Christ, Adi Sankaracharya, an eighth-century Hindu religious leader, Einstein and Karl Marx. The first two had at least one thing in common with Sanjay: they, too, had died at thirty-three. But how any comparison could be made with Marx and Einstein could never be unravelled.

The posthumous personality cult built around Sanjay proved ephemeral. It was brought to an abrupt halt in circumstances even more unseemly than those surrounding its start.

India had been a house divided against itself from the time Indira first split the Congress in 1969. It was the imposition of the Emergency by her five years later that made the breach between the two sides, her ardent supporters and equally determined opponents, bitter and seemingly unbridgeable. Her resounding defeat in the 1977 General

Election engendered enormous relief at her eclipse and the restoration of democracy. It also created the hope that politics, with all their turbulence and tensions, conflicts and compromises, would soon return to normal or what they used to be before the destructive polarisation had begun.

But this hope was dashed, as we have noted, by the Janata's vendetta against Indira which, ironically, had hastened her return to power. By now the hopes that had been belied by the Janata were being pinned on her. But the people, yearning for a return to normal and civilised political behaviour, were disappointed yet again. Instead of working for a grand national reconciliation, Indira embarked on a vengeance of her own. Higher bureaucracy was a major target. To make matters worse, those who had stood by her in her 'darkest hour' made it their business to insist that no one outside their ranks be given any quarter, let alone any consideration. Indira could have treated this demand with contempt, had she so wished. But she found it handy to do what in any case her own instinct and Sanjay's strong advice had dictated. Anyone whom Sanjay had disliked was liable to be harassed through the misuse of government investigation and enforcement agencies.

Of course, the pattern was not uniform. There were interesting variations, even exceptions to the rule. For instance on coming back to power, Indira included in her cabinet Vereendra Patil, a Congress leader from Karnataka who had parted company with her in 1969, had joined the Janata in 1977 and a year later had opposed her in the Chickmagalur by-election which she had won handsomely. Chand Mohammed Ibrahim, a Muslim leader from the same state, was made a minister in the provincial government even though he had repeatedly used unprintable language about Indira from the public platform. And yet Y. B. Chavan, a much more important leader from Maharashtra, who had been Minister for Home, Defence, Finance and Foreign Affairs in Indira's successive cabinets and had become estranged from her in 1978, was allowed to return to the fold in a nondescript position in 1981 after a protracted and humiliating wait. All this was a measure as much of Indira's complex personality as of the complexity of Indian politics but the message it conveyed to the people, especially to the middle-class intelligentsia, the backbone of Indian society, was deeply disturbing.

It also destroyed the last, lingering hope that, having won the votes of the common people, Indira would have the good sense also to win back the confidence of the intelligentsia.

At the time of Indira's return to power at the start of 1980, there was a three-way division in the intelligentsia. In the first place, there was a core of journalists, bureaucrats, academics, lawyers and so on totally and irreconcilably opposed to her. Secondly, there was an equally determined group which had made it its business to beat Indira's drum in season and out of season; in its view, she could do no wrong. There was, however, an important difference between these two rival groupings. Indira's inveterate critics included a large proportion of persons eminent in their respective disciplines and professions. With very few exceptions, Indira's dogged supporters were intellectual lightweights and were generally seen to be self-serving toadies.

The third group, which was also the largest, held the middle ground. It deserved greater attention than Indira cared to bestow on it. Its members, though uneasy about what she might do, nursed the hope that, having learnt her lesson, she would heal old wounds and redeem herself. Far from sustaining this hope, Indira smashed it in next to no time, by her rough treatment of the higher bureaucracy and the parliamentary opposition.

This was a sad culmination of Indira's remarkably ambivalent attitude towards Indian intellectuals, as against her warm friendliness for foreign men and women of letters and thought. On the one hand, she craved for their approval, if not approbation. As we have seen, even during the Emergency she had sought, albeit unsuccessfully, the cooperation of the renowned film-maker Satyajit Ray and others to counter the West's criticism of the Emergency. On the other hand, she professed contempt for the intellectuals, presumably as an essay in reciprocity. She scoffed at them for being purveyors of 'borrowed ideas'. The press collectively she considered her enemy, and she blamed it for being under the 'influence of foreigners' and the ownership of 'domestic vested interests'.

Even so, as in the past, so now, she kept up the practice of seeking a meeting with intellectuals wherever she went. A request for such a get-together in London during her visit in March 1982 to open the Festival of India caused 'embarrassment' in the Foreign Office and 'hilarity' in Fleet Street. However, forty British intellectuals, including Lord Zuckerman, Jean Floud, Malcolm Bradbury, Hugh Casson and Iris Murdoch, did meet her.

Back home, the majority of intellectuals were by this time once again unremittingly hostile to her. This hostility escalated in direct proportion to the mounting political conflicts in the country. There were people, though not many within her immediate circle, who tried to persuade her to do something to mitigate the inflamed feelings of those who would happily respond to any attempt at conciliation by her. But she seemed impervious to this suggestion, as my own experience underscored.

As early as 1980 I had spoken to her twice about the need for reconciliation with the intelligentsia – barring perhaps the intransigent fringe. The first discussion took place in early June in the presence of six other editors and her information adviser; the second one some six months later when no one else was present. On both occasions she was unrelenting. Many of those abusing her, she argued, had 'always been against us'. (She invariably used first person plural in such matters.) 'Nothing that I do will change them. They have been joined, moreover, by some who were with us but left us when we were in difficulty. They continue to be bitter. I do not know why.'

'But what about those who have no reason to be against you personally but are understandably concerned about much of what is going on?' I persisted.

'You do not seem to understand,' she went on patiently. 'Half the people calling themselves intellectuals are under American influence which works to our disadvantage. The other half, under Russian influence, have also changed.' She wouldn't concede that people could have misgivings on their own without being under the influence of either the US or the USSR.

About the bureaucracy she said she had reason to believe that after her victory in the elections some of the senior officers had blandly stated that they would not 'move a little finger to help me. In the circumstances, am I to blame if I entrust sensitive jobs to men who may not be very bright but on whom I can rely?'

All the fault did not lie on Indira's side. Some of her critics, especially in the press, were also going to extremes, their anger sometimes driving them to irrationality. Nor was the situation improved by Indira's proclivity to lash out at all her critics and even to brand them as 'anti-national' while defending vigorously the most outrageous activities of her own supporters.

# 15   Dynasty Above All

Dark shadows of the grim troubles that were eventually to overwhelm Indira had begun to fall well before Sanjay's death, indeed right from the start of her new tenure as Prime Minister. Religious, regional, ethnic, linguistic, caste and other divisive conflicts were nothing new in India. But an ominous change was now taking place in the pattern with which Indira had been accustomed to dealing. Instead of remaining sporadic and largely localised, as in the past, these conflicts were becoming more frequent, sustained and widespread. Too many parts of the country had begun to face turmoil at the same time. The concomitant violence was also escalating in extent, intensity and viciousness.

Ironically, the first notable irruption after Indira's return to power was directed against her special constituency, the Harijans. Their decision to desert her after the Emergency had contributed materially to her defeat in the 1977 General Election. She had then assiduously wooed them and won back their support. In fact, she had embarked on the come-back trail with a visit to the venue of a particularly nasty outrage on Harijans in a remote hamlet in Bihar called Belchi. But hardly had rejoicing over her triumphant return subsided when Belchi was re-enacted in two other villages of the same benighted state, Parasbigha and Pipra. At both places, land-owning upper-caste Hindus shot Harijans in cold blood or burnt them alive, along with their huts and hovels.

Police brutalities from one end of the country to the other compounded the shock of those who, taking Indira at her word, were expecting a return to effective and orderly government. On the day she was sworn in, two hundred policemen in the village of Narainpur in UP went on a rampage, killing two men, torturing scores of others and raping women, all because the villagers had had the temerity to complain about an earlier misdemeanour of the local police. In New Delhi, at a stone's throw from the Prime Minister's house, a procession of blind people, marching to present a petition to her, was mercilessly beaten up. Other typical incidents included an assault on lawyers at Gwalior in Central India and an attack by West Bengal policemen on nine villages of the Islampur area, all of which were set ablaze. Here the villagers had earlier beaten two policemen to death to give vent to their frustration over the failure of the police to protect them from the depredations of dacoits.

Judicial inquiries and changes in police administration in the affected states did nothing to stem the tide of lawlessness of those duty-bound to uphold and enforce the law. The nadir was reached in November 1980 when it was revealed that the police in the Bihar town of Bhagalpur had, for the preceding four months, been blinding suspected criminals in their custody by pouring acid into their eyes. Indira declared that she was 'sickened' by the disclosure which was indeed nauseating. The chief minister of Bihar suspended fifteen policemen responsible for the Bhagalpur blindings. Indira's Home Minister, Giani Zail Singh, later to become the republic's President, promised stern action against the guilty. But in Bhagalpur hundreds of policemen demonstrated in defence of their suspended colleagues and demanded their reinstatement. Although articulate opinion all over the country was in full cry against the barbarity at Bhagalpur, a section of local opinion openly sympathised with the culpable policemen. Its argument was that the prisoners, known to be dangerous criminals, just could not be successfully prosecuted in the notoriously slow-moving courts because no one was likely to tender evidence against them.

This reasoning was unacceptable, of course. But it could not be denied that the shocking police behaviour was at least partly the outcome of the havoc played with the morale, cohesion and discipline of the force by reckless political interference with it. The pernicious process had begun with the Emergency, when favoured policemen could commit excesses with impunity. The situation had worsened later when the Janata government's attempt to call the Emergency 'culprits' to account had turned into an often selective vendetta. By 1978, in most places the police had tended to be riven into two intensely hostile factions along political lines.

In the early months of 1980 the police also found themselves at the receiving end in Hindu–Muslim killings which had once again erupted in full fury.

The first outbreak took place on August 13th, two days before the thirty-third anniversary of independence at Moradabad, a teeming town in UP only a hundred miles away from Delhi and famous for its brassware. A pig, believed by Muslims to be an unclean animal, strayed into a mosque when the faithful were at prayer. Somehow convinced that it had been directed to their place of worship by a nearby police picket, an irate Muslim mob attacked the police rather than the rival community. The trouble at Moradabad lasted a whole month, taking a toll of 144 lives. It also immediately spread not only to nearby towns and to Delhi but also to Allahabad, Mhow in Central India and even the distant Muslim-majority state of Jammu and

Kashmir, traditionally free from the madness that leads to religious carnage, frequently for apparently trivial reasons.

The Moradabad riots became a sensation of sorts also because, for the first time in her political career, Indira departed from her normal style of rushing to the scene of every major communal conflagration to condole with the bereaved, console the victims of loot and arson and censure negligent local authorities. Though Moradabad was only a few minutes away from Delhi by helicopter, she just would not go there despite appeals by parties and groups horrified by the carnage. Nor could it be said that she was paralysed by grief over Sanjay's death because she was travelling to other places in the country. In the end, she did go to Moradabad. But it was a classic case of too little, too late. For by then ulterior motives were being read into her earlier reluctance. She was accused of pandering to Hindu chauvinists who had long grumbled that she, like her father, tended to 'pamper' Muslims and other minorities at the cost of the Hindu majority.

A shining secular image and a capacity to arouse hope and confidence in the minds of the minorities, the weak and the oppressed had been among the more attractive qualities of Indira whether in power or out of it. Moreover, Muslims and other minorities and the Harijans had formed her main power base and this had proved to be a winning combination. Her debacle in 1977 had owed a great deal to the alienation from her of both Muslims and Harijans who had, however, rallied to her support again in 1980. Gratuitously to give up this great advantage made no sense from her point of view. But her critics and some people not particularly antagonistic to her held that she was becoming unsure of retaining the loyalty of the Muslims and Harijans and was therefore trying hard to build an alternative power base by uniting behind her the hitherto fragmented upper-caste Hindu vote which had, on balance, been hostile to her in the past. Shrewd political calculation, it was said, had been reinforced by a recently acquired personal predilection towards religiosity. It had not gone unnoticed that during the first six weeks after her return to power, Indira had worshipped at no fewer than a dozen shrines from the north to the south and the east to the west. All except one of these were Hindu temples. With the passage of time, the view that Indira was acquiring, by deliberate design rather than default, more and more of a 'Hindu role' was steadily to gain ground.

No less persistent than communal and caste killings or police misconduct were tribal insurgencies in the sensitive north-eastern region, some of them dating back twenty years or more. Secessionists and terrorists continued to be active in Manipur, Tripura and Mizoram. Indira managed to defuse the situation in Mizoram but in Tripura she could not prevent a massacre of Bengalis by the tribals. However, it was in the state of Assam, the most populous and important in the north-east, that much deeper trouble, with vast explosive potential, had broken out in the form of powerful agitation, just before the parliamentary election at the end of December 1979. The point at issue was the inclusion in the state's electoral register of large numbers of 'foreigners' or immigrants from what was now Bangladesh and had earlier been the eastern wing of Pakistan. So inflamed was Assamese feeling that in fourteen of the sixteen parliamentary constituencies, elections could not be held. Political parties, unable to withstand the fury of the agitation or the tide of mass sentiment, were reduced to irrelevance. Leadership of the increasingly violent movement passed to the All Assam Students' Union (AASU) and a non-political body, the Assam Gana Sangram Parishad (GSP) or People's Struggle Council. Heady with their initial success, AASU and GSP announced that they would paralyse all normal activity in the state until their demands were fully met. These were summed up as four Ds: that the central government must *detect* the foreigners in Assam, *disfranchise* them immediately and then either *deport* them to Bangladesh or *disperse* them in other Indian states.

On the face of it, there was much justice in the stand taken by people apprehensive of being swamped in their own home, much as had happened in neighbouring Tripura where the indigenous tribal majority had within a generation been outnumbered three to one by immigrants from Bangladesh as well as from the Indian state of West Bengal. In reality, however, the problem was exceedingly complex. Not all the justice was on the side of the agitators.

For one thing, though ostensibly directed against aliens only, the Assam movement had led almost instantly to the intimidation of all non-Assamese-speaking groups which could, by no stretch of the imagination, be called foreigners. The regional sentiment was particularly strong against Bengali-speaking fellow Indians. This obviously had something to do with the cultural snobbery of the Bengalis who tend to behave towards their neighbours much as Frenchmen do towards theirs.

In any case, there was no easy way of determining who exactly was a foreigner. The long and tangled history of demographic movement from the heavily overpopulated East Bengal to the relatively empty and fertile lands of Assam dated back to the beginning of the century when both areas formed part of British India. A passport system, introduced at the time of partition, was defeated by reality. Migrations continued, and not only because the newly demarcated frontier was long, meandering and palpably unpoliceable. Landlords and plantation owners in Assam also persisted in encouraging immigration because penurious newcomers provided them with cheap labour in a state where local workers were scarce. Moreover, nothing had happened to weaken the vested interest Congress party politicians had acquired in the migration because immigrants tended to be their vote-banks.

Even so, after the 1961 census, which revealed an abnormal rise of population in Assam compared with the rest of the country, there was an uproar. Under popular pressure, the state government appointed seventeen tribunals to detect and deport illegal immigrants. But the effort was promptly frustrated by employers profiting from immigrant labour and politicians benefiting from their votes.

When, in 1971, East Pakistan revolted against exploitation by the western wing, more than a million refugees poured into Assam. Most went back after the liberation of Bangladesh but well over 100,000 remained, exacerbating local sentiment. The newly-established Bangladesh government, conscious of the situation's ramifications, signed an agreement with India providing that it would not accept illegal immigrants who had entered Assam before March 25th, 1971 (the date on which Bangladesh had first proclaimed its independence) and would accept those who had entered Assam after that date only if it was 'satisfied that they were Bangladesh citizens'.

During the routine revision of the Assam electoral rolls in 1979, the inclusion of no fewer than 346,000 voters was questioned on the grounds of 'doubtful nationality'. Almost all of them were abysmally poor and totally illiterate. They had never heard of the official documents they were asked to produce to establish their citizenship. A majority of the immigrants from Bangladesh were Muslims. This introduced into the strife the highly emotive communal dimension. Two successive state governments collapsed under the weight of the ensuing crisis. President's rule was introduced, but the problem would not go away.

AASU and GSP militants, insisting on the immediate and wholesale exclusion from the electoral register of all alleged aliens, stepped up their agitation. Repeated general strikes and picketing of government offices, banks, post offices and so on brought normal life to a standstill for prolonged periods. The most powerful weapon in the hands of the agitators was forcibly to stop the flow of oil from Assam, which then supplied a third of the country's needs. Since the agitation enjoyed the overwhelming support of the Assamese, including the local administration, large contingents of the Border Security Force and the Central Reserve Police had to be rushed to Assam to control the spreading violence.

Indira Gandhi tried to reason with the leaders of the agitation and persuade them to accept that those who had been enrolled as voters before March 25th, 1971 – the 'cut-off date' agreed to by Bangladesh –

should be allowed to stay while the others should be sent away. She also promised to ensure a more effective policing of the border and the introduction of identity cards with photographs for all border districts to make illegal immigration difficult. All major political parties welcomed her approach as eminently reasonable, but the students rejected it out of hand, insisting that March 1951 should be the decisive date. It was their voice that counted where it mattered the most.

When no agreement could be reached and violence in Assam mounted fast, Indira decided to act. In April she declared the whole of Assam, except a Bengali-majority district that had remained unaffected by the agitation, to be a disturbed area. This enabled the armed forces to go to the aid of the civil authorities against any threat to public order and, if necessary, to use their weapons. Sweeping restrictions on strikes in public services and the assembly of more than four people were also imposed. But the agitators treated the prohibitory orders with contempt and started a mass civil disobedience movement.

Only massive use of force enabled the central paramilitary formations to seize control of the oil pipeline headquarters and slowly to restore the flow of oil. Army troops stood by. Worse was yet to follow.

In the meantime, neglected complexities of the Assam problem came into play. The backlash in West Bengal to the anti-Bengali undertones of the Assam agitation had been kept in check by the Communist Party (Marxist), CPM, ruling the state. But in March 1980, the youth wing of the Congress (I) and the Chhatra Parishad, the party's student organisation, launched an 'economic blockade' of Assam to make the Assamese students 'realise the folly of their ways'. They disrupted road and rail traffic bound for Assam, which is linked to the rest of the country by only a narrow neck of territory. This led to an orgy of violence and clashes with the police, while the Assamese were incensed. The blockade was called off only after an Assamese student leader warned that if it was continued, 'all Bengali families' in Assam would be 'blockaded and not allowed to buy even food and milk'. Indira's declaration that her party had done nothing to encourage the blockade was contradicted flatly by West Bengal's chief minister, Jyoti Basu, who insisted that the Congress (I) was 'trying to create a law and order problem' with a view to discrediting the Marxist ministry.

Around the same time the Assam agitation encountered stiff opposition also from the tribal population living in the plains of the Brahmaputra valley who rightly claimed that they, rather than the Assamese-speaking Hindus, were the original inhabitants of Assam and that they had been exploited most ruthlessly over successive generations. The All Assam Tribal Youth League denounced the agitation as a ploy 'to perpetuate the domination of high-caste Assamese on the tribals on whom Assamese language and culture have been imposed'. It also demanded the eviction from tribal lands of all 'unauthorised occupants' and the redistribution of these lands among landless tribals. The schism between the tribals and the agitators was also to lead to gruesome consequences later.

Two features of the reaction of Indira Gandhi's government to the Assam agitation and turbulence in tribal areas of the north-east, to say nothing of caste, communal and other conflicts elsewhere, attracted wide notice and some opposition.

First, not content with the vast punitive and preventive powers in its legal armoury, the Indira government sought more. A National Security Ordinance was issued in 1980 and soon converted into a parliamentary act. It authorised detention without trial for up to twelve months to prevent acts prejudicial to the security of the state or to maintenance of public order or to essential supplies and services. The Essential Services Maintenance Act banning strikes in key public utilities and providing for summary trials of strikers followed. A countrywide trade union strike against the two measures in 1981 was crushed; 23,000 activists were arrested but were released after the strike was over.

Secondly, and more significantly, from the word go Indira blamed foreign powers for fomenting trouble in her country, especially in its sensitive areas. Her Home Minister, Zail Singh, speaking in Parliament in March 1980, openly blamed the United States and China. A few days later, Home Ministry officials claimed to have 'definite information' that the US Central Intelligence Agency was 'pumping money' into the north-eastern region through Christian missionaries. Indira herself spoke of a 'foreign hand' behind the upheavals. And though derided by some of her critics, as time went on the 'foreign hand' became the *leitmotiv* of her pronouncements.

Myriad and multiplying problems were crowding in on Indira. She tried to cope with them as best she could, but the paramount issue on her mind in the latter half of 1980 was the vacuum left behind by Sanjay and how to fill it. Basically, this vacuum was of her own creation. Unable to trust anyone except her son – her paranoia had been accentuated by the 'betrayals' following her fall from power three years earlier – and unwilling to have around her anyone even remotely capable of turning into a potential rival, she had formed a cabinet of yesmen content to do her bidding and to speak only when spoken to. Not all of her ministers were nonentities and time-servers. Some, though not many, were men of ability and substance. But none had a power-base of his own, Indira having seen to it, well before 1980, that anyone trying to build himself up was put in his place.

As one of them candidly admitted, even senior ministers were not the Prime Minister's colleagues in any sense of the term but only 'super-bureaucrats' serving at her pleasure. The ruling party, the Congress (I), was in even worse shape than the cabinet. It had become a bunch of loyalists, most of whom were perversely proud of advertising their servility to, and abject dependence on, Indira. They admitted unabashedly that they could never have got elected on their own and therefore owed their privileged positions entirely to Indira's pull with the people and kindness to themselves.

Under the circumstances, it would have been absurd to expect either the cabinet or the Congress (I) to influence in any way the shaping of the post-Sanjay dispensation. The initiative lay entirely with Indira. She could have, if she had so wished, returned to the system prevailing in the time of her father, Jawaharlal Nehru, whose towering position had remained utterly unaffected by the wide auton-omy and authority he allowed to his cabinet colleagues and the democratic functioning of the Congress party that he insisted upon. Party elections were held regularly and healthy dissent was welcomed during inner-party discussions. But Indira had no interest in 'revert-ing' to such a pattern.

Her mind was made up in favour of beckoning her elder and sole surviving son, Rajiv Gandhi, to be by her side to take Sanjay's place even though she was not sure if he had the necessary political acumen. However, once again she refrained from making any direct move herself but let others, ever anxious to anticipate her wishes, to start a 'draft Rajiv' campaign.

Indira's decision that Rajiv should step into Sanjay's shoes and become her principal adviser and putative successor caused no surprise nor much comment, though the intelligentsia did demur that India was being transformed into a 'dynastic democracy' because of her apparent determination to keep power within her bloodline.

Interestingly, Rajiv himself was rather hesitant in responding to his mother's call. As an airline pilot he had been content to live quietly with his Italian wife, Sonia, and their two children. He had studiously stayed out of the limelight while his younger brother had hogged it. He was reluctant to take the plunge into politics even though he realised that he could not deny his mother the help she needed and was asking for. His request that he be allowed time to make up his mind aggravated a problem that would have been serious even if he had obeyed mama's command instantly.

Sanjay's young, ambitious and fiery widow, Maneka, considered herself to be the rightful heir to his mantle and was prepared to fight for what she believed to be her right. In her view, Rajiv was not only a usurper but also unfit for the role expected of him. Sanjay's acolytes, anxious to preserve the positions of power and influence they had managed to occupy, would also have preferred Maneka to be their new mentor. But they were left in no doubt that the very idea was anathema to Indira. Not only was Maneka not a member of the Nehru –Gandhi clan, her marriage to Sanjay notwithstanding, she was also intensely disliked by her mother-in-law – who was extremely fond of Rajiv's wife, Sonia. Indira was deeply suspicious of Maneka's motives, affiliations and 'designs', and would give her no quarter.

How sensitive Indira was on this score was best illustrated by the fate of Khushwant Singh, author, journalist and Sikh historian and a well-liked individual, with a flair for writing very readable prose and cracking the most bawdy jokes. Despite his initial aversion to the Emergency, he had endeared himself to Indira and even more to Sanjay, by lending them powerful support through thick and thin, so much so that even his best friends started calling him a *chamcha*, a particularly wounding Indian pejorative for a sycophant. Sanjay saw to it that Khushwant was nominated to the Rajya Sabha, the upper house of Parliament. Sanjay and his wife would visit him often; Maneka was also distantly related to him.

After Sanjay's death, Khushwant wrote in his widely-read column that Rajiv, being wholly uninterested in politics, would make a poor substitute for Sanjay and that the void would best be filled by Maneka, a born politician. In praise of Maneka, Khushwant went so far as to say that when roused, she was 'like Durga on the tiger', a tribute that the country had hitherto paid only to Indira and no one else.

Indira was furious. She completely dropped Khushwant and told a great many people, including his friends, that Khushwant had been 'our enemy all along'.

With Rajiv still making up his mind and Maneka fuming and fretting, Indira acted fast to strip Sanjay's key associates of whatever power, influence and privilege they had acquired. She was shrewd enough to know that the crowd Sanjay had collected he alone could have controlled. Akbar Ahmed ('Dumpy'), a particularly favoured Sanjay supporter who had enjoyed free access to the Prime Minister's house, was flabbergasted one day when his way was barred by security men normally used to greeting him obsequiously. He lost his temper. They told him they were under orders to keep him out. 'Who has dared give you this idiotic order?' demanded 'Dumpy'. 'I have,' said Indira, brought to the gate by the commotion and shouting. According to 'Dumpy', she also accused him of hatching the most diabolical plots against her.

A quiet campaign first to stop and then to reverse the rather bizarre personality cult being built around Sanjay also began. The high platform on which his cremation had taken place was demolished and rebuilt more modestly some distance away. Ritual tributes continued to be paid to him, however, on his birth and death anniversaries. It was at the turn of the year that Rajiv eventually made up his mind to accept the maternal summons. He gave up not only his job but also his jacket and necktie and took to the traditional Congress garb of a loose collarless shirt, pajama and the white Gandhi cap. He was elected to Parliament from his brother's constituency, Amethi in UP, in June 1981 and appointed a General Secretary of the Congress (I) a few months later. Maneka might have challenged him, and thus her mother-in-law, at the hustings were it not for the fact that at twenty-three she was below the statutory minimum age for an MP. But the breach between her and Indira as well as between her and Rajiv was now complete.

The daily conflict between mother-in-law and daughter-in-law is an integral part of life in India. It is also a staple of popular Indian films which mint millions by churning out tear-jerkers on the tyranny of mothers-in-law on the hapless wives of their sons, oblivious of the days when they themselves were tormented daughters-in-law. But the enactment of the endemic Indian drama in the country's first family was an altogether different thing, a source of much juicy gossip and fevered speculation. Stories of door-slamming, bosom-heaving rows between Indira and Maneka started trickling out of the Prime Minister's house as some kind of a real life soap opera. The underlying struggle for the Sanjay legacy lent a political edge to an essentially personal scandal.

Even so, Maneka, while complaining of ill-treatment and even insults, stayed under Indira's roof. Indira too wanted her to stay, if only because she adored Sanjay's and Maneka's little son, Feroze Varun Gandhi, and could not think of being separated from him.

By and large, the country's reaction to Rajiv's formal anointing as the new Crown Prince was remarkably relaxed. Though leaders of the opposition and newspaper commentators condemned Indira for trying to impose dynastic rule, this criticism was not echoed by the people at large. The entire Indian history and even mythology is an unbroken saga of rule by hereditary monarchs. Family connection is also of the utmost importance in every Indian's life. It may no longer be the case today but tradition enjoins that a man must follow the vocation of his forefathers. For centuries, master craftsmen and maestros of music have taught their skills to their progeny and to no one else. In grooming her son as her successor therefore, Indira was doing nothing wrong in the eyes of the masses, whatever the upper classes might say.

Even the intelligentsia was not uniformly critical. Several writers, not necessarily belonging to the Congress (I), argued that the old, established democracies in the developed world, too, had had their ruling dynasties. They cited all the known examples of the Roosevelts, Kennedys, Churchills, Pitts and Salisburys. As late as 1986, two years after Indira's assassination and Rajiv's ascent to the office of Prime Minister, Professor John Kenneth Galbraith, American economist and former Ambassador to India, was repeatedly asked, during a visit to New Delhi, to comment on India's dynastic succession. 'Don't ask me to insult the memory of the Roosevelts and the Kennedys' was his invariable reply.

Against this backdrop, how does one explain the undoubted and at times fierce opposition in the mid-Seventies to Sanjay's projection as Indira's ideal, indeed inevitable, successor? The explanation is indeed simple and clear. Sanjay's grooming did not take place under normal circumstances but during the terrible days of the Emergency. What is more, he was seen to be not only a beneficiary of the Emergency but also the principal architect of this outrage. After all, wasn't it he who, more than anyone else, had advised his mother to suspend the constitution, jail her opponents, censor the press and rule by fiat? Distaste for the hereditary principle had thus little to do with the hostility evoked by Sanjay during the Emergency and soon afterwards. Moreover, as we have noted, by 1980, when circumstances were back to normal and Sanjay had won a parliamentary election, his acceptance as heir apparent had increased.

In Rajiv's case, the popular reaction had been vastly more favourable at least partly because his personality contrasted with his brother's so refreshingly.

Sanjay was abrasive, aggressive, ruthless and often vulgar in the display of his power. Rajiv was a mild young man with impeccable manners. He was respectful to his elders, courteous to those of his own age and content to work at his mother's elbow unobtrusively. Not only had Sanjay's Maruti car project been a scandal but he had also acquired a malodorous reputation as a wheeler-dealer with a penchant for money-grabbing. Rajiv was totally free from any such blemish. In fact, he was quickly hailed as 'Mr Clean'. Sanjay's lieutenants, notorious for their corrupt and high-handed ways, were known as the mafia. Rajiv's coterie, which moved into the corridors of power along with him, would have been readily admitted into the Carlton Club. Like him, Rajiv's close friends had gone to the élite Doon School in the Himalayan foothills, now being dubbed 'India's Harrow'. Comparisons flattering to the new heir apparent began to be drawn between 'Sanjay's goons and Rajiv's Doons'.

Maneka, however, was unimpressed and unamused. She treated

239

Rajiv with disdain and gave interviews to magazines claiming that her 'indolent' brother-in-law, unable to get ready before ten in the morning, was not of prime ministerial timbre. The unvoiced, but clear, implication of her statements was that she, an heiress to the Gandhi name and mother of Sanjay's only child, was more than capable of succeeding Indira if only her mother-in-law would have the sense to see this simple point.

Maneka, therefore, started needling and defying Indira without pushing things to the breaking point. She seems to have succeeded in getting under her mother-in-law's skin. For Indira, who had cheerfully taken on and worsted the wiliest of opponents, seems to have been unduly rattled by Maneka who was, after all, no more than a chit of a girl. In an article, published four days after Indira's assassination, Marie Seton, a friend of hers for several decades, wrote that during her last years nothing and nobody had 'troubled' Indira so much as Maneka. Others in the know, including members of the Prime Minister's household staff, concurred with this view.

Maneka was nothing if not persistent and pugnacious. She also had, as an astute writer has said, the 'killer instinct'. She indeed believed herself to be a match for her formidable mother-in-law. Convinced that she would have no place in the power structure presided over by Indira, she decided to step up her defiance of her mother-in-law on the one hand and, on the other, to build up a base for herself by mobilising the now dispossessed, and therefore disgruntled, Sanjay supporters.

One of her first acts was to sell off *Surya*, the magazine that Sanjay had started for her, to a group consisting of the Prime Minister's inveterate political foes. Dhirendra Brahmachari intervened, on Indira's behalf, to buy back the journal at whatever price the new owners would care to quote. But they refused. Inside Indira's house tension became palpable.

The breaking point between Indira and Maneka was not far. It was reached at the end of March 1982 when the daughter-in-law was thrown out of the mother-in-law's house in circumstances even more unsavoury than are usually depicted in the Indian cinema. For once life was ahead of art.

Indira was in England earlier that month, to open the Festival of India, when Maneka announced that she would address a convention of Sanjay loyalists at Lucknow on March 29th. A day earlier, on her return home from London, the Prime Minister denounced the proposed convention and forbade her daughter-in-law to attend it. Maneka disregarded the advice and went to the convention though the speech she made there was conciliatory to her mother-in-law. But Indira's fury knew no bounds and she served Maneka with notice to quit.

In a letter, leaked to the press by the Prime Minister's news managers, Indira accused Maneka of disrespect and defiance not only after Sanjay's death but also when he was alive. 'Although you came from a different background,' wrote Indira, 'we accepted you because of Sanjay, but now we see you cannot adjust.' Indira accused Maneka of being a 'willing tool of my enemies and those of Sanjay's' and told her that there was no place for her in the Gandhi household any longer. Her luggage was dumped in the compound and she eventually left, with her sister, amidst scenes that did no good to Indira's image.

The next day Maneka released her stinging reply to her mother-in-law's missive. It began: 'Mummy, as usual, you have written for the press and posterity.' Maneka denied all charges against her and complained instead that she had been subjected to 'indignities and abuse, physical and mental' which 'no, and I repeat, no human being would have suffered'. The letter went on: 'You have insulted me in front of the servants, ordered my luggage searched, abused me in public (and) called my family names . . .'

The slanging match between the two continued though from afar. Indira accused Maneka of denying her access to her grandson. Maneka claimed that her mother-in-law, misusing her enormous powers, was trying to deprive her of Feroze Varun's custody.

On one occasion Maneka likened Indira to the goddess Kali 'who drinks blood'. Indira stated that her son's marriage to Maneka was part of a 'conspiracy to plant her in the inner circles'. She herself, Indira said, had always opposed the marriage and that 'latterly her son, too, had discovered the truth'. Maneka's rejoinder to this was that Indira's 'mind was affected by age and that she wished her a happy and speedy retirement'.

The Lucknow convention of Sanjay supporters that had so infuriated Indira had led to the formation of the Rashtria Sanjay Vichar Manch (National Forum of Sanjay Thoughts) as a pressure group. Maneka now converted it into a political party, as an instrument for fighting her mother-in-law and brother-in-law.

If she had expected disgruntled Congress (I) members to flock to her camp, she must have been disappointed because few did. But she must have been pleased with the welcome she received from the leaders of opposition parties, many of whom had heaped on her the choicest abuse in the past. They had always held Sanjay to be the 'evil genius' of the 'hated' Emergency and Maneka to be his 'partner in crime'.

Early in 1984 Maneka was elated by her party's victory over a Congress (I) candidate in a by-election to the UP state assembly from the Malliahabad constituency, not far from Amethi, represented in Parliament by Rajiv. This encouraged her to announce that whenever

241

a parliamentary election was held, she would personally run against her brother-in-law and defeat him. She had by then reached the minimum qualifying age.

As it happened the election was held after Indira was dead and Rajiv had become Prime Minister. Maneka did stand against him and, carrying her infant son in her arms, campaigned vigorously. But so great was the sympathy wave for the slain Indira that Maneka lost miserably and Rajiv won the biggest mandate in Indian history.

# 16    Lengthening Shadows

By the time Rajiv had responded to the maternal summons and become Indira's principal lieutenant, all the woes tormenting the country and her had become steadily worse. The unending caste conflicts provided an instructive instance in point.

Harijans, the former untouchables, and Girijans or Adivasis, the tribal people living in remote jungles, were doubtless at the receiving end of ruthless exploitation and vicious caste violence. But, strangely, they had also aroused some resentment among relatively affluent upper castes because of independent India's policy to reserve government jobs and seats in educational institutions for Harijans and Adivasis. The rationale behind the policy was sound. Some 'positive discrimination' in favour of the most depressed and dispossessed of Indians was necessary if they were to overcome the crushing backlog of centuries of backwardness. But national consensus behind the policy, easily evolved at the time of independence, had broken down because the temporary expedient, expected to last no more than fifteen years, was being perpetuated. Moreover, 'backward castes', other than Harijans and Adivasis, using their political clout, had secured reservations for themselves, too, considerably reducing the area where merit alone was supposed to prevail.

It was against this backdrop that, at the beginning of 1981, the Harijan issue was turned upside down, so to speak. Ironically, this happened in Gujarat, the home state of Mahatma Gandhi, an indefatigable champion of the Harijan cause. A dispute over the reservation issue in the state's premier medical college in its capital, Ahmedabad, led to a series of riots which shook eighteen of its nineteen districts for four months and left nearly four hundred dead.

The immediate provocation for the upheaval was the denial of admission to a highly specialised medical course to an upper-caste student with very high marks because the solitary seat was reserved that year, under a rota system, for Harijan or Adivasi students for whom qualifying marks were low or else they would not have got in at all.

Medical college students went on strike against this 'injustice' and this action immediately degenerated into an orgy of violence, largely because of the underlying resentment in Gujarat against the sudden surge of Harijan militancy, until then unknown in that state. This new militancy was encouraged partly by the Dalit (Downtrodden)

243

Movement in the neighbouring state of Maharashtra where Dalit Panthers, *à la* Black Panthers of America, had tended to go on a rampage from time to time. Partly it was accentuated by Indira Gandhi's strategy of cobbling together an alliance called KHAM – the acronym standing for Kashtriyas (a less privileged upper caste), Harijans, Adivasis and Muslims – to end the traditional dominance of Gujarat's politics by the powerful land-owning caste, called Patels.

A fortnight before the row over admissions in the Ahmedabad medical college, in a nearby village, a Harijan youth, accused of petty theft, had been burnt alive. In retaliation, Harijans from Ahmedabad raided the village and thrashed its upper-caste inhabitants, mostly Patels. Nothing like this had happened in Gujarat before. The volcano of upper-caste fury burst as soon as the medical college strike began. A succession of anti-Harijan pogroms followed. Harijans, outnumbered in the city, once again hit back in the countryside.

Through various emissaries, Indira mollified the medical students but they went back to their classes only after the state government had raised their stipend. At the same time she got a resolution passed by Parliament 'reiterating its firm commitment to the national policy on reservation as enshrined in the constitution'. This was her way of reassuring her Harijan followers that the adverse reaction of upper-caste Hindus to reservation policy would not deflect her from it. She also took steps to ensure that perpetrators of atrocities on Harijans, accustomed to going scot free, were at last punished.

As early as May 1980, two men were sentenced to death and fifteen others to life imprisonment for the infamous outrage on the Harijans of Belchi. In August 1981, fifty people were sentenced to life imprisonment for the massacre of Harijans at Pipra, which had coincided with her return to power. But the deterrent effect of these stringent sentences was negligible. The killings of Harijans did not abate.

In February 1982, the government ruefully informed Parliament that during the preceding two years, 960 Harijans had been done to death in various parts of the country. Nor did the situation improve during subsequent years.

No less recurring than atrocities on Harijans was the nightmare of Hindu–Muslim riots which kept breaking out in some place or the other with a regularity that would have been monotonous, were the riots themselves not so monstrous.

In April 1981, Harijan-bashing and Hindu–Muslim strife showed signs of overlapping. The conversion to Islam of nearly thirteen hundred Harijans of Meenakshipuram, a village in the southern state of Tamil Nadu, raised hackles all over the country.

Such conversions to Christianity, Islam and Buddhism were not new. Harijans had resorted to these for centuries in the hope of

244

escaping the degradation that was their fate under the Hindu caste system. But it had never worked. The stigma of untouchability could not be shaken off.

In the surcharged atmosphere of the early Eighties, conversions of Harijans to Buddhism might have passed muster. But those to Islam were a different matter. Many Hindus perceived them as a provocative merging of Harijan and Muslim militancies. They also made the angry accusation that Muslim fundamentalists, flush with money received from oil-rich Arab states, were using it to lure poor Harijans into their fold.

Conversions to Islam produced a chain reaction of renewed atrocities on 'offending' Harijans and more conversions. This led to a clamour by some Hindu zealots that India be declared a 'Hindu state' and all conversions banned by law. Indira Gandhi's government responded by declaring that India was and would 'remain a secular state', that a ban on conversions would be 'incompatible with the religious freedoms guaranteed by the constitution' and that there was 'no evidence to show that conversions to Islam were being encouraged by Arab money'. At the same time, the government acted strongly in the industrial town of Kanpur in UP and arrested, under the National Security Act, a dozen Dalit Panthers encouraging Harijans to convert to Islam.

Religious fanatics and caste warriors were not the only ones out to create mayhem. Indian Maoists, called Naxalites, also gleefully got into the act.

Ruthlessly crushed in their birthplace and one-time citadel, West Bengal, nearly a decade earlier, badly let down by China's own repudiation of the Cultural Revolution, from which they had derived inspiration, and splintered into feuding factions too numerous to keep count of, Naxalites had lain low for some years. Soon after Indira's return to power, thirteen factions had met and decided to give up violence and individual terror and take to political action instead. But the resolve had not lasted. By the end of 1980 reports of Naxalite depredations had started coming in from many different places. During 1981, in as many as 324 incidents, Naxalites took a toll of ninety-two lives. They shrewdly concentrated on remote tribal pockets in Andhra, Bihar and West Bengal where aboriginal populations, totally at the mercy of rapacious landlords and forest contractors, tended to welcome the young 'revolutionaries' as their only 'saviours'.

Not all of Indira's troubles were caused by circumstances and conflicts beyond her control. Some were entirely of her own making and some others part of the late Sanjay's legacy.

Her supremacy in her party was undisputed and indisputable. But this in no way diminished her paranoia and innate sense of insecurity. Her own position might be invulnerable, but she worried that some of her ambitious followers, biding their time, might try to block her son's succession to her when the time came. To keep everyone on tenterhooks and not to let anyone build up a power-base for himself was the obvious answer to her problem. She reshuffled her cabinet at least once every three months and changed chief ministers in states ruled by the Congress (I) at the drop of a Gandhi cap.

Instead of enforcing a modicum of discipline in the party, she allowed rival factions – each vying with every other to swear loyalty to her – to run riot. Massive abuse of transitory power inevitably followed. There was also the sad spectacle of instability even in the states where her party had overwhelming majorities. To make matters worse, several of the chief ministers hand-picked by Sanjay just before his death turned out in a matter of months to be major embarrassments. Indira found it necessary to sack, amidst derision by the press and the public, Jagannath Pahadia in Rajasthan because his government's incompetence and corrupt ways had become too much even by the prevailing permissive standards.

More messy than the dismissal of Pahadia was the removal of the chief minister of Andhra Pradesh in Southern India which, along with the neighbouring state of Karnataka, had solidly stood by Indira even during her nadir in 1977. This fact had placed the chief ministers of these two states, Chenna Reddy in Andhra and Devaraj Urs in Karnataka, in a rather special position.

Although Urs had invited Indira to get elected to Parliament from his state, he was the first to fall out with her, largely because of his resentment of Sanjay's influence on his mother. The parting of the ways in 1979 was acrimonious.

Chenna Reddy in Andhra did not match up to Urs in adroitness but he was no political novice. Nor was he without local support. His besetting sin, however, was inordinate conceit, compounded by ambition and disdain for scruples. During Indira's years in the wilderness he stayed ostensibly loyal to her but made no bones about the fact that 'roles were now reversed' because Indira 'needed his support more than he needed hers'. Her return to power meant therefore that his time was up. But he did not leave without putting up some resistance.

With a Pavlovian reflex Andhra Congressmen united in requesting Indira to nominate Chenna Reddy's successor. She could not have made a worse choice than she did when she picked T. Anjiah, a well-meaning but thoroughly ineffectual person. It was Anjiah's misfortune to be chief minister of a major state at a time when the ruling party's main task was to build up Rajiv Gandhi. Apparently unaware of Rajiv's distaste for the crudities his brother used to relish, Anjiah gave the new Crown Prince a fawning welcome at Hyderabad, the state capital.

Rajiv, who ought to have known better, flew into a rage and gave Anjiah a terrible tongue-lashing right on the tarmac within the hearing of hundreds of people. There was an instant outcry against this display of bad manners and all opposition parties jointly declared that discourtesy to Anjiah was an 'insult' to the whole of Andhra.

A prominent and locally popular Andhra film star, N. T. Ramarao, better known by his initials, N.T.R., promptly announced the formation of a new party, Teluga Desam or the party of Telugu-speaking people. Its sole objective, he said, would be to 'restore Andhra's dignity and self-respect'.

Indira was keenly conscious of the political potential of film stars. She used to say, accurately, if also half-jokingly, that Indian film stars – for some inexplicable reasons always called 'matinee idols' – had made their mark in politics long before Americans had thought of electing Ronald Reagan as their president. Indeed, Tamil Nadu, a state next door to Andhra, had been ruled by film personalities, actors and scriptwriters, since 1967. Of them the most glamorous and powerful had turned out to be M. G. Ramachandaran – M.G.R., to millions of his fans – who had been chief minister since 1977. But, curiously, Indira did not take Ramarao's entry into Andhra politics seriously, in the apparent belief that 'Andhra was not Tamil Nadu and N.T.R. was no M.G.R.'.

This was to prove to be a costly miscalculation. In the meantime Indira's attempt to salvage things in Andhra by sacking the luckless Anjiah had had precisely the contrary result. His successor, B. Venkataram Reddy, turned out to be equally bumbling and was replaced within a few months by Vijay Bhaskar Reddy. While others drew parallels with the French Fourth Republic, N.T.R. went on hammering home the message that Indira and her son were treating Andhra as their 'personal fiefdom'.

Even more damaging than the goings-on in Andhra was a major scandal that erupted in August 1981 in the state of Maharashtra which includes the booming city of Bombay, the country's commercial capital. The villain of the piece was Abdul Rahman Antulay, Sanjay's nominee as the state's chief minister.

Antulay, who fancied himself as some kind of a modern-day 'Sultan of Bombay', was apparently in a tearing hurry to consolidate his power which, until then, was based on nothing more than the late Sanjay's benevolence. Antulay was not alone in believing that control of big money was vital to a politician's power. But he went about acquiring such a control with breathtaking brazenness.

He set up a network of trusts the kingpin of which, the *Indira Gandhi Pratibha Pratishthan*, was named after the Prime Minister and thus enabled him to pretend that his entire venture had her support. He then proceeded to 'extort' huge donations to this trust from industrialists and businessmen in return for allocation of scarce materials such as cement and industrial alcohol, building permits and exemption from income tax as well as from the law imposing a limit on the size of the individual urban land holding. Cooperative sugar factories, the mainstay of rural Maharashtra's economy, making appropriate contributions to the trust, were given generous loans which were subsequently written off in some cases. The stated objective of the *Pratishthan* – to provide the poor with housing, schooling and medical aid and to help writers and artists – was nothing more than a convenient cover for the use of funds for political and partisan purposes.

The exposure of Antulay's antics, first by the press and then in Parliament and the Maharashtra legislature, was thorough and extremely well documented.

At this stage Indira could have limited the damage and perhaps turned the situation to her advantage, had she readily agreed to the demand for Antulay's resignation and a judicial inquiry into his conduct. But she dug in her heels in defence of her late son's, and now her own, protégé, though she denied having allowed him to use her name while forming his trust. Her government stonewalled all attempts by the opposition to discuss the tarnished Antulay trusts in Parliament. Outside the House she declared that Antulay would 'stay' because the 'people wanted him'.

Rajiv, who had entered politics as 'Mr Clean', was unhappy over the way the Antulay affair was being handled. But this made no difference to his mother's apparent resolve to shield the errant chief minister. Many of Indira's followers grumbled privately about this but dared not take up the matter with her or speak out in public. An official adviser of Indira, a former academic, alone asked her whether it was wise to go on defending Antulay and taking heavy flak in the bargain. He was tersely told: 'To win and retain the loyalty of followers, a leader has to stand by them.'

Other people's explanations of the Prime Minister's attitude were less charitable. By protecting Antulay, they speculated, she was seeing to it that he refrained from making damaging disclosures about her or about the late Sanjay.

Frustrated by their inability to call Antulay to account through the political process, his detractors took the issue to court. In January

1982, the Bombay High Court held that he had indeed abused his power by making cement quotas and various official permits a medium of exchange. Antulay had to resign. But this did not end the Antulay scandal.

At the time of his involuntary exit, Antulay, using the clout he had built up because of the huge resources at his disposal, made sure that his place was taken by an obscure nonentity, Babasaheb Bhosale. This way he hoped to stage a comeback before long. But evidently he had underestimated his critics' resolve to pursue him as well as Bhosale's ineptitude.

Consequently, while Indira was compelled to replace Bhosale by a more substantial figure, opposition legislators sought the governor's permission to prosecute Antulay privately under the Prevention of Corruption Act, because the government was refusing to do its duty of launching the necessary prosecution. For some time Indira even toyed with the idea of amending the relevant law to save Antulay from a trial on criminal charges. But wiser counsels prevailed. The law was not amended and Antulay's prosecution was sanctioned.

In February 1982, while the sordid Antulay drama was still dragging on, another big scandal burst into the open and caused a terrible stink. The scale of wrongdoing in this case was modest, compared with Antulay's shenanigans, but Indira's embarrassment was much the greater because of the involvement in this scandal of several close associates of the late Sanjay, some of whom, such as Kamal Nath, were also her confidants.

It transpired that within a few days of Indira's return to power, cronies of her younger son had managed to browbeat the Petroleum Ministry to agree, in utter disregard of persistent expert advice, to import huge quantities of petroleum products from a Singapore company called Kuo Oil. The glaring flaw in the deal was the Singapore firm's insistence on a fixed price throughout the period of the contract while a steadily declining trend in world oil prices could be easily foreseen. The result was a bonanza for Kuo Oil and the Indian middlemen and a predictable loss to the government which, on its own admission, amounted to over Rupees nine *crore* or five million pounds.

Attempts by Parliament's Committee on Public Undertakings to examine the deal were contemptuously thwarted. The Petroleum Ministry informed it that the relevant file was 'missing' and could not be traced. After several protests by the committee, the file finally surfaced in, of all places, the Prime Minister's office. Information culled from it was conveyed to the committee precisely twenty-four days before its tenure was to end. Its report, finalised and presented to the House on the last day of its existence, was heavily doctored by the Congress (I) majority, eliminating from it the minutes of the committee's discussions. All references in Parliament to this 'shocking departure' from normal routine were ruled out of order. But this blatant 'Operation Cover-Up' was of no use. The government was exposed to ridicule because someone leaked out the entire Kuo Oil file. Its juicy contents were splashed by newspapers and magazines, in one case under the smart heading: 'Quid Pro Kuo'.

Once again, as during the years leading to the Emergency, corruption in high places became a major issue, furiously discussed all over the country. Searching questions also began to be asked about defence deals such as the purchase from West Germany of the HDW submarine which was known to have had 'Sanjay's blessing'. Indira's response to the growing revulsion against the 'tidal wave of corruption' was the bland declaration that corruption was a 'global phenomenon'.

In any case, the Prime Minister was more worried about safeguarding Indian security than fighting corruption. The Iran–Iraq war, beginning in September 1980, had brought superpower rivalries and military deployments too close to Indian shores for comfort. A greater source of perturbation was the US decision, in the wake of the Soviet military intervention in Afghanistan and the collapse of the Shah of Iran, to pump highly sophisticated weaponry into Pakistan which had previously used US-gifted arms against India. And a personal level, her estranged daughter-in-law, Sanjay's widow, Maneka, had become a thorn in Indira's side.

All her torments were soon to be overtaken, however, by the developing cataclysm in Punjab that had stemmed from evidently widespread discontent among Sikhs. As sinister as it was searing, the Punjab upheaval was to become, from the latter half of 1981 onwards, Indira's principal preoccupation; it was also to take her life.

A detailed study of the bewildering complexities and deep roots of the Sikh problem that erupted with elemental fury in Punjab cannot possibly be attempted within the confines of this book. And yet a brief résumé of the historical background to the problem is needed, if only to comprehend the calamity of such gigantic proportions which it turned into.

Founded by Guru Nanak (1469–1539) less than five hundred years ago, the Sikh religion spread largely in undivided Punjab where he was born, at Talwandi, a small town not far from Lahore, now in Pakistan. Nanak's message, preached through superlative poetic compositions in Punjabi, combined the best of both Hinduism and Islam while rejecting their dogma and bigotry.

Followers who flocked to Nanak were called Sikhs (disciples) which meant that the Guru (teacher) was to be an essential institution of

Sikhism. To this Nanak added the *gurdwara* (Sikh shrine) and *Guru ka langar*, or the Guru's kitchen, where all believers were to eat together to break down the caste barriers.

In choosing his successor in his own lifetime, Nanak bypassed his own sons and named a bright pupil, Angad, whose lasting contribution was to devise a distinct script called *Gurumukhi* in which Nanak's hymns were rendered.

It was during the time of the fifth Guru, Arjun Dev, that the Golden Temple was built and around it developed the holy city of Amritsar. Guru Arjun also compiled the Sikh holy book, called Adi Granth at first and later renamed Guru Granth Sahib, and installed it in the shrine he had built. This is what made the Golden Temple for Sikhs what Mecca is to Muslims and the Vatican to Catholics.

Guru Arjun's son and successor, Hargobind, built within the Golden Temple complex another shrine, Akal Takht or Eternal Throne, symbolising the Sikh temporal power. Thus was born one of the basic tenets of Sikhism: that 'spiritual and temporal, religion and politics are inseparable'. Three and a half centuries later this doctrine was to clash head-on with independent India's resolve to be, and remain at all costs, secular.

The spread of Sikh religion and the heyday of the Mughal rule overlapped. The relationship between the two, far from being happy or harmonious, was one of intense hostility, even hatred, although the land for the Golden Temple was given by Akbar, the most enlightened of Mughal emperors, and its foundation stone was laid by a Muslim Sufi, Mian Mir.

The bitter divide between Sikhs and Muslims began in 1606 when the fifth Guru, Arjun, the builder of the Golden Temple, was tortured in the Lahore fort under orders from Emperor Jehangir, Akbar's son. Enraged by Guru Arjun's martyrdom, Sikhs turned 'militant and militaristic' and started maintaining a 'standing army of the faithful'.

Other martyrs of Sikhism included the ninth Guru, Tegh Bahadur, whose son, Gobind Singh, the tenth and the last Guru, welded the Sikh army into a 'formidable fighting force' and founded a new order called *Khalsa* or Pure – hence the name 'Khalistan' for the independent Sikh state dreamed of by today's Sikh militants – and made it the core of his highly motivated army.

He did more. Enjoining upon his followers to 'preserve their identity at all costs' he 'externalised' this identity by making it obligatory on Sikhs never to cut their hair or shave their beards.

The two threats from which the tenth Guru wanted jealously to guard Sikh identity were the reality of Muslim persecution – shortly after his father's execution his own two sons were entombed alive – and the fear of the reabsorption of Sikh faith by Hinduism.

251

This fear was by no means fanciful. Much older religions, such as Buddhism and Jainism, had indeed met the fate Sikhs feared for their faith. Moreover, from Nanak's time to that of Gobind Singh, Hindus had regarded Sikhism as 'part and parcel of the wider Hindu framework'. Significantly, this Hindu belief remains unchanged till today. Ties of blood and kinship between Hindus and Sikhs, as strong and widespread now as then, tend to blur the lines of demarcation, no matter how aggressively drawn.

Historically, the fear of reabsorption by Hinduism has proved to be the more enduring. During the first two decades of independence, for instance, orthodox Sikhs perceived the 'safety razor' to be the 'principal threat' to Sikh identity. But at the time of the tenth Guru, persecution by Muslims was much the greater danger. He and, after his death in 1708, his devoted disciple, Banda Bahadur, fought a succession of 'fierce but inconclusive battles' with the declining Mughals and other Muslim potentates. But their battle-cry, *Raj Karega Khalsa* (the Khalsa Shall Rule) remained an empty dream; and so it was to remain until the end of the eighteenth century.

It was in the time of Ranjit Singh (1780–1839) that the first and only Sikh kingdom in Indian history was established in 1799 and the Sikh political power reached its apogee.

The backbone of Ranjit Singh's empire, stretching to the frontiers of Tibet in the north and to the Khyber Pass in the west, though stopping well short of Delhi in the east, was his famous army which he had reorganised along Western lines with the help of two captains of Napoleon's defeated armies.

So great was Ranjit Singh's military might that even the British, now happily ensconced in Delhi where the Mughal emperor had become their pensioner, thought it 'prudent not to tangle with him'.

Ranjit Singh ruled in the name of the Sikh faith and paid due obeisance to the religious authority of the Golden Temple. But in matters temporal he allowed no religious interference. His approach to government was secular, born of his shrewd awareness that 'a majority of his subjects and much of his army were non-Sikh'.

Within ten years of Ranjit Singh's death his mighty empire collapsed ignominiously. By 1849, following several Anglo-Sikh wars, Punjab was annexed by the expanding British power. This was a trauma to the proud Sikhs. What infuriated them the most was that they had been beaten by an army only a third of which was of British stock, the majority being *purbiyas* or East India Company's sepoys from eastern provinces.

Herein lies a clue to the Sikhs' strange behaviour barely eight years later, during the Mutiny of 1857, when the fate of the British in India

252

hung in the balance and one more push could have driven them into the sea. Instead of pouncing on the tottering British, Sikhs rallied to their defence. The motive behind this was their desire to 'get even' with the *purbiya* whom they 'despised and whose presence in Punjab they resented'.

For this, Sikhs were rewarded with the grant of fertile lands in Punjab and a pride of place in the British Indian Army. Consequently, a mutually supportive bond between the two sides developed, which endured, by and large, until the end of the Raj in 1947. The British also quickly developed a vested interest in preserving and even playing up the separate Sikh identity. This was not just another strand in the classic imperial policy of divide and rule. Sikh separatism took care also of British concern about the reliability of their Indian Army in the post-Mutiny era. To ensure the Sikh soldiery's total loyalty to the Crown the Raj found it expedient to enforce on it all the rigid rules and rituals of the *Khalsa* orthodoxy and to encourage Sikhs, as a top British intelligence officer candidly wrote, 'to regard themselves as a totally distinct and separate nation'.

During the First World War, Sikh representation in the Army 'shot up threefold' and Sikh soldiers fought valiantly on all fronts. At the end of the war, however, a very large number of Sikhs turned hostile to the British. This change in their attitude was triggered by the infamous massacre at Jallianwalla Bagh in Amritsar in 1919 that had, as we have noted, so thoroughly appalled Indira's grandfather, Motilal Nehru.

Like Motilal, hundreds of thousands of Sikhs, including demobbed soldiers, joined Mahatma Gandhi's non-violent crusade to drive the British out. By contrast, priests in control of Sikh shrines, evidently out of touch with the community's nationalist sentiment, 'honoured' General Dyer, the perpetrator of the Jallianwalla Bagh outrage, in the Golden Temple. In sheer disgust, Sikhs started a mass movement to free their *gurdwaras* from the control of 'corrupt and degenerate' priests who were loyalists of the Raj and often 'more Hindu than Sikh'. It was a big success.

It also turned out to be a watershed in Sikh history because the Gurudwara Act, passed in 1925, 'institutionalised Sikh communal separatism'. This it did by forming a body called Shiromani Gurudwara Prabadhak Committee (SGPC) or the Central Managing Committee of Sikh shrines. What made the SGPC unique and gave it, apart from complete control of Sikh shrines and their vast wealth and incomes, great authority over the Sikh community was that it was chosen exclusively by a Sikh electorate, divided into small constituencies. It thus became something of a Sikh Parliament.

Along with SGPC, and in a symbiotic relationship with it, was born the Akali Dal or the Akali party, its political wing. Once again the doctrine of the inseparability of religion and politics was at work. Since then every political activity of the Akali Dal has had highly emotive religious overtones, with a heavy accent on martyrdom by which Sikhs set great store.

Remarkably, during the six decades since their birth, the Akali Dal has never once lost control of SGPC and the two organisations, regardless of their unending factional feuds, have together conducted countless Sikh agitations – on every occasion called *dharma yudh* (holy war) – throughout this period.

In the Eighties there was a seemingly small but actually profound change in the established pattern. In the 'holy war' that became Indira Gandhi's 'last battle', the Akali Dal and SGPC were in the forefront only nominally. In reality, they had 'surrendered the leadership of the agitation' to a young, fundamentalist preacher, Jarnail Singh Bhindranwale, whose fanaticism promptly earned him the nickname 'Sikh Khomeini'.

The painful story of Bhindranwale's rise to some kind of a messianic figure and his diabolical role must wait until we have surveyed the developments between the Twenties and the Eighties.

In the wake of the successful Gurudwara agitation, the nationalist fervour among Sikhs and their consequent cooperation with the Indian National Congress alarmed Akali leaders who regarded the Congress as a 'Hindu organisation' and were haunted by the frightening, if familiar, vision of the Sikh identity being 'swallowed up by Hinduism'. In a bid to preserve this identity, the Akali Dal reverted to collaboration with the Raj. The Second World War widened the breach between the Congress and the Akali Dal. Nationalist India boycotted the British war effort; the Akali party joined it wholeheartedly. But, as the war drew to a close, Akalis were in for a rude shock.

India's independence was now round the corner. The only question was whether the British would leave behind a united India or carve out of it the state of Pakistan, demanded by the Muslim League. Sikhs discovered to their dismay that they were being left high and dry. Belatedly the Akali Dal raised a demand for a Sikh state independent of India and Pakistan. But no one took it seriously; Sikhs were too few and too scattered to sustain it.

Independence and partition were accompanied by massacres and migrations unparalleled in history in peacetime. Hindus, Sikhs and Muslims all suffered grievously. However, partition did bring about a consolidation of the Sikh community, raising its proportion in Indian Punjab to over a third of the state's total population. But even this was nowhere near a majority; the basic Sikh problem, that there were not enough of them, remained. Freedom also meant disappearance of the separate communal representation and preferential treatment enjoyed by Sikhs during British days.

Once again the thoughts of Akali leaders turned to a sovereign Sikh state. But realising that 'so soon after the 1947 holocaust no one would countenance a second partition', they asked for an 'autonomous' state within India. They also 'camouflaged their craving for a Sikh-dominated state' by claiming that they were asking for only Punjabi *suba* or a Punjabi-speaking state.

Though entirely transparent, the linguistic cover for an essentially communal demand had its uses. The redrawing of the internal political map of the country along linguistic lines – so that provincial adminis-tration could be carried on in the language of the people – had been an integral part of the Gandhian blueprint for independent India, a land of fourteen major and several hundred minor languages, to say nothing of thousands of dialects.

No one saw through the Akali game more clearly than Jawaharlal Nehru, the titan-like Prime Minister of the day, whose worst enemies would not accuse him of communal or religious prejudice. He rejected the Akali demand for Punjabi *suba* at once and resolutely resisted it right until his death in 1964, despite a succession of virulent Akali agitations.

It was not Punjabi *suba* alone that Nehru opposed. He had developed 'serious second thoughts' on the very concept of linguistic states. But popular sentiment for such states forced him, in 1953, to appoint the States Reorganisation Commission. The Akalis were delighted and pressed hard their demand for Punjabi *suba*. But the commission, while conceding the linguistic principle in the rest of the country, ruled that Punjab, a sensitive border state where both Punjabi and Hindi were used, should stay bilingual. Master Tara Singh, the dominant Akali leader from 1935 until his eclipse in the early Sixties, denounced the commission's verdict as a 'decree of Sikh annihilation'. His rhetorical excess was not liked but many sympathised with him in his complaint that denial of Punjabi *suba* smacked of 'discrimination' against, and 'distrust' of, Sikhs.

This much was indeed said to Nehru's face by Ajoy Ghosh, the highly respected leader of the Communist Party of India from the early Fifties until his death in 1961, who also pleaded that the Akali demand be accepted.

'I envy you, Ajoy,' Nehru had replied. 'You do not have to run the country. It is my responsibility to do so. Sikhs are fine people but they are led by separatists and fanatics. I cannot hand over a state to them on the border with Pakistan. But such things are not permanent. As national integration proceeds, we will surely have a Punjabi-speaking state.' Ghosh was disarmed but Akalis went on fuelling Sikh discontent which was mitigated however, by Punjab's 'phenomenal prosperity' by Indian standards.

It was Nehru's daughter, Indira Gandhi, who conceded the Punjabi-speaking state in March 1966, less than two years after his death. Her bold decision, doubtless influenced by the valour with which Sikh soldiers had fought in the 1965 war between India and Pakistan and the way in which the Sikh population in the border areas had rallied to the Army's support, was widely acclaimed.

By now the Akali leadership had passed from Master Tara Singh to Sant Fateh Singh, a Jat and therefore a more authentic steward of a party drawing its support from the Jat Sikh peasantry. Fateh Singh was also a bachelor, but this did not prevent him from proclaiming: 'A handsome baby has been born in my household.'

Soon, however, Fateh Singh was to discover that his was a Pyrrhic victory. Akalis had got the 'Sikh homeland' but they could not rule it. The dynamics of both demography and democracy were against them.

Even after Hindi-speaking areas of Punjab had been transferred to Haryana, Sikhs constituted only fifty-six per cent of the remaining population. This obviously was not enough for the Akali party to capture power. For although all Akalis were doubtless Sikhs, all Sikhs, contrary to bombastic Akali claims, were not Akalis, judging by the community's voting pattern.

In 1967 and 1969, the Akali party did manage to scrape to power by entering into a coalition with its antithesis, the Hindu chauvinist party, the Jana Sangh (now called the Bharatiya Janata Party or BJP). On both occasions, the 'marriage of inconvenience' proved sadly shortlived. In the 1971 General Election the Akali rout in Punjab was complete while Indira won hands down there, as all over the country.

To fill the Akali cup of misery to the brim, Punjab's new chief minister, Giani Zail Singh, a Sikh who was later to become Home Minister of India and later still the President of the Republic, started stealing the Akalis' clothes. This he did by 'ostentatiously pandering' to Sikh religious sentiment. Many of his Congress colleagues were alarmed and 'complained' against him to Indira.

The Akalis were, of course, furious and started looking for issues on which even Zail Singh would not be able to give satisfaction to the Sikh community, a danger he should have anticipated but obviously did not.

It was at this time that the renewed cry of 'Khalistan', an independent Sikh state, also began to be heard. It was raised most notably by Jagjit Singh Chauhan, who had been Finance Minister in one of the transient Punjab ministries. He had then migrated to London where

Portrait of Indira at the
height of her power and
glory.

At her desk surrounded
by a phalanx of
petitioners.

With her main rival in the power struggle, Morarji Desai, who led the Janata government after Indira's fall from power in the 1977 General Election. This picture was taken barely three months before Indira divested Desai, then Deputy Prime Minister, of the finance portfolio, leaving him no option but to resign.

Jayaprakash Narayan, generally known as J.P., who led a powerful movement in 1974-5 for Indira's removal, being welcomed on arrival at Calcutta's Howrah station.

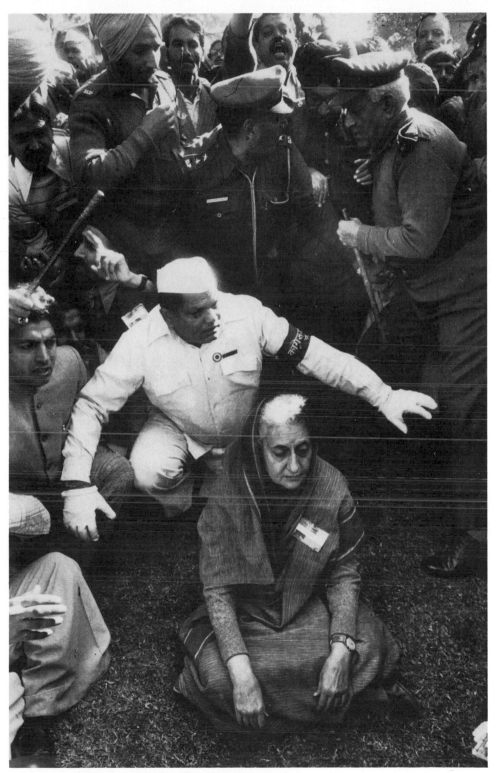

After her defeat and arrest by the Janata government.

After being out of power for nearly three years, Indira Gandhi on the come-back trail.
She addresses a mammoth public meeting in Haryana State in December, 1979.

Being greeted by supporters and admirers after her return to power in January, 1980.

On the day of her younger son Sanjay's death, Indira being consoled by her surviving son and eventual successor, Rajiv Gandhi.

With Queen Elizabeth
II and the Duke of
Edinburgh in New
Delhi in November,
1983.

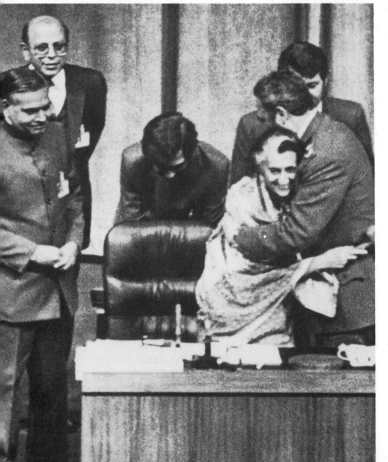

Fidel Castro hugs
Indira Gandhi on
handing over to her the
chairmanship of the
Non-Alignment
Movement at NAM's
seventh summit, in
New Delhi, March,
1983.

Crowds jostling for a last glimpse of Indira before her funeral.

Consigned to the flames of the funeral pyre, watched by Rajiv and other members of her family.

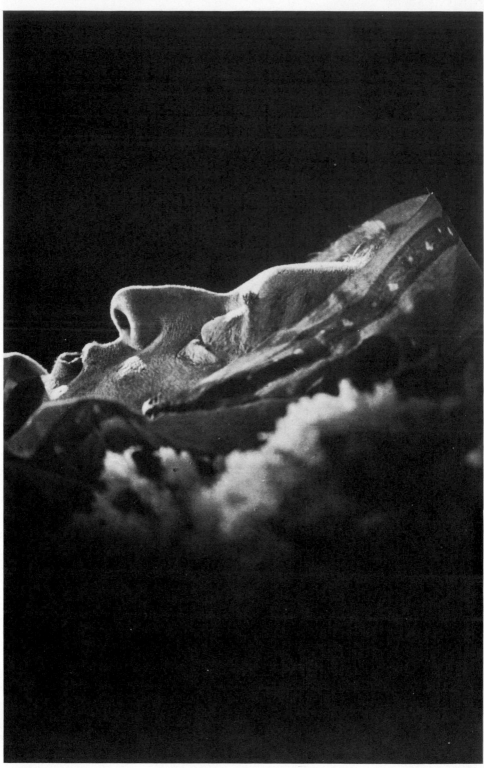

Lying in state.

he styled himself, as he continues to do, as 'President' of the 'Republic of Khalistan'.

In a resolution, drafted in 1973 at Sri Anandpur Sahib, the very spot where the tenth and the last Guru had held the first assembly of the *Khalsa*, the Akali Dal demanded, on behalf of the 'Sikh nation', that there must be an area in India where the *'Khalsa* must be pre-eminent'. Towards this end, the resolution demanded that the central government's 'interference' in Punjab should be limited to defence, foreign relations, currency and communications. The resolution thus stopped short of endorsing the demand for 'Khalistan' but with such skilful resort to ambiguity as to blur the dividing line between autonomy and independence. For instance, the resolution blandly declared that Sikh religion 'was not safe without sovereignty'.

Two years later, the Emergency suspended all political activity. In the 1977 General Election, Indira met her Waterloo. In Punjab the Akalis won a comfortable majority for the first time. Even so, they chose to rule the state in partnership with the Janata party with which they were already sharing power in New Delhi.

Nobody heard anything about the Anandpur Sahib resolution or any other Sikh grievance during the succeeding three years until the Akali hope of ruling Punjab uninterruptedly until 1982 and then hopefully returning to power was shattered by Indira.

Once again the Akalis were on the warpath, this time with far greater fury than ever before. Hitherto, they had studiously ignored the Anandpur Sahib resolution. But they now made it their main battlecry, though they had little difficulty in compiling a catalogue of forty-five Sikh grievances – religious, political and economic, real or imaginary – which they themselves later reduced to fifteen.

The Akali 'holy war' did not formally begin until the middle of 1982. But portents of the ghastly events to come had started darkening the horizon in Punjab more than a year earlier. Groups of militant and armed Sikh youths had taken to mindless violence in the countryside to force the issue of Sikh grievances. In an obvious attempt to widen the Hindu–Sikh divide, severed heads of cows were thrown into Hindu temples.

Critically important to the gathering storm in Punjab was the emergence, as the most powerful Sikh figure, of Bhindranwale, a classic example of Frankenstein's monster, if ever there was one. For, soon after Indira lost power and the Akalis realised their dream of ruling Punjab, Zail Singh and Sanjay had started looking for a Sikh leader who, by striking extreme positions, would embarrass the Akali government and divide the Akali ranks. Their choice fell on

Bhindranwale, until then a relatively obscure preacher. It is inconceivable that they could have acted without Indira's approval.

Bhindranwale fulfilled his assigned task only too well. At first he concentrated on the physical elimination of Nirankaris or followers of a Sikh sect considered apostate by the orthodox. But by the time Indira returned to power and Akalis started preparing for a 'holy war', he was ready to turn on his former mentors and indeed on the Indian state.

The assassination on September 9th, 1981, of Jagat Narain, a Hindu Punjabi owner-editor of a chain of newspapers opposed to 'Khalistan' and intrepid in his criticism of it, became the proverbial spark that lights the prairie fire. Bhindranwale was suspected of masterminding this murder and a warrant for his arrest was issued. But even though he drove two hundred miles across Punjab and Haryana he was not taken into custody because Zail Singh, now Home Minister of India, was 'protecting him still', despite horrified protests all over the country.

On September 20th, Bhindranwale dramatically submitted himself to arrest on his own terms and in his own stronghold, the Mehta Chowk *gurudwara* near Amritsar. As soon as he was whisked away, his heavily armed followers, carrying the banner of 'Dal Khalsa' or Army of the Pure, clashed with the police. Seventeen of them were killed. A spate of violent protests followed. An Indian Airlines aircraft was hijacked to Lahore in Pakistan. It was clear that a sufficiently large and efficient organisation to do Bhindranwale's behest already existed.

It was at this precise moment that Akali leaders submitted their revised and shortened charter of demands to the government. Significantly the first demand on the new list was for Bhindranwale's 'immediate and unconditional' release.

Without waiting for the submission of charges against Bhindranwale to a court of law, Indira's government released him on October 14th. This was a Himalayan blunder. It was also a 'major turning point' in Bhindranwale's career and Punjab's history. His supremacy in Sikh politics was now complete and unshakeable. He moved into the Golden Temple complex where, surrounded by his armed acolytes, he held court, spewed venom against the government and Hindus, contemptuously called Indira 'that Brahmin woman' and ordered murder squads where and when to strike next. TV crews and journalists from all over the world converged on the Golden Temple and Bhindranwale wallowed in the prodigious media attention paid to him. Akali leaders were dazzled by the unprecedented support he managed to mobilise for them, though this also made them 'hostages to his whims and extremism'.

\* \* \*

Ironically, as the Punjab situation grew increasingly worse, Indira's capacity to deal with it was correspondingly eroded. One of the reasons for this was that Zail Singh, as Home Minister in Delhi, and Darbara Singh, also a Sikh hand-picked by Indira to be chief minister of Punjab, were constantly working at cross purposes. This inevitably confused and paralysed an administration and a police force already demoralised and in almost total disarray because of prolonged political manipulation and contamination by communal prejudice.

Above all, Indira's own credibility with a bulk of the intelligentsia and therefore with articulate opinion had slumped sharply. The harder she tried to draw attention to Akali intransigence the more she was disbelieved by her political opponents and media critics who also regularly ridiculed her repeated warnings about a 'foreign hand' out to 'destabilise and disrupt' India. She was criticised for wilfully promoting crises to 'justify her absolute power'. An even harsher charge against her was that she had knowingly allowed the Punjab crisis to 'worsen' in order to 'unify behind her the Hindu vote in Punjab, in the Hindi-speaking state of Haryana and in the Hindi-heartland as a whole'. Those who said so, and there were many of them, obviously overlooked the fact that she was being blamed by a very large number of Hindus for 'not dealing with Akali agitators and terrorists forcefully enough'.

However, the theme of 'Indira in a Hindu Role' had come to stay. It indeed became a refrain which was taken up also by the Communist Party of India (CPI), previously a habitual supporter of Indira even during the Emergency. Later, presumably to 'wash the filth of Emergency from its hands', it turned intensely hostile to her. Even pleading by Leonid Brezhnev, the Soviet leader, could not persuade it to soften its attitude. The CPI went on attacking Indira for her 'authoritarian style', 'dynastic politics' and 'anti-democratic policies'. By the middle of 1982, the party General Secretary, C. Rajeswara Rao, was publicly upbraiding her for having become a 'Hindu communalist'.

Indira was infuriated by this charge. But what troubled her more was the loss of Communist support. Even at the height of her populist-socialist phase, she had never ceased to be a 'hard-headed pragmatist'. But she was always sensitive to the uses of maintaining a left-leaning image in a poor country like India. To do so became difficult in view of the consistent badgering by the once loyal CPI. She hit back by describing the Communists as a bunch of 'opportunists' who had joined hands with 'reactionaries and communalists' against her. Among those she said this to was Tariq Ali, Britain-based Pakistani author and Left activist who had close contacts with Indian Communist leaders. He was not the only foreigner to whom she poured out this grievance. She took it also to the highest in the

international Communist hierarchy, Yuri Andropov, who had succeeded Brezhnev in 1982.

On June 21st, 1983 – forty-second anniversary of the Nazi invasion
of the Soviet Union – Indira sent a 'My Dear General Secretary'
letter to Andropov criticising the CPI for having 'ganged up' with
right-wing and reactionary forces against her. More intriguing than
the content of the letter was the mode of its delivery. It was sent to
Moscow with a CPI leader, Yogendra Sharma, a dissenter from
Rajeswara Rao's anti-Indira line. Sharma, she told Andropov in
her letter, could explain the 'Indian situation' to him in 'greater
detail'.

In other words, the messenger was the message. But things went
awry. Sharma suddenly developed cold feet over his role as Indira's
'secret emissary' to Andropov and 'confessed all to an Indian comrade'
who was already in the Soviet capital before his arrival.

As the news of the curious correspondence leaked out, the Russians
gently washed their hands of Sharma. In India there was a predictable
uproar that Indira was 'inviting Soviet interference in the country's
internal affairs'. Yogendra Sharma was disciplined by his party and
deprived of his membership of its National Executive. Indira made
absolutely no comment.

To blame Indira for deliberately allowing Punjab to burn in order to
make political capital out of the tragedy in the rest of the country was
unfair. But her handling of the crisis was doubtless inept, often
shockingly so. At first she was slow to realise the gravity of the
situation, mistaking the outbreak of violence as a passing spasm of
Akali anger over loss of power. But even after she knew what was
what, she was slow to negotiate with the Akali leaders.

Moreover, the negotiations, which took place by fits and starts,
against a background of steadily escalating Hindu–Sikh violence in
Punjab, were singularly sterile. Indira first met the Akali leaders in
late 1981, indeed a day after Bhindranwale's release. This was followed
by a six-month lull in talks. The second meeting, which took place in
April 1982, was particularly 'frosty' and therefore fruitless. Thereafter,
Indira did not personally meet the Akali leaders again though her
senior cabinet colleagues, top official aides, several mediators and
even her son and heir apparent, Rajiv Gandhi, continued to talk,
secretly or openly, to second-rank Akali leaders without being able to
make any headway.

This caused widespread dismay to those who passionately believed,
and loudly proclaimed, that the 'legitimate' Akali demands should be
met forthwith. If this was done, they argued, the Akali leaders could
be persuaded to abandon 'illegitimate' demands, notably that for

implementing the Anandpur Sahib resolution's scheme of radical devolution which would all but destroy the central authority in India, and leave terrorists and extremists isolated.

However, conceding even legitimate demands was not as easy or simple as it was being made out to be. There was, for instance, the emotive question of Chandigarh which was to have served as a joint capital of both Punjab and Haryana. Under a 1970 award, given by Indira in the wake of bitter strife between the rival claimants, Chandigarh was to go to Punjab in return for transferring to Haryana Abohar and Fazilka, two small but agriculturally rich areas of Punjab where Hindus were in a majority.

It was a clumsy arrangement and also marked a departure from Nehru's sensible approach that territorial adjustments must not be based on religion, but it was acceptable to all concerned, including Akalis. Curiously, for a whole decade nobody implemented the award although Indira's party was in power in both Punjab and Haryana until 1977 and the Akalis and their partners, the Janata, ruled in the two states during the subsequent three years.

In the Eighties, the Akalis insisted that Chandigarh be given to Punjab without any territorial compensation to Haryana, which could be given a generous financial grant to build a new capital instead. Indira declared that she could not make any change in the unimplemented award that was not acceptable to Haryana. Her critics blamed her for 'encouraging her party's government' in Haryana to be 'intransigent'. But her point was that forcing a decision on Haryana would lead to violent agitation there.

Similarly, on the river waters issue, a matter of great concern to the prosperous Sikh peasantry, Akalis were not content with the assurance that Punjab's needs would be met. They insisted that Rajasthan, a rain-starved desert state, should be deprived of whatever share it had been getting and denied any claim on the waters subsequently. To accept this would have destroyed the basis on which, under a 1960 treaty between India and Pakistan, the three eastern rivers of the Indus Basin were allotted to India in the first place.

Ironically, as bickering over river waters went on, huge quantities of 'unutilised' Indian water continued to flow into Pakistan because the 'Indian government could not complete the necessary irrigation schemes'.

Meanwhile the slaughter of the innocent in Punjab also went on. Motorcycle-borne Sikh terrorists went on shooting Hindus and Sikhs 'like quails and partridges in the open season' without apparently anyone being able to do anything about it.

Frustration over the failure of talks beween the government and Akalis and impotent rage over the government's inability to do anything about Bhindranwale's killer gangs combined to create in the country a mood of deep despondency, indeed despair. But rather than unite behind a programme of defeating terrorism at whatever cost, the people got bitterly divided into two. One section blamed Indira for not making enough concessions to Akalis which they thought would have weaned the majority of Sikhs away from the influence of Bhindranwale and the terrorists; the other denounced her for doing nothing to curb the terrorists and particularly for 'allowing' Bhindranwale and his killer gangs to use the Golden Temple as a sanctuary in circumstances which made nonsense of the convention that the police should not ordinarily enter this holiest of the Sikh shrines. She was indeed having the worst of both worlds.

Horrendous happenings in Punjab, Assam and elsewhere did not mean that Indira's second innings as Prime Minister was a period of unrelieved gloom and doom. It had its bright spots, but these were few and far between.

During her first tenure, India had become the sixth member of the Nuclear Club, the most exclusive in history, when it had conducted, in May 1974, an underground peaceful nuclear experiment (PNE) which others called an atomic test. Now, six years later, largely as a result of the impetus provided by her in the past, the country successfully blasted off, on July 18th, 1980, its own satellite launching vehicle, SLV-3, placing in orbit an indigenously designed and built thirty-five kilogram satellite, Rohini-I. Barely three weeks had elapsed since Sanjay's death and Indira was still shell-shocked, but she was beaming when she rose in Parliament to announce that it had been a 'great day for India and Indian science'. She dismissed as 'unwarranted inferences' any thoughts that SLV-3 might have been designed for military purposes, though the military potential of the venture was obvious enough.

Other achievements in space followed. In cooperation with France, scientists of the Indian Space Research Organisation successfully put a communication satellite called APPLE (Ariane Passenger Payload Experiment) in its final geostationary position. Indira congratulated them. In another three years, in April 1984, Squadron-Leader Rakesh Sharma became India's first spaceman by joining the crew of the Soviet Salyut-7 space station. Indira led the country in applauding this. She also said that the joint space flight had added a 'new dimension' to Indo-Soviet friendship.

On becoming Prime Minister a second time Indira took the unusual decision of retaining the Defence portfolio for herself. This was a measure of her concern over the deteriorating security environment not merely in India's immediate neighbourhood but also in the entire region vital to it, especially the Indian Ocean. She never ceased to campaign for keeping big power rivalries out of this ocean and making it a zone of peace.

Her biggest worry remained, however, the US decision to rearm Pakistan with highly sophisticated weaponry. She remonstrated with the US both publicly and privately but, in view of America's need of Pakistani manpower and military installations for the defence of US interests in the Gulf and the Middle East, without success. She saw to it therefore that the US military supplies to Pakistan were more than matched by necessary acquisitions by her country. Mig-29 aircraft, T-72 tanks, armoured personnel carriers and other items were obtained from the Soviet Union. Mirages were bought from France, Sea Harrier 'jump jets' from Britain and HDW submarines from West Germany. Though she believed these purchases to be unavoidable, self-reliance in defence remained Indira's real objective. She increased the outlay on defence R & D and speeded up projects of indigenous defence production, devoting special attention to missilery and nuclear propulsion of ships and submarines.

For these efforts and exertions she did not get many thanks. Far from seeing any merit in what she was doing, the intelligentsia, alienated from her and generally innocent of matters military, blamed her for spending 'too much on defence'. To make matters worse, some of the defence purchases became controversial because of suspicions of 'kickbacks' and 'payoffs'. This was particularly the case with the submarine deal with West Germany, the 'inspiration for which had come from Sanjay almost immediately after his mother's return to power'.

Indira was one of those world leaders – Kennedy, Nasser, Sukarno and Willy Brandt may be cited as other examples – who find it easier and more congenial to shine in the realm of foreign policy and international relations than to make their mark by grappling with the more daunting and demanding internal problems. She loved to travel abroad, at least partly because the elaborate and often effusive welcome in host countries impressed the people back home. During the four and a half turbulent years between her return to power and assassination, she went overseas no fewer than eighteen times, visiting close to three dozen countries including the US, the USSR, Britain, France, Norway, Denmark, Finland, Austria, Switzerland, Yugoslavia, Greece, Cyprus, Mexico, Zimbabwe, Mozambique, Kenya, Australia, Indonesia, Philippines, Fiji, Saudi Arabia, Tunisia and Libya.

Not all these journeys were jaunts by any means. Some were put to skilful use to further Indian interests. During a short visit to the United States in July–August 1982, for instance, she managed to get out of the way a nagging dispute with the Reagan administration over the supply of nuclear fuel to the US-built atomic power station at Tarapur in Western India. The row had started four years earlier because of US insistence that the 1963 Indo-US agreement guaranteeing fuel supplies to Tarapur had been overriden by subsequent US laws forbidding nuclear fuel supplies to Tarapur until India either signed the Nuclear Non-Proliferation Treaty (NPT) or accepted 'fullscope' safeguards on all its nuclear installations. Both preconditions were totally unacceptable to Indira on the grounds that they were 'discriminatory and unfair'. She also held that it was illegal and unethical for the US to renege on its 'contractual commitment'. In any case, she did not want to forswear India's nuclear option because of the continuing Chinese nuclear threat and the developing challenge of the Pakistani bomb, called the 'Islamic bomb' by some.

Even so, she did not want 'avoidable bickering' with the US and over the Tarapur issue she avoided it by opting for a compromise. Under it, the responsibility for fuelling Tarapur was transferred from the US to France on the strict understanding that nothing would be added to, or subtracted from, the terms and conditions agreed to by India and the US in 1963.

Indira's meeting with Reagan in Washington was not the first encounter between them. They had met ten months earlier, in October 1981, at the famous North–South Summit at Cancun in Mexico where leaders of fourteen developing and eight developed nations had gathered in the hope of breaking the deadlock between rich and poor nations over a new and just international economic order. The summit achieved little. The 'chasm' between rich and poor nations remained 'as wide as ever', but rapport among the leaders, especially between Indira and Reagan, had been established. Leaders of industrialised nations appreciated Indira's 'sagacity' in persuading developing nations not to insist on Cuba's presence at Cancun. She had argued with them that though Cuba was then chairman of the Non-Aligned Movement (NAM) and therefore entitled to be at the summit, its presence would invite a US boycott of Cancun and thus defeat the very purpose of the whole exercise.

It was in the same spirit that during her talks with Reagan at the White House in August 1982 she tried to reduce the areas of Indo-US disagreement, even though there was no 'give' from the American side on the all-important issue of the renewed US–Pakistan military relationship. For the first time in many years the possibility of transfer of high technology, including military technology, from the US to India was discussed seriously.

The principal US concern about India – too close a proximity to the Soviet Union, considered by Reagan to be the 'evil empire' – was raised not only in private talks but also publicly. At a press conference an American reporter asked Indira why did India 'always tilt towards the Soviet Union?'

'We don't tilt on either side,' she replied laconically, 'we walk upright.'

Looking upon herself as the leader of India as well as of the Third World, especially the Non-Aligned Movement, of which she was to become chairperson later, Indira did not allow herself to be disheartened by the failure of the Cancun summit. She decided instead to keep up the pressure on the rich nations and, for this purpose, convened a ministerial conference of 122 developing nations in New Delhi to press for a proper 'restructuring of international economy'. At the three-day conference which began on February 22nd, 1982, she regretted the 'visible deterioration in the global economy since Cancun', deplored the 'protectionism of the Western countries' which amounted to 'victimisation of developing nations' and called for a world conference on food security, energy and finance. It was at this conference that the need for 'collective self-reliance' by the poor nations was recognised and the concept of South–South cooperation was born.

There was a certain contradiction between Indira's efforts to improve relations with the US and her repeated protests that 'inimical' foreign forces 'were out to "subvert" and "harm"' her country and herself. Of course, she never identified the US by name in such denunciatory declarations, but those speaking on her behalf left no one in any doubt that the accusing finger pointed at least to the CIA, if not at the US government. Nevertheless, she persevered with her 'damage limitation' policy in relation to the US.

An even more important foreign policy initiative Indira took was that for improving relations with her country's most powerful neighbour, China. These relations, having remained frozen in mutual hostility since the 1962 border war, had thawed just a little during her previous tenure. The Janata government, anxious to outdo her in this respect, had sent its foreign minister, Atal Bihari Vajpayee, to Beijing in February 1979. But the exercise had turned sour. China attacked Vietnam, a close friend of India's, at a time when Vajpayee was still on Chinese soil. He cut short his visit abruptly. Soon thereafter the Janata government fell.

Within a month of her return to power, Indira flew to Belgrade for President Tito's funeral. She took the opportunity to meet Hua Guofeng, then Chairman of the Chinese Communist Party, and the two agreed to resume the interrupted India–China dialogue. Huang Hua, the then Chinese Foreign Minister, was to come to Delhi for talks in the autumn of that year. But the visit was postponed because of China's pique over the recognition by Indira's government of the

Vietnam-backed Heng Samrin regime in Kampuchea. The Chinese ought to have known that she would do this because she had clearly stated her intention in her party's election manifesto.

However, the quest for India–China rapprochement was resumed soon and Huang Hua duly arrived in Delhi in June 1981. There was a divergence between the Indian and Chinese positions. India gave primacy to the vexed boundary issue and wanted it solved first. China wished to put this on the back burner and suggested instead immediate improvement of relations in other fields.

Indira proposed a neat compromise. Both the border problem and relations in other fields were to be taken up together, provided that both sides recognised that progress towards a border settlement would have a multiplier effect on improvement of relations in general. Further talks were to take place between senior officials, alternately in New Delhi and Beijing.

Both sides knew that on the vexed boundary dispute they would have to compromise. Neither could hope to have its way fully. There was no way China would accept the traditional Indian position that it must vacate 'every inch' of Indian territory it had occupied before and during the 1962 war. Nor could China expect India to accept the Chinese 'package deal' envisaging the perpetuation of status quo in Ladakh in return for Chinese withdrawal of its claim on 90,000-square-kilometres of territory in the eastern sector which was under Indian control in any case.

A ticklish task before Indira therefore was to define the parameters of the acceptable compromise and indeed the contours of the line that would eventually be the frontier between India and China. But she remained circumspect and at first gave no precise idea of her thinking even to the officials negotiating with the Chinese.

However, early in 1982, when I took up this issue with her in a private conversation, she was remarkably frank in discussing it. She readily agreed to the suggestion that, apart from the acceptance of the existing situation in the eastern sector, the irreducible minimum India would have to insist on in Ladakh was Chinese withdrawal at least from the areas occupied during the actual fighting in 1962. But she added that she would like this suggestion to come from the Chinese. 'After all, they are sitting on our territory, not we on theirs.' She also felt that a settlement along the suggested lines would be acceptable to the people though the opposition parties were 'bound to shout'.

Some time later she told the chief Indian negotiator that he should go ahead with his negotiations and try to seek agreement on the principles and criteria to govern the boundary demarcation. As for the actual line, she added, 'I will have to sit down with Deng [Xiaoping] and draw it.'

Her underlying confidence in the feasibility of an agreement with China that would be fair to both sides and acceptable to Indian public opinion seems to have lasted all through 1982 and a large part of the following year. It was just before the end of 1983, when another round of the India–China dialogue was due, that she apparently had second thoughts. The various crises crowding in on her had worsened alarmingly and the next parliamentary election was no more than thirteen months away. She told the leader of the Indian delegation somehow 'to keep the talks going' without committing himself to 'anything specific'. The Chinese were quick to perceive the change and thereafter the talks continued only in name.

In dealing with Pakistan, Indira was clear-headed, firm and resolute. But she was not always adroit. This was particularly the case in September 1981 when Pakistan, having consistently rejected for thirty-three years an Indian offer of a no-war pact, suddenly reversed its position and invited India to sign precisely such an agreement. The purpose behind Pakistan's somersault was clear. It wanted to neutralise the Indian objection, being pressed hard in Washington, that the resumed US arms supplies to Pakistan would endanger Indian security. In fact, the Pakistani offer to India was only a small part of a long statement by the Pakistani government accepting the $3.2-billion package of American military supplies and economic aid.

Both Indira and her Foreign Office were caught off guard. They could not reject out of hand a pact India itself had been commending to Pakistan for more than three decades. On the other hand, to welcome the idea would have been to walk into a Pakistani trap. For in that case Indian efforts to dissuade the US from arming Pakistan and thus disturbing the balance of power in the region would have become meaningless.

After humming and hawing for a few days, Indira did produce a deft response to the Pakistani proposal. She offered to sign with Pakistan a comprehensive treaty of 'peace, friendship and cooperation' instead of just a non-aggression pact. The then Pakistani foreign minister, Agha Shahi, was in New Delhi on the day Indira made the counter-offer. After only a brief hesitation he agreed that the Indian and Pakistani proposals could be considered together in the hope that the two drafts could be 'married' to produce an agreed one.

This turned out to be a fruitless and frustrating exercise. Numerous rounds of talks to produce an agreed draft of a treaty or otherwise to improve India–Pakistan relations proved to be the proverbial 'task of Sisyphus' – Sisyphus being the mythical Greek character condemned to roll a rock up the hill and trying again when it rolled down. The situation was exacerbated when Pakistan, while emphatically denying it, started giving Sikh terrorists in Punjab support, sanctuary, cash, arms and training.

Discord between India and Pakistan was rooted in deep-seated and impersonal mutual suspicion and misgiving, born of historical experience, recent and remote, not in personal predilections or foibles of leaders on either side. Even so, the situation was aggravated by Indira's total distrust of the Pakistani military dictator, General Zia-ul-Haq. He reciprocated the compliment but, in his public pronouncements at least, was restrained. With the passage of time, Indira's statements about dangers to India from the US arms aid to Pakistan and the Pakistani quest for nuclear capability became increasingly strident. But Zia, in a virtuoso display of diplomatic skills, managed to maintain a stance of being on a 'peace offensive' in relation to India.

Indira had had no particular reason to like Zia's predecessor, Z. A. Bhutto, with whom she had signed, as we have noted, the Simla agreement five years before his overthrow by Zia in July 1977. Two years later, in April 1979, Zia executed Bhutto after what a former US attorney-general, Ramsay Clark, called a 'travesty of a trial'. Indira was then out of power. The Janata government, headed by Morarji Desai, in pursuit of its own concept of 'good-neighbourliness', would not even comment on Bhutto's 'judicial murder'. Indira, however, kept up a one-woman campaign on his behalf. At first she wrote to world leaders friendly to Pakistan requesting them to use their influence with Zia to get Bhutto's death sentence commuted. When the sentence was carried out she protested vigorously.

Her return to power, preceded by the precipitate fall of the Desai government, was a 'big shock' to Zia. But he was quick to congratulate her by telephone and she thanked him graciously enough, though she was not particularly happy to receive his call.

Three months later, in April 1980, she and Zia met for the first time during Zimbabwe's independence celebrations at Salisbury, now Harare. Unfortunately for Zia, the morning papers had repeated some of his earlier uncharitable remarks about her. Indira, however, was all smiles and courtesy when he arrived.

'Madam, please do not believe everything you read in newspapers,' was Zia's opening gambit.

'Of course not,' replied Indira. 'After all, aren't they calling you a democrat and me a dictator?'

Neither this nor the subsequent three conversations between them led to any meeting of minds or even to a mitigation of mutual suspicions and distrust. To make matters worse, Zia chose to be surprisingly tactless on two issues to which Indira was particularly sensitive.

At their first encounter in Salisbury, he presented her with an autographed, coffee-table publication on Pakistan. A map in it showed not only the whole of Kashmir but also three small former principalities in India's Gujarat state, far away from the Pakistani border, as parts of Pakistan. Indira was not amused.

Secondly, Zia was so full of his understanding with 'Desai Sahib' that he would bring it up in the talks repeatedly until Indira retorted: 'You do not seem to realise that Mr Desai is no longer in charge of our government.'

Zia's claim that, except for a lunatic fringe, no one in his country any longer believed that Pakistan could attain near-parity of power with the much larger India had apparently impressed Desai. In the hope of creating a similar impression on her, Zia made the same elaborate presentation to Indira. She listened patiently and went on doodling on a scratch-pad. (She had already told him, as she had said to many other interlocutors, that she concentrated best when she doodled.) Having said his piece, Zia paused both for effect and Indira's response. She looked up, gave him a smile that was both bewitching and enigmatic and said: 'I am listening, General Sahib, please continue.'

In November 1981, the Commonwealth Heads of State and Government met at Melbourne. Pakistan, having walked out of the Commonwealth in a huff in 1972 when Britain recognised the newly liberated Bangladesh, was most anxious to return to the fold. The host Prime Minister, Malcolm Fraser, was keen to accede to the Pakistani request and other Commonwealth leaders seemed to have no strong objection.

Even the Indian Foreign Office gave Pakistan's Ambassador, Abdul Sattar, who later became his country's Foreign Secretary, the impression that India would 'go along with the consensus'. But Sattar, an able and astute diplomatist, evidently knew Indira better than her own officials did. He asked to see her and she saw him immediately. She was cordial but told him firmly that if she agreed to the Pakistani request, the Commonwealth would become 'yet another forum' for Pakistan to 'rake up' Kashmir and other bilateral disputes and to 'malign' India generally.

Sattar told her that he would get her his President's written undertaking that nothing of the kind would be done. She replied that she had to go by what Pakistan 'was doing' and had been doing 'all along', not by what President Zia might say or write to her. At Melbourne, neither Fraser nor anyone else raised the question of Pakistan's readmission to the Commonwealth. Instead, Commonwealth leaders readily agreed to holding the next meeting in New Delhi in November 1983. It was also announced that a visit to India by Queen Elizabeth would coincide with the Commonwealth meeting.

*     *     *

Even before inviting the Commonwealth Heads of State and Government to Delhi Indira had taken care to ensure that the seventh summit of the Non-Aligned Movement (NAM) would also take place in the Indian capital a good eight months earlier, in March 1983. Normally, NAM should have met in Baghdad in September 1982. But the war between Iran and Iraq – both members of the movement, ironically – had made that impossible. Indira cut short the consequent quest for an alternative venue by offering to host the summit in New Delhi. The discerning were quick to notice that this would also mean that the prestigious chairmanship of NAM would pass to her from Fidel Castro of Cuba, the host of the previous summit at Havana in 1979.

Her critics said, plausibly enough, that by trying to dazzle her dispirited countrymen with grand and gala gatherings of world leaders, she was covering up her failure to come to grips with the burning problems that were troubling the people. The more uncharitable ones compared the proposed 'jamborees' to the 'circuses' in vogue in Ancient Rome.

Neither the Commonwealth Heads of State meeting, nor the Non-Aligned Movement summit, however, was the first such 'circus'. That distinction went to the Asian Games, the most spectacular sporting event ever to be staged in India, which began in New Delhi on November 19th, 1982, Indira's sixty-fifth birthday. In her scheme of things these games were vitally important because they provided the first opportunity to her inexperienced son and heir-designate, Rajiv Gandhi, to prove his mettle. Having entrusted to him the entire management of the whole undertaking, from the construction of the infra-structure to the completion of the last fixture, she was determined to see to it that he made a complete success of his first major assignment. Expense was no consideration; nor was red tape to be allowed to impede him. Rajiv did eventually pass the test. The Asiad went through without a hitch, indeed with clockwork precision and great pomp and pageantry. But this success was achieved at a very heavy price: an amalgam of countrywide embarrassment over the seamy side of the extravaganza and appalling but easily avoidable aggravation of the situation in Punjab.

To stage the games on time, a string of modern stadia, several five-star hotels, an entire Olympic village and sundry flyovers and bypasses had to be built at break-neck speed. New Delhi was to be given a facelift the like of which it had never before received. Charges of corruption and favouritism in the disbursement of lucrative contracts inevitably followed. But the stink they raised was nothing compared with the shock and revulsion over the brutal, indeed in-human, treatment meted out to tens of thousands of construction

workers who toiled night and day to complete the magnificent struc-
tures on schedule.

Most of these hapless workers had been brought in from remote
and poverty-stricken regions because, unlike the workforce in Delhi's
vicinity, they were unaware of their rights under the law and uncom-
plaining about their abysmal plight. They were made to work horribly
long hours in stone quarries or at construction sites. All of them – men,
women and children – lived under incredibly unhygienic conditions in
makeshift shanties and they were compelled to give up a part of their
measly wages to greedy contractors.

When some outraged social workers took the matter to the Supreme
Court, it delivered a searing judgment, declaring that the workers
were being treated as 'serfs' and 'denied' the freedom of movement
allowed 'even to animals'. But the stunning impact of the judgment
did not last long. There was only a marginal improvement in the
condition of the 'bonded labour'. Work went on, and the whole thing
was forgotten by the time the spectacle of sport began.

Not so easy to forget, however, was the Asiad's vastly more damaging
fall-out in Punjab.

All through 1982 the situation in the problem state had continued
to deteriorate. There was a steady escalation of the daily death toll at
the hands of Sikh terrorists. For their part, Akalis went on protesting
that the police were 'killing innocent Sikhs' in cold blood and pretending that the deaths had occurred in armed clashes. In the negotiations
between the government and the Akali leaders there were sharp ups
and downs but no real progress.

In the summer of 1982 Indira released 25,000 Akali prisoners who
had courted arrest during the preceding months in the hope that this
'goodwill gesture' would pave the way for a settlement. But the hope
was short-lived. On the contrary, Akalis started a campaign physically
to obstruct the digging of a canal without which the water dispute
between Punjab and the neighbouring states could not have been
resolved. In October, Akalis brought their violent demonstrations to
Delhi, which led to bloodshed close to Parliament House. They were
protesting against the deaths of thirty-four of their comrades who
were killed when a lorry carrying them to prison collided with a railway
train at an unmanned crossing. Bhindranwale screamed that this was
no accident but 'preplanned murder'. Nevertheless, talks between
Indira's aides and Akali leaders went on but collapsed on November
6th, 1982, barely a fortnight before the start of the Asiad.

On that very day, Longowal, the 'dictator' of the Akali 'morcha'
(battlefront) announced that his party would stage daily demonstrations at the Asian Games. Indira's colleagues and advisers panicked. Even a single Akali demonstration could lead to violence and

disrupt the games. This they could not afford even to contemplate because Rajiv Gandhi's prestige was at stakc. Their answer to the Akali threat was a stringent security ring around the capital so that no demonstrator from Punjab could get to Delhi, let alone anywhere near the venue of the games.

Since all roads from Punjab to Delhi pass through Haryana, it was in that state's territory that all comers had to be stopped and screened. Haryana's chief minister, Bhajan Lal, now a member of Rajiv Gandhi's cabinet, seized this 'opportunity' to display his 'loyalty to Indira' and to 'settle scores' with Sikhs. Thus emboldened, the state's generally uncouth and high-handed police force treated all Sikh travellers with rank discourtesy and often with intolerable rudeness. Almost literally no one was spared. A former chief of the Indian Air Force, the General who took the surrender of the Pakistani troops in Dacca in 1971, judges of the Punjab and Haryana High Court and even leading Sikh supporters of the Prime Minister were at the receiving end of the insulting behaviour of Haryana police. The entire Sikh community felt humiliated and was furious. Bhindranwale was not alone in exploiting the hurt sentiment to engender hatred for the government and the Hindus and sympathy for the extremists.

# 17   Calamity After Calamity

With the worsening crisis in Punjab, continuing turmoil in Assam and other north-eastern states, paralysis of several Congress (I) ministries because of acute factionalism, a sluggish economy necessitating a huge loan of six billion dollars from the IMF on terms considered 'humiliating' by many Indians and a general mood of despondency in the country, 1982 ended for Indira on a dreary note. But worse was yet to come in the new year.

In the very first week of 1983, in state assembly elections there, she lost her bastions in South India, the states of Andhra and Karnataka, which had voted solidly for her even during her lowest point in 1977. Now, more than five years later, her party, the Congress (I), lost heavily in both. In Andhra it was routed almost completely. The newly formed Telugu Desam party, founded by film star N. T. Ramarao (N.T.R.) to 'avenge' the 'indignities' heaped on Andhra by Indira and her son, won an overwhelming majority. The defeat in Karnataka, at the hands of the Janata, was not so crushing but this could be only cold comfort to the Congress (I).

The resounding rebuff to Indira in her former strongholds boosted the morale of the opposition, fragmented as it was into numerous notoriously fractious parties and groups. Enthused by the expectation that what had happened in Andhra and Karnataka could perhaps be repeated in the parliamentary election, due in less than two years, these parties yet again revived their efforts to unite on a common platform. Opposition unity, they knew, was an essential prerequisite for victory over the Congress (I) at the national level. Two combinations, the National Democratic Alliance and the United Front, were quickly cobbled together by parties with a following in North India. In the south, N.T.R. took the initiative to convert his purely regional Telugu Desam into 'Bharat Desam' (Bharat is an ancient name for India) by bringing together all national and regional parties opposed to Indira. He made no secret of his belief that he would be the combined opposition's 'choice' to replace Indira as Prime Minister. His position as chief minister of a large state did give him an edge. But almost every other opposition leader considered his own claim to that office superior to Ramarao's or, for that matter, to that of anyone else. Under the weight of these and other contradictions, efforts at opposition unity foundered, though N.T.R. continued to hold 'conclaves' of non-Congress (I) chief ministers and prominent opposition leaders from time to time.

A bizarre touch was added to the opposition's exertions when it became known that in the privacy of his home N.T.R. was dressing up as a woman, complete with sari and diamond ear-rings, because his astrologers had assured him that this mumbo-jumbo would 'hasten his elevation' to prime ministership!

Indira was not wrong therefore in describing the move to unite the opposition as a 'joke' and an attempt to 'fool the people'. But she remained rather paranoid about it, complaining repeatedly that everyone, from extreme Right to extreme Left, was 'ganging up' on her.

One indication of her 'siege mentality' was her criticism of the press which, she complained, acted 'as the opposition' rather than discharging its legitimate functions. There was a grain of truth in her allegation, although it tended to be smothered by chaff. After all, reporters, commentators and editors belonged to the intelligentsia, the bulk of which, as we have noted, was hostile to her, and sometimes carried this hostility too far. On the day of her assassination I felt compelled to record that some of her inveterate critics appeared to have adopted, in a perverse way, the 'stupid slogan', 'Indira is India and India is Indira', abandoned even by those sycophants who had coined it in the first place during the Emergency. For these critics would not 'hesitate to hurt India if they could thus hurt Indira, too'. On the other hand, the lady protested too much and often could be as irrational as her detractors. She knew very well that the Indian press, like India, was extremely diverse and reflected a wide variety of shades of opinion. But, in denouncing it, she treated it as a malign monolith.

To Bihar's chief minister, Jagnath Mishra, who was having problems of his own with the newspapermen in the state capital, Patna, Indira's allergy to the press came in handy. He enacted in July 1982 a Press Bill providing for imprisonment for 'scurrilous writings' and tightening up some other restrictions on freedom of expression. Since the bill amended sections of the Indian Penal Code, it needed the President's (in reality the central government's) assent to become law. This assent Indira was inclined to give. But she could not ignore the countrywide uproar against the measure. Almost all journalists had united as one, presumably because of the traumatic memories of the Emergency, to demand that the Bihar Bill be scrapped. Giving it presidential assent was therefore kept pending.

Meanwhile, by a delicious though not entirely unexpected quirk of irony, the bill's begetter, Mishra, fell from grace. On July 21st, 1983, he withdrew the bill as abruptly as he had sponsored it almost exactly a year earlier. He did it to spite Indira but obviously could not say so openly. She turned the situation to her advantage and 'contrived' to take credit for the bill's demise. Three weeks later she eased Mishra out of office.

Despite her blanket condemnation of the press and avowal of 'utter indifference' to what it said about her – she would never admit even to reading newspaper articles concerning herself – Indira was not averse to using skilful PR to consolidate the far from insignificant support she did have in the press and, where possible, to soften her critics.

Radio and television were, in any case, under the government's complete control which Indira was totally averse to loosening. TV was set up in India on an 'experimental basis' less than two decades earlier when she was Information and Broadcasting Minister in Lal Bahadur Shastri's cabinet. Since then it had made only limited headway. Realising its potential, she ordered its phenomenal expansion as well as a change-over from black-and-white to colour television. By 1982 TV had been made accessible to seventy per cent of the population. Inevitably it also became the principal instrument for the building up of Indira's image. There was on the small screen a nightly projection in colour of the formidable personality cult that had already been built around her.

In sharp contrast to this blatant misuse of the state-owned electronic media, Indira's handling of the privately owned press was remarkably subtle. It was also highly selective. The crude task of 'news management' almost on a daily basis, by planting pro-government stories or seeking deletion or dilution of critical despatches, was left to official and political aides. Her own role in influencing opinion-makers was limited and played in her usual lofty style.

She would receive selected journalists in small groups or individually for off-the-record briefings, but rather than volunteer any statement, she would encourage them to ask questions. Her carefully crafted answers to easily anticipatable queries were apparently expected to serve her purpose. However, old habits die hard. Indira's deeply ingrained reticence would sometimes assert itself even at meetings engineered by herself, as I had occasion to experience at both group and one-to-one meetings.

At times, she would start by being fairly forthcoming and candid and then suddenly turn monosyllabic and about as communicative as a clam afflicted with laryngitis. At other times, the process would be reversed. Sometimes she would be relaxed and quite willing to talk throughout the meeting.

Her selection of journalists asked to meet her individually was more rigorous than that of those asked to group meetings which usually included one or two critics she might not have written off as wholly malicious. Summonses to meetings of both categories were considered quite an honour and envied even by those who professed to hate Indira.

For her part, despite all the elaborate trouble she took to meet journalists she found expedient to keep in touch with, Indira maintained the façade that it was the journalists who had asked to see her, not vice-versa. The technique used to ensure this was astonishingly simple. Whenever a journalist's presence was required, he would be rung up by someone in her office and told: 'You wanted to see the Prime Minister. Can you please come at such-and-such time on such-and-such day?' The individual placed in this delicate position could hardly be so churlish as to blurt out the truth that he had sought no meeting, especially if he wanted to retain his privileged access to the Prime Minister.

During her three years in the wilderness this technique had, of necessity, to be varied but it was changed only slightly. In those days someone from her circle would turn up or telephone to announce: 'It appears you haven't seen Indiraji for a long time. Would you call so-and-so or should I fix a meeting?'

In one respect alone – which became particularly pronounced during the Eighties – were Indira's dealings with the press totally devoid of subtlety. Every time she embarked on one of her frequent foreign journeys she would invite hand-picked reporters and even editors and proprietor-editors to accompany her, wholly or partially at the government's expense. Relevant newspapers accepted the practice nonchalantly, largely because they were happy to save money on the coverage of the Prime Minister's visits. The chosen journalists had to endure the jibe that they were being 'rewarded' for their 'loyalty'.

From the stunning blow of electoral defeats in Andhra and Karnataka, Indira recovered partially a month later, in February 1983, when her party won an impressive victory in the essentially local but politically prestigious municipal elections in Delhi. Her elated supporters proclaimed gleefully that the Delhi voter had reflected the mood of the people in the entire Hindi heartland, the Congress (I)'s power-base.

This impression was confirmed in June when assembly elections were held in the sensitive state of Jammu and Kashmir. In the Hindu-dominated Jammu region of the otherwise Muslim-majority state, the Congress (I) did extremely well, winning as many as twenty-four seats in an area where it had held only eleven in the outgoing assembly. All the additional seats were wrested from the Bharatiya Janata party (BJP), the traditional and militant champion of the Hindu cause. While Indira and her followers rejoiced, her critics pointed out sarcastically that Jammu had only confirmed that Indira was 'outdoing even the BJP' in cynically appealing to Hindu chauvinism.

Moreover, the good that the outcome of the poll in Jammu might have done to Indira in the Hindi region had to be balanced against the harm it was causing elsewhere, most notably in the Kashmir valley. Still a bone of contention between India and Pakistan, the valley also decided who would rule Jammu and Kashmir. Its verdict was therefore vital. Looked at from this standpoint, the Congress (I) performance in Jammu was a tragedy, not a triumph.

As the country's ruling party, the Congress, with or without the appellation (I), had almost always had its problems with the Jammu and Kashmir National Conference which, under the leadership of the towering Sheikh Abdullah, had masterminded Kashmir's accession to India in 1947. As early as 1953 New Delhi had found itself driven to dismissing Abdullah as Kashmir's chief minister and detaining him. He spent fourteen of the subsequent twenty-two years in prison before returning to power in February 1975 as a result of an accord with Indira.

All through this period, irrespective of whether Abdullah was in jail or out of it, the Congress and the National Conference had managed to maintain their uneasy partnership, especially in elections, to keep at bay pro-Pakistan elements and religious fanatics infesting the sensitive state. Three wars fought with Pakistan between 1947 and 1971, largely over the lovely vale of Kashmir, had only underscored the need for this cooperation.

However, the Sheikh's return to power, instead of fostering the Congress–National Conference bonds, caused renewed bitterness between him and Indira. The most important reason for this was the Emergency which, apart from its other unwelcome features, frustrated Abdullah's plans to hold early state assembly elections in Kashmir. Indeed, they could not be held until June 1978. By that time, Indira was out of power and the Congress party in Kashmir was in even greater disarray than in the rest of the country. For the first time, the National Conference and the Congress were on opposite sides in the electoral battle in Kashmir. The National Conference, led by the Sheikh, won hands down.

With Indira's return to power at the start of 1980, conflict between her and the Kashmir leader grew but both sides took care not to let it get out of hand. In fact, when the Sheikh died in September 1982, Indira not only saw to it that he was paid the highest national honours but also smoothed the succession of his son, Farooq Abdullah. Even those inveighing against her for her 'dynastic designs' praised her for putting Farooq into power in Kashmir. Interestingly, the only other contender was his wily and ambitious brother-in-law, G. M. Shah.

277

Farooq had known Indira since his childhood. Her father, a highly civilised and sensitive man, having agreed to Sheikh Abdullah's dismissal and arrest with great reluctance and regret, looked after the jailed Kashmir leader's family with almost paternal care. During his visits to Delhi, Farooq usually stayed under Nehru's roof. He and Rajiv, being roughly of the same age, became friends. Like Rajiv, he started calling Indira 'Mummy' and continued to do so even after becoming Kashmir's chief minister.

This was of no help to him, however, in his official and political dealings with her. For Indira's hope of being able to mould the young and inexperienced Farooq according to her wishes was soon belied. He had his own exaggerated notions of his importance, though his somewhat hedonistic lifestyle left him very little time to attend to the state's administration. This, Indira complained, enabled Sikh extremists and Pakistani agents to make the state a 'safe base' for their 'nefarious activities'. Farooq denied this. Tension between the two grew.

In course of time, Farooq got alarmed that he might be toppled as so many chief ministers had been in the past. He was being troubled by his brother-in-law, G. M. Shah, furious over being 'cheated' out of the chief ministership. Shah started dropping dark hints that he might make common cause with local Congress leaders, then desperate to recapture power in Kashmir by fair means or foul.

To forestall this Farooq called state assembly elections in June 1983, a year earlier than he had to. The announcement of the poll produced a sudden lull in the strife between the Congress (I) and the National Conference and revived in both parties the old impulse that 'nationalist and secular' forces should fight the elections as partners, not antagonists. But mutual suspicions were too strong. Each side demanded too high a price for unity in terms of seats in the legislature. The talks for an alliance – between Indira and Rajiv on the one hand and Farooq and his mother on the other – ended in bitterness and discord. Worse followed.

Kashmir, like the rest of India, was no stranger to violent and venomous election campaigns. This time, however, the electioneering set a new record in viciousness which often degenerated into 'downright vulgarity'. Muslim fundamentalists and pro-Pakistani elements, previously opposed to him, rallied round Farooq. This infuriated Indira and she denounced him as 'anti-national'. He hit back in kind and called her 'dictatorial'.

It was against this background that the good showing of Indira's party in Jammu was completely overshadowed by its debacle in the Kashmir valley where it won only two seats, compared with forty-six captured by the National Conference under Farooq's leadership. With a comfortable overall majority in the legislature, he was sworn in as chief minister again, this time in his own right. But Indira seemed determined not to let him rule in peace because the abusive election campaign and Farooq's victory had made her angrier with him than ever before. He went round claiming that he simply could not understand why she 'bothered' about a 'nobody' and a 'provincial politician' like him.

While the Indira–Farooq strife was starting to develop into a fight to the finish, with disastrous consequences both before and after her assassination, most people paid scant attention to the poisonous aftermath of the Kashmir elections. These were minor matters compared with the calamities following one another elsewhere.

People had been killed in pre-poll violence in Kashmir, no doubt. But their number was smaller than a single day's toll taken by terrorist gangs in neighbouring Punjab.

Moreover, four months earlier, around the time municipal elections were taking place in Delhi, a monstrously deadly and destructive election in Assam had left behind several thousands dead and hundreds of thousands homeless. The country had watched the gruesome tragedy helplessly and, in some cases, callously. The most chilling part of it all was that there was absolutely no justification for holding an election in Assam at that time though Indira, driven by the compulsion of circumstances and her own political calculations of partisan gain, had opted for it.

Thanks largely to her own misuse of the central government's power to impose President's rule in states, the constitution had been amended during the Janata rule to provide that no state could be so governed for longer than a year. By this yardstick election to the Assam assembly, last elected in 1978, could not be delayed beyond mid-February 1983. On the other hand, conditions for holding an election simply did not exist. Feelings over the unresolved issue of detecting and disfranchising 'foreigners' in Assam had now reached a fever pitch. All efforts throughout 1982 to find a negotiated settlement of the problem had failed. The state remained paralysed because of repeated strikes. Oil could flow from Assam's oilfields to refineries only under very heavy protection by the paramilitary forces.

A sensible way out of the dilemma could have been one more amendment to the constitution to provide for an extension of President's rule in Assam alone. But this required the cooperation of the opposition parties because Indira, on her own, did not have the necessary two-thirds majority in Rajya Sabha, the upper house of Parliament. And this cooperation was not easily forthcoming, at least partly because she sought it rather half-heartedly. Both sides were once again busy playing politics. Indira succumbed to the temptation of holding an early election in the belief that it would return a Congress (I) government which might control the situation more effectively than officials sent from New Delhi. This was a horrendous mistake. Since a major complaint of the Assam agitators was that her party was habitually using illegal immigrants as 'vote-banks', the consequences of an election based on old electoral rolls could have been easily foreseen.

No sooner had Indira announced that the election in Assam would be held on February 13th, 17th and 20th than leaders of the Assam movement declared that they would 'not allow the elections to be held'. The Janata party and the BJP promptly proclaimed a boycott of the poll and offered to help Indira get the constitution amended to prolong President's rule and postpone the poll in Assam. But she was not interested. She had somehow convinced herself that a massive show of force would see the election through. This too turned out to be a dangerous delusion.

The violence that wrecked the elections was mind-boggling in both scale and savagery. It took place mostly in remote parts of the state and reached its apogee around the time the votes were being cast. Such was the state of communications in Assam and so busy were the authorities in trying to hold the election, by hook or by crook, that the news of the holocaust percolated to Gauhati, the state capital, several days later.

Unable to take on the armed might of the state, enraged Assamese had turned on hapless immigrants, mostly Muslims, living in penury in makeshift villages and townships. However, it was not a case merely of Hindus and Muslims killing each other. Hatreds in Assam were more complex than that. Hindu Assamese were at the throats of Bengali Hindus as well. Bodo tribesmen were caught in the crossfire and, in retaliation, slaughtered whoever they thought had attacked them.

Official figures put the death toll at 1,482 with another 2,000 reported missing. But the actual casualties were much higher, perhaps exceeding 5,000 dead. Sixteen villages were virtually wiped out.

The worst carnage, at a remote and small refugee town, Nellie, was described by Tariq Ali as the 'My Lai massacre in Vietnam magnified by ten'. But, shamefully, Indians did not display over Nellie even a small fraction of the remorse witnessed in America over My Lai.

On February 21st, Indira flew to Assam. 'I cannot find words to describe the horrors,' she declared in a choked voice while her audience sat benumbed by shock. But in Parliament in New Delhi four days later she asserted that an elected government in Assam would be 'better able to handle the situation'; that in holding elections in Assam and thus 'restoring the political process' she had 'only fulfilled a constitutional obligation'; that it was 'mere guesswork' that there would have been no violence had elections not been held; and that 'violent opponents' of the poll could not be allowed to 'hold the country to ransom'.

Some of these sentiments would have been unexceptionable in normal circumstances. In the abnormal context of Assam, they appeared hideously heartless. In any case, the poll had turned out to be a gigantic farce, indeed a fraud. Except in a small Bengali-majority area where ten per cent of the electorate voted, the voting average in the state was a mere two per cent. Many polling stations reported 'nil voting'; many others were burnt down. And yet a Congress (I) government in Assam was supposed to have been 'duly elected' and was installed in office.

Because of slow communications and equally slow printing processes, heartrending colour photographs of massacred Nellie children, hacked to death in cold blood and then laid side by side in fields, appeared on the cover of *India Today*, the country's largest-selling English newsmagazine, in the first week of March just as presidents and potentates, military dictators and elected prime ministers of non-aligned countries were assembling in New Delhi for the seventh Non-Aligned Summit.

If Indira suffered any twinge of conscience or embarrassment she showed no sign of it. The NAM summit was a glittering affair and she, as its presiding deity, was at her radiant best. Impeccably groomed and attired, she exuded an air of supreme calm and confidence as if she did not have a care in the world.

While taking over the chairmanship of NAM from Castro, she extended her hand to him. But the flamboyant Cuban leader ignored it and embraced her instead, calling her 'My sister'. The delegates rose to their feet and gave her an ovation.

For five days, Indira conducted the NAM summit with remarkable dexterity, reconciling conflicting opinions and patiently evolving consensus on all contentious issues, including Kampuchea, Afghanistan, the Gulf war and Latin America, which later became part of the elaborate documents adopted by the delegates.

All through the summit and more notably at her concluding press conference, Indira conspicuously steered the Non-Aligned Movement away from the Cuban concept that the Soviet Union was a 'natural ally' of NAM. 'We have,' she declared, 'neither natural allies nor natural adversaries. We have tried not to be openly critical [of anyone] or use a strident type of voice.'

As at Cancun and follow-up conferences in Delhi and elsewhere, so during the NAM summit, Indira pressed hard the demand for a re-structuring of the world economic order. The non-aligned countries, she declared, sought 'not charity or philanthropy', only that rich nations should look at the world's economic problems with 'sound commonsense'. Nuclear disarmament was her second major theme and it formed the nucleus of the 'New Delhi Message' adopted by the summit. It called for a freeze on the production of nuclear weapons as a first step towards a total elimination of the nuclear menace.

It was not at the NAM summit or in front of TV cameras alone that Indira exuded an air of carefree self-confidence and bright-eyed briskness. Most of the time, though by no means always, she did so even when she was not under public gaze, whether in her office, surrounded by acolytes, or at home, in the bosom of her family. In the company of her grandchildren she could even be elated.

A friend of mine who saw her on a day in early 1983 when news from both Punjab and Assam was extremely bad, came back exclaiming: 'Her nerves must be made of steel.' In the last week of July 1983 serious ethnic riots broke out in Sri Lanka, causing Indira much anxiety and anguish because forty-five million Tamils in South India were incensed and started demanding immediate Indian intervention to save the island republic's Tamil minority. At the same time, Foreign Ministers of six countries in India's immediate neighbourhood, including Sri Lanka, were in Delhi to set up the South Asian Association for Regional Cooperation (SAARC).

I was present at a reception Indira gave in honour of the assembled Foreign Ministers in the convention hall of Ashok Hotel. During this social function came the news of a particularly gruesome anti-Tamil pogrom near Colombo. An aide passed on the information to the Prime Minister which she received with stoic calm.

'What a shame,' I said to her, 'that, on top of so many other problems, this one should land on your plate!'

She smiled and remarked: 'It's part of life. In fact, of the day's work. I must cope with it as best I can.' Saying this, she turned to a visiting Foreign Minister to enquire if he had tried a particular snack and to suggest that he must, if he had not.

Indira's grief over Sanjay's death had not gone away. But she had apparently quietly learnt to live with it. The twinkle in her eye was back; so was her sense of fun. She laughed at other people's jokes and seldom missed an opportunity to pull the leg of a friend or associate.

Typically, while ruling out any criticism of her own government on Indian TV, she had encouraged the screening by it of the famous British serial, *Yes, Minister*. On the morning after the night when the first instalment was telecast, she asked her principal secretary, P. C. Alexander, later High Commissioner in London and now Governor of Tamil Nadu, whether he had seen the episode.

'Yes, Madam,' he replied.

'Did you recognise yourself in it?'

While entertaining at home, Indira took a keen personal interest in the menu, the laying of the table and, above all, the flower arrangement, as we have seen. She was particular that in the case of guests invited more than once dishes served previously were not repeated.

Special guests, including foreign dignitaries, were sometimes shown round her tastefully decorated home, where a major attraction was the 'Map Room'. It had had its beginnings in December 1965 when neither Indira nor anyone else could have foreseen that within a month she would be Prime Minister. As mere Minister for Information and Broadcasting, she had gone to Rome to attend a conference. Being short of money because of foreign exchange restrictions, she had gone window-shopping, accompanied by Darina Silone, wife of famous Ignazio, who later became her friend.

At the Piazza Navona, they browsed in a shop famous for old maps which interested Indira greatly but which she could not buy. But the shop's 'charmingly eccentric proprietor', Signor Nardecchia, having learnt from Darina who the 'strikingly handsome lady from the Orient' was, insisted on presenting a sixteenth-century map of East Asia to 'Nehru's daughter'. Around this work of a Venetian cartographer developed a remarkable and rare collection of old maps. These included some bought from Nardecchia in November 1981 when, during a state visit to Italy, Indira drove off to the 'little map shop' in the Piazza Navona, throwing Italian and Indian security into panic and confusion.

However, Indira's mood could change mercurially. Charm and graciousness could instantly turn into irritation and cold disdain, wit and humour into sullen silence.

James Callaghan, former Labour Prime Minister of Britain, has written that while Indira had a 'taste for the sharp retort', she could also be the 'mistress of an eloquent silence'. He could have added that she seemed to have the additional gift of the 'glacial glance'. At a state banquet once, as guests stood in a line waiting for the President, Indira espied someone whom she used to like at one time but had started detesting later. She made it a point to talk cordially to the people to the poor man's right and left but looked through him as if he did not exist or was made of glass.

The volatility of Indira's mood and temper, partly inherited perhaps, dated back to her childhood. But it grew worse with the passage of time and reached its peak after the trauma of the electoral defeat in

1977. Thereafter she was haunted by the thought that those she had 'trusted' had 'betrayed' her.

This made her virtually incapable of trusting anyone except her son and a very small coterie of aides. Sadly, it also accentuated a vindictive streak in her make-up, something her father had lacked almost completely.

We have noted already the awful treatment meted out to the family of P. N. Haksar, unquestionably the ablest and most dedicated of chief advisers ever to serve her. Rajni Patel, a one-time favoured confidant and fund-collector, was later flung on the scrap-heap so cruelly that when he died in 1982 Indira refused to send a condolence message to his widow.

By contrast, in one of the almost constant reshuffles of her cabinet, she included in it Veerendra Patil, an old political foe who had gone so far as to oppose her in the Chickmagalur by-election that briefly brought her back to Parliament in November 1978.

No less striking than these contradictions were spells, if not of depression, at least of bafflement which punctuated the glad, confident image that Indira projected most of the time. Such fits were neither frequent nor prolonged but they were indubitably there.

She would just sit and stare vacantly into space, as if at a loss about what to do or say – a trait which had first become noticeable during the later stages of the Emergency. Sometimes, the far-away look would appear even during the meetings of her 'think tank' or council of advisers on high policy. It consisted of the three ministers who, despite the centralisation of power in Indira's own hands, had retained a modicum of independent authority of their own – P. V. Narasimha Rao, Pranab Mukherjee and R. Venkataraman – and three officials, P. C. Alexander, principal secretary to the Prime Minister, Krishnaswamy Rao Saheb, cabinet secretary, and R. N. Kao, security adviser. With Indira looking blank or inattentive the 'think tank' was apt to stop in its tracks.

What disconcerted the 'think tank' even more was the curious fate of many of the decisions arrived at after the most elaborate consultations with it. Within hours of a decision being taken, Indira's top advisers would discover to their dismay that a totally different, indeed even contrary, course of action had been followed.

The worst sufferer from this state of affairs, Darbara Singh, then chief minister of Punjab, was to lament later that no sooner would he get Indira's clearance for a contemplated course of action – such as sending the police to an outhouse in the Golden Temple complex, far away from the holy shrine, to apprehend a dangerous criminal hiding there – than someone from her office would telephone tersely to tell him to desist.

'Eight out of every ten decisions on Punjab that we took those days,' recalled a 'think tank' member a year after Indira's assassination, 'somehow underwent a strange metamorphosis by the time they were conveyed to the state government for implementation.'

The woman whose name had become synonymous with decisiveness in the early Seventies was falling prey to vacillation and indecision a decade later.

In September 1983, in their weekly programme *South Asia Survey*, the external services of the BBC asked me whether Indira was 'losing her grip'? I replied: 'No, I don't think she is losing her grip. Her trouble is that since her return to power she has not been able to re-establish her grip at all.'

In dealing with the crisis arising from the ethnic conflict in Sri Lanka, however, Indira did not waver in the least and firmly took control of a highly explosive situation.

Sri Lanka's Tamil minority, forming about a tenth of the total population and concentrated in the north and the east of the island, having despaired of getting justice from the Sinhalese majority, had started clamouring for Tamil Eelam (independence). Moderate groups, which might have settled for less, were quickly marginalised and the leadership of the Tamil movement passed to a ferociously separatist organisation called the Liberation Tigers of Tamil Eelam (LTTE) which was heavily armed and never reluctant to take on the Sri Lankan Army, often getting the better of the government troops in combat. In sheer frustration, the security forces killed unarmed Tamil civilians.

Unsurprisingly, the LTTE enjoyed wide support in Tamil Nadu, the Southern Indian state whose people had ties of blood, kinship and culture with the Tamils of Sri Lanka. The state's phenomenally popular chief minister, M. G. Ramachandaran (M.G.R.), was the LTTE's patron saint and gave the 'Tigers' sanctuary, arms and cash on a generous scale. This was obviously embarrassing to Indira, then busy denouncing Pakistan for its aid and assistance to Sikh terrorists in Punjab, but she could do nothing about it, for a tidal wave of Tamil opinion was supporting the actions of M.G.R. who was, moreover, Indira's only political ally in the whole of South India, now ruled by non-Congress (I) parties. In any case, she herself was not averse to using M.G.R.'s support of the LTTE as leverage on the Sri Lankan government.

At the same time she was not prepared to countenance the demand for Tamil Eelam or that for converting Sri Lanka into another Cyprus, partitioning it *de facto* rather than *de jure*. What she wanted was that within the framework of a united Sri Lanka, the Tamil minority should have equal status with the Sinhalese majority as well as adequate autonomy.

Towards this end she acted fast. She asked her own Foreign Minister, Narasimha Rao, to fly to Colombo without waiting for an invitation. She then rang up President Jayewardene of Sri Lanka to inform him that Rao was coming to discuss how best to end the anti-Tamil violence quickly and find a just and durable settlement of the ethnic problem.

Inevitably, there were cries of 'interference in Sri Lanka's internal affairs' and not by Sri Lankans alone. Indira's critics at home said the same thing. But she disregarded it. She also made it clear that, apart from justice to the Tamil minority, she was worried also about the undermining by Sri Lanka of wider Indian interests in the region. To train his forces to be able to cope with Tamil insurgency and terrorism, Jayewardene had brought in the Israeli intelligence agency, Mossad, former SAS personnel from Britain and some military officers from Pakistan. There were persistent reports that he was about to enter into a deal with the United States under which America could have the use of Sri Lanka's superb port of Trincomalee in return for giving him military and political support.

It was against this background that at the height of anti-Tamil riots, a correspondent of the United Press International (UPI) was expelled from Sri Lanka for having reported that Jayewardene had asked for help from 'the United States, the United Kingdom and several South Asian countries' in the event of an 'Indian invasion'. Jayewardene denied the story. But Indira believed that 'it was not without basis'.

She therefore declared that in relation to Sri Lanka, India was 'not like just any other country'. She added that arrival of foreign troops in Sri Lanka would be a matter of serious concern to India and that, if Sri Lanka needed troops for internal security, it should ask for Indian help or 'invite others only with Indian consent'.

A fashionable comment at that time was that Indira had proclaimed a 'South Asian Monroe Doctrine'. But this was an erroneous view. To keep South Asia free of foreign military presence had been her father's policy since before the independence and partition of the subcontinent.

Jayewardene saw the logic of the situation and the strength of Indira's determination. He accepted her offer of Indian good offices to promote an agreement between the Sri Lankan government and various Tamil groups. This task she gave to her trusted foreign policy adviser, G. Parthasarthi. The Sri Lankan president named his own brother, Hector Jayewardene, as his emissary. The tripartite negotiations dragged on until Indira's death and even beyond without producing any result.

\* \* \*

However, it was in Punjab, not in Sri Lanka, that the real test of Indira's leadership and statesmanship lay, and it cannot be said that she withstood it with any degree of credit. On the contrary, by design, default or drift she allowed the crisis to deteriorate until the military assault on the Golden Temple became unavoidable. And once Operation Blue Star, as the military action at the shrine was codenamed, took place other grim and gory events unfolded themselves as inexorably as in a Greek tragedy.

Even so, it would be unfair to put all the blame at Indira's door. No less responsible for the catastrophe that engulfed Punjab was the 'Akali Trinity', consisting of Harchand Singh Longowal, the party leader and 'dictator' of the agitation, Gurcharan Singh Tohra, who controlled the Sikh shrines including the Golden Temple, and Prakash Singh Badal, a former chief minister of Punjab. At first because of their rivalries and clashing ambitions and then because of their collective cowardice they allowed Bhindranwale and his murder gangs to prevail.

After the breakdown of talks between the government and the second-rank Akali leaders in early 1983, the pace of terrorist violence quickened. There is no point going into all the grisly details. Some of the salient developments should suffice.

On April 23rd, 1983, killers entrenched inside the Golden Temple shot dead the most senior police officer in Amritsar, Deputy Inspector-General A. S. Atwal, a believing Sikh, as he came out of the temple after praying there. This was a lot more than the brazen murder of a police officer in broad daylight, for it demonstrated both the rising power of the terrorists and a virtual collapse of the authority and the prestige of the Indian state. Atwal's police bodyguard, waiting for him while he prayed, fled as the first shot was fired. His body lay at the main entrance to the Sikhs' holiest shrine for two hours before the District Magistrate, the most senior civilian official in the city, could 'persuade the Temple authorities to hand it over'.

Darbara Singh, Punjab's chief minister, realised that Atwal's murder had given him an opportunity to enter the residential part of the Temple complex and round up Bhindranwale and his gangs. He believed – and no one has ever disputed his assessment – that in the circumstances the Sikh community, despite its alienation from and resentment against the government, would not be up in arms. But once again New Delhi discouraged him. He alleges that Mrs Gandhi was at first 'inclined to agree' with him but later changed her mind on the advice of his arch rival, Zail Singh.

Atwal's murder and the government's failure to do anything about it spread panic in Punjab and demoralisation in the rest of the country. Bhindranwale's power and popularity among the Sikh youth soared.

This alarmed even Longowal and his associates who had so far been 'meekly kowtowing' to him. Tension within the Golden Temple grew, with the two sides installed in opposite buildings in confrontation. By September 1983, eight dead bodies were found in the sewers of the Golden Temple. By May 1984 the number of such bodies, tossed out of the Temple complex, rose to nineteen.

A far-reaching effect of this internecine violence was Bhindranwale's decision to move from the residential area to Akal Takht, the second holiest structure inside the sacred precincts. Surrounded by armed followers, he could safely direct the campaign of terror and murder from there. Not only was Longowal going on appealing to Sikhs all over the world to resist any attempt by the police to enter the Golden Temple complex but Indira's Home Minister, P. C. Sethi, was repeatedly assuring Parliament and the Sikhs that the government had no intention of sending the police or paramilitary forces into the shrine.

Curiously, apart from making such statements – even after the government had realised that entry into the Temple was unavoidable – Sethi had little to do with the making of Punjab policy or implementing it. Even background briefings to editors were handled by other ministers, principally Narasimha Rao, the Foreign Minister, who later replaced Sethi as Home Minister.

At one of my meetings with Indira I took up this bizarre situation with her. Never reluctant to run down even the most loyal of her colleagues, she shot back: 'You know that the Home Minister is usually either drunk or doped or both.'

I pointed out that she alone had appointed him and given him perhaps the most crucial portfolio. She only gave a wan smile.

On October 5th, 1983, in a diabolical attempt to force Hindus to flee Punjab, terrorists stopped a bus and selectively killed six Hindu passengers. Next morning Indira dismissed the Darbara Singh ministry and brought Punjab under direct central rule. Far from improving, the situation in Punjab worsened. In one night in April 1984, terrorists burnt down no fewer than thirty-seven isolated railway stations.

Meanwhile Bhindranwale, realising that public opinion might force the government to enter the Golden Temple to arrest him, started fortifying the building in such a way as to make the operation extremely difficult and costly. In fortifying the temple and accumulating the arms his followers would need to fight the Army, Bhindranwale had the professional help of retired Major-General Shahbeg Singh, a hero of the Bangladesh war who was later cashiered for corruption. Neither Longowal nor any other leader moved a little finger to stop Bhindranwale.

As early as in January 1984, Indira's government had reconciled itself to the inevitability of military action and started planning for it. But strangely neither Indira nor anyone else did anything to prepare public opinion. Opposition leaders, meeting under the auspices of N. T. Ramarao in successive 'conclaves', were more critical of the Prime Minister than of the terrorists. So was the bulk of the press.

In the first week of April 1984 I was invited to see Indira for a private discussion on Punjab. The suggestion came from T. N. Kaul, a former Foreign Secretary close to the Prime Minister, who also asked to sit through the meeting and meticulously prepared a summary record of the conversation.

Repeatedly I asked Indira why she was not meeting the opposition leaders, individually and collectively, to win over as many of them as possible in favour of the grave action from which there was now no escape.

She argued that as a seasoned observer of the political scene I should know that it would be a useless exercise. 'They hate me so much that they don't even care for the national interest.'

I pointed out that this might be true of some opposition leaders, but not of all and that an effort to build up a consensus on Punjab should be made in any case. But she insisted that I was wrong. 'You should know that if I invite them, they won't even come.'

I pleaded that as the person 'in the driving seat' she must be seen by the country to have made the effort and failed. But she remained adamant.

Unknown to me at that time, a similar conversation took place between her and the well-known historian, Bipan Chandra. Chandra suggested that she should start a political crusade against terrorism in Punjab with the cooperation of 'like-minded' parties. She countered that no party was prepared to help and her own party could also do little. Chandra persisted that she had waged admirable struggles with the same instruments in the past.

'Maybe, I am not so strong as I then was,' she replied.

Despite all such pleas of helplessness, she did make one other effort to explore the possibility of a settlement with the Akalis. Early in May 1984 what Mark Tully and Satish Jacob of the BBC called the 'last-ditch negotiations' started.

There is no doubt that on the previous three occasions when an agreement with the Akali negotiators was all but reached, it was she who had backed out at the last minute. This has been attributed to her desire to keep the 'Punjab pot simmering' for political reasons and even to Zail Singh's 'cunning advice' that a settlement should be reached only when the 'credit' for it could be given to Rajiv and no one else.

Indira's own explanation for her backtracking was that the Akali leaders were in no position to make an agreement 'stick' because of opposition from Bhindranwale. She never answered the question as to why she bothered to negotiate at all and failed to make her apprehension public.

However, at the beginning of May, Longowal talked to her on the telephone and asked her to help him because the 'situation has gone out of my control'. She responded by making a major concession to the Akalis on the transfer of Chandigarh to Punjab. Instead of giving Haryana two fertile sub-divisions of Punjab, a single town would do. But she laid down one condition: Bhindranwale must accept the deal before it was announced.

The 'Akali Trinity' was delighted. It wanted to clinch the agreement at once. But how to secure Bhindranwale's consent? Tohra, who had installed the once obscure preacher in Akal Takht, undertook the task. Bhindranwale hoist him and his two colleagues with their own petard. Only cowards, betrayers and office-seekers, he said, would settle for anything other than full compliance with the Anandpur Sahib resolution. This would have meant the creation of a theocratic state within secular India which was as abhorrent as an independent 'Khalistan'.

The die was now cast. There was no alternative to Blue Star. The date for the start of the military action was set, ironically, by Longowal. After the collapse of the last-ditch negotiations, he announced that, beginning from June 3rd, the anniversary of the martyrdom of Guru Arjun, the builder of the Golden Temple, Akalis would stop shipments of grain from Punjab and start cutting electric transmission lines.

On June 2nd, Indira went on TV and radio to make a last appeal to Akalis to call off their agitation and return to the negotiating table. She concluded her broadcast with an impassioned appeal to all sections of Punjabis: 'Don't shed blood – shed hatred'. But those concerned were not listening. Hatreds were running high. Bloodshed, a daily routine in Punjab, was about to acquire a new dimension.

To flush out the terrorists from the Temple turned out to be tougher than originally expected. The quality of the fortifications, the quantity of arms with terrorists operating from commanding heights and the strength of the resistance, all came as a surprise. Tanks and artillery had to be used.

Casualties, as we have noted, were heavy. Akal Takht was razed to the ground. Harmandir Sahib, the holiest shrine, was also damaged slightly. The Sikhs the world over were outraged as never before.

# 18   Those Fateful Shots

When Indira authorised Operation Blue Star she knew that she had also signed her own death warrant. But the conviction that she was destined to die a violent death had been with her for a very long time.

I first heard of it as early as 1972 from one of the two officials who, apparently under instructions, had invited me to write a 'profile' of the Prime Minister to be included in the 'press kit' to be distributed during Indira's visit to Stockholm in the June of that year to address the first UN Conference on Environment, a subject 'close to her heart'.

What happened next year is best left to Fidel Castro to describe. On November 11th, 1973 Castro was in New Delhi, on his way to Vietnam. An extremely pleasant banquet Indira gave in his honour was rudely interrupted by the 'stunning news' from 'far-off Chile where it was still morning' that Salvador Allende had been killed in a *coup d' état*.

'At that dramatic moment,' recorded the Cuban leader twelve years later, 'Indira Gandhi, in a proof of her intimacy and confidence, said to me: "What they have done to Allende they want to do to me also. There are people here, connected with the same foreign forces that acted in Chile, who would like to eliminate me".'

Thereafter, time and again she was to repeat publicly a sanitised version of what she had told Castro privately. As constant as her warnings against the 'foreign hand' – which, according to sneering critics, was 'home-made' – was her refrain that 'they' wanted to do her in. She took care never specifically to identify who 'they' were. But, by innuendo and insinuation, she left little doubt that the accusing finger pointed to the CIA, if not to the government of the United States.

Understandably, the oft-repeated accusation was not popular at the Potomac. But, curiously, it did not interfere with the complex love-hate game New Delhi and Washington kept playing all along. Even at the height of the Emergency, when the American media were depicting Indira as an ogress and her verbal attacks on the US were particularly strident, behind the scenes there was much cordiality between her and American leaders and diplomats. So much so that, throwing protocol to the winds, she went to the American Embassy to dine in honour of a relatively junior US senator.

On the other hand, Daniel Patrick Moynihan, having been at the

291

receiving end of the poisoned darts during 1972–4 as US Ambassador to India, decided to hit back in kind. In a book, published after Indira was voted out of office, he confessed that the CIA had indeed 'interfered in Indian politics twice'. But he added that on both occasions the intervention was on the side of the Congress and that once at least the CIA 'money was paid directly to Indira as Congress President'. She angrily repudiated his claim as 'mischievous, motivated and absolutely baseless'.

It is not possible to prove or disprove conclusively the assertion of some that Indira would have relaxed, if not withdrawn, the Emergency on the twenty-eighth anniversary of independence on August 15th, 1975 – barely fifty days after its imposition – were it not for the massacre in Dacca that very morning of President Sheikh Mujibur Rahman and several members of his family. But the fact remains that from then onwards she started saying that what 'they' had done to Mujib 'they' wanted to do to her and her family also. When General Zia-ul-Haq executed Bhutto in Pakistan on April 4th, 1979, she conjured up visions of a noose being prepared for her own neck, too.

Her return to power barely ten months later did not improve matters. On the contrary, the fear of an unnatural death was aggravated. Blood-curdling threats by Sikh extremists were still some time away. But there were at least two apparent attempts on her life.

The first took place as early as mid-April 1980 when Ram Bulchand Lalwani, an unemployed youth from Baroda in distant Gujarat, was arrested in New Delhi for throwing a spring-knife at the Prime Minister at a public meeting. The next day, his elder brother, a political activist known to be opposed to Indira, and three others were arrested in Baroda, but later released on bail. They, along with Lalwani, about whose mental state there was some doubt, were charged with conspiracy to murder Indira. The conspiracy charge did not hold, but in October 1981 Lalwani was sentenced to three years' imprisonment for intent to cause bodily harm.

Six months before Lalwani was sentenced, Parliament was informed of an 'outrageous act of sabotage' of a Boeing-707 on which Indira was due to leave on a foreign tour some days later. The official theory that this, too, was an attempt on the Prime Minister's life was widely disputed because the plane's crucial cables were cut a good fortnight before the date of Indira's departure, and every aircraft likely to be boarded by her was bound to be checked thoroughly for three days continuously before take-off. Suresh Inamdar, a senior Air India technician, arrested for the crime, admitted to cutting the wires but maintained that he had done so to 'spite his bosses who had declined to recommend his promotion'.

Claims by Indira or on her behalf that conspiracies were being hatched to kill her were not the only ones to be disbelieved. Almost everything she said was being greeted with scepticism by articulate opinion. Her credibility, never very high after the halcyon days of the early Seventies, had reached a new low. The military action she took at Amritsar at great risk to herself did win her some sympathy and support. There was a body of opinion which maintained that she had courageously done her duty, even if belatedly. The contrary opinion, however, was more voluminous and more vocal. Her critics alleged that she herself had created, or at least escalated the problem, until the 'disastrous assault' on the Golden Temple had become unavoidable. The conduct of Blue Star also came under heavy fire. It had, the critics said, caused the 'maximum hurt' to the 'Sikh psyche'.

Several of Indira's own friends claimed that she was shocked by the unexpectedly heavy casualties and damage caused by Operation Blue Star though she herself said little except to appeal to 'all Indians' to 'heal the wounds' of Punjab and went about her job, as always, with apparent calm.

On the evening of June 5th, while the battle of the Golden Temple was still raging and tanks and artillery were being used, Indira and the West German socialist leader, Willy Brandt, had a long talk, sitting in the garden at whose gate she was to be gunned down six months later. The next morning, Brandt received me and four other journalists and gave us, in strict confidence, an account of his conversation with Indira which, he said, had 'impressed him immensely'.

Punjab was mentioned during this talk. Indira explained to the former West German Chancellor the reasons which left her with no option except to order the Army to clear the Holy Temple of those who had made it the citadel of terror and secession. The bulk of the discussion related, however, to the 'nuclear menace to mankind', especially to the Six-Nation Appeal for Nuclear Sanity which was her last major initiative in international affairs.

The appeal, issued on May 22nd, 1984, and presented to the representatives in the UN of the five nuclear-weapon powers the same day, had been drafted after quiet preparatory work lasting four years. Apart from Indira its sponsors were President Alfonsin of Argentina, Prime Minister Papandreou of Greece, President Miguel de la Madrid of Mexico, Prime Minister Olof Palme of Sweden and President Nyerere of Tanzania, 'straddling all continents and all differences of size, wealth and development'. Stating that 'agreements which merely regulated an arms build-up are clearly insufficient', the appeal called for an immediate 'freeze' on the 'testing, production and deployment of nuclear weapons', a message Indira went on hammering home till the last.

Quoting Julius Nyerere, she told Brandt that peace was 'too important to be left to the White House and the Kremlin', and asked Brandt whether and, if so, when Europe would 'finally join' the Non-Aligned Movement – the 'biggest peace movement in history', according to her – in 'pressurising the superpowers' on the issue of disarmament and development.

By the time Operation Blue Star ended on the evening of June 6th, it was clear that Sikh anger had 'spread' far beyond the ranks of the 'orthodox and the Akalis'. The gloom and foreboding in Delhi that evening was palpable. Indira briefly attended a reception for the members of India's third expedition to Antarctica and spoke to them about the vast wealth of the frozen continent. Some of them told me the next day, with unconcealed amazement, that she had shown 'not the slightest trace of tension'.

Two months earlier she had asked to dinner a Hungarian friend, Dr Joseph Friedman, whom she had known for forty years because his sister, Fory, had married Indira's cousin, B. K. Nehru, veteran administrator and diplomat. The Nehrus were therefore also invited to the dinner though Indira's relations with her cousin were strained at that time. As Governor of Jammu and Kashmir, B. K. Nehru had refused, despite repeated pressure from the Prime Minister's office, to dismiss Farooq Abdullah, Kashmir's chief minister, on 'flimsy' grounds.

Even so, conversation at the dinner table was light and relaxed and food superb. Friedman asked Indira a question that had repeatedly occurred to many others: How did she manage to be so free from tension in circumstances that were so terribly trying?

'Tension, Dr Friedman, is within. One never wears it on one's sleeve,' she had replied.

A few days after Blue Star Indira flew to Ladakh. This visit to some of the most strategic outposts on the border with China had been fixed several months earlier. Just before her arrival, there was tension because a detachment of Sikh soldiers originally assigned to guard the helipad where she was to land was replaced at the last minute by non-Sikhs. There was no mistaking the unhappiness of the troops whose loyalty and discipline had been questioned so openly. But those who made the sudden switch cannot be blamed, for by then a rash of mutinies had broken out among Sikh soldiers in different places, underscoring the countrywide Sikh indignation. The worst of these irruptions had taken place at the Sikh Regimental Centre at Ramgarh in Bihar where the Commandant, Brigadier S. C. Puri, was shot dead.

Despite their loud complaint that their representation in the Army was being 'reduced unfairly', Sikhs, who comprise only two per cent of the population, constituted a tenth of India's million-strong Army.

They were also the 'only Indians to have infantry regiments made up entirely of their own community' though not exclusively officered by Sikhs.

Of the 100,000 Sikh troops less than 3,000 in all mutinied. Almost all of them belonged to exclusively Sikh formations and nearly two-thirds were raw recruits. At least some of them were forced to join the mutineers at 'gun point', as subsequent court martials established. Inquiries also indicted senior officers for failing to keep in touch with their troops and explain to them what was going on in Punjab. The government's own folly in excluding all foreign correspondents from Punjab and controlling the outflow of news from there inevitably meant that Sikh troops, like their community in general, started believing the wildest of rumours. Things were made worse by motiv-ated propaganda over Pakistan TV and radio, viewed and heard in large parts of India. As a result of this there was a renewed rupture in the India–Pakistan talks aimed, ironically, at concluding a treaty of peace, friendship and cooperation.

On her return from Ladakh, Indira called in half a dozen editors of Delhi newspapers, including me, for one of the group 'briefings' she liked to hold. Her Information Adviser, H. Y. Sharada Prasad, was also present.

We found that more than Punjab, it was Kashmir that was on Indira's mind. She made no secret of her conviction that Farooq's continuance as chief minister of Kashmir was bad for the state and the country. This shook most of us. After what had happened in Punjab it was hardly prudent to embark on a clash course in Kashmir. Some others and I had, in fact, been writing in our newspapers for some time pleading against any precipitate action against Farooq. George Verghese, who had been Indira's Information Adviser from 1966 until 1969, had later turned a critic of hers and was editing *The Indian Express* in 1984, had been making the point more sharply than others.

He and I repeated our arguments, by way of questions, but she was not impressed. She told us that Farooq had allowed 'anti-national forces' in Kashmir to be encouraged to an extent that was intolerable.

As the meeting dispersed, I asked to stay on for a few minutes in the hope of making a little more impact with my plea in private. She countered by saying: 'You know the military rather well. Why don't you ask the Generals what is happening? We have ceased to get information about Pakistan's designs and doings even from sources which were active until last year.'

In some ways this conversation with Indira was not a surprise. She had been wanting Farooq Abdullah to be sent packing for a long time.

B. K. Nehru, the Kashmir Governor, as we have noted, was refusing to fall in line with the central government's stratagem. This was that G. M. Shah and his cronies would leave Farooq's party, reducing it to a minority in the Kashmir legislature, whereupon the Governor should dismiss Farooq and install Shah as chief minister with the Congress party's support.

Nehru took the position that if Farooq lost his majority in the legislature, the constitutional course would be to ask him to face the assembly within three days rather than dismiss him right away. Indira argued, or rather G. M. Shah, itching to replace his brother-in-law, did, that a three-day reprieve would enable Farooq to 'unleash the mobs' on his would-be topplers. Nehru responded by saying that, as governor, he would see to it that no one took the law into his own hands.

Tired of this impasse, Indira transferred Nehru to Gujarat in February 1984 and in his place appointed Jagmohan, a dynamic, no-nonsense administrator, then working as Lieutenant-Governor of Delhi, who had become very controversial during the Emergency and was later pilloried by the Janata government. Jagmohan's appointment as Governor of Kashmir was generally taken as a signal that Farooq's days were numbered. But hopes persisted that, with the crisis in Punjab reaching its climax, Indira would hold her hand in Kashmir. This was an erroneous reading of the situation.

On the morning of July 2nd, G. M. Shah and thirteen other members of the National Conference party in the legislature, until then consisting of forty-seven members, arrived at the governor's residence in Srinagar, announced that they had split from the parent party, produced a letter of support by the twenty-six-member Congress (I) party and demanded that Shah be sworn in as the new chief minister immediately. The Governor sent for Farooq and brought him face to face with the defectors from his party who reiterated that they were totally opposed to his continuance as chief minister. On Farooq's refusal to resign – he kept saying: 'Please do not hand over the government to these thieves' – he was dismissed a few hours later and G. M. Shah became chief minister of a minority government that could exist only on the sufferance of the Congress (I).

To have engineered the installation of such a government in Kashmir was one of Indira's worst mistakes in the last few months of her life. Farooq's main faults were his inexperience and immaturity though, in her eyes, his most heinous crime was to have made common cause with N. T. Ramarao and other non-Congress (I) chief ministers who were constantly holding 'opposition conclaves' with a single-point programme of defeating Indira in the parliamentary elections which had to be held, at the latest, by January 1985.

296

Farooq's presence and fiery speeches at these conclaves infuriated Indira because she felt that he was trying to take away from her the votes of the Muslims, already more than somewhat alienated from her. Her attempt to dub him 'anti-national' cut no ice because, unlike other Kashmiri leaders, including his father, he would shout from the housetops that Kashmir was an integral part of India and that 'he was born an Indian and would die an Indian'.

By contrast, G. M. Shah's position on his Indian nationality was ambiguous. Worse, his past record as a minister in his father-in-law's cabinet was far from savoury and even his best friends were not willing to vouch for his probity. Under him the Kashmir ministry sank to the lowest depths of corruption and capriciousness. Some said that there was no difference between the 'Shah of Kashmir' and the late, unlamented Shah of Iran.

Indira was fully informed about Shah's antecedents as well as his activities. Why then did she install him in power simply to get rid of Farooq? The more one explores this question the more convinced one is that she was virtually blinded by her intense dislike of Farooq. Arun Nehru, a cousin of Rajiv Gandhi, had wielded great power during Indira's last years and had become even more powerful during the first two years of Rajiv's prime ministership until the two cousins fell out. According to him, 'Indira *puphi* (aunt) asked us to get rid of Farooq at all costs and we did.'

Why then did they not just sack Farooq and impose Governor's rule, rather than deliver Kashmir to G. M. Shah's untender mercies? Indira and her 'think tank', it seems, were keen to maintain the façade that the change in the state was 'brought about by Kashmiris themselves, not engineered by New Delhi.'

In Kashmir, as well as in the rest of the country, Farooq's dismissal and Shah's 'coronation' touched off a wave of revulsion and protest. Opposition parties organised a mass rally in New Delhi to denounce this 'shabby manoeuvre'. Its size and exuberance were reminiscent of the public meeting held in January 1977 just after Indira had announced fresh elections and relaxed the Emergency.

A few days later, the National Development Council – consisting of the Planning Commission and all state chief ministers, which has the last word on all issues relating to economic planning in India – met in the Indian capital under Indira's chairmanship. On behalf of the chief ministers belonging to parties other than the Congress (I), N. T. Ramarao of Andhra rose to read out a short statement deploring the ousting of their colleague, Farooq. Indira tersely told him to desist because the NDC was not a 'political forum'. When he persisted in having his say, she ordered that his statement should not go on the

297

Council's record. Thereafter Ramarao and all other non-Congress (I) chief ministers staged a walk-out.

This could easily have been the end of the unhappy episode. But Indira, and even more than she, the Congress (I) chief ministers fawning on her, would not let it be. They insisted on passing a resolution condemning the 'undignified behaviour' of the chief ministers who had left the meeting. Nor was this allowed to be the end of the affair. Indira ordered out of the meeting officials from non-Congress (I) states who, not being involved in any political dispute, had quite properly stayed on even after the walk-out by their political bosses.

All this was a measure of the bitter divide between Indira and her opponents which had also vitiated the political discourse. Each side was painting the other in the 'blackest of black hues'. Moreover, the parliamentary election, which could not be delayed beyond seven months, had now become the focus of ceaseless bickering.

From all accounts the wind was blowing in favour of the opposition. Articulate opinion was overwhelmingly against Indira. In a by-election to the UP assembly at Malliahabad, not far away from her son's parliamentary constituency, her party had lost badly to a candidate set up by her estranged daughter-in-law, Maneka.

Even so, it was the opposition that showed signs of nervousness while Indira confidently told her associates: 'Of course, we will win the election.' One reason for this was that the frantic efforts to unite the opposition parties were not bearing fruit. Opposition leaders, several of whom had been Indira's colleagues or followers at one time or another, were therefore afraid that she might take them by surprise and order a snap poll before they were able to put their act together.

This fear had become particularly pronounced after June 1983 when Margaret Thatcher had held elections in Britain a good twelve months before schedule. The talk in Delhi those days used to be: 'If Mrs T. takes the plunge, can Mrs G. be far behind?' But by the end of March 1984 a totally different apprehension had gripped the opposition parties. During that month, in biennial elections to a third of the seats of Parliament's Upper House, the Rajya Sabha, Indira had regained the coveted two-thirds majority required to amend the constitution. Her critics were convinced that she was likely to use this power to delay the elections by at least a year.

No one paused to ask whether, after what the Emergency had done to her, she would wish to repeat the mistake. Her credibility had sunk so low that anything said against her was apt to be believed, so much so that Pran Chopra, a former editor of *The Statesman* and a sober political commentator, had no hesitation in writing that never since India became independent 'has there been a time when it has been so widely feared, and so openly said by so many, that the Prime Minister of the country has become a danger to national unity'.

Those who had thought that, with the toppling of Farooq in Kashmir, they had witnessed the last of Indira's penchant for using crises and confrontation as a 'vehicle of her power' were in for a shock.

On August 16th, shortly after lunch, a news agency flash was brought to my desk. It made no sense whatsoever, but there it was – the agency could not have dreamed it up – announcing that Ram Lal, Governor of Andhra, had dismissed the state chief minister, N. T. Ramarao, and sworn in N. Bhaskara Rao in his place. Bhaskara Rao had defected from Indira's party in 1983 and become finance minister in N.T.R.'s Telugu Desam ministry. Now he had re-ratted, this time on his new mentor, and had apparently convinced the Governor that with the support of those who had crossed the floor with him and, of course, the Congress (I) he was in a position to form an alternative government.

Almost all of India was appalled. Andhra was no Kashmir. N.T.R., for all his administrative shortcomings and political high-handedness, remained extremely popular. While protest poured in from all parts of the country, a strange statement was issued on Indira's behalf. It said that she had no prior knowledge of what had happened in Hyderabad, the Andhra capital. Hardly anyone believed her. In Hyderabad, the Governor, now rattled by the countrywide reaction to his stupidity, bleated that he had acted only after 'clearance by New Delhi' – as clear a confirmation as there could be of the oft-repeated charge that governors had become promoters of Indira's partisan politics.

Despite a number of ministerial posts and vast sums of money at his disposal to buy support for himself, Bhaskara Rao simply could not tempt enough followers of N.T.R. to his side to be able to secure a vote of confidence in the state assembly. He therefore went on postponing its session on the flimsiest of pretexts. N.T.R., on the other hand, confident of retaining his majority in the legislature, flew to Delhi, along with the legislators backing him, and paraded them before the President.

A large number of eminent Indians, including retired judges and bureaucrats, lawyers and academics, journalists and social workers, descended on Hyderabad to make sure that Indira could not get away with 'this rape of democracy'.

On August 21st Indira personally told Parliament that she first heard of Ram Lal's action in Andhra only from agency reports and before she could 'ascertain facts', 'proceedings' to swear in Bhaskara Rao had been 'set into motion'. Noisy protests greeted her remarks and opposition leaders left her in no doubt that they did not believe a word of what she had said.

I, for one, believed her though I knew that she was not a stickler for the truth and never hesitated to dissimulate whenever it suited her. Even so, I felt, as did many others, that having been expelled from Parliament for making false statements, among other things, she was unlikely to mislead the House a second time.

However, as I pointed out in my writings and said to her personally during a brief conversation in Parliament's lobby, what she had said indicated a situation far more alarming than it would have been had the blunder in Andhra been committed by her or with her knowledge. That decisions of grave import could be taken and implemented behind her back had implications too terrible even to contemplate. As became clear later, Ram Lal had spoken on the telephone with Arun Nehru who had encouraged him to sack N.T.R. The Governor was too timid to inquire whether Nehru had taken Indira's approval. He simply 'assumed' that this must have been done. For his pains he was later dismissed.

While the Andhra crisis was still raging, even more lurid speculation about what Indira might do next gripped political India. Typical of the prevailing tension, even hysteria, was a conversation I had on August 23rd with Karan Singh, the scholarly and urbane former Maharaja of Kashmir, who had served Indira loyally as the youngest member of her cabinet for ten years until he, like so many former admirers, had parted company with her following the post-Emergency political debacle.

Both he and I were at a dinner where other guests included some prominent politicians and eminent lawyers. As in most drawing rooms in Delhi those days, talk at the dinner party focused on Indira.

Karan Singh was emphatic in predicting that within weeks Indira would either 'engineer a military scrap' with Pakistan or detonate a second nuclear device, the first one having been exploded ten years earlier.

Anyone with Karan Singh's experience and background, even if lacking inside knowledge, should have known that both possibilities had to be ruled out. But unfortunately – thanks largely to deep suspicion of Indira among the intelligentsia – both forecasts had acquired a certain plausibility.

Indira had for some time been protesting against Pakistani inter-ference in Punjab by way of help to Sikh terrorists. She had also been warning the country about 'war clouds on the horizon'. In April 1984, she had found it necessary to order the deployment of an Army brigade at Siachen, the world's largest glacier outside the polar regions, along the line of control in Kashmir, to forestall its occupation by Pakistan.

In Pakistan itself fears of an 'Indian attack' were being voiced, though mildly.

But, as I explained to Karan Singh and others who joined the discussion, there was no way Indira could start a war with Pakistan even if she wanted to – which, I knew, she did not. Senior commanders of all three defence services met in Delhi twice a year. On every such occasion, she used to have a meeting with the military leaders with no one else present. At every such session in 1983 and 1984, she clearly stated that India had 'nothing to gain by attacking or dismembering Pakistan and that the unity of Sri Lanka also had to be maintained at all costs'.

As for a second nuclear explosion, the flurry was caused by a misleading report in American newspapers that a US satellite had noticed 'preparations for a test' at the old test site at Pokharan in Rajasthan. The false alarm was to subside soon enough.

I told Karan Singh that with six infantry divisions badly bogged down in internal security work in smouldering Punjab, India was in no position to start any military adventure. An even bigger constraint on Indira was that she was chairperson of the Non-Aligned Movement and could not possibly attack a fellow non-aligned country unless it could convincingly be shown to be an act of self-defence. Moreover, the US, which, during the 1971 war, had sent a naval task force to the Bay of Bengal from the South China Sea now had massive deployments close to the Indian shores.

Karan Singh, however, was not impressed. So convinced was he of Indira's propensity to do anything outrageous to win the next election that he offered to take a bet. He even fixed the deadline at September 30th, 1984, after which I would have automatically won the bet if nothing happened on the Pakistan front. His reasoning for fixing the time-limit was also interesting. Delhi's grapevine had it that Indira had been advised by her astrologers to go to the polls in late October or early November.

I informed Karan Singh that since I was leaving for Britain and the United States early in September I would like to collect the bottle of Scotch we had wagered whenever I came back. To his credit he sent me a bottle of premium Scotch after the mourning for Indira was over.

Before leaving for overseas I went to see Indira on August 31st. How was I to know that this was going to be our last meeting? I spent very little time on Andhra because only a few days earlier she had confided to Girilal Jain, Editor of *The Times of India* and my senior colleague, that she was trying to 'rectify' the Andhra situation and that, if Ramarao retained his majority for another fortnight, 'he would be back'. This meant that though she realised that the folly in Andhra had to be undone, she was still not averse to seeing N.T.R.'s majority melt away if this could somehow be made possible.

What was weighing on my mind at that time was not Andhra but the nuclear issue. Right from the Sixties Indira's nuclear policy had been clear and consistent. Left to herself she did not want to make the bomb but wanted to keep the nuclear option alive. Towards that end she encouraged Indian nuclear scientists to maximise Indian proficiency in all branches of nuclear technology. She had resolutely refused to sign the Non-Proliferation Treaty (NPT). Equally persistently she had maintained that the Pakistani nuclear bomb would be a serious threat to India and would invite 'appropriate Indian response'. On what this response would be she was deliberately ambiguous.

In the last week of August, however, in reply to a parliamentary question, she made the extraordinary statement that India 'need not go nuclear even after Pakistan has acquired the nuclear bomb'. Among those concerned with nuclear policy there was alarm and dismay. But she seemed not to notice.

When I raised the matter with her she replied, as was her wont in such circumstances, rather tersely: 'What security will nuclear weapons give us or them?' I replied that absence of nuclear weapons on one side while the other side had them could cause a lot of insecurity and scope for blackmail. She kept quiet.

I asked whether she really wanted to convey to Pakistan the message that was contained in her statement in Parliament. This time she perked up.

'Do you realise,' she asked, 'that I was answering a question on the Six-Nation Appeal for Nuclear Sanity we have issued calling for a total elimination of nuclear weapons? Someone brought in the Pakistani bomb. Did you expect me to say that we would make the bomb?' After a pause, she added: 'In any case I do believe that nuclear weapons can do no good to us or the Pakistanis; nor have they done any good to the Chinese.'

We then talked briefly about Punjab where things were again going wrong. Indira's party had organised *kar seva* (voluntary service) to rebuild the Akal Takht destroyed during Operation Blue Star through Baba Santa Singh, a pro-government Sikh leader. The majority of the Sikh community intensely disliked this and lampooned the *kar seva* as *sarkar seva* or the service of the government. Nor did an officially sponsored *Sarbat Khalsa*, a grand assembly of Sikhs, do much good. It added to the bitterness sweeping Punjab. Sikh high priests excommunicated President Zail Singh and the most senior Sikh minister in Indira's cabinet, Buta Singh. Such Akali leaders as were out of jail were threatening a civil disobedience movement and worse if the Army did not vacate the Golden Temple immediately. Indira felt that the situation could somehow be tided over.

As I rose to take my leave, she said: 'I gather you are going away for a while. When you come back, try and convert me to your view on the nuclear question.'

At London's Heathrow airport on September 16th, while catching a plane for New York, I heard from an Air India official, to my great relief, that N. T. Ramarao had been sworn in as chief minister of Andhra once again.

Exactly forty-five days later, it was in a hotel room in London that I received the early-morning phone call about those fateful and fatal shots fired in Indira's lovely garden.

A few days after Indira's death some sheets of paper covered with her spidery handwriting were found in a pile of notes and documents she had kept aside. It turned out that these pages comprised her will. Undated but penned apparently not long before the assassination, her last testament began: 'I have never felt less like dying and that calm and peace of mind is what prompts me to write what is in the nature of a will.'

And yet, as we have noted, the thought that she might be killed had occurred to her frequently, especially in recent months. Her friends and aides had become even more worried on this score. As the summer of 1984 began, Darina Silone, holidaying in a remote Greek island, suddenly wrote to her: 'Somehow I have begun to pray for your safety. Don't bother to answer this.'

It was around this time that her Defence Minister R. Venkataraman – later to become Vice-President and later still President – sought her permission to transfer the responsibility for her security from the police to the Army. She firmly told him 'never even to entertain this idea'. In a democracy, she added, the armed forces should be kept 'well out of such matters'.

Shortly after Blue Star, some of her associates noticed that, unlike in the past when she would accept engagements even three years in advance, Indira was now declining to make appointments on relatively distant dates. Her reminder to Pupul Jayakar, that she wanted her ashes strewn over the mountains she loved, not immersed, as is customary among Hindus, in the Ganges, has already been noted. In her will she was to write: 'If I die a violent death as some fear and a few are plotting, I know that the violence will be in the thought and the action of the assassin, not in my dying . . .'

Even so, there seems no basis for the legend that Indira did not expect to see her sixty-seventh birthday on November 19th, 1984, which grew rather fast after she was gunned down. Her two-day visit to Kashmir, the land of her ancestors, in the last week of October, indeed her last but one foray outside Delhi, is often quoted in support of this belief.

She had gone to Srinagar, Kashmir's capital, primarily to see an old chinar tree, a variant of the maple family, she had greatly liked since her childhood. Chinar, much loved by all Kashmiris who call it 'universal mother' sheds its leaves at the end of October after they have turned crimson. This is what Indira had wanted to watch. But she discovered that the tree had died some time earlier. This, according to the authors of the legend, was the omen that convinced her of the imminence of her own end.

Available evidence does not warrant this conclusion. For, immediately after learning of the tree's demise, Indira went through a host of engagements most cheerfully until late into the night. Early next morning, accompanied by a solitary security officer, she went to pay her respects to an ascetic, widely hailed as a saint. She took with her an offering of yellow rice she herself had cooked in the kitchen of Raj Bhavan, the official residence of Governor Jagmohan. When she came back she was in a buoyant mood. She joked with those present, particularly twitting the balding Governor for the elaborate care 'bestowed by him' on his disappearing hair.

Before leaving Srinagar for Delhi she spent a long time discussing with Jagmohan not only Kashmir's problems but also her elaborate plans to take her grandchildren on holiday in Ladakh in June 1985.

My first inclination was to have ended the narrative here and to leave it to the reader to draw his own conclusions. But, on second thoughts, it seemed to me that having written, as best I could, the life story of a person as complex, as controversial and as compelling as Indira, to say nothing of the turbulent times she was both shaped by and helped to shape, a short summing-up is called for. Thankfully, the essential points can be made briefly.

While opinions about Indira's role and place in independent India's history differ violently, there can be no two opinions that for nearly half the post-independence period, she was incomparably the most dominant figure on the Indian scene. She occupied the centre of the stage even when out of power. From the mid-Sixties to the end of her life, she was the principal 'point of reference' for most Indians, including her bitter opponents and critics. It was usually in relation to her that they defined their positions.

Also, irrespective of whether her countrymen were applauding her or barracking her, she was heard with affection in the Third World and with respect in the First and the Second.

It is equally indisputable that Indira's failings were many and some of them grew worse as time went by. She could be capricious, imperious and, in pursuit of her ends – which sometimes meant holding on to power and, in later years, to ensure dynastic succession – supremely indifferent to the means adopted. But while this has been driven home almost continuously since the Seventies, astonishingly little attention has been paid to the other side of the coin: what she was up against.

There was, to begin with, the awesome, indeed mind-boggling, responsibility for ruling a vast, volatile and, at times, ungovernable country. As far back as 1963, Welles Hangen had written that the burdens on the shoulders of the Indian Prime Minister 'dwarf the Himalayas'. Two decades later these burdens had increased immeasurably, if only because the population had nearly doubled and production had barely kept pace with reproduction. Not for nothing did Helmut Schmidt, West German Chancellor, tell Indira in 1983: 'Your job isn't what I would want to do.' Even so, this was only a part of the problem.

A bigger difficulty arose because those whose job it was constructively to oppose her – in order that India could be run democratically – chose to be extraordinarily obstructive and obstreperous. This reinforced her instinct to be inordinately harsh to them, touching off a disastrous chain reaction.

Author V. S. Naipaul, no great admirer of Indira's, made an interesting point when he stated, after her death, that he had learnt to 'sympathise' with her on the day when he discovered, during a visit to the Rajasthan desert, that local politicians were 'opposing vehemently' her plans to bring piped water to the thirsty because tradition sanctified only well-water.

To draw attention to all this is not to deny that, in creating an atmosphere of relentless confrontation in which neither side was willing to concede even an iota of merit in the other's point of view, Indira's responsibility was much the greater. But this cannot absolve the legion of her adversaries of their share of blame. Eventually, it was she, not any one of them, who fell victim to the hatreds bred by the steadily escalating and increasingly embittered polarisation of Indian politics.

The declaration of the Emergency was unquestionably the worst of Indira's blunders. But here again, it must be asked whether Jayaprakash Narayan (J.P.), the saintly leader of the movement to dethrone her, was right in driving her to the wall by virtually asking the Army and the police to disobey her and insisting on precipitate dissolution of duly elected legislatures. Moreover, while the Emergency must be denounced, does not Indira merit any credit for having held elections and 'gracefully yielded power' after predictably losing them?

However, none of the extenuating circumstances can excuse, let alone justify, the body blow to Indian democracy she chose to deliver and from which the Indian system has yet to recover fully.

This is the most important of several reasons for which, in India's estimation, Indira will always suffer in comparison with her father whose benign and civilised rule is remembered by two generations of Indians with nostalgia. Nehru, no less impatient than her, especially when he felt thwarted by 'obscurantist' and 'retrograde' forces, would not countenance the idea of abandoning the democratic path even temporarily. Indira had no compunction in doing so, on the specious plea that she was really trying to put back on the track India's 'derailed democracy'.

Curiously, she tried to explain away the sharp contrast between her father's values and her own by saying, quite wrongly, that Nehru was a 'saint strayed into politics' who, 'never having had to struggle' to stay at the top, could be indulgent even to his enemies. The unstated corollary of this statement, that her resort to rough and ruthless tactics was due to the struggle for survival forced on her, was at best a half-truth. Her intractability and belief in her 'indispensability' were at least partly responsible for many of her own and her country's misfortunes.

On the other hand, while Indira did err grievously, equally grievously did she pay for it. All the more reason therefore that her great services to her country, the good she did to it, are recognised, instead of being ignored, brushed aside or played down, as is happening at present.

She gave India stability that appeared to have been lost for ever in the 1967 General Election which, in the words of *The Times*, London, was to have been 'India's last'. In the final analysis, in spite of the outrage of the Emergency, she kept the country on the democratic path. She won the Bangladesh war and made India the pre-eminent power of the region and a respected member of the comity of nations. In the Non-Aligned Movement and the Third World's struggle for a just world economic order, she took over her father's leadership role.

In her time, India became the third largest reservoir of highly skilled technical manpower in the world, the fifth military power, the sixth member of the Nuclear Club, the seventh to join the race for space and the tenth industrial power.

Her economic failures were also many and stark. Far from narrowing, economic disparities widened dangerously and added to social upheaval. Corruption, a part of India's life from times immemorial, became rampant. She tolerated it blandly and, at times, seemed to be encouraging it.

At the same time, Indira did successfully push through the 'Green

Revolution' which enabled India to feed itself and do away with demeaning dependence on the largesse of others.

Transcending all this, however, were her two most outstanding contributions which – it can be said without fear of contradiction – could not be equalled by any of her contemporaries, friend or foe.

To take them up in the reverse order of importance, her empathy with the Indian people, especially the poor, the deprived and the downtrodden, had to be seen to be believed. Millions, from one end of the country to the other, would squat on bare earth to listen to her speak from high rostrums, bewitching them even when most of what she said was above their heads. Or they would line the roads for hours, under scorching sun or pouring rain, to catch a glimpse of her.

At work here was something much more than the charisma and magnetism she had inherited from her father. Her radical rhetoric might have been phony, her populist promises utterly unmatched by performance, but right until the end, the poor of India never ceased to believe that she cared. Rajiv Gandhi's unprecedented victory in the parliamentary election in December 1984 was, in reality, a posthumous homage to her by a grateful and grieving nation – minus perhaps its cynical upper crust.

Worthy of even greater honour and more enduring was her second shining attribute: her deep and unswerving devotion to India and to the cause of its unity. Advocates of large-scale devolution, as we have noted, felt that she herself was endangering national unity by concentrating too much power in her own hands. But her conviction was exactly the opposite. She believed that excessive regional autonomy would destroy the central unity of the Indian state at a time when it was under stress from myriad challenges.

There is scope for honest difference of opinion on the issue and some of her policies and tactics could be open to objection. But there could be no doubt about the soundness and sincerity of her overriding objective. She could not have demonstrated her commitment to Indian unity more convincingly. After all, she laid down her life for it.

To say that she 'incarnated her country' – this is not a hyperbole by one of her sycophants but an assessment of *The Observer*, London – is perhaps an exaggeration. But about her total identification with India there cannot be any doubt. In this respect, no twentieth century leader, 'with the solitary exception of Charles de Gaulle', came anywhere near her, according to John Kenneth Galbraith, leading US economist and Ambassador to India in the Sixties. She herself was to say in her will: 'No hate is dark enough to overshadow the extent of my love for my people and my country; no force is strong enough to divert me from my purpose and my endeavour to take this country forward . . . I cannot understand how anyone can be an Indian and not be proud.'

All through her long and chequered political career, in good times and bad, Indira worked tirelessly to build up India's power. Constantly she strove to enlarge and expand the areas of Indian autonomy in all walks of human endeavour – political, economic, scientific, technological and cultural. She would have readily killed or swallowed poison herself than even think of compromising with her country's honour. India, in short, was her God.

Some say that both India and Indira would have been better off if she had loved it a little more and her sons, especially Sanjay, a little less. Even if there is a point to this, to harp on it is needlessly to get lost in the thicket of the ifs and buts of history.

# Notes

## 1 Murder in the Morning

... When a carefully cultivated dishevelled look served a political purpose ... *The Observer*, March 21st, 1982. Also Sunanda K. Datta-Ray in *The Statesman*, Calcutta & New Delhi, November 2nd, 1984.

Sikhs, a community 'Mrs Gandhi regarded with great affection'. Mark Tully and Satish Jacob, *Amritsar, Mrs Gandhi's Last Battle* (Jonathan Cape, London, 1985), p. viii.

'Intolerable desecration'. Statement by Air Chief Marshal (retired) Arjan Singh, Lt.-Gen. (retd.) J. S. Aurora, Inder Gujral and others, *The Indian Express*, June 8th, 1984.

'... Every single drop of my blood ...' Tully and Jacob, *op. cit.*, p. 2.

A wish to die 'on my two feet'. Orissa Governor, Bishamher Nath Pandey to Author; later repeated by him on All India Radio, October 31st, 1986.

'I have done what I had to do ...' Tully and Jacob, *op. cit.*, p. 2.

Ustinov's account of Indira's assassination. *The Guardian*, November 1st, 1984.

Violation of elementary norms of security. Tully and Jacob, *op. cit.*, p. 10.

Top Secret file on which Indira scribbled 'Aren't we secular?' Author's article, *The Times of India*, November 8th, 1984.

'No two armed Sikh guards should ever be posted together ...' Several security officers to the Author; none of them wanted to be quoted by name.

'... fled in different directions ...', *ibid.*

'Those supposed to save me will be the first to run away.' A most reliable source close to both Indira and R. N. Kao who spoke on the condition that he would not be identified by name.

There is reason to believe that this incident as well as the directive that no two Sikh armed guards be posted together are recorded in the report of Justice Thakkar of the Supreme Court who was appointed to hold an inquiry into the circumstances of Indira's assassination but whose report, at his own request, was being kept secret at the time of writing.

Rajiv first hearing of his mother's death from the BBC. Tully and Jacob, *op. cit.*, p. 3.

For past practice in the event of the Prime Minister's death, see Author's article, *The Statesman*, June 10th, 1964 and January 20th, 1966. Also Michael Brecher, *Succession in India* (OUP, London, 1966).

Leisurely succession ... a luxury India could hardly afford ... This conclusion was reached at highest-level conclaves in Delhi on that fateful morning in which R. Venkataraman, P. V. Narasimha Rao, V. P. Sathe, Sita Ram Kesari and several others participated. Accounts of these consultations given to the Author by several participants were broadly the same.

Zail Singh's statement: 'If Madam asks me to pick up a broom . . .' *The Statesman*, July 6th, 1982.

Zail Singh's decision, during the flight from Sa'na to Delhi to swear in Rajiv as Prime Minister. Tarlochan Singh, the President's Deputy Press Secretary and confidant to Author.

The Mahatma's murder shocking the country out of its madness. M. J. Akbar quoted by Tully and Jacob, *op. cit.*, p. 8.

Nearly 2,500 people, mostly Sikhs, were killed . . . Fifty thousand . . . fled the capital of their country . . . Tully and Jacob, *op. cit.*, p. 7.

Inaction of police or its collusion with rioters, *ibid.*, p. 5.

'Most overpopulated area on earth'. James Cameron, *New Statesman and Nation*, June 5th, 1964.

'Daughter of the mountains' wanting her ashes scattered in the Himalayas. Pupul Jayakar to Author. For Indira's love for mountains from an early age, also see Chapter 3.

## 2  Invaluable Inheritance

Motilal's palatial house called Anand Bhavan. For a graphic description of it, see Zareer Masani, *Indira Gandhi, A Biography* (OUP, 1975), pp. 5–6.

'Father . . . would have remembered to celebrate . . . with champagne.' Krishna Hutheesing, *Dear to Behold* (Macmillan, 1969), p. 10. Mrs Hutheesing was Indira's aunt, the younger of Nehru's two sisters.

'It's a bonnie lassie . . .' to '. . . better than a thousand sons', *ibid.*, p. 18.

'May he be a worthy successor to Jawaharlal . . .' to . . . 'without knowing that he had held a girl, not a boy', K. A. Abbas, *Indira Gandhi, Return of the Red Rose* (Hind Pocket Book, Delhi, 1966), p. 12.

'New soul of India', letter by Sarojini Naidu to Nehru, December 17th, 1917. Quoted in Jawaharlal Nehru, *A Bunch of Old Letters* (Asia Publishing House, Bombay, 1958), p. 1. These letters were selected and edited by Nehru during a brief vacation that year in the Kulu Valley in North India.

'Indian in blood and colour, but English in taste . . .' Quoted in M. J. Akbar, *Nehru* (Viking, 1989), p. 27.

'More an Englishman than an Indian'. Quoted in Masani, *op. cit.*, p. 4.

Anand Bhavan 'a delight for children . . . for play and hiding', Arnold Michaelis, Interview with Indira Gandhi, *McCall's*, April 1966.

Motilal's 'fiery' temper 'softened by quick forgiveness . . .', *ibid.*

Jibes and jeers aimed at Indira's mother, Kamala, by the Nehru women. Masani, *op. cit.*, p. 7. Also see Uma Vasudev, *Indira Gandhi, Revolution in Restraint* (Vikas, Delhi, 1974), pp. 22–3.

Vijayalakshmi Pandit's denial of having ill-treated Kamala. Interview with Shailja Bajpai, *Gentleman*, Bombay, May 1986.

On Nehru's indifference to his wife's suffering, he himself was to say: 'An unkindness to her would have been better than this semi-forgetful, casual attitude.' Quoted in Masani, *op. cit.*, p. 8.

Indira repaying Aunt Vijayalakshmi Pandit 'in kind' for barbs directed at Kamala, *ibid.*, p. 7. Also see, in greater detail, Uma Vasudev, *op. cit.*

'I loved her [Kamala] deeply . . . and quarrelled with people.' Quoted in Promilla Kalhan, *Kamala Nehru, An Intimate Biography* (Vikas, Delhi, 1973), p. 141. It was known to quite a few people in 1973 that Indira had asked Promilla Kalhan to write this biography. Later, Mrs Kalhan confirmed this to Author.

'Morning coats, top hats'. Michael Edwards, *Nehru* (Penguin, 1972), p. 25.

Conflict between Jawaharlal and his father. Krishna Hutheesing, *With No Regrets* (Padma Publications, Bombay, 1946), p. 33.

Motilal's view of *satyagraha* as 'midsummer madness', Masani, *op. cit.*, p. 10.

No one in Motilal's family 'dared to utter a word for fear of rousing Father's anger or irritating Jawaharlal'. Hutheesing, *With No Regrets, op. cit.*, p. 11.

On the Jallianwalla Bagh Massacre and General Dyer's arrogant statement to the Hunter Committee, that if more were not killed it was because he had 'exhausted his ammunition', see Tariq Ali, *The Nehrus and the Gandhis, An Indian Dynasty* (Picador, 1985), pp. 24–5.

'Nationalist Trinity . . .' Quoted in Masani, *op. cit.*, p. 10.

'Half-naked Fakir'. Quoted in Vincent & Sheean, *Lead Kindly Light* (Random House, 1949), p. 36.

'He came, we saw, he conquered . . .' Vijayalakshmi Pandit's description of Gandhi's entry into the Nehru family. Interview with Shailja Bajpai, *op. cit.*

Indira's memories of Mahatma Gandhi when she was a child of five. Indira Gandhi, *My Truth*, presented by Emmanuel Pouchpadass (Vision Books, Delhi, 1981), pp. 18–19. The book, first published in French in Paris, was based on a series of interviews Indira gave Pouchpadass, a former Indian diplomat. Like so many other interviews of Indira's, these were singularly unrevealing.

Bonfire of foreign clothes at Motilal's mansion and Indira's discovery of her power over her parents, Uma Vasudev, *op. cit.*, p. 29–30. The searing sequel to bonfire, Indira's burning of her favourite foreign doll, *ibid.*, pp. 30–31. Also see Indira Gandhi, *The Story of Swaraj Bhavan*, an article in the Motilal Nehru Centenary Souvenir, available at the Indira Gandhi Memorial Trust, New Delhi.

'Livery of freedom'. Quoted in Author's article on Nehru, *The Guardian*, May 28th, 1979.

Nehru's belated realisation that he must have been a 'burden and trial' to his wife whose response was to show 'amazing patience and tolerance'. See Nehru, *An Autobiography* (Bodley Head, London, 1936), p. 77.

Indira on her mother's role in the freedom struggle. Speech at a women's seminar at Tanjore in South India, June 1965, quoted in Masani, *op. cit.*, p. 12.

Indira's fantasies identifying herself with Joan of Arc. Hutheesing, *Dear to Behold, op. cit.*, p. 44.

Indira: 'Everybody has gone to jail'. Quoted in Uma Vasudev, *op. cit.*, p. 66.

Little Indira 'greatly annoyed' with the police carting away family furniture in lieu of unpaid fines. Nehru, *Autobiography*, p. 91.

Indira becoming 'more and more intractable . . . ' Nehru's letter to Motilal, quoted in Masani, *op. cit.*, p. 19.

Indira's withdrawal from St Cecilia's after a row between her father and grandfather. Masani, *ibid.*

Indira's reaction to her father's letters to her, later published as *Glimpses of World History*, see Indira Gandhi, *My Truth*, *op. cit.*, p. 22.

Dandi March, as part of Salt *satyagraha*. See Michael Brecher, *Nehru, a Political Biography* (OUP, London, 1959), p. 66.

'Rather curious approach . . .' Brecher, *ibid.*, p. 67.

Kamala Nehru's arrest in 1931 and her elation mixed with concern for her daughter, see Promilla Kalhan, *op. cit.*, pp. 72–3; also Nehru, *Autobiography*, pp. 240–1.

*Vanar Sena* acting, 'not unlike monkeys . . .' Michaelis, *op. cit.*

Indira seemed 'quite happy'. Quoted in Masani, *op. cit.*, p. 30.

Mrs Vakil, perhaps the only Indian in a position to admonish Indira during the Emergency. One of Indira's aides who heard Mrs Vakil do so, to Author. The source did not want to be identified by name.

For Indira's happiness at Santiniketan and Tagore's letter to Nehru, see Tariq Ali, *op. cit.*, p. 119. A more detailed account of her life at Tagore's academy, where she also learnt the Manipuri style of Indian dancing, is to be found in Uma Vasudev, *op. cit.*, p. 115–16.

'No influence even remotely comparable to Kamala's'. Pupul Jayakar to Author.

Iris Murdoch contributed her comment on Indira's stay at Badminton and Somerville to *Indira Gandhi, Statesmen, Scholars, Scientists and Friends Remember*, published on the first anniversary of her death (October 31st, 1985) by the Indira Gandhi Memorial Trust and Vikas, New Delhi. Edited by G. Parthasarthi and H. Y. Sharada Prasad, p. 308. Hereafter this book will be referred to as *Indira Gandhi Remembered*.

Indira's failure to pass the Latin examination at Oxford. Dhiren Bhagat, himself a young Oxonian, in *Illustrated Weekly*, Bombay, February 1985.

Toast to the 'first Somerville Prime Minister'. Naomi Mitchison in *Indira Gandhi Remembered*, p. 299.

Rejecting advice that she should not become a mere 'appendage' to her father. Quoted in Welles Hangen, *After Nehru, Who?* (Hart-Davis, London, 1963), p. 161.


## 3 *Against the Whole World's Wishes*

'She does not speak, she squeaks.' Indira to Lord Chalfont in an interview for the BBC, October 1971. Quoted in Masani, *op. cit.*, p. 52. The text of the interview at the Indira Gandhi Memorial Trust, New Delhi.

Indira 'lambasted' both the racist South African rulers and Indian businessmen there. Dom Moraes, *Mrs Gandhi* (Vikas, 1980), p. 74.

Stafford Cripps's offer to India 'a post-dated cheque . . .' Tariq Ali, *op. cit.*, p. 69.

Subhas Chandra Bose's Indian National Army, *ibid.*, p. 71.

Feroze Gandhi's 'devotion' to Kamala Nehru. Moraes, *op. cit.*, pp. 64–5.

Indira 'did not like Feroze but she loved him'. Quoted in Anand Mohan, *Indira Gandhi, a Personal and Political Biography* (Meredith Press, New York, 1967), p. 241.

Indira finally said yes to Feroze's proposal of marriage at the Sacré-Coeur in Paris. 'Paris was bathed in sunshine . . .' Indira Gandhi, *My Truth*, *op. cit.*. p. 45.

For Nehru's complex objections to Indira's decision to marry Feroze, see Tariq Ali, *op. cit.*, pp. 124–5.

Nehru to Feroze: '*If* you have taken these photographs . . .' Moraes, *op. cit.*, p. 75.

For Nehru's reference to the different 'backgrounds' of Indira and Feroze, see Tariq Ali, cited above.

'I would welcome as wide a breach . . .' Quoted in Tariq Ali, *ibid.*, p. 124.

Indira carrying out her threat of 'not speaking to her father'. Nayantara Sahgal, *Indira Gandhi: Her Road to Power* (Macdonald, London, 1982), p. 23.

Indira's claim: 'the whole world was opposed to my marriage'. Pupul Jayakar to Author.

Gandhi's defence of the Indira–Feroze marriage. See Tariq Ali, *op. cit.*, p. 126.

'And now a rather delicate matter . . . Feroze . . . has got into hot water with his people . . .' Nehru's letter to Vijayalakshmi Pandit, quoted in Sahgal, *op. cit.*, p. 22.

During the Bangladesh war Indira's mind 'suffused with reds'. Pupul Jayakar to Author.

'Do have some potato cripps, Sir Stafford'. Quoted in Masani, *op. cit.*, p. 63.

'The loveliness of the land enthralled me . . .' Nehru, *The Unity of India* (Lindsay Drummond, London, 1941), p. 223.

Indira as 'mountain goat'. Masani, *op. cit.*, p. 71.

For amusing exchanges between father and daughter during her honeymoon, see K. A. Abbas, *op. cit.*, p. 93.

For a complete account of the Quit India movement, 1942, see *History of the Freedom Movement*, by Dr Tara Chand (Publications Division, Delhi, 1972), pp. 362–423. This book (p. 357) also quotes Gandhi's remark 'free India would join Britain . . .'

For Feroze's exploit in escaping arrest through impersonating a British soldier, see Moraes, *op. cit.*, p. 82.

The scene of Indira's arrest. Feroze Gandhi to Author in 1956.

'I had made up my mind that I had to go to prison . . .' Indira to Michaelis, *op. cit.*

'. . . the matron came in excitedly announcing "Mrs Indira is here" . . .'
Vijayalakshmi Pandit, *Prison Days* (Signet Press, Calcutta, 1945), p. 60.

Indira 'considered so dangerous . . . etc.' Quoted in Sahgal, *op. cit.*

For Mrs Pandit's account of life in prison along with Indira and others,
all sharing a dormitory, which belies Indira's claims of excessive hardship,
see Sahgal, *ibid.*, pp. 16–18.

Indira's joy in motherhood. From an article by her, quoted in Masani,
*op. cit.*, p. 74.

Indira's displeasure with adulatory biographies because of suggestions that
her marriage was far from happy. Interview to Promilla Kalhan, *Hindustan
Times*, July 10th, 1973. Mrs Kalhan, as she later confirmed to Author, was
invited to interview Indira.

Whether 'Indira would become a Gandhi . . .' Quoted in Tariq Ali,
*op. cit.*, p. 123.


## 4  Father's Châtelaine and Confidante

'Wreck it from within'. Durga Das, *India: From Curzon to Nehru* (Collins,
1969).

Sanjay's delivery 'difficult and painful'. See Masani, *op. cit.*, p. 77.

A minor sideshow at Sanjay's birth, pregnant with symbolism. Feroze
Gandhi to Author in 1959.

Indira's overwhelming 'pride and excitement' on Independence Day.
Quoted in Masani, *op. cit.*, p. 79.

'Wounded in body and spirit . . . ' Vimla Sindhi, herself a refugee who
fled Pakistan after her parent had been murdered and knocked at Nehru's
door, to Author. She stayed on at the Prime Minister's house as an aide
throughout the Nehru era and later served Indira. She now lives in retirement.

. . . rescued a poor man chased by a 'howling mob evidently intent on
hacking him to pieces'. Subhadra Joshi, then working with Indira, to Author.
Mrs Joshi, an articulate and activist Congress MP for many years, remained
close to Indira until the Emergency when they drifted apart.

GBS: 'This comes of being too good'. Quoted in the *Hindustan Times*,
January 31st, 1948.

'The light has gone out of our lives . . .' Nehru, *Independence and After*, a
collection of speeches (Delhi, 1947), p. 17.

'. . . With Gandhi gone, her father's dependence on her had increased'.
K. D. Malaviya, a colleague of both Nehru and Indira, and a close friend of
Feroze, to Author shortly after Feroze's death in September, 1960.

'Famous toothless smile'. Quoted in Masani, *op. cit.*

'Reputation for a roving eye'. See Dom Moraes, *op. cit.*; also Uma Vasudev,
*op. cit.*

'Near-disasters narrowly averted . . .' Quoted in Masani, *op. cit.*

Indira on her reasons for her decision to help her father because he had
'real need' for this help and connected quotations, see Indira Gandhi, *My
Truth, op. cit.*, pp. 107–8.

Indira introduces a subject her father was embarrassed to mention during Nehru's talks with Soviet leaders. Pupul Jayakar, who had been told of the incident by Indira, to Author.

Indira's elevation to the post of Congress President a 'Machiavellian move by Nehru'. Morarji Desai, *Story of My Life*, Vol. II (Macmillan, India, 1974), p. 121.

'. . . not a good idea for my daughter to come in as Congress President while I am Prime Minister . . .' Nehru quoted in *National Herald*, January 8th, 1959.

Indira 'bullied into accepting the post' to '. . . that was the clinching argument'. Interview with Lord Chalfont, in 1971, quoted in Masani, *op. cit.*, p. 114.

Alarm over the election of the Communist government in Kerala. Nachiketa, a Bombay publishing house, actually published in 1959, a book, *Kerala, the Yenan of India*, by Prof. Eric Fic of Singapore University.

For a summing up and analysis of the agitation against the Communist ministry of Kerala, see Author's article, 'Twenty-six Months of Kerala's Communist Ministry', *The Statesman*, August 1st, 1959. Also *Kerala's Red Riddle* by D. R. Mankekar (Manektala, Bombay, 1960).

Nehru's aloofness with Feroze and Indira's tense relationship with him. See Moraes, *op. cit.*, pp. 84–5 and pp. 98–9.

Feroze as 'son-in-law of the nation', first put into print by Tariq Ali, *op. cit.*, p. 135.

Nehru's invitation of Siqueiros to lunch and Author's criticism of it. *The Statesman*, September 7th, 1956.

'*I* did not bring *my* wife here.' Quoted in Moraes, *op. cit.*, p. 98.

Feroze: 'I am not going to talk to her.' Tara Ali Baig to Author.

A two-volume biography of Nehru: Dorothy Norman, *Nehru, the First Sixty Years*, Volumes I and II (London, 1965).

'I can tell you things which I wouldn't dream of telling anyone'. Dorothy Norman, *Indira Gandhi, Letters to a Friend (1950–1984)* (Weidenfeld & Nicolson, London, 1985), p. 8. In later notes, this book will be called *Correspondence with Dorothy Norman*.

'I am in the midst of a domestic crisis', *ibid.*, p. 25.

'I have been and am deeply unhappy . . . to have missed . . . perfect relationship . . .', *ibid.*, pp. 28–9.

'On the domestic front, Feroze has always resented my very existence . . . The Kerala situation is worsening', *ibid.*, p. 57.

Feroze took his 'defeat' over Kerala 'badly'. Author's impression shared by several of Feroze's friends.

Whenever Indira was 'so pleased, something terrible usually took place'. Quoted in Masani, *op. cit.*, p. 117.

Author's reference to Feroze as 'a lonely and unhappy man' killed by 'overwork'. Feroze Gandhi's Obituary, *The Statesman*, September 9th, 1960.

Feroze's death a 'heart-rending blow' to Indira. *Correspondence With Dorothy Norman*, pp. 77–9. Dorothy Norman's own comment on the tragedy (p. 77) was: Feroze Gandhi's death 'had represented a heart-breaking blow to her. Despite their early closeness, they had drifted apart. Yet it was Feroze she loved . . . and it was the greatest comfort to her that she learned from him, shortly before his death, that he had always truly loved her, and no one else.'

'The most important death in my life was my husband's.' Quoted by Moraes, *op. cit.*, pp. 146–7. She added: 'Whatever happened between us, Feroze never made a fuss.'

'The Nehrus were very unmusical . . . Feroze . . . introduced us to . . . Western classical music.' H. Y. Sharada Prasad to Author.

'Voice of reason and sanity'. James Cameron, *Point of Departure* (London, 1966), p. 14.

Indira's books 'were not numerous and in some the leaves were uncut'. Moraes, *op. cit.*, p. 47.

'Voracious and amazingly rapid reader'. H. Y. Sharada Prasad to Author; endorsed by several others who worked for Indira for many years.

Mathai, an 'adventurer from Kerala' who first started 'pushing Indira into limelight'. Masani, *op. cit.*, p. 98.

Feroze's role in exposing Mathai's misuse of the power that proximity to Nehru gave him. Author's personal knowledge through almost daily contact with Feroze.

Philip Ziegler's claim that Mountbatten was not a 'complaisant husband' and that too much should not be read into the Nehru–Edwina–Lord Mountbatten 'triangle'. Philip Ziegler, *Mountbatten* (Collins, London, 1985), pp. 474–5.

'Dressed in a housecoat'. An Indian security officer who usually accompanied Nehru but did not want to be quoted by name to Author in 1964.

Widespread belief in India that Mountbatten 'encouraged' the romance between Nehru and Edwina because it served his political purpose. Dr S. Gopal, Nehru's official biographer, to Author. Gopal had been told by one of Mountbatten's former ADCs that the latter had overheard conversation between the Lord and his Lady confirming that he expected his wife to 'soften' Nehru.

Indira's warm relationship with Edwina and exchange of gifts, including pieces of jewellery, between them. Vimla Sindhi, who had loyally served Nehru and Indira, and also knew the Mountbattens well, to Author.

For Mountbatten's dismay over the abolition of the privy purses of princes and his anger over the imprisonment and ill-treatment of Gayatri Devi, the dowager Maharani of Jaipur, see Ziegler, *op. cit.*, p. 654.

Mountbatten wondering whether he could bear to go to India at all. Ziegler, *ibid.*

Sita Ramaswamy, a protocol officer of Air India and a friend of the Author, was present when Mountbatten, during a brief halt at Bombay airport, rang up Gayatri Devi but conspicuously refrained from calling Indira.

Indira's advice against 'hysteria' in relation to tension with China in the late Fifties. Quoted in the *Congress Bulletin*, November, 1959.

The Chinese would do 'nothing big'. See Author's three-part article, *The Times of India*, October 20th–22nd, 1982, twentieth anniversary of the India–China war.

President Radhakrishnan's criticism of Nehru's 'credulity and negligence.' *Ibid.*

'My father always liked neatness . . .' Author's article, *The Statesman*, January 20th, 1966.


## 5    The Shastri Interlude

Desai, a man 'physically resembling Cassius and spiritually Calvin'. Moraes, *op. cit.*, p. 80.

Desai's belief that he was the 'natural successor' to Nehru, . . . 'cheated out' of his due. See Author's article on succession, *The Statesman*, June 10th, 1964. Also Michael Brecher, *Succession in India*, p. 32.

The powerful collective of Congress party bosses nicknamed 'the Syndicate', *ibid.* Brecher graciously notes that the expression 'the Syndicate' was first used in print by Author.

The Kamaraj Plan, *ibid.* Also see Francine Frankel, *India's Political Economy 1947–77* (OUP, 1978), pp. 229–30. Morarji Desai's version is to be found in Volume II of his *Story of My Life, op. cit.*, pp. 199–205.

Shastri's own feeling that Nehru's first preference as his successor was his own daughter Indira. Quoted by Kuldip Nayar, *Between the Lines* (Allied, Delhi, 1968), p. 8.

Nehru's unhappiness that Hangen in his book *After Nehru, Who?, op. cit.*, had 'dragged in' Indira's name into the succession stakes and that she had met 'that American journalist'. First hinted to Author in 1970 by T. T. Krishnamachari, Nehru's Finance Minister whom Nehru trusted and consulted. Later, in 1980, Nehru's official biographer, Dr S. Gopal, confirmed to Author that Krishnamachari had conveyed Nehru's opposition to Indira being his successor explicitly and in greater detail to President Radhakrishnan, Gopal's father.

Nehru's hope that as a minister under Shastri Indira would be an 'instrument of continuity' . . . , *ibid.*

Nehru: '. . . dynastic succession . . . repulsive to my own mind'. Quoted in Uma Vasudev, *op. cit.*, p. 302.

'No public figure disclaims . . . none is more disbelieved'. Hangen, *op. cit.*, p. 162.

Indira's craving for 'privacy and anonymity . . . I cannot ignore without some kind of self-annihilation'. *Correspondence with Dorothy Norman, op. cit.*, p. 96.

Depression over inability to buy a London flat 'she had fallen in love' with. *Ibid.*, p. 97.

'I am not running away from anyone or anything . . .' *Ibid.*

'Desire to be out of India . . . overwhelming . . .' *Ibid.*, p. 103.

'Should he not have consulted me . . .' Indira to Author, in the presence of the ladies mentioned in the text.

'Slighted and ignored'. Indira to Author and a host of others.

'Strengthened this impression'. In a speech in Parliament on June 18th,

1964, Shastri said that he would not necessarily stick to the 'beaten track'. Indira and others interpreted it as abandoning the Nehruvian path.

For causes and dimensions of the language agitation in South India, see Author's article. 'Eleven Weeks to Hindi', *The Statesman*, November 1st, 1964.

'Jumping over' (the Prime Minister's head): general impression, to Author's knowledge, among Shastri's colleagues.

'Do you think this government can survive if I resign? . . .' and allied remarks. Indira to Author. The substance of this conversation was included in Author's Political Commentary, *The Statesman*, February 2nd, 1965, without any attribution to her.

'. . . the only man in a cabinet of old women'. Frank Moraes, not to be confused with his son and Indira's biographer, Dom, in *The Indian Express*, of which he was then Editor-in-Chief, August 10th, 1965.

'*Is ka kaya karein?*' (What should we do with it?). The incident was first related to Author and Pran Sabbharwal by Indira. Later confirmed by Dharma Vira, then Cabinet Secretary to whom Shastri handed over Indira's note.

For background to the Sikh demand for Punjabi Suba, see Chapter 16.

'I will be the next to be thrown out . . .' etc. Indira to Author on December 31st, 1965.

'No English, no Hindi? How?' Kamaraj quoted in C. S. Pandit, *End of an Era* (Allied, Delhi, 1977), p. 21.

'Terrified' of having to answer parliamentary questions. Pupul Jayakar to Author.

'Guided by the wishes of the Congress President'. *The Statesman*, January 14th, 1966.

'That's exactly how I feel . . .' Indira stressing her reluctance to be Prime Minister. To Narayana Menon, quoted in Uma Vasudev, *op. cit.*, p. 316.

'To be king is within the situation and within me . . .' Frost's verse, quoted by Indira in her letter to her son, Rajiv. J. Anthony Lukas, *The New York Times* Magazine, March 27th, 1966.

'*Lal Gulab Zindabad*' (Long Live the Red Rose), K. A. Abbas, *op. cit.*, p. i.

'Will someone, please, give me a glass of water?' H. Y. Sharada Prasad to Author.


## 6   The Dumb Doll

Start of the Mizo insurgency. *The Statesman*, February 23rd, 1966.

Harold Wilson's . . . factually wrong and partisan comments . . . *Ibid.*, September 7th, 1965.

Shift in Soviet policy towards India and Pakistan. See Author's article on the Shastri–Mikoyan talks in Delhi, July 14th, 1964, *The Statesman*.

Indira's discomfiture at the Jaipur AICC over food policy. See in *The Statesman*, 15th February, 1966; also Masani, *op. cit.*, pp. 151–2.

The churlishness and downright discourtesy with which Indira was treated in Parliament. See Author's article, 'Decline of Parliament', *Illustrated Weekly of India*, August; also Hiren Mukherjee, a long-time Communist Member of Parliament, *The Statesman*, June 10th, 1986.

Indira developing for Parliament the kind of 'disdain it had shown her'. *Ibid.*

Indira follows Shastri's economic and social policies which she used to criticise . . . Francine Frankel, *op. cit.*, pp. 294–7.

'. . . easier for a conclave of cardinals . . . than . . . for [Indira's government] . . . to . . . give up Emergency [powers].' Author's article, *The Statesman*, March 5th, 1966.

'Pragmatism' as watchword. D. P. Mishra told the Author that even at the height of her 'radical phase' Indira would often invoke 'pragmatism' to give concessions to big business. When one day he needled her for this, she burst out: 'Yes, I am a pragmatist and proud of it.'

Annual plan outlay lowered from that in the preceding period 'for the first time since the start of the planning process'. Francine Frankel, *op. cit.*, p. 295.

'Don't publish this but . . .' Indira to Author.

Madame 'would be our *Mon Général*'. Minoo Masani quoted in *The Statesman*, April 8th, 1967.

'No harm comes to this girl . . .' In Author's presence.

Johnson's decision to stay to dinner. *Ibid.*

Enabling Indira to 'concentrate almost all powers . . . in her hands'. Ram Subhag Singh in the Lok Sabha, lower house of Parliament, November 21st, 1969. Also see Kuldip Nayar, *Judgment* (Vikas, 1977), p. 22–3.

'Sharing' versus 'understanding' by India of 'America's agony' in Vietnam. P. N. Haksar to Author. Confirmed by L. K. Jha.

'We must get her elected . . . whatever you say.' B. K. Nehru to Author.

'Steel in her spine'. *Daily Mirror*, November 1st, 1984.

'Her countrymen wouldn't approve . . .' Author's despatch in *The Statesman*, March 30th, 1966.

'How can you expect the Americans . . .' to 'Americans are thinking of a way to save face.' Quoted in Tariq Ali, *op. cit.*, p. 157.

Charge of 'sell-out' and Indira's reply to critics, led by Menon, with the punch line: 'Even Lenin had taken American aid . . .' Quoted in Masani, *op. cit.*, p. 159.

'If it is necessary to deviate from past policies . . .' etc. Indira at AICC meeting in Bombay, quoted in *The Times of India*, May 22nd, 1966.

'Inflation and rising prices'. In Author's presence.

Last-minute attempt to postpone the devaluation decision. B. K. Nehru to Author.

'A big man's daughter, a small man's mistake.' Kamaraj's remark to his associates. Confirmed to Author by Atulya Ghosh and R. Rangarajan, a journalist colleague very close to Kamaraj.

'Strings without aid.' Rajinder Puri, in the *Hindustan Times*, September 10th, 1966.

She came to believe she could 'trust no one' and (everyone) was 'capable of betraying her'. Romesh Thapar, then a close friend and staunch supporter of Indira, later to turn her bitter critic, to Author.

Indira's Vietnam initiative, especially the joint statement in Moscow condemning the 'imperialist aggression' in Vietnam. Author's despatches and article from Moscow, *The Statesman*, July 10th–17th, 1966.

The Pope and U Thant 'do not want our wheat'. B. K. Nehru to Author.

'If food supplies stop these ladies and gentlemen . . . will not starve . . .' Indira to Author.

'Behaving like a capitalist in Washington and a socialist in Moscow.' Quoted in *The New York Times*, September 30th, 1966. The MP had, in fact, used an Indian proverb to the effect that a fickle pilgrim while bathing in the Ganga calls himself Ganga Ram and when taking a holy dip in the Jamuna assumes the name Jamna Dass.

'Futile, silly and ridiculous' demand, in Author's presence in Parliament on March 12th, 1956.

Refusing to be 'cowed down by cow-savers'. Quoted in *The Times of India*, December 13th, 1966.

Nanda's protest that he was being made a 'scapegoat'. See Author's despatch, *The Statesman*, November 10th, 1966.

'. . . This pretty woman does not have to suffer . . .' Quoted in *The Statesman*, January 23rd, 1967.

'A degree of detachment . . .' Interview with Michaelis, *op. cit.*, Indira had gone on to say: 'I do remove myself from a place if I have to or if I am tired. I do have the feeling sometimes, if I am addressing a meeting, that I am watching the whole procedure from the outside.'

' . . . My position among the people is uncontested.' Quoted in *The Times of India*, December 26th, 1966.

'Go and ask the Maharajas . . .' *Ibid.*, January 21st, 1967.

For the stone-throwing in which Indira's nose was fractured and her disappointment over the surgeon's refusal to give her a 'beautiful nose' through plastic surgery, see Hutheesing, *Dear to Behold*, *op. cit.*, pp. 195–6.

'My burden is manifold . . .' Quoted in Masani, *op. cit.*, p. 171.

The 'Mother Indira' legend. Within a few days of the slogans at Rae Bareli, Indira was again called Mother Indira at Cochin, some 2,000 miles away, in the Author's presence.

'After the broken nose, a slap in the face.' *The Times*, March 7th, 1967.

'From Calcutta to Amritsar . . .' and allied analysis of elections, including Kamaraj's 'fantastic fall', see Author's article, *The Statesman*, February 24th, 1967.

'Better-suited and better qualified . . .' Desai to journalists, February 22nd, 1967, in Author's presence.

Party feeling against a 'damaging contest' and Syndicate's success in imposing a compromise. See Author's article, 'Syndicate Rides a Divided Congress', *The Statesman*, March 3rd, 1967.

Desai seen as the 'Syndicate's Trojan Horse'. See Kuldip Nayar, *India, the Critical Years* (Vikas, 1971), p. 28.

## 7   Short-Cut To Supremacy

Desai's exchange with journalists. In Author's presence.

'Indiraben, you don't understand . . .' P. N. Haksar to Author.

Desai's reluctance to invite a charge of 'disloyalty' and his dual policy to see Indira's position undermined. Several of Desai's associates to Author. The most notable of these sources, Tarakeswari Sinha, was a Deputy Minister in Nehru's days. She was one of Indira's sharpest critics and very close to Desai. The words she used to me in 1967–8 were 'Morarjibhai (the respectful way of using his name) wants us to bring prime ministership and dump it in his lap. He would not even soil his fingers.'

Subba Rao's judgment on fundamental rights, known as the Golak Nath case, is printed in P. L. Lakhanpal, *Two Historical Judgments* (Delhi, 1972).

'When people want to know why Zakir Sahib . . .' H. Y. Sharada Prasad to Author.

Appeal to the 'natural constituency' of the Left, and downgrading of 'pragmatism'. Several associates of Indira, including Dinesh Singh, Inder Gujral and Nandini Satpathy, to Author. D. P. Mishra, who did not particularly like leftism, went along with the strategy, according to his statement to Author.

A compromise ten-point programme, failure of the 'Young Turks' to push through bank nationalisation and their 'landmark victory'. *The Statesman*, June 24th, 1967. For the text of the ten-point programme, see Francine Frankel, *op. cit.*, pp. 397–8.

Reactions of leaders to the adoption of the late-night demand for the abolition of privy purses: summed up by Francine Frankel, *op. cit.*, pp. 398–9.

For AICC proceedings at Jabalpur, see *The Statesman*, April 9th, 1968.

For the circumstances of Nijalingappa's selection as Congress President, see C. S. Pandit, *op. cit.*, p. 52.

Nijalingappa's diary entry – that Indira's enforced resignation would 'break the party', quoted in Kuldip Nayar, *Critical Years, op. cit.*, p. 26. The entry was dated August 24th, 1968.

*Gherao* was included in the Oxford Dictionary in 1968.

Impact of the Green Revolution, see Frankel, *India's Green Revolution, Economic Gains and Political Costs* (Princeton, 1971). 'Green Revolution might turn red'. Report of Ministry of Home Affairs, New Delhi, October 1968.

Desai's advice to Indira not to take sleeping pills. Harsukh Pandit, an astrologer with free access to Indira, to Author in 1967. Since then confirmed by several other confidants of Indira.

'Constitutional coup'. Author's description of the dismissal of the Marxist-led ministry in West Bengal, *The Guardian*, November 22nd, 1967.

Nijalingappa's diary entry April 12th, 1969. Kuldip Nayar, *Critical Years, op. cit.*, p. 27.

For the text of Nijalingappa's presidential address, censure motions and Indira's rejoinder, see *Congress Bulletin*, April–May 1969.

Walk-out by D. P. Mishra and Uma Shankar Dikshit 'in disgust'. D. P. Mishra to Author, confirmed by Dikshit.

Desai's 'isolation' in a small committee of leaders. Frankel, *Political*

*Economy*, *op. cit.*, p. 403. She cites C. Subramaniam as the source of her information.

Fire at Faridabad may not have been 'accidental'. C. S. Pandit, *op. cit.*, p. 55.

Indira initially non-committal about Sanjiva Reddy's candidature. Kamaraj to Author. Confirmed by P. N. Haksar. Also late Sushital Banerjee who was with Indira in Tokyo.

Converting the personal power struggle into an ideological one. In 1986 Haksar confirmed to the Author what had been known all along and had indeed been published in almost every biography of Indira, that the advice to follow this strategy had come primarily from him though others among her advisers felt the same way.

Some of Haksar's critics, however, accused him of being a conduit of advice from the 'Soviet Embassy to the Prime Minister'. See Kuldip Nayar, *Critical Years*, *op. cit.*, p. 3. In support of this charge, Nayar had quoted S. K. Patil.

This was, of course, an absurd and unwarranted slur on a patriotic Indian. In 1986 Haksar told the Author that he had thought of suing Nayar and Patil for libel but was advised by the government's law officers as well as eminent lawyers to desist because the Indian libel laws are 'heavily weighted' against the aggrieved complainant.

For his part, Desai made no allegation against Haksar but told Francine Frankel in 1973 that to maintain herself in power Indira would 'sell India to the Russians'. Frankel, *Political Economy*, *op. cit.*, p. 401.

'Stray thoughts, hurriedly dictated'. *The Times of India*, July 11th, 1969.

Indira's father, too, had been similarly outvoted . . . in 1957. Nehru wanted S. Radakrishnan to become President that year. But the Prime Minister's colleagues in the Parliamentary Board preferred to give a second term to the incumbent President, Rajendra Prasad.

A 'wounded tigress'. For Indira's reactions to Parliamentary Board's decision, see C. S. Pandit, *op. cit.*, p. 33.

. . . Would smack of 'personal vendetta' . . . D. P. Mishra to Author.

For the text of the correspondence between Indira and Desai over the latter's removal from the Finance Ministry, see A. M. Zaidi, *The Great Upheaval, '69–'72* (New Delhi, 1972), pp. 92–3.

Attempt to make out that bank nationalisation was a 'personal act' of the Prime Minister. Sahgal, *op. cit.*, p. 46.

Popular enthusiasm over bank nationalisation . . . 'genuine and largely spontaneous'. Author's article in *The Guardian*, July 22nd, 1969. The article acknowledged that there was some organisation behind the show.

Bank nationalisation law in 'indecent haste'. Quoted in Sahgal, *op. cit.*, p. 59.

Accused of being a 'Communist fellow-traveller . . .' to . . . 'Nothing could have prevented me from doing so'. Quoted in Frankel, *Political Economy op. cit.*, pp. 421–2.

'They drove me to the wall . . .' Pupul Jayakar to Author.

C. D. Deshmukh, a distinguished ICS officer who was knighted and made Governor of the Reserve Bank during the British Raj. After independence he was a much respected Finance Minister in Nehru's cabinet. In 1956, over the issue of including Bombay city in Maharashtra state, he resigned and became a critic of Nehru and, later, of Indira.

For a detailed account of the 'War of Midnight Missives' over the demand for a 'conscience vote' in the presidential election, see Zaidi, *op. cit.*, pp. 105–10.

Kamaraj's statement on Chavan's 'slipperiness'. To Author at Cochin in February 1971.

Prime Minister's supporters add a few 'forged signatures' on requisition. Inder Gujral and several others to Author.

For the text of the Nijalingappa letter of October 28th, containing the prophetic punch line, 'You have made personal loyalty to you the test . . . ' see *Congress Bulletin*, November 1969.

For a detailed account of the two rival meetings of the Congress Working Committee and for the ugly demonstration against the Nijalingappa faction, see *The Times*, November 2nd, 1969; also Sahgal, *op. cit.*, pp. 49–50.

After the Congress split, it was alleged that most Congress MPs who took Indira's side were 'misled' by All India Radio into believing that she was winning. But this only confirms the point that to most Congressmen what mattered was power, not programme or ideology.

For Jagjivan Ram's unpaid taxes, see Author's article on 1969 in retrospect, *The Statesman*, January 1st, 1970.

'Creeping dictatorial design'. Sahgal, *op. cit.*, p. 150.

For Nijalingappa's charge, see note (above) on allegation against Haksar.

For a description of the *'durbari* (courtier) culture,' see Romesh Thapar, *Economic and Political Weekly*, March 14th, 1970.

Indira: The Prime Minister's secretariat was not 'invented' by her. *National Herald*, July 30th, 1970.

Replicating the 'Kerala pattern' in Delhi. *New Wave*, March 30th, 1971. Also several CPI leaders to Author though they took care to add that, at the national level, the combination would have to be led by Indira. As subsequent chapters show, these hopes were dashed.

For the reaction of the 'Young Turks' and other radicals among Indira's supporters to the Supreme Court judgment *Political Economy* and their demand for revising the constitution, see Frankel, *op. cit.*, p. 113.

Indira's refusal to follow the radicals' advice . . . 'I am against certain attitudes of mind . . .' to '. . . against such Congressmen also'. AICC publication, *From Delhi to Patna*, pp. 148–9.

'I am the issue', *'Indira Hatao'* and *'Garibi Hatao'*. *Newsweek*, cover story, February 5th, 1971.

Dual electoral strategy of rousing the masses and reassuring the classes, Masani, *op. cit.*, p. 224.

'Damned close run thing.' Estimates of several newspapers, including *The Statesman* and *The Times of India*, privately confirmed by several of Indira's cabinet colleagues.

## 8   Her Finest Hour

Geographical monstrosity. Mountbatten, the last British Viceroy of un-divided India told Dominique Lapierre and Larry Collins, co-authors of *Freedom at Midnight* (Vikas, Delhi, 1975), that he did not expect the tenuous partnership between Pakistan's two wings to endure more than twenty-five years. Lapierre and Collins to Author in Bombay.

For the prelude to the struggle for the liberation of Bangladesh, see Pran Chopra, *India's Second Liberation* (New Delhi, 1973); Anthony Mascarenhas, *Rape of Bangladesh* (Vikas, 1972); G. W. Choudhry, *India, Pakistan and Great Powers* (New York, 1975), which gives the Pakistani point of view; and Raunaq Jahan, *Pakistan: Failure of National Integration* (Dacca, 1973), a Bangladeshi account of what happened.

Defenceless East Pakistan, saved in the 1965 India–Pakistan war only by Indian fears of 'Chinese intervention'. Sheikh Mujibur Rahman knew that when the Pakistani Air Force bombed Kalaikunda Indian air base near Calcutta, Air Chief Marshal Arjan Singh was restrained from retaliating in East Pakistan by Prime Minister Shastri, arguing that this would give the Chinese an excuse to intervene. A key aide of Shastri to Author in 1965. Later confirmed by Arjan Singh.

'Pakistan is now dead and buried under a mountain of corpses.' Quoted by Surjit Mansingh, *India's Search for Power* (Sage Publications, Delhi, 1984), p. 215.

Lack of even a contingency plan in New Delhi. Author's information, checked and rechecked with several military leaders of the period who wanted their anonymity respected.

'. . . determined not to be stampeded . . .' D. P. Dhar and P. N. Dhar, both top aides of Indira at that time, to Author.

For Indira's speeches and statements on Bangladesh, see *India and Bangladesh: Selected Speeches and Statements of Indira Gandhi* (Orient Longman, Delhi, 1972).

Indira's strategy of avoiding warlike noises even while realising that war was unavoidable and giving primacy to the refugee issue. Explained to Author by D. P. Dhar, P. N. Haksar, P. N. Dhar, General (later Field-Marshal) Manekshaw and Air Chief Marshal Pratap Lal. During the war Manekshaw was Chief of the Army Staff and Lal headed the Indian Air Force.

What was 'claimed to be an internal problem in Pakistan . . .' Quoted in Surjit Mansingh, *op. cit.*, p. 217.

Competent handling of the refugee problem enabling 10 million people quickly and smoothly to return home. See Surjit Mansingh, *ibid.*, p. 218, and Pran Chopra, *op. cit.*, p. 85.

Attitude of Army commanders. Field-Marshal Manekshaw told Author later, but during Indira's lifetime, that he had specifically requested Indira to beware of 'sawdust Caesars' raring to march into Bangladesh and she had agreed.

Intensification of concern over Chinese intentions after Kissinger's visit. Diplomats and politicians who took part in the talks with Kissinger to Author.

For the working and scope of the Indo-Soviet treaty see Chapters 17 and

18. It is noteworthy that immediately after the Indo-Soviet document was concluded, Indira publicly offered all other countries to sign identical treaties with them. See Indira's interview to *Link*, New Delhi, August 15th, 1971.

In 1981, Indira offered a Treaty of Peace, Friendship and Cooperation to Pakistan, in response to the Pakistani proposal for a non-aggression pact. The twin suggestions were still under discussion between the two countries until the death of General Zia-ul-Haq.

Indira's refusal to open negotiations in Moscow in Brezhnev's absence and her remarks to him and other Soviet leaders. T. N. Kaul, then Foreign Secretary, now Ambassador to Moscow for a second time, as well as other Indian diplomats who were accompanying her. The incident about Brezhnev's absence was recalled by Girilal Jain after Indira's return to power, *The Times of India*.

Conversation between Indira and Sir Alec Douglas-Home. H. Y. Sharada Prasad, who was present during the talks, to Author.

Her government's restraint 'despite such tremendous provocation' . . . 'when Hitler was on the rampage . . .' to '. . . let the Jews die'. Interview with BBC, quoted in *Years of Endeavour, Selected Speeches of Indira Gandhi, From August 1969 to August 1972* (Publications Division of the Government of India, 1973), pp. 547–8.

'A classic dialogue of the deaf'. Henry Kissinger, *White House Years* (Little Brown & Co., Boston, 1979), p. 848.

Kissinger's book makes no bones about the Nixon administration's 'tilt' towards Pakistan (p. 910); it also confirms that Kissinger expected China to send India some kind of an ultimatum and was therefore surprised when Huang Hua, the Chinese Foreign Minister, at a secret meeting in New York, stated that China would like the Bangladesh war ended on the lines of a resolution then being discussed by the UN Security Council.

Could not possibly 'shake hands with a clenched fist'. Quoted in Masani, *op. cit.*, p. 242.

'If that woman thinks . . .' Quoted in Masani, *ibid.*, p. 242.

K. A. Abbas, *That Woman* (Kitab Mahal, Bombay, 1972).

'. . . sitting on top of a volcano . . .' Indira's speech at the India League in London, reported in *India Weekly*, London, November 6th, 1971.

. . . 'clinch' the issue . . .' J.P. quoted in *The Times of India*, November 1st, 1971.

Yahya's 'unlucky strike', see Author's article, 'Look Back With Pride', in *The Times of India*, December 27th, 1971; also Air Chief Marshal P. C. Lal, *My Life with the IAF* (Lancer, New Delhi, 1986).

It was Air Chief Marshal Lal who first told Author that had Pakistan not started the war on December 3rd, India would have been compelled to do so the next evening. Later this was confirmed by Field-Marshal Manekshaw.

Indira utterly relaxed and busy . . . choosing a bedspread . . . Dr K. P. Mathur to Author.

American attempt to 'browbeat' India. Expression used by S. K. Singh, Official Spokesman of the Indian Foreign Office at that time, now Foreign Secretary in New Delhi, at a press briefing on December 12th, 1971. Singh also called the American action a form of 'psychological warfare'.

Scene in Indira's office at the time of Pakistani surrender in Dacca. H. Y. Sharada Prasad to Author.

'I must order a cease-fire on the western front . . . not be able to do so tomorrow.' *Ibid.*

'Proper lesson' to Pakistan. Indira Gandhi to Tariq Ali, *op. cit.*, p. 175.

Indira calling General Manekshaw privately and then holding a meeting of the cabinet's Political Affairs Committee. Manekshaw to Author; later Haksar confirmed this to Author.

Cabinet committee's proceedings. Described to Author by Manekshaw and later confirmed by Haksar. P. C. Lal's version to Author was roughly the same except that he did not know that Manekshaw had had a prior private talk with the Prime Minister.

'I am not a person to be pressured – by anybody or any nations.' Indira to *Time* news magazine, quoted in Masani, *op. cit.*, p. 248.

## 9 Down the Hill, Dismally

Bhutto's disparaging remarks about Indira. To Oriana Fallaci, reproduced in *The Statesman Weekly*, June 10th, 1972.

'Really her father's daughter . . .' Quoted in Abbas, *op. cit.*, p. 214.

Unwritten informal understanding at Simla. Account is based on interviews with Indira, principal Indian negotiators, Bhutto and some Pakistani officials and journalists. The substance of a 75-minute talk with Bhutto in Rawalpindi on December 21st, 1973, was contained in Author's articles, 'Journey Through Pakistan', *The Times of India*, January 10th, 1974, and 'Pakistan's One-Man Democracy', *Illustrated Weekly of India*, February 1st, 1974.

Indira's party accused of collecting 'tons of black money' and her supporters' rejoinder that this was 'character assassination' by 'vested interests'. See C. S. Pandit, *op. cit.*, p. 111.

'Forces of reaction . . .', 'big money . . .', 'Character assassination'. Rajinder Puri, *Crisis of Conscience* (New Delhi, 1973), pp. 131–2.

Indira's supporters 'denied' funds by the Syndicate during the 1967 General Election. Indira's letter to P. N. Haksar, then in London, in April 1967. Haksar to Author.

'. . . suitcases full of currency notes . . .' '. . . she did not return even the suitcase'. S. K. Patil, quoted in Nayar, *Critical Years*, *op. cit.*, p. 3.

'Nearly half the currency in circulation' . . . Generally accepted estimate though the report of the K. N. Wanchoo Committee on Black Money (Government of India, 1970) placed the estimate a little lower.

Nagarwala allegedly acting at the behest of the CIA. The *Hindustan Times*, November 11th and 12th, 1986.

'. . . Even her father had never been able to do . . .' etc. H. Y. Sharada Prasad to Author. Also confirmed by Abdul Ghafoor.

Party elections cancelled because of egregious malpractices and manipulation. See Frankel, *Political Economy*, *op. cit.*, pp. 482–3.

Heightening conflict within Indira's radical supporters. For a description of this struggle, see *ibid.*, pp. 404–14.

The Kumaramangalam thesis was only vaguely talked of until, in 1972, it was published in full, along with a long introduction, by Satindra Singh, an enterprising journalist and himself a former Communist, under the title *Communists in Congress, Kumaramangalam's Thesis*. Singh wrote, in the introduction, that he hoped the 'exposure' of the thesis would 'help Mrs Gandhi see the light before it is too late for her as well as for democracy'.

Indira accepted Dikshit's advice and rejected D. P. Mishra's. Both Dikshit and Mishra to Author.

Maruti car project of Sanjay and dubious help given to it by Lalit Mishra, Bansi Lal, Indira's government and businessmen anxious to curry favour with him and his mother. See Moraes, *op. cit.*, pp. 195–7; also Sahgal, *op. cit.*, pp. 216–25.

Of all the commissions of inquiry appointed by the Janata government against Indira and Sanjay, only one, the Gupta Commission on Maruti, produced findings adverse to mother and son. The report painstakingly detailed the undue favours shown to Sanjay and his project by his mother's government, resulting in 'a decline in the integrity of public life' whereby the 'purity of administration had been sullied'. (The *Report of the Gupta Commission on Maruti*, Government of India, 1979.)

However, Indira could treat this document with disdain because it was published in September 1979, less than four months before her return to power.

Poverty could not be banished 'overnight'. Quoted in Mary Carras, *Indira Gandhi, In the Crucible of Leadership* (Beacon Press, Boston, 1978), p. 153.

The Supreme Court's judgment 'an attack on Parliament and the Prime Minister', etc. . . . 'Necessary brake' on the executive's 'capriciousness' and other heated exchanges, see Kuldip Nayar, *Supersession of Judges* (Delhi, 1974), pp. 28–9, 36–7.

Criticism answered by Kumaramangalam rather than Law Minister, H. R. Gokhale. See Frankel, *Political Economy*, *op. cit.*, p. 488.

'Clown Prince of India'. Martin Woollacott in *The Guardian*, March 21st, 1977.

For a detailed discussion of Indira's economic policy changes, under pressure from the IMF and the World Bank, and their political consequences, see Mary Carras, *op. cit.*, pp. 168–70; also Jeremiah Novak's two articles, *The Times of India*, July 1st and 5th, 1977.

. . . 'struck by the courage . . .' to '. . . must be done'. Manmohan Singh, then Economic Affairs Secretary in the Finance Ministry, now Member-Secretary of the Geneva-based South Commission, to Author.

'Equality of sacrifices'. Mary Carras, *op. cit.*, p. 171.

'Nav Nirman' agitation turned the challenge to the legitimacy of Indira's power into one to the 'legitimacy of the entire system she presided over'. Rodney and Dawn Jones, 'Urban Upheaval in India: The 1974 Nav Nirman Riots in Gujarat', *Asian Survey*, November 1976.

'Powerful conspiracy . . .' to '. . . cause a political setback to Mrs Gandhi'. Frankel, *Political Economy*, *op. cit.*, p. 527.

Total collapse of belief in each other's good faith. 'Each side became convinced that the other would no longer abide . . .' *Ibid.*

For J.P.'s life and work, see Ajit Bhattacharjea, *Jayaprakash Narayan: A Political Biography* (Vikas, Delhi, 1975).

For J.P.'s naive endorsement of Field-Marshal Ayub's 'basic democracy', see Tariq Ali, *op. cit.*, p. 183.

For letters exchanged between J.P. and Indira on judicial supersessions, see Kuldip Nayar, *Supersession of Judges, op. cit.*, pp. 169–74.

Indira: J.P. a 'frustrated man' . . . '(on) Morarji Desai's bandwagon'. *Correspondence with Dorothy Norman, op. cit.*, p. 138.

A 'vast armed camp' . . . 'a lakh of rupees . . . a day'. Quoted in Frankel, *Political Economy, op. cit.*, p. 534.

'Well-laid conspiracy'. *Ibid.*

Campaign to crush the railway strike 'personally conducted by Indira . . .' Tariq Ali, *op. cit.*, p. 181.

Anti-Smuggler crack-down. Walter Schwarz and Inder Malhotra, *The Guardian*, September 18th, 1974.

'Pakistan's protector and armourer'. See Author's cover story, 'Guns and Gold for Bhutto', *Illustrated Weekly of India*, March 2nd, 1973.

Joy and gloating over the Peaceful Nuclear Experiment (PNE). Author's despatch in *The Guardian*, May 20th, 1974.

Desai's refusal to undo 'annexation of Sikkim'. His first press conference as Prime Minister, March 23rd, 1977. Text available from the Press Information Bureau, New Delhi.

J.P.'s movement into crusade against 'widespread corruption' etc. See *Bihar Shows the Way* (a publication of *The Statesman*, 1975), p. 11.

Chinks in J.P.'s own shining armour. Most accounts of J.P.'s movement, in keeping with the temper of that time, are highly sympathetic to him. A thoughtfully critical one is by Mary Carras, *op. cit.*, pp. 175–7 and 180–4.

'What kind of revolution can it be . . .' to '. . . for anarchy'. Sham Lal, *The Times of India*, May 20th, 1975.

Account of the Indira–J.P. meeting. R. K. Karanjia, *Indira–J.P. Confrontation*, based on interviews with both the Prime Minister and J.P. (Bombay, 1975), pp. 38–71.

J.P. hands Indira her mother's letters to his wife, Prabha Devi, who had died a year earlier. L. C. Jain, a close associate of J.P. to Author in 1986. Confirmed by H. Y. Sharada Prasad.

For circumstances of Mishra's murder and his family's complaints about lax security and delayed medical aid, see Sahgal, *op. cit.*, pp. 128–9.

'When I am murdered . . .' Quoted in *The Statesman*, January 8th, 1975.

Dharia's removal from the council of ministers boosted his popularity 'even among Congressmen'. Moraes, *op. cit.*, p. 216.

'Rape of Democracy'. Quoted in Frankel, *Political Economy, op. cit.*, p. 538.

'See you in Mexico . . .' to '. . . that judgment yet to come'. Pupul Jayakar to Author.

For operative parts of the Allahabad judgment, see *The Times of India*, June 13th, 1975.

## 10 Emergency: The Cardinal Sin

'. . . As though a head of government should go to the block for a parking ticket'. James Cameron in *The Guardian*, June 16th, 1975.

'. . . Incompatible with the survival of democracy'. Quoted in the *Indian Express*, June 18th, 1975.

For past practice in such cases, see Author's article, 'Indira Gandhi, What Next?', *Illustrated Weekly*, June 24th, 1975. My advice to the Prime Minister was temporarily to step down and return to office only after exoneration.

Indira's justification for staying on in office despite the Allahabad judgment. Moraes, *op. cit.*, p. 220. 'It was my duty to stay though I didn't want to,' she said, among other things.

Jagjivan Ram's objection to Swaran Singh as temporary Prime Minister. For this and other events preceding the declaration of a State of Emergency, see Kuldip Nayar, *Judgement* (Vikas, 1977), Uma Vasudev, *Two Faces of Indira Gandhi* (Vikas, 1977), C. S. Pandit, *op. cit.*, and the Shah Commission's Reports Interim I, Interim II and Final, published by the Government of India in March, April and August 1978, respectively.

Sanjay's decisive role in putting an end to the 'nonsensical' talk about his mother's withdrawal from office. Quoted in Frankel, *op. cit.*, p. 543.

Palkhivala's book, *The Constitution Defaced and Defiled* (Macmillan, 1975).

The text of Justice Krishna Iyer (*The Times of India*, June 25th, 1975) gives the full flavour of his style.

For J.P.'s exhortations, see notes regarding page 166–7 above.

Desai's vision of coming struggle. Interview to Oriana Fallaci, *The New Republic*, July 1975.

For Indira's political psycho-analysis and its conclusions, see Mary Carras, *op. cit.*, especially chapters II and III.

Desai's commitment to 'restoring democratic decencies and norms'. Statement at his first press conference after being released from captivity, Bombay, January 21st, 1977.

Crude police methods won't do. Swaran Singh's remark was first mentioned to Author by one of his friends soon after he was dropped from the cabinet. Later confirmed by him.

Chavan–Haksar conversation about the Emergency. Haksar to Author. When I brought up this subject with Chavan shortly before his death in 1985, he neither denied nor confirmed what I had been told. 'Why rake up such things?' was all he said.

L. K. Advani: On the behaviour of the press during the Emergency. Statement to a press conference, New Delhi, March 25th, 1977.

Indira: Intellectuals 'dupes of foreign elements and ideas hostile to us'. To Author repeatedly in 1979, 1980, 1981 and 1983. In June 1980, shortly before Sanjay's death, she said so to six Delhi editors, including the Author.

Typical of Indira's attitude was an incident in latter half of 1983. One of her advisers, Arjun Sen Gupta, rushed to her to say that he was hearing alarming reports of an impending Indian military intervention in Sri Lanka. If so, he pleaded, it must be stopped, or else international opinion would be outraged. Indira gave him her characteristically cool look and remarked that no intervention was in the offing. But if it became necessary, she would not be deterred by 'whining' intellectuals like him. (The incident, narrated to Author by another Indira aide, was confirmed by Dr Sen Gupta.)

Indira's claim that the Emergency was temporary and would be ended as soon as the 'derailed democracy' was 'put back on the track' was almost completely disbelieved in India. But Michael Foot, then a senior cabinet minister, after one talk with her in Delhi, was convinced that she was sincere.

Foot later told Author that the British Foreign Office had advised him not to raise with Indira either the question of elections in India or the subject of the arrest and maltreatment of George Fernandes, Foot's comrade in the Socialist International. To his surprise, said Foot, Indira herself brought up both the subjects.

Dorothy imploring Indira to rescind the Emergency. See *Correspondence with Dorothy Norman, op. cit.*, p. 48.

Twenty-Point Programme. For the text of this programme, see J. S. Bright, *Emergency in India and the 5 plus 20 Point Programme* (New Delhi, 1976). The additional five points Bright, an enthusiastic supporter of Indira and the Emergency, included in the title of his book were the ones announced by Sanjay.

For a discussion of the number of arrests during the Emergency, see *The Times of India*, July 8th, 1977.

'Dropouts, drifters and roughnecks' surrounding Sanjay. See Sahgal, *op cit.*, p. 226. She quotes Girilal Jain and Kuldip Nayar on this point at some length.

Text of J.P.'s brother's letter to Indira. Quoted in Sahgal, *op. cit.*, p. 169.

'Something had been done to J.P. in prison'. *Ibid.*, p. 168; also see Dom Moraes, *op. cit.*, p. 245.

Because of Rajan's mysterious disappearance the Home Minister in the Kerala government had to resign. Some police officers were sentenced to life imprisonment for murder but were acquitted of the charge on appeal.

For a detailed and shocking account of the inhuman treatment of George Fernandes's brother, Lawrence, and friend, Snehlata Reddy, see Moraes, *op. cit.*, pp. 246–8.

Sanjay's excesses, Turkman Gate, reaction by Sheikh Abdullah and President Ahmed etc., *ibid.*, pp. 231–7.

Speculation about the secret of Sanjay's extraordinary hold on his mother. Ian Jack, *The Sunday Times*, June 20th, 1977.

For the apology to Indira, in a libel case, by Salman Rushdie and his publishers, see *The Guardian*, August 1st, 1984.

K. D. Malaviya's version. To the Author in 1978 and 1980. Malaviya said that, in his presence once during her three years in the wilderness, Indira held Sanjay's hands and said, 'These are the hands which saved me'.

'Stray incidents of no great consequence'. To Sheikh Abdullah who repeated the remark to Author; also see Carras, *op. cit.*, p. 252.

## 11   The Matriarch At Home

'. . . Always bathed and fed' her children to 'bedside stories'. Indira Gandhi, in an article, 'On Being a Mother', published in 1957.

Anu Kunte, Professor of French literature at the Jawaharlal Nehru University, New Delhi, and Indira's interpreter in her conversations with French leaders, told Author that, visiting Indira one evening in 1984, she told the Prime Minister that she was taking her children to the club for dinner because her cook was on leave. 'No, Anu,' Indira had reacted, 'never do that.' She had gone to add: 'When my cook is not there, I cook for the children myself.'

Wanted all 'friends of my husband' to be present at Rajiv's wedding. Message to Author through Harsukh Pandit.

The only regret was that by the time she got home the children were 'asleep'. Novelist R. K. Narayan, *in Indira Gandhi Remembered, op. cit.*, p. 310.

Motilal saw the country 'through Jawaharlal'. Mahatma Gandhi quoted in B. R. Nanda, *The Nehrus* (Allen and Unwin, 1962), p. 43.

*Chamchas* or spoons as a synonym for sycophants. The most plausible explanation for this is that the first toadies of the British Raj were the wealthy Indians who stopped eating with their fingers and imitated the British rulers by using spoons and forks.

'Fish-bowl existence' ruling out 'liaisons' on the quiet. Pupul Jayakar to Author. Also quoted by Moraes, *op. cit.*, p. 96. This view is strongly endorsed by Vimla Sindhi and several others who did not wish to be quoted by name.

Feroze's role in unearthing M. O. Mathai's malfeasance. Author's personal knowledge.

Mathai's statements, insinuations and innuendoes about the 'escapades' of Indira in 'Dwarka suite' and elsewhere, including an alleged love affair with him. M. O. Mathai, *My Days With Nehru, Volume II* (Vikas, 1977), pp. iv, v and vi, p. 173, p. 205.

Withheld chapter 'She', *ibid.*

'Diary of a *Namark Haram*' Khushwant Singh, *Illustrated Weekly*, December 18th, 1977.

'Double-distilled combination . . .' *The Times of India*, December 25th, 1977.

Was the first to put into print what 'many had been saying for years that . . . Dinesh Singh'. Mathai, *op. cit.*, p. 202.

Printed in facsimile. *Ibid.*, between pp. 203–4.

'Now greying . . .' to '. . . she had a rival'. *The Observer*, March 25th, 1984.

For Dhirendra Brahmachari, including his reputation, see *Illustrated Weekly*, cover story 'Rasputin', June 8th, 1986.

In the Fifties Indira asked Lal Bahadur Shastri to help Brahmachari set up his *ashram*. See K. K. Birla, *Reminiscences of Indira Gandhi* (Vikas, Delhi, 1987), p. 8.

'. . . exceedingly good-looking Yogi . . .' to '. . . so full of superstition.' *Correspondence with Dorothy Norman, op. cit.*, p. 48.

Customs accepting Brahmachari's word uncritically, etc. Malik, *The Times of India*, June 27th, 1980.

D. P. Mishra finding it 'impossible' to talk to Indira alone because of constant intrusion by Sanjay and Brahmachari. Mishra to Author in 1977. Later he was to tell me that on one occasion he spoke to Indira in some detail about what was being said about Brahmachari's proximity to her. According to him, she listened politely, but 'did not say a word'.

Abrupt stoppage of Brahmachari's TV programme reportedly at Rajiv's instance and denial of access to first Indira and then Rajiv. See *Illustrated Weekly*, *op. cit.*

Brahmachari at Indira's funeral. Seen by millions during the funeral's live coverage by TV.

'another human being . . .' Dorothy Norman, *Letters to a Friend*, *op. cit.*

Nehru's long and satisfying relationship with Edwina Mountbatten. Apart from Mathai, *op. cit.*, see Chapter 4, and Notes above.

'I am a person with a job to do.' Indira's statement at her first press conference after being elected leader of the Congress Parliamentary Party, January 19th, 1966.

'. . . Whether it is sex, religion or caste'. Indira's interview with Lord Chalfont, *op. cit.*

Indians' dismay at the country's destiny being entrusted to a woman. Khushwant Singh, 'Indira Gandhi', *Illustrated Weekly*, March 17th, 1971.

'. . . not right' to 'shake hands' with foreign men, etc. *The Times of India*, Delhi Diary, December 26th, 1983.

Indira did not like being called Madam Prime Minister. Lukas, *The New York Times Magazine*, March 27th, 1966.

'. . . Some of my cabinet ministers call me "Sir". He can do so, too, if he likes.' B. K. Nehru to Author.

Sad 'fate of Sultana Raziya'. *Economic and Political Weekly*, August 20th, 1966.

'*Zoon politikon*'. Helmut Schmidt, in *Indira Gandhi Remembered*, *op. cit.*, p. 383.


## 12   The Empress Overthrown

A cautiously worded despatch to *The Guardian*. The censors in those days were more tolerant of what appeared in the foreign papers than in the Indian press.

'Her place in history' . . . Girilal Jain, *The Times of India*, May 11th, 1981, after Indira had got the 1978 resolution unseating and imprisoning her rescinded by the new House on May 7th, 1981. The resolution was passed unanimously after most opposition members had walked out.

Patil: Indira's sudden decision to hold a General Election a 'trap'. To Desai and other opposition leaders at first and publicly on January 21st, 1977 at Desai's press conference in Bombay in Author's presence.

'*Mein kya karoon?* What should I do?' Fory Nehru to Author.

For Pupul Jayakar's account of Indira's conversation with the savant, see Pupul Jayakar, *J. Krishnamurthi, A Biography* (Penguin India, 1987), pp. 347–8.

Jagjivan Ram's resignation from the cabinet and Indira's party. *The Indian Express*, February 3rd, 1977.

Contents of Sanjay's interview to the proscribed issue of *Surge*. Uma Vasudev to Author.

Sanjay's anti-Communism welcome to big business. See Sahgal, *op. cit.*, p. 164. 'Close and cordial relations' between Sanjay and Delhi-based American diplomats. Author's personal knowledge. Also see *New Age*, official journal of the CPI, March 31st, 1977. Also *New Wave* and several other leftist journals in the immediate post-Emergency period.

For various vignettes and details of the election campaign, see despatches by Author, *The Times of India*, February 18th to March 18th, 1977; also Myron Weiner, *India at the Polls, 1977* (Princeton), and Kuldip Nayar, *Judgement, op. cit.*, pp. 168–75.

Unsuccessful attempt to get the counting of votes in Indira's constituency suspended. Nayar, *ibid.*, p. 57.

Crowds dancing with joy at Indira's defeat at the polls, see Author's articles, 'The Nation's Verdict', *Illustrated Weekly*, March 27th, 1977 and 'Exit Indira, Enter Morarji', *Surge*, April, 1977.

Scene at Indira's official residence. Pupul Jayakar to Author.

Rumours of attempted coup to thwart the people's verdict. Ram Pershad, a leading hotelier and man of influence whom Jagjivan Ram asked to investigate the matter because of his close contacts with Ashwini Kumar, then Chief of the Border Security Force, to Author. Later confirmed by Jagjivan Ram.

Choice of Desai as Janata Prime Minister. *The Times of India*, March 23rd, 1977.

'Consigning Indira to the dustbin of history'. *Ibid.*, March 24th, 1977.

For the *Kissa Kursi Ka* case, see Chapter 14. Also Sahgal, *op. cit.*, pp. 201–2.

'. . . tons of weight have been lifted from my shoulders'. Quoted by Khushwant Singh, *Illustrated Weekly*, April 4th, 1977.

'Exemplary punishment . . . without delay'. See Sahgal, *op. cit.*, *The Indian Express*, April 2nd, 1977 and June 5th, 1977.

'Betrayed' by friends and hemmed in by enemies 'determined' to 'destroy' her. Pupul Jayakar, Vasant Sathe and Khushwant Singh to Author. Indira had made these remarks to them and many others.

Under surveillance by intelligence agencies. Author's own experience while visiting 12, Willington Crescent, Indira's residence during the years she was out of power. K. Natwar-Singh, now Minister of State for Foreign Affairs and then High Commissioner to Zambia, said to Author that when he told some colleagues that he was going to Indira to 'pay his respects,' they were flabbergasted. They told him that his name and car number would be noted by the Intelligence Bureau and he would be in 'serious trouble'.

## 13   Return of Mother Indira

'A revolution by the ballot box'. Press Trust of India's despatch, March 21st, 1977. Also see Lawrence Veit, *India's Second Revolution* (New York, 1977).

'Prosecution of Indira turned into persecution.' Girilal Jain, in *The Times of India*, December 17th, 1978.

The Janata government lax and lenient in investigating charges against Indira. See Arun Shourie, *The Indian Express*, January 22nd, 1979. Shourie alleged, for instance, that Indira's hoard of 'ill-gotten wealth' was buried in her farm house in Mehrauli, on the outskirts of Delhi; only unconscionable delay and worse on the part of the investigating agencies enabled her to carry it away before the search of the farm house could start.

For the details of Indira's constitutional changes undone by the Janata, see Sahgal, *op. cit.*, pp. 195–6.

'. . . light musical accompaniment . . . sombre theme of prime ministerial power.' *Ibid.*, p. 156.

For suicides of T. S. Anand and Kishan Chand, see Khushwant Singh, *Indira Gandhi Returns* (New Delhi, 1979), p. 152.

Indira: When would people bring her back? 'After I am dead.' Aruna Asaf Ali, in *Indira Gandhi Remembered*, *op. cit.*, p. 46.

Campaign of 'hatred and harassment'. Author's article, *The Times of India*, December 17th, 1978. The article pointed out that, left to himself, Morarji Desai would not have persecuted Indira but he had succumbed to pressure by the 'Janata hawks'.

Charan Singh's charge that Indira had 'planned' to kill imprisoned opposition leaders during the Emergency. *The Times of India*, May 24th, 1977.

Indira's rejoinder, call for ending the 'smear campaign' and taunt to the Janata to attend to the people's problems. Quoted at length in Tariq Ali, *op. cit.*, pp. 204–5.

For demoralisation and discontent in Indian police, see *The Guardian*, April 17th, 1978.

Indira's elephant-ride to Belchi. Her companion, Prathiba Singh on Indian TV after Indira's return to power.

Contradictory despatches on Indira's visit to her constituency by Simon Winchester and correspondents of most Indian papers quoted in Moraes, *op. cit.*, p. 277.

Charan Singh advocating 'stringent action' against Indira. See his letter to Morarji Desai, *The Times of India*, June 12th, 1978; also Tariq Ali, *op. cit.*, p. 203.

'I already feel imprisoned.' Moraes, *op. cit.*, p. 281.

American girl refusing to leave until Indira accepted her ring as a gift. H. Y. Sharada Prasad to Author.

'No, . . . those for whom something was done are nowhere to be seen.' Tariq Ali, *op. cit.*, p. 202.

Commenting on Sanjay's position as his mother's 'main protector', Sahgal (*op. cit.*, p. 194) calls it a 'curious reversal of roles'.

For Indira's feeling that her former senior colleagues had 'betrayed' her, see Moraes, *op. cit.*, p. 249. 'I don't think I want to say anything about them, because I don't know *what* I might say'. (Emphasis in original.) In 1979 she said to me, in reply to my question, that nothing done to her by her former colleagues and subordinates came to her as a surprise except that she had 'never thought that Morarjibhai (Desai) would turn out to be so incompetent'.

Swaran Singh left with 'party files while the ranks had gone over' to Indira. Swaran Singh to Dr V. P. Dutt who repeated the remark to Author.

Failure of unity talks because Indira wanted a party 'completely under her control'. Syed Mir Qasim, her negotiator, to Author.

For the Shah Commission's main findings against Indira see Interim Report, Part II, *op. cit.*, p. 24.

J.P. felt 'neglected by Desai'. Chandra Shekhar and several other associates of J.P. to Author.

Shah Commission in no position to 'hold anyone guilty of anything'. Part II of Commission's Interim report, *op. cit.*, p. 26. On an earlier page, the Commission did recommend to the government to 'ensure that the administrative set-up is not subverted in future in the manner it was done . . .'

A 'collection of impotent men'. *The Times of India*, June 6th, 1978.

For details of the Chikmagalur by-election campaign, see Moraes, *op. cit.*, pp. 304–11 and 314–17.

The only official to meet Indira at Moscow airport was Y. Pegov, Deputy Foreign Minister and former Ambassador to India.

For the Janata government's efforts to dissuade foreign statesmen and heads of government from showing any consideration to Indira, see James Callaghan, in *Indira Gandhi Remembered, op. cit.*, p. 96. After recounting these, Callaghan adds: 'Later, I had the honour [to tell the Indian Parliament] that the ultimate mark of a true democracy is the willingness of a government defeated at the ballot box to surrender power peacefully to its opponents.'

'. . . I have only two alternatives . . .' Pupul Jayakar in J. Krishnamurthi, *op. cit.*, p. 353.

For the Charan Singh-led campaign to charge Desai's son with 'dubious business deals', see Arun Gandhi, *The Morarji Papers* (Bombay, 1987), pp. 215–20.

Abusive exchange between Charan Singh and Bahuguna. First quoted in *The Indian Express*, July 13th, 1979. Later confirmed in Arun Gandhi, *The Morarji Papers, op. cit.*, pp. 106–9.

The highest price rise during the four months preceding the poll. Sahgal, *op. cit.*, p. 209.

'It's Indira All the Way'. *The Times of India*, January 7th, 1980.

## 14   Triumph Into Tragedy

Sanjay seen as having won his spurs. Even newspapers previously critical of him praised him this time, though with some reservations. In one such article, *The Times of India*, June 9th, 1980, just a fortnight before his death,

Sanjay's influence on the Indian youth was compared to that of Mahatma Gandhi in his time.

'If Sanjay tells me to do so, I will even put my head in an oilseed crusher' . . . see Sahgal, *op. cit.*, p. 226.

For the kind of faithfuls Sanjay had collected around him, see Romesh Thapar, *Economic and Political Weekly*, January 12th, 1980; Girilal Jain, *The Times of India*, May 7th, 1980; and Tariq Ali, *op. cit.*, p. 209.

For the abortive move to make Sanjay UP chief minister, see *The Times of India*, June 12th, 1980.

'Wheel of political fortune' turning full circle a second time in Punjab. Some authors and commentators, such as Robin Jeffrey, *What's Happening to India?* (Macmillan, 1986), have assumed that Indira went out of her way to sack the Akali ministry in Punjab and thus invited the wrath of Sikhs. As noted, Punjab was one of the nine states where provincial governments were dismissed in retaliation for what the Janata had done in 1977.

Refusing to be sworn in until the day considered auspicious by her astrologers. One of these astrologers, as Indira said to the Author, was her cabinet colleague, Kamalapati Tripathi.

For Indira's addiction to astrology and superstitious behaviour, see Sahgal, *op. cit.*, pp. 227–8.

Carrington 'much impressed' by what Indira had to say about Afghanistan. Sir Donald Maitland, who was present during the talks, to Author.

Refusal to join the 'chorus' of condemnation of the Soviet Union. See Author's articles in *The Times of India*, May 22nd, 1980 and January 29th, 1981.

Indira's tough response to Andrei Gromyko: 'On this [the Afghan issue] I cannot help you.' Inder Gujral, then Ambassador to the Soviet Union and privy to the talks, to Author.

Indira's public demand for the withdrawal of the Soviet troops from Afghanistan on Soviet soil. Press conference in Moscow September 22nd, 1982. She was quoted in the Indian newspapers the next day but not in the Soviet press.

Pakistan's conversion from a 'pariah' to a 'frontline state' in the US scheme of things. See Tariq Ali, *op. cit.*, p. 210.

Short shrift given to civil servants after Indira's return to power. See Author's article, 'Ministers and Civil Servants', *The Times of India*, August 17th, 1980.

Disqualification of themselves by the special courts of Justices Jain and Joshi, see Sahgal, *op. cit.*, pp. 200–1.

Quashing of the convictions of Sanjay and Shukla after the new government lawyer had taken 'fifteen minutes' to dispose of the 6,500-page record. For this and a succinct summing up of the *Kissa Kursi Ka* case, see A. G. Noorani, *Economic and Political Weekly*, June 14th, 1980.

Nahata's volte-face. *The Times of India*, March 28th, 1980.

For Sanjay's death underscoring all that had 'gone wrong' and for Air Marshal Zaheer's letter as well as subsequent fate, see Arun Shourie, *Mrs Gandhi's Second Reign* (Vikas, 1983), p. 3.

'Straight-backed, dry-eyed . . .' H. C. Sarin, a distinguished civil servant and former defence secretary, then administering Assam, placed under President's rule. Incidentally, Indira's earlier decision to appoint Sarin as Governor of Bihar was vetoed by Sanjay who said, in a scribbled note to his mother: 'Does not listen to advice.' Sarin to Author. Confirmed by N. K. Seshan, one of Indira's aides.

Joke about the Israel Symphony Orchestra and Indian bureaucracy. J. J. Bhaba, in *Indira Gandhi Remembered, op. cit.*, p. 74.

'. . . One has to learn to live with grief.' Quoted by Jayakar in the text accompanying Raghu Rai's photographs of Indira, *Indira Gandhi* (Delhi, 1985), p. 22.

Indira's search for Sanjay's wristwatch and keys allegedly to get hold of his 'vast wealth' stashed abroad – see Sahgal, *op. cit.*, p. 229; also Tariq Ali, *op. cit.*, p. 214.

'Janata's vendetta against Indira . . .' parallel with other defeated prime ministers in the region. During her visit to London in 1978, Indira had publicly stated that her adversaries wanted to do to her not only what had happened to Mrs Bandaranaike (she was deprived of her civil rights for six years) but also what awaited Bhutto in Pakistan: execution.

Ibrahim's unprintable language against Indira included such expressions as 'international prostitute'. See Arun Shourie in *Sunday*, Calcutta, November 22nd, 1981. Shourie gave his article to the Calcutta weekly because his own paper, *The Indian Express*, wouldn't print it. S. Nihal Singh, then Editor-in-Chief of the paper, to Author.

Meeting with British intellectuals. See Ian Jack's article in *Sunday Times*, March 28th, 1982.


## 15   Dynasty Above All

Merciless beating up of a procession of blind people. *The Times of India*, March 17th, 1980.

Sickening Bhagalpur blindings. See *The Indian Express*, November 26th, 1980, and *Sunday*, December 2nd, 1980.

For Moradabad Hindu–Muslim riots, see *The Times of India*, August 18th, 1980.

The feeling that Indira was taking on a 'Hindu role', starting from the time of the Moradabad riots was to become steadily stronger. See Chapters 16 and 17.

For the 'four Ds' (*detection* of foreigners, their *disfranchisement*, their *deportation* to Bangladesh or their *dispersal* in the rest of India) demanded by the leaders of the Assam 'anti-foreigners' agitation and the grim progress and ramifications of it, see Tariq Ali, *op. cit.*, pp. 224–6; also *India Today*, New Delhi, April 15th, 1981.

'Economic blockade' to make Assamese students 'realise the folly . . .' See *Keesing's Contemporary Archives*, 1982. Vol. xxxvi, p. 3033.

'All Bengali families . . .' *Ibid.*

'Trying to create a law and order problem'. *Ibid.*

'Perpetuate the domination of high-caste Assamese over tribals . . .' to 'unauthorised occupants'. *Ibid.*

The tendency to assume more and more Draconian powers was accentuated by the Punjab crisis. See Chapters 16 and 17.

Nearly 23,000 arrested for striking against the National Security Ordinance. *The Indian Express*, January 20th, 1982.

Foreign instigation behind the trouble in Assam: Zail Singh's statement in Parliament and statement of Home Ministry officials quoted in *The Statesman*, May 6th and 8th, 1981.

For 'foreign hand' being the *leitmotiv* of Indira's pronouncements from 1980 to 1984, see Pran Chopra, 'Our "home-made" foreign hand' *Far Eastern Economic Review*, August 23rd, 1984; also 'Foreign Hand Strikes Again', *Sunday*, August 21st, 1984.

As one of them admitted . . . 'only super-bureaucrats'. To Author. The minister did not want to be identified by name.

Maneka considered Rajiv a 'usurper'. Tariq Ali, *op. cit.*, p. 215.

Khushwant Singh's praise of Maneka, comparing her to 'Durga on the tiger'. *Hindustan Times*, June 25th, 1980.

'. . . our enemy all along'. Indira to Author and many others.

Akbar Ahmed 'Dumpy': Humiliating expulsion from the Prime Minister's house where he used to have a free run earlier. 'Dumpy' to Khushwant Singh and Author.

Galbraith on dynastic rule. To Author; also see his interview to Nandini Mehta, *The Indian Express*, January 16th, 1986.

'Sanjay's goons and Rajiv's Doons'. Author's article in *The Times of India*, August 23rd, 1984.

Marie Seton on how deeply troubled Indira was by Maneka. *The Sunday Times*, November 4th, 1984.

Maneka's 'killer instinct'. Tariq Ali, *op. cit.*, p. 215.

The story of *Surya*'s sale to Indira's foes by Maneka has been told most gleefully by the new owners. *Surya*, August 1981.

For letters exchanged between Indira and Maneka and other details of Maneka's expulsion from the Prime Minister's house, see *The Guardian*, Ajoy Bose's despatch, March 31st, 1982.

Irate Maneka–Indira exchanges from . . . 'who drinks blood' to '. . . speedy retirement'. See *Daily Mail*, November 1st, 1984.

It is a measure of the Janata leaders' anger with Maneka that they confiscated her passport and launched a number of cases, including some for defamation, soon after her mother-in-law lost power. In early 1988, she was admitted to the Janata party and made one of its general secretaries.

## 16  Lengthening Shadows

Temporary expedient expected to last no more than fifteen years, being 'perpetuated'. In the euphoria of constitution-making for the Indian Republic, national leaders had convinced themselves that not only the problem of untouchables but many others would be over soon. Hence, 1965 was fixed as the deadline for ending reservations for Harijans and tribals, for the introduction of free and compulsory education and for the replacement of English by Hindi as the sole official language. There is little hope of any of these things happening even at the end of the first quarter of the twenty-first century.

For details of the Gujarat anti-Harijan riots, see Author's two articles, 'Gujarat's Caste War', May 7th and 8th, 1981; also *The Crooked Mirror*, a privately circulated report by the Editors' Guild of India on the bias against Harijans shown by most Gujarat newspapers during the agitation.

Reiteration of 'national policy on reservations'. Resolution by Lok Sabha, lower house of Parliament, May 10th, 1981.

Meenakshipuram conversions of Harijans to Islam and their repercussions, see *India Today*, March 15th, 1982.

For Indira's response to the demand for declaring India a 'Hindu state' and to her refutations that conversions to Islam were being 'encouraged by Arab money' from oil-rich countries, *ibid.*

For the 324 incidents in which the Naxalites (Indian Maoists) killed ninety-two people, see *The Statesman*, April 14th, 1982.

Chenna Reddy's belief during 1977–80 that Indira 'needed his support more than he needed hers'. To several journalists in Author's presence.

For Anjiah's brief career as Andhra chief minister and Rajiv's public tongue-lashing to him which was seen as an 'insult' to the whole of Andhra, see *The Times of India*, May 29th, 1982.

For the formation of Telugu Desam party by film star, N. T. Ramarao, better known as N.T.R., see S. Venkatanarayan, *N.T.R., A Biography* (New Delhi, 1983).

For Indira's awareness of the political clout of Indian film stars, preceding that of Ronald Reagan in America, see Tariq Ali, *op. cit.*, p. 231.

And yet she underestimated N.T.R., believing that he was no 'M.G.R.', the then chief minister of Tamil Nadu. To Mohit Sen, an Andhra-based Communist theoretician who used to see her frequently. Sen, who told Author in 1982 what Indira had said to him, indicated that he shared her assessment that Andhra would not go the Tamil Nadu way.

For the Antulay scandal, first exposed in *The Indian Express*, see Shourie, *Mrs Gandhi's Second Reign op. cit.*, pp. 107–53.

For Indira's decision that Antulay would stay because 'people wanted him', Rajiv's unhappiness with this stance and the damage caused by it see *The Times of India*, June 17th, 1982.

'To win and retain the loyalty of followers, a leader has to stand by them'. Indira to Arjun Sen Gupta. Dr Sen Gupta to Author.

Indira toyed with the idea of amending the law on corruption to save Antulay. Vasantdada Patil, then chief minister of Maharashtra, to Author.

For lurid details of the Kuo Oil scandal see Shourie, *Second Reign, op. cit.*, pp. 158–69.

'Quid Pro Kuo'. *India Today*, July 31st, 1982.

HDW submarine deal having 'Sanjay's blessing'. C. P. N. Singh, a Sanjay crony and then minister of state for defence to the cabinet Committee on

Political Affairs in July 1980 'with tears rolling down his cheeks'. Quoted in *India Today*, October 31st, 1981.

Indira: Corruption 'a global phenomenon'. See Author's two articles, *The Times of India*, December 20th and 27th, 1981.

From the birth of the Sikh religion to the present-day Sikh politics, the background has been extracted, apart from Author's own study, from the following extremely useful books: Khushwant Singh, *A History of the Sikhs*, Volumes I and II (OUP edition, New Delhi, 1977; original edition: Princeton, 1966). All quotations are from the Indian edition; Rajeev Kapur, *Sikh Separatism* (Allen & Unwin, 1987); M. J. Akbar, *India: The Siege Within* (Penguin Books, 1985); and Paul R. Brass, *Language, Religion and Politics in North India* (London, 1974).

Hereafter only the most essential quotations on the historical background will be given specific references.

In Sikhism 'spiritual and temporal, religion and politics are inseparable'. Quoted in Tully and Jacob, *op. cit.*, p. 20.

Martyrdom of Guru Arjun at the hands of the Moghuls and its consequences, *ibid.*, p. 19.

Guru Gobind Singh, the tenth and the last Guru, the welding by him of the Sikh army into a 'formidable fighting force' and the founding by him of a new order called the *Khalsa* or Pure, *ibid.*, p. 20.

Sikhs enjoined to 'preserve their identity at all costs', *The Siege Within*, *op. cit.*, p. 121. M. J. Akbar, *op. cit.*, p. 121.

Hindu belief that Sikhs are a 'part and parcel of the wider Hindu framework'. Tully and Jacob, *op. cit.*, p. 17.

The safety razor 'principal threat' to Sikh identity. M. J. Akbar, *The Siege Within*, *op. cit.*, p. 145.

Even the British . . . found it 'prudent not to tangle' with Ranjit Singh. Tully and Jacob, *op. cit.*, p. 23.

Ranjit Singh essentially a secular ruler. *Ibid.*, p. 25.

Sikhs' desire to 'get even' with the *purbiyas* 'whom they despised and whose presence in Punjab they resented'. Philip Mason, *A Matter of Honour: An Account of the Indian Army, its Officers and Men* (Jonathan Cape, London, 1974), p. 236.

To ensure Sikh soldiery's total loyalty to the Crown, it became British policy to encourage Sikhs to 'regard themselves as a totally distinct and separate nation'. Top Secret note by Intelligence Chief, Petrie (1911) quoted in Tariq Ali, *op. cit.*, pp. 238–9.

'Surrendered the leadership'. Tully and Jacob, *op. cit.*, p. 218.

Sikh agitation to free their shrines from 'corrupt and degenerate priests'. *Ibid.*, p. 31.

The Gurudwara Act, 1925, 'institutionalised Sikh separatism' . . . symbiotic relationship between the SGPC and the Akali Party. Rajeev Kapur, *op. cit.*, p. xv.

In the Twenties Akali leaders regarded the Congress as a 'Hindu organisation' and reverted to a policy of collaboration with the Raj. Tully and Jacob, *op. cit.*, p. 33.

Akali tactic of camouflaging their demand for a Sikh-dominated state as a 'linguistic' province and Nehru's total refusal to concede. M. J. Akbar, *The Siege Within, op. cit.*, pp. 158–9.

Nehru's 'second thoughts on linguistic states'. His speech at the Hyderabad session of the Indian National Congress, in Author's presence, quoted in *The Statesman*, December 6th, 1953.

Sympathy with Akalis when the States Reorganisation Commission rejected their demand for a Punjabi *suba*.

Author said in an article that to deny Punjabi *suba* while conceding linguistic states elsewhere did smack of 'discrimination', *The Statesman*, January 30th, 1964. Khushwant Singh wrote him a letter saying just one word, '*Shabash* (Bravo)'. Some years later Khushwant was to write in his *History of the Sikhs* that the Punjabi *suba* demand was in fact for an 'independent Sikh state'. The talk of a province was only 'sugar-coating'. Khushwant Singh, *op. cit.*, p. 245 volume II.

'I envy you, Ajoy' ... to 'Punjabi-speaking state'. Ajoy Ghosh to distinguished journalist Nikhil Chakravartty and Chakravartty to Author.

'A handsome baby has been born in my household.' Fateh Singh quoted in Tully and Jacob, *op. cit.*, p. 43.

Zail Singh, as Congress chief minister of Punjab, 'steals' Akalis' clothes by 'ostentatiously pandering' to the Sikh religious sentiment. M. J. Akbar, *The Siege Within, op. cit.*, p. 189.

For an analysis of the Anandpur Sahib resolution and the Sikh disregard of it until the early Eighties, see *ibid.*, p. 178–80.

Bhindranwale initially brought into politics by Sanjay and Zail Singh, see Tully and Jacob, *op. cit.*, pp. 57–8. The two authors also cite evidence to show that Zail Singh helped the formation of the Dal Khalsa, later to become a militant advocate of the cause of 'Khalistan', an independent Sikh state.

'Protecting him still'. Darbara Singh, chief minister of Punjab at the time, to Author.

For a description of Bhindranwale's functioning from the Golden Temple, see M. J. Akbar, *The Siege Within, op. cit.*, pp. 199–200; also Tavleen Singh quoted in Tully and Jacob, *op. cit.*, pp. 98–100.

Charges against Indira that she was promoting the Punjab crisis or allowing it to worsen in order to 'exploit' it for her own purposes: to justify her 'absolute power', unify the 'Hindu vote' behind herself and so on. See Pran Chopra, *The Telegraph*, Calcutta, 'Mrs Gandhi in a Hindu Role', June 20th, 1983; Rajni Kothari and G. Deshingkar, 'Punjab: The Longer View' in Abida Samiuddin ed., *The Punjab Crisis: Challenge and Response* (Delhi, 1985) and Dipankar Gupta, 'The Communalising of Punjab', *Economic and Political Weekly*, July 13th, 1985.

At the same time blamed by Hindus for 'not dealing with Akali agitators and terrorists forcefully enough'. *India Today*, May 15th, 1984.

The CPI, wanting to 'wash the filth of the Emergency from its hands', attacks Indira. Tariq Ali, *op. cit.*, p. 217.

Indira calls Communists 'opportunists' and complains about their behaviour to Tariq Ali, *ibid.*, p. 218.

For Indira's letter to Yuri Andropov, see Author's article 'Mrs Gandhi, CPI and Moscow', *The Times of India*, September 29th, 1983.

Dismay over Indira's failure to accept the 'legitimate' Akali demands so that the illegitimate ones could then be rejected and terrorists and secessionists 'isolated' (ignoring that Bhindranwale, the arch-extremist, was in command) was the leitmotiv of the bulk of comment then on Punjab and Sikhs. This is duly reflected in Khushwant Singh and Kuldip Nayar, *Tragedy of Punjab* (Delhi, 1984).

. . . Huge quantities of unutilised Indian water continued to flow into Pakistan because 'the Indian government could not complete the . . . irrigation schemes'. Tully and Jacob, *op. cit.*, p. 50.

'Like quails and partridges'. Phrase used to Author by a member of the Prime Minister's 'think tank' who did not wish to be identified by name.

'Great day for India and Indian science', to 'unwarranted inferences'. Indira's statement in Lok Sabha, July 18th, 1980.

For the details of US military supplies to Pakistan and for Indian acquisitions during 1980–4, see Col. R. G. Sawkney, *Zia's Pakistan* (New Delhi, 1985), pp. 34–7.

Spending 'too much on defence'. See G. Deshingkar, 'Is India Overarmed?', *Illustrated Weekly*, January 22nd, 1984.

Allegations of payoffs on defence deals 'inspiration for which came from Sanjay . . .' See notes concerning page 250 above.

'Unfair and discriminatory'. Repeated pronouncements by Indian government summed up in K. Subrahmanyam, *India's Nuclear Predicament* (Institute of Defence Studies and Analyses, New Delhi, 1984).

For the first time, the transfer of military technology from the US to India was discussed seriously. Nothing came, however, of Indian attempts to buy American TOW anti-tank missiles, howitzers and some other equipment.

'We don't tilt on either side; we walk upright.' Indira quoted in USIS publication on her US visit, (New Delhi, 1981).

'I will have to sit down with Deng and draw' the line. Indira to Indian negotiators. K. S. Bajpai, first member and then leader of the Indian delegation to Author.

Indira's instruction to negotiators to 'keep the talks going' without agreeing to 'anything specific'. *Ibid.* By this time, domestic problems and the approaching General Election had made it difficult for her to do a deal with China.

Improving India–Pakistan relations the 'task of Sisyphus'. See Author's articles in *The Times of India*. March 13th, 1980; November 11th, 1981; and June 12th, 1984.

For Zia's virtuoso display of diplomatic skills and stance of peace offensive, *ibid.*

'Madam, please do not believe . . .' to '. . . me a dictator'. H. Y. Sharada Prasad to Author; confirmed by a Pakistani diplomat who did not wish to be mentioned by name.

'You do not seem to realise that Mr Desai is no longer . . .' *Ibid.*

'I am listening . . .' *Ibid.*

Indira's reasoning for keeping Pakistan out of the Commonwealth. R. D. Sathe, then Foreign Secretary at the Indian Foreign Office, confirmed by Abdul Sattar, then Pakistani Ambassador to India, later Foreign Secretary in Islamabad.

For the massive expenditure on Asian games and terrible exploitation of workers, see Tariq Ali, *op. cit.*, pp. 218–21.

Asiad and the great affront to Sikhs which complicated the Punjab problem. See Tully and Jacob, *op. cit.*, pp. 86–8.


## 17 Calamity After Calamity

Whopping IMF loan on terms considered 'humiliating' by many Indians. For most detailed coverage and comments see *The Hindu*, Madras, October 31st and November 3rd, 7th and 10th, 1981.

For details of Indira's defeat in Andhra and Karnataka, see *The Times of India*, January 6th, 1983.

N.T.R. dressing as a woman in the expectation that this would hasten his elevation to prime ministership. See Tariq Ali, *op. cit.*, p. 232.

For Indira's criticism of the opposition and of the press, see *India Today*, September 30th, 1983; also Girilal Jain, 'Mrs Gandhi and the Press', *The Times of India*, July 1st, 1983.

Her critics would not 'hesitate to hurt India, if they could thus hurt Indira, too'. Author's article, 'Survival of a Mystique', *The Guardian*, November 1st, 1984.

For the Bihar Press Bill and its withdrawal see Arun Shourie, *Mrs Gandhi's Second Reign, op. cit.*, pp. 60–72.

That Indira would never admit to having read any book or article about her was the experience of all who raised the subject with her. However, Dom Moraes, *op. cit.*, records (p. 279) that whenever he quoted to her 'accusations and allegations' from books she claimed never to have read, she 'appeared to know' where the 'quotations had come from'.

Phenomenal expansion of TV network. At one stage, one new relay transmitter was being made operational every day.

Sheikh Abdullah vehemently gave expression to his anger and frustration over his inability to hold elections in Jammu and Kashmir in Bombay in his talks with Author and A. G. Noorani all through the Emergency.

Farooq's succession and Indira's role in seeing to it that he did succeed his towering father. B. K. Nehru, then Governor of Kashmir, to Author.

Farooq calling Indira 'Mummy'. Farooq, whom Author has known since he was a medical student, to Author. Confirmed by Indira's aides .

Indira gave expression to her unhappiness with Farooq, especially with Kashmir having become a 'safe base' for Sikh extremists, both publicly and in off-the-record briefings to editors at which Author was usually present.

For the viciousness and 'downright vulgarity' of the Kashmir election campaign, see *India Today*, September 15th, 1983; for the other side of the case, *Onlooker*, Bombay, October 20th, 1983.

For failure of efforts to change the constitution to stave off elections in Assam, see *The Times of India*, January 5th, 1983.

Unspeakable savagery of the massacres in Assam during the poll and only two per cent voting. See Tariq Ali, *op. cit.*, pp. 225–6.

For Indira's rebuttal of her responsibility for the Assam carnage, see *The Times of India*, February 23rd, 1983.

For documents of NAM and Indira's concluding press conference, see *The Times of India*, March 13th, 1983.

*Yes Minister* episode. Mentioned to Author that very day by some of Indira's aides. Later confirmed by Dr P. C. Alexander.

For the Map Room, originating from the gift of a map in Rome's Piazza Navona, see Darina Silone, in *Indira Gandhi Remembered, op. cit.*, p. 392.

'Taste for the sharp retort' and for 'eloquent silence'. Callaghan, in *Indira Gandhi Remembered, op. cit.*, p. 97.

Several of the 'think tank' members have mentioned Indira's blank, baffled look to me but none wanted to be identified by name. In the Eighties, P. N. Haksar was consulted by Indira rarely. But he was aware of her fits of vindictiveness and spoke of them to me more in sorrow than in anger.

'Eight out of every ten decisions . . .' To Author.

Indira's Sri Lanka policy, explained to me by G. Parthasarthi, Chairman of the Policy Planning Committee and special envoy to Sri Lanka, K. S. Bajpai, then secretary at the Foreign Office in charge of relations with Sri Lanka and S. J. S. Chhatwal, then High Commissioner in Colombo.

UPI despatch later denied by Colombo. See *The Times of India*, August 3rd, 1983.

In relation to Sri Lanka, India 'not just any other country'. Quoted in *India Today*, August 31st, 1983.

For the faults of omission and commission of the Akali leadership, especially the 'Akali Trinity', see Tully and Jacob, *op. cit.*, p. 218.

For Atwal's gruesome murder and New Delhi's obstruction of Darbara Singh's decision to enter the Golden Temple and arrest Bhindranwale, Darbara Singh to Author. Also see Tully and Jacob, *op. cit.*, pp. 96–9.

Till today no satisfactory explanation is available for the government's repeated declaration that the authorities would not enter the Golden Temple even after it knew it to be unavoidable.

General Sunderji, the overall commander of the Operation Blue Star, later told Author that the Defence Minister had told him to start planning for the operations on January 15th, 1984, the Army Day.

'Maybe, I am not so strong as I then was.' Indira to Bipan Chandra. Prof. Chandra to Author.

'Situation has gone out of my hand'. Quoted in Tully and Jacob, *op. cit.*, p. 134.

The 'last-ditch negotiations'. Tully and Jacob, *ibid.*, p. 122.

For details of Blue Star and worldwide Sikh reaction, see Khushwant Singh and Kuldip Nayar, *Tragedy of Punjab op. cit.*; Tully and Jacob, *op. cit.*, and, for the government's point of view, *The White Paper on Punjab* (Government of India, 1984). *The Times of India*, in its editorial, August 3rd, 1984, called it an 'unforthcoming document'.

## 18   *Those Fateful Shots*

. . . Also signed her own death warrant. Pupul Jayakar to Author.

H. Y. Sharada Prasad and S. K. Singh had talked to Author about writing the Prime Minister's profile. It was Singh who mentioned Indira's 'premonition'. The profile, *Indira Gandhi, Prime Minister of India*, was published by the Government of India in 1972.

'Close to her heart', Salim Ali, the ornithologist, in *Indira Gandhi Remembered, op. cit.*, p. 15.

'Stunning news from far-off Chile' . . . to '. . . "like to eliminate me".' Fidel Castro, in *Indira Gandhi Remembered, op. cit.*, p. 103.

Moynihan's allegation that the CIA had financed the Congress while Indira 'was its President'. See Daniel Patrick Moynihan, *A Dangerous Place* (Allied, Bombay, 1978), p. 41.

Indira's rejoinder. *The Times of India*, May 19th, 1978.

'They' would treat me and my family as 'they' treated Mujib and his family. Indira to sculptor Sankho Chaudhuri, son-in-law of 'Auntie Vakil'. Chaudhuri to Author.

Hurling of spring-knife at Indira by Ram Bulchand Lalwani. See *The Times of India*, April 15th, 1980.

Alleged sabotage of Makalu, the Prime Minister's Boeing 707. Zail Singh's statement to Parliament. April 27th, 1987.

Inamdar's statement that he was only trying to 'spite his bosses'. *The Statesman*, April 30th, 1981.

Indira shocked by the consequences of Blue Star. Indira aides who wanted their anonymity respected.

The Six-Nation Appeal for Nuclear Sanity. See *The Times of India*, May 23rd, 1984.

Peace 'too important to be left to the White House and the Kremlin'. Indira quoted to Author and four other journalists by Willy Brandt in New Delhi, June 1984.

Indira: When will Europe 'finally join' . . . in 'pressurising the superpowers'. Brandt in *Indira Gandhi Remembered, op. cit.*, p. 88.

'Not the slightest trace of tension.' S. Z. Qasim and several others present at the function to Author.

'Tension, Dr Friedman, is within . . .' Narrated to Author by B. K. Nehru.

Replacement of Sikh detachment by non-Sikhs during Indira's Ladakh visit. Confirmed to Author by Indira.

For the details and dimensions of mutinies by Sikh soldiers in the wake of Blue Star, see Tully and Jacob, *op. cit.*, pp. 196–200.

B. K. Nehru's differences with Indira over sacking Farooq Abdullah. Nehru to Author; confirmed by T. N. Kaul and P. N. Haksar, also consulted by the Prime Minister.

In relation to B. K. Nehru's transfer away from Kashmir, it is only fair to add that his replacement as Governor, Jagmohan, cited as a source of information below, is the Author's cousin.

Account of Farooq's dismissal and replacement by his brother-in-law. Reconstructed from newspaper accounts and briefings by Jagmohan,

Farooq and Devi Das Thakur, deputy chief minister in Shah's government.

Farooq's claim that he was 'born an Indian and would die an Indian'. Quoted in M. J. Akbar, *The Siege Within*, p. 198.

'The Shah of Kashmir'. See Author's article, *The Times of India*, July 8th, 1984.

'Indira *puphi* (aunt) asked us to get rid of Farooq . . . and we did.' Arun Nehru to Author.

'Think tank' keen on a 'façade' in Kashmir. Two members of the 'think tank' to Author. Confirmed by Jagmohan.

For graphic account of the meeting of the National Development Council, see Ashok Mitra, former Finance Minister in the Marxist government of West Bengal, in *Illustrated Weekly*, December 15th and 22nd, 1985 and January 15th, 1986. These are among the most scathing articles ever written about Indira. They were published soon after the first anniversary of her death.

'Of course, we will win the election.' Indira to Mohit Sen in the first week of October. Sen to Author.

'If Mrs T. takes the plunge, can Mrs G. be far behind?' See Author's article, *The Times of India*, March 29th, 1984.

Never before has it been 'so widely feared, and so openly said by so many . . .' Pran Chopra in *Far Eastern Economic Review*, August 11th, 1984.

For details of the sacking of N.T.R.'s ministry, see Author's article, *The Times of India*, August 23rd , 1984.

Indira opposed to an attack on or dismemberment of Pakistan. Also keen on preserving Sri Lanka's unity. Several military leaders, of whom none was prepared to be identified by name, to Author.

Trying to 'rectify' the Andhra situation and if Ramarao could retain his majority 'he would be back'. Girilal Jain to Author.

'Need not go nuclear'. Quoted in *The Times of India*, August 24th, 1984.

'Somehow I have begun to pray . . . Don't bother to answer this.' Darina Silone, *op. cit.*, p. 396.

Indira's refusal to countenance the idea of her security being entrusted to the Army. A source very close to Mr Venkataraman to Author.

To see an old chinar tree . . . which had died. Pupul Jayakar and Jagmohan to Author.

Plans for a holiday with grandchildren in Ladakh in June 1985. Jagmohan to Author. The allegation that Indira did not expect to 'see' her next birthday was made by P. N. Lekhi, defence counsel of her alleged assailant in mid-November 1984.

Indira as Indian people's 'principal point of reference'. Girilal Jain, in *The Times of India*, November 8th, 1978. M. V. Kamath, former editor of *Illustrated Weekly*, who turned very critical of Indira since 1977, lamented after her assassination: 'Who will I criticise now?' (*Sunday Observer*, Bombay, November 11th, 1984).

'Dwarf the Himalayas'. Welles Hangen, *op. cit.*, p. 22.

'Your job isn't what I would want to do'. Helmut Schmidt in *Indira Gandhi Remembered*, *op. cit.*, p. 383.

V. S. Naipaul's comment. *Daily Mirror*, November 1st, 1984.

'Gracefully yielded power'. James Callaghan in *Indira Gandhi Remembered*, *op. cit.*, p. 96.

Indira's description of her father as a 'saint strayed into politics'. Quoted and refuted by Author in an article on Nehru's fifteenth death anniversary, *The Guardian*, May 28th, 1979.

'India's fourth and last General Election'. Neville Maxwell, in *The Times*, March 8th, 1967.

Indira 'incarnated her country', *The Observer*, March 21st, 1982.

'With the solitary exception of Charles de Gaulle . . .' Professor Galbraith to Author in New Delhi in January 1986.

'No hate is dark enough to overshadow the extent of my love for my people and my country . . . how can anyone be an Indian and not be proud.' Indira's will. Text at the Indira Gandhi Memorial Trust, 1, Akbar Road, New Delhi.

# Index

# INDEX